D0743660

RENEWALS 458-4574

DATE DUE			
MAY 0 7			
OCT 2 3 2008			
DEC 2 2 2008			
GAYLORD			PRINTED IN U.S.A.

HOSPITALITY TODAY

WITHDRAWN
UTSA LIBRARIES

Educational Institute Books

HOSPITALITY TODAY

An Introduction

Rocco M. Angelo, CHA
Andrew N. Vladimir

A nonprofit educational foundation

Disclaimer

This publication is designed to provide accurate and authoritative information in regard to the subject matter covered. It is sold with the understanding that the publisher is not engaged in rendering legal, accounting, or other professional service. If legal advice or other expert assistance is required, the services of a competent professional person should be sought.

—From the Declaration of Principles jointly adopted by the American Bar Association and a Committee of Publishers and Associations

The authors, Rocco M. Angelo and Andrew N. Vladimir, are solely responsible for the contents of this publication. All views expressed herein are solely those of the authors and do not necessarily reflect the views of the Educational Institute of the American Hotel & Motel Association (the Institute) or the American Hotel & Motel Association (AH&MA).

Nothing contained in this publication shall constitute a standard, an endorsement, or a recommendation of the Institute or AH&MA. The Institute and AH&MA disclaim any liability with respect to the use of any information, procedure, or product, or reliance thereon by any member of the hospitality industry.

© Copyright 1991
By the EDUCATIONAL INSTITUTE of the
AMERICAN HOTEL & MOTEL ASSOCIATION
1407 South Harrison Road
P.O. Box 1240
East Lansing, Michigan 48826

The Educational Institute of the American
Hotel & Motel Association is a nonprofit
educational foundation.

All rights reserved. No part of this
publication may be reproduced, stored in
a retrieval system, or transmitted, in any
form or by any means—electronic,
mechanical, photocopying, recording, or
otherwise—without prior permission of the
publisher.

Printed in the United States of America
    4 5 6 7 8 9 10 95 94 93 92

Library of Congress Cataloging-in-Publication Data

Angelo, Rocco M.
    Hospitality today : an introduction/Rocco M. Angelo and Andrew
N. Vladimir.
        p.   cm.
    Includes bibliographical references and index.
    ISBN 0–86612–060–2
    1. Hospitality industry—Management. I. Vladimir, Andrew.
II. Title.
TX911.3.M27A54 1991
647'.94'068—dc20   91–15548
                                              CIP

Editor: Jim Purvis

**Library
University of Texas
at San Antonio**

Contents

About the Authors

Rocco M. Angelo (left) is the Associate Dean of the School of Hospitality Management at Florida International University. Prior to joining FIU in 1974, Mr. Angelo spent six years as manager of Laventhol & Horwath's Management Advisory Services division in New York City. At that time he was responsible for supervising and conducting economic feasibility studies, operation and control analyses for hotels and restaurants, and tourism studies in the United States, Canada, and the Caribbean. He has also worked in various management positions with ARA Services (a food service management company), Loews Hotels, and Pannell Kerr Forster. He received B.S. degrees from Fordham University and the School of Hotel Administration at Cornell University, and an M.B.A. from the University of Miami. He has taught courses at Cornell University, New York University (Continuing Education), and the Centre International de Glion in Switzerland.

From 1985 to 1989, Mr. Angelo was advisor to the Club Management Institute of the Club Managers Association of America. Since 1988 he has been a Member of the Corporation of the Culinary Institute of America. He is also a member of the advisory board of Dade County's Academy for Tourism and serves on the Market Research and Feasibility Studies Committee of the American Hotel & Motel Association and the Scholarship and Grants Committee of the American Hotel Foundation.

Mr. Angelo is the author of *A Practical Guide to Understanding Feasibility Studies*. He resides in Key Biscayne, Florida.

Andrew N. Vladimir has a diverse background in advertising, travel, and tourism. He is Assistant Professor at the School of Hospitality Management of Florida International University, where he teaches sales, marketing and advertising courses and graduate seminars in management and marketing.

Before joining FIU's faculty in 1986, Mr. Vladimir served as Director of Tourism for the Government of Bermuda, the only non-Bermudian ever to hold that post. Part of his responsibilities as Bermuda's chief tourism regulator was to oversee the government's marketing, advertising, and public relations programs.

Mr. Vladimir has spent most of his career in the advertising business, with a special emphasis on hospitality, travel, and tourism. He has held senior management positions with some of America's best advertising and public relations agencies, including Young & Rubicam, Norman Craig & Kummel, Kenyon & Eckhardt, and Ruder and Finn. In addition, he has headed his own advertising and public relations agencies and has owned two travel agencies.

In the course of his career Mr. Vladimir has worked for such hospitality clients as Delta Airlines, Air France, TravAlaska Tours, Sonesta Hotels, Resorts International, and McDonald's. He has been a featured speaker at three world congresses of the American Society of Travel Agents.

Mr. Vladimir is the author of *The Complete Travel Marketing Handbook* and *Advertising Age's Professional Development Program in Advertising*. According to *Advertising Age* he is considered "a recognized expert on marketing management and the advertising agency business." He has a biography in the new edition of Marquis's *Who's Who in Advertising*.

Mr. Vladimir holds a B.A. degree from Yale University and an M.S. degree from FIU's School of Hospitality Management. In 1987 he was elected to membership in Delta Delta Phi, the hospitality honor society. He is also a graduate of the Harvard Business School's Advanced Management Program, and a former president of the Harvard Business School Club of Seattle. He is currently the secretary and treasurer of FIU's Hospitality Society and the editor of its newsletter. He resides in Coconut Grove, Florida.

Preface

In our more than 80 combined years of teaching and practicing hospitality management, we have watched the industry grow and diversify at a lightning pace. This bodes well for students seeking to enter the industry. Today there are more kinds of jobs and places to work than ever before. Students with an interest in the field can find opportunities in a variety of hotels, restaurants, institutions, private clubs, cruise ships, airlines, consulting firms, travel agencies, and government tourist bureaus. This book's purpose is to present and describe these opportunities while at the same time preparing students for a hospitality management career.

The book has been divided into four parts. Parts I and II describe the dimensions and scope of the industry and depict many of the career opportunities. These sections tell why and where people travel, and describe various kinds of hotel and food service operations and how they are organized and managed. Readers will find current, practical information on hotel and food service product concepts, descriptions of the industry's major players, and advice on developing or planning new hotels and restaurants.

Part III focuses on management theory and practical management techniques. It describes such key areas of management responsibility and concern as human resources, marketing, sales, and advertising. Franchising and management contracts are expected to continue to play an important role in the growth of the industry and a chapter is devoted to each.

Part IV concentrates first on social responsibility and then takes a look at the future of hospitality. In today's climate, in which corporations are judged as much for what they stand for as what they offer to consumers, we feel it is important to give students a framework for making ethical business decisions. Moreover, with the advent of the European Economic Community and the globalization of society, the hospitality industry faces some dramatic changes in the next decade that future managers must understand in order to develop appropriate responses.

This book could not possibly be the work of only two authors. A great many people have contributed their ideas and time to conceiving and shaping it. We would first like to acknowledge the active support and encouragement of Anthony G. Marshall, Dean of the School of Hospitality

Management at Florida International University. His understanding gave us the time and resources needed to accomplish this project. Ute Vladimir's assistance in researching and consolidating our material has been invaluable. Many of our colleagues at FIU have helped as well by reviewing material and suggesting directions for us to pursue. We are especially grateful to professors Joseph Gregg and Theodore White.

Our friends in the industry have provided many ideas and examples, which we have used extensively. We would like to particularly thank (in no particular order) Tom Hewitt, President of The Continental Companies; Bob James, Chairman of Regal-AIRCOA; industry consultants M. L. Dayton and Lee Dayton; Bob Hamel, General Manager of the Sheraton Bal Harbour Hotel; Paul Breslin, FIU alumnus and Director of Human Resources of the Fontainebleau Hilton; and Jim Potter, Vice President of Inter-Continental Hotels. Finally, our editor, Jim Purvis of the Educational Institute, has shown great insight and patience in working with us. Many of his suggestions have been incorporated into this text.

Rocco M. Angelo
Andrew N. Vladimir
North Miami, Florida

Part I

Introduction

Chapter Outline

1 The Travel and Tourism Industry

The hospitality industry is only one of several industries that together make up the travel and tourism industry. In Chapter 1 we will take a close look at the travel and tourism industry. We will present a brief history of travel, then look at the scope and economic impact of travel and tourism. We will also see how businesses within the industry are interrelated. We'll conclude the chapter with a discussion of why people travel and travel and tourism's effect on society.

A Brief History of Travel

Since the word "travel" suggests pleasure and adventure to most people, it is not often remembered that "travel" is derived from the French word "travail," which means "toil and labor." Prehistoric travelers moved about in search of food and shelter. Their travels were by no means pleasant. Travel has been an arduous task for much of recorded history. In fact, it has only been in modern times that travel has become relatively comfortable.

Commerce was an important motivator of early travel. By 3000 B.C., caravan routes from Eastern Europe to North Africa and on to India and China were well established. Camels were the favored pack animals in those days—a healthy one could carry up to 600 pounds of cargo. By 1200 B.C. Phoenician merchant vessels were plying the Mediterranean, following sea routes stretching from Britain to Africa.

The Romans were the first to travel on land on a large scale. Their desire to expand the Roman Empire resulted in expeditions of discovery and conquest followed by massive road building. The first important Roman highway was the Via Appia, started in 312 B.C. By A.D. 200 the Romans could travel all the way from Hadrian's Wall in northern Britain to the Sahara Desert on highways that had wheel-changing stations and rest houses every 15 to 30 miles.

People in ancient times traveled for pleasure as well. Hundreds of years before the birth of Christ, Greeks and barbarians (defined by the Greeks as anyone who was not Greek) traveled to the Olympic Games. Health, too, provided an impetus for early travel. Doctors believed that waters in certain locations possessed healing qualities and would send

Exhibit 1.1 A Roman Spa

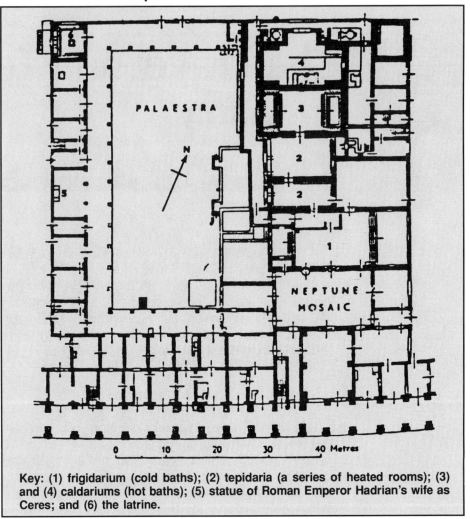

Key: (1) frigidarium (cold baths); (2) tepidaria (a series of heated rooms); (3) and (4) caldariums (hot baths); (5) statue of Roman Emperor Hadrian's wife as Ceres; and (6) the latrine.

Source: Russell Meiggs, *Roman Ostia*, 2nd ed. (Oxford: Clarendon Press, 1973).

their patients there. By the time of the Romans it was not unusual to travel to spas as far away from Rome as Bath, England (Exhibit 1.1).

With the growth of organized religion, pilgrimages became common in many parts of the world. Muslims traveled to Mecca; Christians traveled to shrines all over Europe and beyond. Christian pilgrimages in the Middle Ages were immortalized in the fourteenth century by Geoffrey Chaucer in his book *The Canterbury Tales*. The book's narrator is a jovial innkeeper who hosts 29 pilgrims staying at the Tabard Inn in Southwark, England, and subsequently offers to accompany them on their journey to help make the trip an interesting one.

The first European traveler to popularize long-distance trips was Marco Polo. It was the desire for wealth that sent this Venetian in 1275 to trade at the "Hall of the Barbarians" in Kublai Khan's empire. Polo returned from the Far East 20 years later to write a book about his adventures, titled *The Description of the World*, which later became known popularly as *Il milione—The Millions*—because of all the wealth he had allegedly acquired abroad. His adventures soon captured the imagination of courts all over Europe. Almost certainly, a reader of *Il milione* who eventually set out to find some of the sights Polo catalogued was Christopher Columbus.[1]

By the thirteenth century trade and commerce had emerged as the prime reason for travel. Improved navigation skills and the development of the magnetic compass took much of the uncertainty out of long, arduous sea trips. Maps of the continents and two- and three-masted sailing ships helped open the oceans to further exploration in the fourteenth and fifteenth centuries.

During the Renaissance period (beginning in the fourteenth century in Italy and lasting in Europe into the seventeenth century), travel for cultural and artistic reasons became common. Soon it was popular for aristocrats, diplomats, scholars, and other young gentlemen and women to take an extended tour of the Continent, which came to be known as "The Grand Tour." Paris, Rome, Florence, Venice, Munich, Vienna, and other cities of central Europe were fashionable tour stops, and resorts and spas were developed to accommodate the tourists.

Travel to the New World for adventure and profit in the seventeenth and eighteenth centuries opened sea lanes and hastened the development of the great trans-Atlantic ocean liners which were to bind Europe and the Americas together in the nineteenth century. The first steamship to cross the Atlantic was the *Sirius* in 1838. In 1840 Samuel Cunard inaugurated regular passenger service across the Atlantic when he formed the British and North American Royal Mail Steam Packet Company, later to take on its founder's name and become the Cunard Line. Sea voyages became the most romantic and luxurious form of travel, but they were confined to the few who could afford them.

The most famous and tragic sea voyage of all was that of the *Titanic*. The 46,000-ton vessel offered a degree of luxury that was unheard of in the shipping world. One writer called the maiden voyage of the *Titanic* "the millionaires' special." The ship left port on April 12, 1912, and more than two thousand passengers and crew partied their way into the North Atlantic. Only 705 passengers survived the voyage. April 14, 1912—the night the *Titanic* struck an iceberg and sank—is the saddest day in the history of passenger shipping. A woman who survived the tragedy later wrote about that Sunday night in her diary:

> We dined the last night in the Ritz Restaurant. It was the last word in luxury. The tables were gay with pink roses and white daisies, the women in their beautiful shimmering gowns of satin and silk, the men immaculate and well groomed, the stringed orchestra playing music from Puccini and Tchaikovsky. The food was superb-caviar, lobster, quail from Egypt, plover's eggs, and hothouse grapes and fresh peaches. The night was cold and clear, the sea like glass. But in a few short hours every man in that room was dead except J. Bruce Ismay, Gordon Duff, and a Mr. Carter.[2]

Despite this disaster, trans-Atlantic passenger service continued, and the great ocean liners such as the *Queen Mary*, the S.S. *France*, and the *United States* became known throughout the world as the flagships of their nations. Ocean liners were the principal form of luxury travel until the

The *Queen Mary*, Long Beach, California. Courtesy of the Long Beach Convention and Visitors' Bureau.

late 1950s, when commercial jets first entered trans-Atlantic service. Soon the great ocean liners became relics of the romantic past. Today the *Queen Mary* is permanently docked and operated as a hotel by The Walt Disney Company in Long Beach, California; the *United States*, which still holds the world's record for the fastest Atlantic crossing of a passenger steamship, is mothballed in Newport News, Virginia; and the S.S. *France* has taken on a new life as Norwegian Cruise Line's *Norway*.

Finally, modern technology became a major force in travel with the development of the locomotive, automobile, and airplane. These new forms of transportation put long-distance travel within the reach of many more people than ever before by decreasing the amount of time and money necessary to take long trips.

The first working locomotive was built in England in 1804. In 1830 the railroad age began with the opening of the Liverpool and Manchester Railway in England. One year later America's first public railway, the South Carolina Railroad, began service. It did not take long for entrepreneurs to sense the potential of the railroad to stimulate travel. In 1841 a Baptist preacher named Thomas Cook organized a rail tour from Leicester to Loughborough and back for 570 people to attend a temperance meeting, thus earning himself a place in history as the world's first recognized travel agent.

In the last half of the nineteenth century, railroads grew rapidly in Europe and elsewhere. An important milestone was reached in 1869 when the Union Pacific and the Central Pacific railroads joined their tracks at Promontory Point, Utah, making a transcontinental rail trip across America possible for the first time. In 1891 construction started on the Trans-Siberian railroad, which would link Europe to Asia.

By the turn of the century the automobile was gaining attention as a new mode of land transportation on both sides of the Atlantic. Pioneers

In the nineteenth century, railroads put long-distance travel within the reach of ordinary Americans. Courtesy of the State of Michigan Archives.

The automobile's potential as a convenient and inexpensive means of travel would not be realized until better roads were built. Courtesy of the State of Michigan Archives.

such as Henry Ford and R. E. Olds in America, Sir Henry Royce in Great Britain, and Karl Benz and Gottlieb Daimler in Germany were making cars an affordable and efficient way to travel. Affordable automobiles allowed more people than ever before to travel great distances inexpensively. Today about 80% of all trips are taken in automobiles.

Commercial aviation captured the interest of the public on both sides of the Atlantic after World War I, but it was the daring exploits of pioneers like Charles Lindbergh, who made the first solo flight across the Atlantic on May 21, 1927, that got financiers enthusiastic enough to invest large sums in developing the industry. That same year a young World War I pilot, Juan Trippe, founded Pan American Airlines with a mail contract from the United States government to fly between Key West, Florida, and Havana, Cuba. The DC 3, the first practical passenger aircraft that met the needs of the flying public, was introduced in 1936. In 1958 the first Boeing 707 went into service. It heralded the start of the jet age and provided a huge stimulus to both the tourist and business traveler markets.

The Nature of the Travel and Tourism Industry

When the United States Senate created the National Tourism Policy Act of 1981 to encourage the growth of tourism, it used the following definition of the travel and tourism industry:

> An interrelated amalgamation of those businesses and agencies which totally or in part provide the means of transport, goods, services, and other facilities for travel outside of the home community for any purpose not related to day-to-day activity.[3]

Another definition that is somewhat similar but a bit clearer, and therefore the one we will adopt for this text, is provided by Douglas Fretchling, former director of the U.S. Travel Data Center and currently president of Guest Plus. Fretchling defines the travel and tourism industry as "a collection of organizations and establishments that derive all or a significant portion of their income from providing goods and services purchased on a trip to the traveler."[4] Exhibit 1.2 lists businesses that make up the travel and tourism industry. The businesses under the headings "Lodging Operations" and "Food and Beverage Operations," along with institutional (generally non-profit) food service operations constitute the hospitality industry. As you can see, the hospitality industry is only a part of the travel and tourism industry.

Size   One way of defining the size of the travel and tourism industry is to add up the amount of money spent on goods and services by travelers. Unfortunately, it is not possible to do this accurately. While just about everyone would agree that airlines, campgrounds, and resorts receive all of their business from travelers, what about gift shops and gas stations? These businesses on the whole have no way of knowing what percentage of their customers are travelers and what percentage are local residents. Depending on their location, there may be a wide variation in the amount of business they get from each source. But, although there is no way of knowing how much of their revenues are from travelers, for statistical purposes the total receipts of these types of businesses are included in projections of the size and scope of the travel and tourism industry.

Exhibit 1.2 The Travel and Tourism Industry

Lodging Operations (17%)*	Food and Beverage Operations (26%)	Transportation Services (38%)	Retail Stores (8%)	Activities (10%)
Hotels	Restaurants	Ships	Gift Shops	Recreation
Motels	Lodging Properties	Airplanes	Souvenir Shops	Business
Motor Hotels	Bars/Taverns	Autos	Arts/Crafts Shops	Entertainment
Resorts	Catering	Buses	Shopping Malls	Meetings
Camps	Snack Bars	Trains	Markets	Study Trips
Parks	Lunch Counters	Bikes	Miscellaneous Stores	Sporting Events
Pensions	Cruise Ships	Limousines		Ethnic Festivals
	Institutions			Art Festivals
	Contract Food Companies			Cultural Events
				Seasonal Festivals

*Rounded percentages indicate each segment's percentage of total U.S. travel and tourism industry revenues.

Although statisticians and economists measure the size of the travel and tourism industry by adding together the receipts of the businesses that compose it, everyone agrees that these figures do not tell the whole story and may in fact be somewhat misleading. For instance, one could argue that the amount of money a hotel takes in is not a true measure of its economic impact on the community. The real impact is measured by the amount of salaries the hotel pays to its employees which they in turn spend on housing, clothes, and food for their families; by the taxes the hotel pays to state and federal government; by the amount of profits generated by local companies who sell goods and services to the hotel; and finally by the number of jobs the hotel creates that may keep people off the welfare rolls and thus save government the cost of supporting them.

Industry analysts have a name for these indirect or hidden benefits—the multiplier effect. The multiplier effect is measured by first adding up all the expenditures of travelers in a given geographic area and then multiplying that figure by a factor (known as the multiplier) to arrive at the amount of income that stays in the area and is generated by these expenditures. While the multiplier effect is highly variable among cities and countries around the world, many industry analysts use a figure of 1.6 as a reasonable multiplier on a general basis.

Travel Expenditures

In 1987 total domestic and international tourism worldwide exceeded $2 trillion and represented about 12% of the world's economy. Spending for world tourism exceeded the gross national product (GNP) of every country in the world except the United States. Travel and tourism can now be considered the world's largest industry.[5] Besides creating economic growth, the travel and tourism industry also creates jobs. It has created more entry-level jobs than any other industry.[6]

On a worldwide basis, travel is flourishing and projections are that it will continue to do so at an accelerating rate. According to World Tourism Organization estimates, in 1987 there were 4.3 billion trips taken worldwide, an increase of nearly 5% over the previous year. Of these, 90% were domestic trips, 10% international. If we look at the 430 million international trips, the world's leading destinations in 1988 were Italy and Spain. Both of these countries received over 50 million travelers. The United States was third with almost 30 million international visitors. As you might expect, in all of these countries a large percentage of the visitors came from the nearest neighboring country: 20% of Italy's visitors came from Switzerland, 23% of Spain's visitors came from France, and 42% of the visitors to the United States were from Canada. A special report issued by *The Economist* in the United Kingdom estimates that international tourism will more than double to 910 million trips by 1999. That growth is expected to come mostly from European countries and Japan.

It is interesting to note the profile of U.S. residents who travel overseas (see Exhibit 1.3). In 1987 California contributed the largest percentage of any state (16%), with New York second (12%) and Florida third (11%). Sixty-one percent of trips abroad by Americans were for vacation purposes, twenty-eight percent for business. Most of these people were experienced travelers. Ninety percent of the trips were made by repeat visitors—only ten percent by first timers. The median annual family income of U.S. overseas travelers was $55,138 and the average trip length was 20.9 nights. It is estimated that the average expenditure outside of the United States on these trips was $971.

The profile of overseas visitors coming to the United States shows that 44% came from Western Europe and 27% from the Far East. As was true of U.S. travelers abroad, more foreign visitors were in the states for vacation than for business. However, more of them—22%—were first-time visitors. Their median family income was somewhat lower than that of Americans traveling abroad—$43,113—but they averaged more nights away from home (25.6) and they spent more money when traveling—an average of $1,384 per visitor.

The Domestic Travel and Tourism Industry. Now let's examine travel expenditures in the United States. If we define the size of the U.S. travel and tourism industry in terms of dollars as the total gross receipts of airlines, bus companies, Amtrak, hotels, motels, eating and drinking places, and amusement and recreation services, then we can say that in 1989 the industry grossed $363.5 billion dollars, or 6.5% of the GNP. As a matter of fact, for the past half decade the U.S. travel and tourism industry has been growing at the same rate as the GNP.

In terms of employment the figures are staggering. Total travel-generated employment in the industry in 1987 reached 5.3 million jobs, up 3.4% from the previous year. The nation's hotels and motels alone created 81,000 new jobs in 1987.

On the whole the industry was very healthy. Approximately 447 million passengers flew on the nation's airlines, generating record profits of $2.5 billion dollars. On average every passenger flew 904 miles and spent $100. In 1989 Americans took more than 664.3 million overnight or day trips more than 100 miles away from home. Of those trips, business and

Exhibit 1.3 U.S. Travelers Overseas versus Overseas Travelers in the United States

U.S. Travelers Overseas		Overseas Travelers in U.S.	
Residence			
California	16%	Western Europe	44%
New York	12%	Far East	27%
Florida	11%	Caribbean	9%
Purpose of Trip			
Business	28%		37%
Vacation	61%		48%
Trip Experience			
First Time	10%		22%
Repeat	90%		78%
Median Family Income	$55,138		$43,113
Nights Away from Home	20.9		25.6
Total Trip Expenditure	$971		$1,384

Source: *Travel & Leisure's World Travel Over 1988/1989,* American Express Publishing Company.

conventions represented 25%; the remaining 75% were pleasure trips. Seventy percent of pleasure trips were made by auto, truck, or recreational vehicle. Because of rising air fares, travel by car has been rising at a faster rate than by air.

The U.S. Travel Data Center also reported that the 1987–1988 winter travel season was particularly strong. From 1983 to 1987 winter vacations increased twice as fast as summer vacations. Another surprising fact was that more people visited cities than beaches for June-July-August vacations.

The lodging industry. The American Hotel and Motel Association (AH&MA) estimates that in 1986 the U.S. lodging industry hosted about one billion guests. There were approximately 3 million hotel rooms in the United States in 1989, and it is anticipated that this number will grow by slightly more than 2% a year through 1991. While hotel room rates and occupancy levels grew very slowly in 1988 because of a boom in hotel construction over the past decade, they did grow. The average occupancy for all properties in the United States was 63.8% in 1989. Through September of 1989 the average room rate was $56.47, up 3.9% from 1988. Honolulu, Las Vegas, Orlando, and New York had the highest occupancy rates, while the lowest figures reported were in Houston, Dallas, Tampa, and Denver. Nationally, leisure travelers comprise about one-third of the demand for accommodations. Business and government represent another 40%, and 20% of the demand is from conference participants.

One of the most important hotel industry trends in recent years has been product segmentation. Chain and independent operators alike have created specialized lodging products to satisfy emerging segments of the market. For example, Marriott offers Resorts, Suite Hotels, standard Marriotts, Courtyard by Marriott, and Residence Inns. Each of these products features different amenities, has different pricing strategies, and caters to a different kind of guest. All-suite and budget hotels are by far the fastest growing lodging niches.

Another industry trend is the emergence of the "yield management" system of setting rates. This pricing system, adopted from the airlines, uses a hotel's computer reservation system to track advance bookings and then lower or raise prices according to demand on a day-to-day basis to yield the maximum average daily rate.

The food service industry. The food service industry has also been remarkably robust in the last decade. The food service industry comprises all of the businesses listed under the heading "Food and Beverage Operations" in Exhibit 1.2, plus institutional food service operations. According to a report prepared for the National Restaurant Association (NRA), industry sales reached $213.5 billion in 1988.[7] Other findings in this same report:

- There are 619,000 food service operations in the United States.

- More than eight million people are employed in the industry.

- Over 40 cents of the guest's food dollar goes to meals and snacks away from home.

- The typical individual eats out 3.7 times a week or 192 times a year.

The NRA report predicts continued growth in the industry but notes that changing lifestyles and demographics will influence the way this growth manifests itself. The number of single-parent households and two-income working families is increasing. Convenience is paramount to these groups and thus fast-food operations and takeout services are likely to show the largest industry gains in the years ahead.

Another significant guest group for the food service industry is mature adults. The number of Americans over the age of 55 will continue to increase during the coming decade. But these senior citizens will not fit popular stereotypes:

> Today's older consumers differ markedly from previous generations.
> They are healthier, more active, and enjoy relatively higher standards
> of living. They like to travel and engage in a variety of other social
> and leisure activities, including dining out, and allocate a larger por-
> tion of their food budget to restaurant meals and snacks.[8]

Nutrition and health are other issues that are affecting consumer behavior. Americans are becoming more concerned about what they eat, and their interest in the health effects of fats, cholesterol, fiber, and alcohol is bound to influence their food choices.

Immigration too has been affecting our food tastes. The popularity of Latin American and Asian foods is increasing. Some food service companies are now spending research and advertising dollars on these foods, which should accelerate the trend.

Amusement and recreation. The amusement and recreation sector of the travel and tourism industry continues to show significant growth.

Attendance at U.S. commercial tourist attractions and amusement parks in 1988 (including multiple visits) reached 249 million—a 6% increase over 1987 attendance. The majority of visits were to Walt Disney World in Florida, Disneyland in California, Sea World in Florida, and Universal Movie Studios in California. Zoos are also major drawing cards for travelers and tourists. For example, more than five million people visit Lincoln Park Zoo in Chicago annually.

Cruise ship industry. The cruise ship industry is also growing rapidly. There had been a growth in booking rates of 9.9% yearly, although this rate slowed to 7.7% in 1989. Construction during the 1984–1990 period added 34,315 berths to the 41,000 that were in the market in 1983, and the industry projects capacity growth of 39% over the next five years. Only 5% of Americans have taken a cruise, but the new super liners and youth-oriented cruise-ship activities have attracted a far younger clientele than ever before. Leaders in the cruise industry hope for as much as a ten-fold increase in the number of people who take a cruise.

The Interrelationship of the Travel and Tourism Industry

An important and unique feature of the travel and tourism industry is the interrelationship of the various parts of the whole. A trip may consist of an airplane flight, a car rental, a stay at a hotel, several restaurant meals, and some gift purchases. Each of these elements must work well in order for travelers to have a pleasant total experience.

For example, suppose the Smiths decide to fly from their home in Minneapolis to vacation at Walt Disney World in Orlando, Florida. The sum total of their experiences determines the quality of their vacation and the likelihood of their becoming repeat guests at Disney World. For instance, the Smiths might have a pleasant flight to Florida, but then their rented car could overheat, leaving them stranded for several hours and cutting short the day they were going to spend at EPCOT. Or their hotel could be undergoing refurbishing so that the pool and the restaurant are closed during their stay and the usually attractive lobby decor is covered with drop cloths and scaffolding. Even worse—suppose they arrive at the Magic Kingdom at a particularly busy time and find that the park has closed its parking lot and is not admitting any more visitors that day. Any of these incidents could spoil their entire vacation.

The point is that travel-industry businesses have a symbiotic relationship, a mutual dependency. For any one of them to be entirely successful in pleasing the Smiths, all of them must do a good job. If the hotel stay was uncomfortable, the Smiths might enjoy Disney World but still feel on the whole that they had a less-than-perfect vacation. If the hotel did its job but Disney's park was overcrowded or over-priced, the net sum of their experience would also be negative. Either way, in the long run, all of the travel businesses in the area would suffer because the Smiths may not return to Disney World and might tell their friends in Minneapolis that a trip to Disney World is a disappointing experience.

Some destinations are so aware of this interrelationship that they go to extreme lengths to control all elements of the travel product. The British Crown Colony of Bermuda, for instance, which is only 20 square miles in size, monitors the standards of all hotels, restaurants, and attractions because it believes that if a visitor has a bad hotel room or a bad meal, he or she will go home feeling critical of the whole island. Since more than 40% of Bermuda's travel business is repeat, it cannot afford to disappoint its visitors.

Owners and operators of hospitality enterprises often underestimate the importance of the interrelationship of the travel and tourism industry when considering how their enterprise is going to attract consumers. Such vacation spots as Hawaii depend on airlines to deliver 100% of their visitors. If airline fares are too high, business suffers, no matter how strong or how effective marketing efforts are. Atlantic City is a highly successful destination now for motorcoach tours from New York City, but that is entirely a function of the gambling industry that has grown in Atlantic City in the last two decades. Now the casinos depend on the buses, and the buses depend on the casinos. Neither could succeed without the other.

Why People Travel

We saw from looking at the history of travel that over the centuries travel has developed for business, health, social, and cultural reasons. But at the most basic level, it can be said that the main reason people travel is to gather information. We want to know how our favorite aunt is doing in Nashville, so we take a trip to visit her. Businesspeople travel to see what is going on in their home office in Chicago or to find out what customers in Madrid think of their products. Some of us travel to France to see how the French vintners grow grapes and produce wine. Others go to Moscow and Beijing to learn more about Russian and Chinese culture.

Travel is a very important part of our lives. It helps us understand ourselves and others. It is both an effect and a cause of rapid change in society. Technology has played a huge part in all of this. Commercial jet aircraft have brought foreign places closer, and communications satellites bring news events from around the world into our living rooms. Both of these technologies have stimulated interest in traveling abroad.

The three most important factors that determine the amount people spend for travel are employment, disposable income, and household wealth.[9] The more money people who want to travel have, the more likely they are to travel, the more frequently they are likely to travel, and the farther they are likely to travel. While business travel is somewhat less susceptible to economic downturns than leisure travel, it is not immune. Companies invariably tighten up their travel budgets during recessions. Research has shown that international travel patterns are very sensitive to shifts in exchange rates. The buying power of a traveler's own currency affects destination choices and the timing of trips.

Conditions at home and in destination countries also affect travel. In 1991 the amount of overseas travel by Americans declined significantly as a result of the war in the Persian Gulf and the fear of terrorist incidents.

It is important to note that not everyone is disposed to travel. Some people by their nature are stay-at-homes. Others don't like to fly or get motion sickness and simply won't travel no matter what their economic circumstances. Dr. Frank Farley, a psychologist at the University of Wisconsin, has studied the behavior of travelers versus non-travelers.

Many people enjoy vacations with lots of sports activities. Photos courtesy of Four Corners Expeditions, Buena Vista, Colorado; and the Aspen Skiing Company.

"People who hesitate to travel may do so because of deep-seated fears," says Farley. "Travelers, though, seem stable enough to expose themselves to uncertainty and adventure. They worry less, feel less inhibited and submissive, and are more self-confident than stay-at-homes."[10] Farley found other differences between people who like to travel and those who enjoy staying at home:

> Most passionate travelers are risk-takers in many areas of life. They're drawn not only to unknown lands but also to taking chances with their investment portfolios. However, their risk taking is rational; it's based on a deep sense that they control their destiny. They enjoy life, love to play, and gravitate towards crowds and parties.[11]

Travel Motivators
Given a predisposition to travel, there are various motivations that prompt people to take trips. Professors Robert McIntosh and Charles Goeldner believe that basic travel motivators can be divided into four categories:

1. *Physical.* Physical motivators are those related to physical rest, sports participation, beach recreation, relaxing entertainment, and other activities connected with health. Additional physical motivators might be a doctor's recommendation or the desire to visit a health spa. People with these motivators have one goal in common: the reduction of tension through physical, health-related activities.

2. *Cultural.* Cultural motivators spring from the desire to know about the culture of other areas—their music, art, folklore, dances, painting, and religion.

3. *Interpersonal.* Interpersonal motivators include a desire to meet new people, visit friends or relatives, escape from routine or from family and neighbors, and make new friends.

4. *Status and prestige.* Status and prestige motivators concern ego and personal development needs. People with these motivators take trips related to business, conventions, study, and the pursuit of hobbies and education. The desire for recognition, attention, appreciation, knowledge, and a good reputation can be fulfilled through travel.[12]

Exhibit 1.4 Travel Tendencies of Americans

Relatively High Tendency To Travel	Relatively Low Tendency To Travel
Married	Widowed
Male	Female
35 to 44 years of age	65 years and older
Graduate studies	Did not complete high school
Professional/managerial	Blue collar
Own their home	Rent their home
$50 to $75,0000 family income	Less than $10,000 a year
Two wage earners	No wage earners

Source: U.S. Travel Data Center.

The U.S. Travel Data Center has done a good deal of research to determine what types of Americans travel and how many of them there are. According to the center, 150 million Americans take one or more trips away from home every year. Some groups, as we have pointed out, have a higher propensity to travel. The data center identified them in a survey (see Exhibit 1.4).

There are some real differences between persons who travel for business and those who travel for pleasure (see Exhibit 1.5). There is a higher percentage of men between the ages of 25 and 44 among business travelers than among pleasure travelers. There are many more college graduates and persons from households with $40,000 income or more per year among business travelers. Business travelers take trips of longer distances but stay away from home fewer nights on each trip and use airlines and rental cars almost twice as often as pleasure travelers.

Changing Travel Patterns

Because the demographics of the United States are changing dramatically, it is important to look at population, income, and social trends to see if the groups that have been identified as having a high tendency to travel are increasing or decreasing in population.

The overall population of America is increasing. Today there are more than 250 million Americans. That number is expected to increase to 266 million by the year 2000. The age group with a high tendency to travel—the 35 to 44 age group—currently numbers approximately 62 million and should increase at the same rate as the general population. The over 65 population is also growing, but these new senior citizens are much more affluent than their predecessors. There is mounting evidence that they can be a very important market segment in the future if the right products are developed for them. There are many studies to show that the average American's personal income and level of education are continuing to rise. All of this bodes well for the travel and tourism industry over the long term. It means that the numbers of potential travelers should continue to grow, thereby increasing the demand for travel services.

Even if there is a demand, we need to know more about where that demand will come from. Often travel and tourism marketers wistfully dream of increasing the number of visitors from far-away places. Many

Exhibit 1.5 Business Travelers versus Pleasure Travelers

	Pleasure Travelers	Business Travelers
Selected Demographics		
Men	48%	62%
Age 25–44	46%	60%
College graduate or more	26%	44%
Professional or managerial	15%	27%
Household income $40,000 plus	29%	42%
Two or more wage earners per household	46%	51%
Selected Characteristics		
Average miles per trip	970	1,190
Average nights per trip	5.4	4.0
Average household members on trip	2.0	1.3
Use an airline	22%	42%
Use a rental car	8%	15%
Stay in a hotel	42%	73%
Used a travel agent in past year	15%	32%

Source: U.S. Travel Data Center's National Travel Survey and Survey of Business Travelers.

have tried it with varying degrees of success. Douglas Fretchling has observed that

> the behavioral regularity closest to a law in tourism is that the farther a person lives from a destination, the less likely he or she is to visit it, all things being equal. The most important corollary is that the farther a population concentration is from a destination, the smaller the proportion of that population that will visit. Indeed, more than half of all personal trips are within a 300-mile radius of travelers' homes. In short, your best markets are usually in your own back yard.[13]

In addition to these observed phenomena there are some changing travel patterns that have emerged from studies done by the U.S. Travel Data Center and other tourism research groups around the world:

• More people travel by air than ever before.

• Trips tend to be shorter than they used to be. More than one-third are to places within a 150-mile radius of home, and 43% are less than three miles away.

• Travel parties tend to be smaller—40% are just two people.

• In general, there is less seasonality in pleasure travel than there used to be. When both members of a household work, they get away when they can.

- People report more trips for sightseeing and entertainment than in the past. Fewer are traveling simply to visit friends and relatives.

- There appears to be a definite trend to combine business and pleasure trips. Approximately 15 percent of business and convention trips include vacation activities.[14]

Another kind of research that is helpful in understanding changing travel patterns is psychographic. Psychographic research attempts to classify people's behavior not in terms of their age or education or sex, but rather their lifestyles and values. Sometimes this information is more useful than demographic information in deciding what kind of amenities to offer in a resort or how to advertise a particular destination. For instance, in 1985 the government of Bermuda conducted psychographic research in the United States to determine what kind of people would be most interested in going to Bermuda on vacation. In a sample of persons who were potential vacationers, three different groups emerged:

- *The price and sights group.* When these people picked a vacation they were interested in seeing the most things for the least amount of money. They wanted tours that covered ten countries in nine days at a bargain price. The best cruises were the cheapest ones that visited the most ports. And a good hotel offered budget-priced accommodations within walking distance of everything they might want to see.

- *The sun and surf group.* These people sought a vacation where they could lie on a beach and get a golden tan. Value was important, but even more important was finding a destination where there was good weather, guaranteed sunshine, and a beautiful beach where they could soak up the sun and swim in clear waters.

- *The quality group.* The quality of the vacation experience was of paramount importance to this group. They felt they had worked hard for a vacation and now it was their turn to relax and be taken care of. This group valued destinations and accommodations that were first class or deluxe. Service was very important—they wanted and expected lots of pampering and were willing to pay a fair price for it. They also wanted gourmet dining and sophisticated entertainment.

Yankelovich, Clancy, and Shulman (YCS) is a firm that specializes in psychographic research. For many years it has studied how social changes affect American consumer behavior. This information is tabulated annually and provided to subscribers to a service called MONITOR, a trademarked study of YCS. MONITOR tracks such trends as whether people are planning more or fewer vacations, dining out more or less often, more concerned or less concerned with going into debt, and desiring more or fewer materialistic purchases and luxury. MONITOR has identified trends that are changing the way people feel and act about traveling:

- *The great-expectations syndrome.* To some extent the new American traveler is a nitpicker. We're more educated than any previous generation, and more of us have traveled to more places more often than at any other time in history. We're not a bunch of country bump-kins anymore willing to settle for bad service because we're away from home. We have greater expectations because we have more travel experience and because we value our leisure time more.

- *The trade-off syndrome.* Because Americans today are so much better traveled than prior generations, they are increasingly inclined to postpone vacations, to trade two weeks in a foreign country for pri-vate school tuition for their child or a down payment on a house. According to MONITOR, even with the increase in two-earner fam-ilies, people are finding they can't really have it all—they have to make trade-offs. The two-week vacation may well be on its way to becoming a dinosaur because of the need to trade off and the diffi-culties of juggling schedules and priorities in today's more complex family structure.

- *The harried traveler.* Working couples and new parents are stretched for time. They don't always have the luxury of planning far in ad-vance. For these reasons, last-minute travel will become more com-mon. The stress in their lives also means that people are more likely to take mini-vacations to escape from pressures for short periods of time.

- *The strategic traveler.* When it comes to the cost of vacations, most American consumers could best be described as strategic in their thinking. Rather than searching for the lowest price, today's (and probably tomorrow's) strategic traveler is looking for the best value. MONITOR shows that strategic travelers are also information-ori-ented consumers. They want more information and more access to information.[15]

The Social Impact of Travel

Hotels, restaurants, and attractions can shape and change life in a com-munity and they are almost always at the center of it. For example, Club Med was the first resort to open in Hutalco, Mexico, a community that did not even exist until Club Med decided to build there. Walt Disney World has changed the character of Orlando and Florida forever.

New travelers to any destination bring new money and jobs, but they also bring problems. Whenever you have increased travel to an area you need to provide additional public services such as police, fire fighters, water treatment plants, and solid waste disposal facilities. This may in-crease the cost of living for residents. Crime may increase. New airports bring with them pollution and noise. Hotels and shopping strips change the character of the community. Residents may have limited or no access to beaches and other property that previously had been public.

For these and other reasons many people feel that their communities have been negatively affected by travelers and are not in favor of de-velopment that encourages more tourism. Some states such as Washing-ton and Oregon have ambivalent feelings about the benefits of the travel and tourism industry, and they have not gone out of their way to attract tourists or develop facilities for them. Other communities, like Monroe County, Florida (where Key West is located), feel that they

Many of today's resorts try to blend in with the surrounding landscape in order to enhance their appeal and minimize environmental damage. Courtesy of Club Med, Cancun, Mexico.

may have let development get out of hand and are belatedly trying to put a cap on it.

In developing and Third World countries there are other problems. One is the enormous gap that exists between the travelers who stay in luxurious resorts and the employees who witness for the first time new life styles and cultural behavior that can change their own expectations and values. Local residents often try to emulate the dress styles and consumption patterns of visitors. An area's culture and traditional values can be eroded. Racial tensions are not uncommon as a result of these conditions. The seasonality of tourism poses another major problem. When the season is over, often there is a large number of dislocated, jobless workers who have no place to go and few other opportunities to earn a comparable living.

Today's hospitality managers are paying more attention to the social costs of travel and tourism. Modern planning methods make more use of impact studies that consider both social and environmental changes brought about by increased demand. Many countries have mounted impressive marketing campaigns in the off-season to attract visitors and keep employment levels high. Countries like Turkey have developed arts and crafts industries so that workers can spend the months when there are no tourists making products to sell to them during the season.

The bottom line is that travel and tourism is an industry that has its benefits and its costs. Ultimately, societies and governments need to recognize both sides of the coin and determine the proper balance for their own situations.

In this text we will look at one component of the travel and tourism industry—the hospitality industry—from a management perspective. The next chapter will introduce you to the hospitality industry and alert you to the many career opportunities that are open to you. Part II will talk about types of hotels, restaurants, and private clubs, and how they are organized. Part III—Hospitality Management—will cover the management process and such areas of managerial responsibility as human resources, marketing and sales, and advertising. Franchising and management contracts will also be discussed. Business ethics and the future of the industry will be examined in Part IV. The book concludes with an appendix useful to students and hospitality managers and employees who desire more information and more opportunities to begin or advance their careers.

Chapter Summary

Looking back in history we learn that people traveled for many reasons:

- Food and shelter
- Commerce
- Conquest
- Pleasure
- Health
- Religion
- Cultural and artistic reasons
- Adventure and profit

The earliest travelers in prehistoric times traveled to find food and shelter. As human society advanced, commerce became an important motivator of travel, and elaborate trade routes were established on land and sea. The Romans were the first to travel on land on a large scale. Their desire for expansion and conquest led to massive road building in order to facilitate communications and support troops in their far-flung empire. Roman roads also made travel for commerce, pleasure, and health easier.

With the growth of organized religion, pilgrimages became common in many parts of the world. For example, Muslims traveled to Mecca; Christians traveled to shrines all over Europe and beyond. Christian pilgrimages became especially popular during the Middle Ages.

During the Renaissance period (from the fourteenth to the seventeenth centuries), it became common for European aristocrats, diplomats, scholars, and other gentlemen and women to take an extended tour of the Continent for cultural and educational reasons. This tour came to be known as "The Grand Tour."

Travel to the New World for adventure and profit in the seventeenth and eighteenth centuries opened trans-Atlantic sea lanes and hastened the development of regular passenger service between Europe and the Americas. Modern technology in the nineteenth and twentieth centuries has made possible rapid expansion and improvement of travel. Steamships, railroads, automobiles, airplanes, and jets are among the technological advances that have contributed to increased travel.

Travel and tourism is now the world's largest industry. We cannot measure its size in receipts alone; expenditures are a truer measure. Moreover, the multiplier effect needs to be added to get a true picture.

There are many components to the travel and tourism industry, including airlines, hotels, restaurants, and attractions. They are all interrelated and the success or failure of one segment can affect all of them.

People travel for many reasons but there are four basic travel motivators:

- Physical
- Cultural
- Interpersonal
- Status and prestige

Travel patterns are changing. These changes include more automobile trips, shorter trips, and smaller parties. MONITOR has tracked some other trends of interest such as the trade-off syndrome and the harried traveler.

All segments of the travel and tourism industry are growing and the outlook for the future is positive. But society must recognize that there are costs as well as benefits associated with tourism and travel.

Endnotes

1. *Encyclopedia Britannica*, 15th ed. (Chicago: Encyclopedia Britannica Inc., 1975), p. 757.
2. Williamson, *When We Went First Class*, p. 112.
3. Waters, *Travel and Tourism Industry World Yearbook—The Big Picture 1988* (New York: Childs & Waters, 1988).
4. Andrew Vladimir, *The Complete Travel Marketing Handbook*, (Chicago: NTC Business Books, 1988), p. 5.
5. Waters, p. 4.
6. Waters, p. 15.
7. *Restaurant Industry Operations Report, 1988 Edition* (National Restaurant Association and Laventhol & Horwath), p. 6.
8. *Restaurant Industry Report*, p. 7.
9. Robert McIntosh and Charles Goeldner, *Tourism: Principles, Practices, Philosophies*, 5th ed. (New York: Wiley, 1986), p. 13.
10. Daniel Goleman, "Head Trips," *American Health*, April, 1988, p. 58.
11. Goleman, p. 58.
12. McIntosh and Goeldner, pp. 124–125.
13. Vladimir, p. 9.
14. Vladimir, pp. 8–9.
15. Vladimir, pp. 43–48.

Key Terms

cultural motivators
great-expectations syndrome
harried travelers
interpersonal motivators
multiplier effect
physical motivators
price and sights group
psychographic research

quality group
status and prestige motivators
strategic travelers
sun and surf group
trade-off syndrome
travel and tourism industry
yield management

Discussion Questions

1. What were some motivators for early travel?

2. What role has modern technology played in travel?

3. How is the travel and tourism industry defined?

4. What are two ways to estimate the size of the travel and tourism industry?

5. What is the current status of the worldwide travel and tourism industry? the domestic travel and tourism industry?

6. What are some of the changing lifestyles and demographics that will affect the growth of the food service industry in the years to come?

7. How are businesses within the travel and tourism industry interrelated?

8. Why do people travel?

9. How are travel patterns changing?

10. What are some of the social impacts that the travel and tourism industry can have on society?

Chapter Outline

A Brief History of the Hospitality Industry
    Early Hotels
    Early Restaurants
    The Impact of Modern Transportation
        Railroads
        Automobiles
        Airplanes
The Nature of the Hospitality Industry
    Size
        Lodging
        Food Service
    Characteristics
        Intangibility
        Inseparability
        Perishability
        Repetitiveness
        Labor-Intensiveness
Careers in the Hospitality Industry
    Selecting an Industry Segment
        Skills Inventory
    Career Options
        Hotels
        Restaurants
        Clubs
        Catering
        Contract Food Companies
        Institutional Food Service
    Your First Moves
    Management Training Programs
Chapter Summary

2 The Hospitality Industry

This chapter focuses on the hospitality industry. The chapter begins with a brief history of the industry, then discusses the industry's size and unique characteristics. The chapter concludes with a discussion of career opportunities in the hospitality field, including some practical advice on how to start and advance your career.

A Brief History of the Hospitality Industry

Few people realize that there are at least two patron saints for those engaged in providing hospitality to others. The first of these is Saint Julian the Hospitaller. While many acknowledge that he may be mythical, he is listed in the *Oxford Dictionary of Saints* and has seven English churches dedicated to him.[1] In addition, he is depicted in stained glass windows in the cathedrals of Chartres and Rouen. He is the patron saint of innkeepers, travelers, and boatmen, although he has no date, no country, and no tomb. He does have a feast day, however, for those who wish to celebrate it: January 29.

The legend goes that while Julian was away from home one day, a traveling couple knocked on the door of his house. His wife answered. She gave the tired travelers food and water and invited them to take a nap in her bed while she went to the market. While she was away, Julian (who was not yet a saint) came home to discover a man and woman asleep in his bedroom. Assuming it was his wife with another man, he killed both of them on the spot. As he left the house he met his wife returning from the market. Because of this experience, he decided to spend the rest of his life being hospitable to strangers!

The second saint, Saint Notburga, has a church dedicated to her in her hometown of Eben/Maurach, Austria. The church literature describes her as a "farm girl who dedicated her life to the welfare of servants," and she is considered the patron saint of food servers.

Early Hotels

No one knows exactly when the first hotels or inns opened. References to them go as far back as recorded history. But certainly the first inns were private homes that offered accommodations to travelers. By 500 B.C. ancient cities such as Corinth in Greece had a substantial number of establishments that offered food and drink as well as beds to travelers.

The early Roman *hospitia* provided rooms and sometimes food, although whether they were provided hospitably is open to question. The Cornell Quarterly, quoting from a 1981 book, *The Laws of Innkeepers*, says, "In ancient Rome, publicans and their houses were held in general contempt, just as they were in Greece. The Romans were a proud race who held that the business of conducting a tavern was a low form of occupation, and the running of such establishments was usually entrusted to slaves."

In the Middle Ages, inns built along the highways were of questionable reputation. There is an anonymous English verse written about an inn in Wales that depicts its lack of hospitality this way:

> If you ever go to Dolgelly,
> Don't stay at the Lion's Hotel;
> 'Cause there's nothing to put in your belly,
> And no one to answer the bell!

During this period, landlords were predatory and robberies of travelers were common.[2] Even today the legend of the unscrupulous innkeeper is a part of our cultural heritage. In the 1985 London and Broadway productions of *Les Misérables*, one of the most colorful characters is the innkeeper Thénardier, who sings:

> Welcome, M'sieur
> Sit yourself down
> And meet the best Innkeeper in town.
> As for the rest,
> All of them crooks
> Rooking the guests
> And cooking the books.

Thénardier himself is not past using a few of these devices, as he tells the audience:

> Charge 'em for the lice,
> Extra for the mice
> Two percent for looking in the mirror twice!
> Here a little slice,
> There a little cut,
> Three percent for sleeping with the window shut![3]

By the middle of the seventeenth century the private inn was well established in England and on the Continent. By this time inns had vastly improved. Samuel Johnson echoed a popular sentiment of the time: "There is nothing which has yet been contrived by man, by which so much happiness is produced as by a good tavern or inn."[4] Inns in those days were important social gathering places, and people congregated at the ones where political and literary figures stayed regularly. One collector of historical anecdotes tells of Thomas Telford, a British engineer who was considered something of a celebrity as well as delightful company: "In London, he stayed at the Ship Inn in Charing Cross, which was always crowded with his friends. A new landlord purchased the inn without knowing that Telford was about to move into a house of his own on Abingdon Street. When he found out he was utterly dismayed. 'Not leaving!' he exclaimed. 'I have just paid seven hundred and fifty pounds for you.'"[5] In France, large buildings that had rooms to let by the day, week, or longer were called *hôtel garni*. The word "hotel" was first used in England in about 1760 by the Fifth Duke of Devonshire to name a lodging establishment in London.[6]

In 1794 the first hotel in the United States opened—the 70-room City Hotel on Broadway in New York City. Daniel Boorstin, an American historian, notes that American hotels played a very different role than European hotels:

> Lacking a royal palace as the center of "Society," Americans created their counterpart in the community hotel. Hotels were usually the centers of lavish private entertainment (which, being held there, acquired a public significance) and of the most important public celebrations. The hotel lobby, like the outer rooms of a royal palace, became a loitering place, a headquarters of gossip, a vantage point for a glimpse of the great, the rich, and the powerful.[7]

One of the first hotels to clearly reflect this purpose in its architecture was the 170-room Tremont House, opened in Boston in 1829. Besides having a colonnaded marble portico, it featured formal public rooms with Ionic columns designed to give the hotel a palatial feeling. The Tremont was also the first hotel to have bellpersons, front desk employees, locks on guestroom doors, and free soap for guests. It is considered the first modern American hotel. Its designer, Isaiah Rogers, went on to build many other hotels and became one of the most influential hotel architects of the nineteenth century.

Hotels were often the first places where the public could experience new technology. The Tremont was one of the first large buildings in America to incorporate extensive plumbing facilities. The first public building to be heated by steam was the Eastern Exchange Hotel in Boston. Elevators were first introduced in hotels (New York's Fifth Avenue Hotel had one installed in 1859), and within three years after Thomas Edison announced in 1879 the commercial feasibility of his incandescent lamp, it was tried in hotels. The Hotel Everett on Park Row in New York City was the first hotel lit by electricity.[8]

Early Restaurants
About the same time that hotels were gaining a strong foothold on both sides of the Atlantic, restaurants were also achieving prominence. According to *Food in History*, professionally cooked food was not a new concept:

> It had been known in Mesopotamia in the time of Nebuchadnezzar, and the population of the Near East still, in medieval times, preferred not to cook at home but to buy forcemeat balls, roast mutton, fish fritters, pancakes, and almond paste sweets from the market. It may, indeed, have been from the Arab world, by way of Spain, that the custom of buying ready made food was reintroduced into Europe. . . .[9]

An interest in preparing delicious food on a large scale was stimulated in Europe by Louis XIV of France, who reigned from 1643 to 1715. He made dining a state occasion. The first restaurant (as distinct from an inn, tavern, or food specialty house) was opened by Boulanger in Paris in 1765. While he was ambassador to France, Thomas Jefferson learned to appreciate French food and wines and used them in White House functions when he became president. In 1829 America's first real continental restaurant opened— Delmonico's in New York City.

The Impact of Modern Transportation

It was the railroads first, and later the automobile and airplane, that changed the face of the hotel industry in the nineteenth and twentieth centuries.

Railroads. After rail travel became popular in Europe, the most desirable place to build a hotel in major European cities was next to the railroad station. In the United States, hotels and restaurants were built beside the railroad tracks as they crisscrossed the country. In many instances, hotels were built well *before* the arrival of the railroad or even before a town had sprung up. The idea was that a proper hotel would attract the railroads and, with them, settlers and commerce. Daniel Boorstin quotes from a Victorian novelist, Anthony Trollope, whose book on North America makes this point:

> In the States of America the first sign of an incipient settlement is a hotel five stories high with an office, a bar, a cloak-room, three gentlemen's parlours, a ladies' entrance and two hundred bedrooms. . . . Whence are to come the sleepers in those two hundred bedrooms and who is to pay for the gaudy sofas and numerous lounging chairs of the ladies' parlours? In all other countries the expectation would extend itself simply to travellers; to travellers or to strangers sojourning in the land. But this is by no means the case as to these speculations in America. When the new hotel rises up in the wilderness, it is presumed that people will come there with the express object of inhabiting it. The hotel itself will create a population, as the railways do. With us railways run to the towns; but in the States the towns run to the railways. It is the same thing with the hotels.[10]

Resorts also had their beginnings with the growth of the railroad. The Catskill Mountains were a popular day trip by rail from New York City and eventually became the home of the "borscht circuit," a group of mountain resorts that spawned many great entertainers in the 1930s, 1940s, and 1950s—Jack Benny, George Burns, Milton Berle, and others. Two of the most famous Catskill resorts were the Concord and Grossinger's. Soon railroad companies started developing resorts of their own. In Florida, Henry Flagler built The Breakers in Palm Beach and other hotels in Miami and Key West to accommodate passengers on his Flagler Line. In West Virginia, the Chesapeake & Ohio Railway company developed the Greenbriar Resort.

Trains significantly increased the amount of business travel. With that growth came a demand from business travelers for a uniform standard of hotel quality so that they could go from one city to another and enjoy similar services wherever they went.

Hotel-chain pioneers. The demand for a uniform standard was first recognized by Ellsworth Statler. He started his hospitality career in 1878 as a bellhop in Wheeling, West Virginia. In 1908 Statler opened the first hotel bearing his name in Buffalo, New York. It featured telephones in every room, advanced plumbing, full-size closets with lights, ice water,

Hotels were sometimes built well before the arrival of the railroad—or even before there was much of a town! Courtesy of the State Archives of Michigan.

and other amenities. Soon he had other Statler hotels in Cleveland, Detroit, St. Louis, and Boston. Statler's genius was his ability to increase service and simplify operations on a chain-wide basis. He started giving free morning newspapers to guests, provided radios at no extra charge, and even developed "The Statler Service Code," which all employees were required to memorize and carry with them.

Another early hotel-chain pioneer was Conrad Hilton, born in 1887 in San Antonio, New Mexico. Young Conrad started his hotel career by renting rooms in his family's home to travelers. In 1919 he bought his first hotel, the Mobley, in Cisco, Texas. Hilton continued to buy hotels throughout his lifetime (he died in 1979), including the Waldorf Astoria, which his company purchased control of in 1949, and the entire Statler chain, acquired in 1954.

The Sheraton chain—at one time the largest hotel chain in the world—was started in 1941 by Ernest Henderson, a Boston investor. The chain began when Henderson, along with associate Robert Lowell Moore, acquired several New England hotels in the mid-1930s. One of the hotels had an expensive electric sign on the roof bearing the name "Sheraton." Deciding it would be too costly to remove, the owners kept the sign and applied the name to all of their future hotels.[11] Henderson was more interested in making money than he was in hotelkeeping or providing hospitable service. His primary interest was in new forms of financing, taxes, and other methods for increasing equity. Sheraton was finally sold to the International Telephone and Telegraph Corporation (ITT) in 1969.

Automobiles. As the automobile became more popular and interstate highways were built, a growing need developed for roadside eating establishments and accommodations. Some of the earliest restaurants were roadside diners, which evolved from the horse-drawn lunch wagons that provided sandwiches and coffee to factory workers. By the 1930s, these stainless steel and porcelain diners were a familiar sight along American highways.

Restaurant- and motel-chain pioneers. Just as the railroads encouraged the development of hotel chains with standardized products, so too did automobiles and highways encourage the development of restaurant and motel chains.

In 1925 Howard Johnson purchased a small drugstore in Wollaston, Massachusetts. He soon started selling a chocolate ice cream product he developed to supplement his drugstore's revenues. The ice cream did so well that soon Johnson added other flavors until he had developed the "28 Flavors" that became his trademark. Johnson was one of the first franchisors. By 1940 he had 100 roadside restaurants selling Howard Johnson's ice cream and other food.

Like Statler, Johnson was interested in standardization and quality control. The building, decor, and seating arrangements for each restaurant in the Howard Johnson's chain were standardized. Johnson also created a central commissary to make sure his restaurants' food products were consistent and of the proper quality. This commissary prepared frozen entrées for delivery to Howard Johnson's franchises all over the country. Johnson insisted that his franchisees buy everything from him (which was legal at that time) and operate their restaurants exactly as he specified.

The concept of standardized roadside accommodations was the brainchild of Kemmons Wilson. Wilson was a movie theater operator in Memphis, Tennessee, who came home very unhappy from a family vacation where he felt he and his wife and children had been overcharged to stay in substandard motel rooms. In 1952 Wilson built his first Holiday Inn in Memphis. Its unique features included a restaurant—most motels did not have one—as well as two double beds in every room. Wilson did not believe in charging for children—he had three of his own and paying extra for them when he stayed at a motel irked him. Other marketing innovations by Wilson included a huge sign (he had learned the value of signs from his years in the theater business). Wilson also recognized the value of his guests. He instructed his managers to offer to make reservations by telephone for departing guests who wished to stay at another Holiday Inn down the road. Like Statler, Wilson offered free "extras" to his overnight guests—free TV, free ice, and a telephone in every room.

Today, Holiday Inns, Inc., is one of the largest hotel chains in the world. In 1990 there were 1,581 hotels, with a total of 314,261 rooms, operating under the Holiday Inn name.[12] The company is no longer American-owned, however. In 1989 the Holiday Corporation sold the Holiday Inn chain to Bass PLC, a British company. The original American firm changed its name and continues to operate its gaming division and sell franchises for its Hampton Inn and Embassy Suites products.

Finally, no discussion of early restaurant and motel chains would be complete without mentioning Ray Kroc, the man who founded McDonald's.

Many World War I pilots started independent, non-scheduled air transportation services after the war. Passenger comfort was not a consideration. Courtesy of the State of Michigan Archives.

Kroc was a milk shake-machine salesman who, at the age of 52, called on two brothers who had set up a hamburger stand in San Bernadino, California. They were not interested in expanding their concept, which featured large lighted golden arches, but Kroc was. Within 40 years of making a deal that allowed him to franchise the operation, Kroc had a chain of restaurants stretching first across the nation and then around the world. The success of McDonald's is due largely to its commitment to QSC&V— quality, service, cleanliness, and value—combined with a simple standardized concept utilizing many of the same ideas originally pioneered by Howard Johnson.

Airplanes. In a sense, the end of the First World War marked the beginning of commercial aviation on both sides of the Atlantic. The impetus, of course, was the experience gained in flying planes during the war and the number of trained pilots and mechanics available to exploit this new form of transportation. In 1919 the British launched their first trans-channel commercial flights linking the business capitals of London and Paris. The flight took two and a half hours and the first planes used were converted bombers in which the pilot and the passenger sat in open cockpits.

In America the first commercial flights were inaugurated in 1918 as joint ventures of the U.S. Signal Corps and the Post Office. These flights delivered mail only. Many pilots who had learned to fly in the war bought surplus planes from the government and started independent non-scheduled service between various points such as New York and Boston, and Los Angeles and Catalina Island. Soon there were regular flights carrying both mail and passengers between major cities. But the air age was really ushered in when a young stunt flyer named Charles Lindbergh, whose act of standing on the top wing of a looping plane thrilled crowds all over the country, decided to compete for a prize of $25,000 being offered to the first person to fly solo across the Atlantic Ocean. At 7:55 a.m. on May 27,

1927, Lindbergh took off from Roosevelt Field on Long Island, New York, and landed at Le Bourget in Paris 33 hours and 30 minutes later. Lindbergh had shown that the airplane was a practical means of traveling over long distances, and, as a result, bankers and others who had been hesitant to put money into this new field of transportation lined up to invest in commercial aviation. The air age had arrived.

Almost from the beginning, commercial aviation has had a substantial impact on the hospitality industry. The airplane made affordable mass transportation over long distances possible. Business travelers were able to leave their homes in New York in the morning and have a luncheon meeting in Chicago, whereas formerly it took a full day of travel by train. Resort areas such as the Caribbean and Hawaii, which had previously been accessible only by boat, now were more convenient to a larger number of tourists. The airplane was a boon to the hospitality industry.

Innovative hotel chains immediately saw an opportunity for a whole new range of lodging and food service products. In-flight food catering services, airport terminal restaurants of all types, and airport hotels became big business.

The Nature of the Hospitality Industry

What exactly is the hospitality industry? This is not an easy question and there are many different answers to be found in different books on the subject. Some view the hospitality industry as being composed of four sectors: lodging, food, entertainment, and travel. If you refer to the first chapter, you can see that this is just about the way the U.S. Travel Data Center defines the travel and tourism industry as a whole! However, usually the hospitality industry is viewed as being confined mainly to lodging and food service businesses—specifically, those that provide short-term or transitional lodging and/or food. If we define the industry this way we can include such facilities as school dormitories, nursing homes, and other institutions. Exhibit 2.1 shows the businesses that constitute the hospitality industry.

Size   The hospitality industry has grown tremendously in recent decades. Some of the reasons for this growth are a generally higher standard of living among Americans, increased leisure time, rapid advances in medicine that have increased life spans, the growth in education, and the greater opportunities available in a rapidly developing society. Today, services and goods that in the past were only available to the privileged few can now be enjoyed by a much larger percentage of the population. In the past ten years, the number of people who have flown on an airplane or taken a cruise has increased dramatically, for example.

We can get an idea of the hospitality industry's size by examining some of the statistics for the lodging and food service industries.

Lodging. The American Hotel & Motel Association estimates that in 1989 there were 44,300 hotels, motels, and inns in the United States, with approximately three million guestrooms. The lodging industry's receipts have been climbing steadily:

Exhibit 2.1 The Hospitality Industry

Lodging Operations		Food Service Operations	
Hotels	Motels	Restaurants	Lodging Properties
Motor Hotels	Resorts	Bars/Taverns	Catering
Camps	Parks	Snack Bars	Lunch Counters
Pensions		Cruise Ships	Institutions
		Contract Food Companies	

Year	Billions
1984	$38.9
1985	$42.1
1986	$43.1
1987	$45.0
1988	$53.8
1989	$57.1

However, there is no doubt that industry growth is slower now, compared to the rapid hotel building and expansion of the early 1980s. In fact, many hotels, after years of comfortable success, are showing red ink for the first time. To understand how this happened we must go back to the 1970s, when the economy was so buoyant that the demand for hotel rooms exceeded the supply. A natural consequence of this was a steep increase in average room rates. The early 1980s brought a recession, and with it came some tax incentives to create new jobs and economic growth by encouraging the building of new hotel properties. The combination of an increase in the number of hotel rooms and (because of the recession) a constraint on raising room rates was lethal to the industry. One result was extensive discounting. Another consequence was that new hotels had to engage in expensive marketing programs, which cut into their operating profits and increased pre-opening costs.

The Tax Reform Act of 1986 slowed down the construction of new hotels. It eliminated the investment tax credit, lengthened depreciation periods, decreased the value of deductions, and eliminated the ability of investors to use losses from real-estate investments to offset active income (in other words, a non-profitable hotel was no longer an attractive tax shelter). Besides this, in recent years fixed operating costs for hotels such as rent, property taxes, and insurance have risen dramatically. This has meant that higher occupancy rates are needed to achieve targeted profit levels.

Food Service. The food service industry is experiencing a healthier growth pattern. Food service sales have risen dramatically since 1970:

Year	Billions
1970	$ 47.8
1975	$ 70.3
1980	$119.6
1985	$178.4
1989	$227.3

Exhibit 2.2 Average Weekly Expenditures for Food Purchased Away from Home

Demographic Group	Average Weekly Expenditure
Age*	
Under 25	$23.93
25–34	29.54
35–44	38.92
45–54	38.40
55–65	28.02
65+	15.51
Income	
Under $15,000	14.99
$15,000–19,999	24.53
$20,000–29,999	29.34
$30,000–39,999	37.46
$40,000+	57.87
Marital Status	
Single	26.41
Married	33.80
Region	
South	26.77
Midwest	27.66
Northeast	30.03
West	33.27
*Head of household	

Source: U.S. Department of Commerce and the Bureau of Labor.

According to the National Restaurant Association, food service industry sales equal nearly five percent of the gross national product. Over 8 million people are employed in the industry. That number is expected to reach 11.4 million by the year 2000.

The U.S. Department of Commerce and the Bureau of Labor estimate the average weekly expenditures per household for food purchased away from home in 1987 was approximately $29. Exhibit 2.2 shows weekly expenditures for various demographic groups. As can be seen from these statistics, the heaviest group of restaurant users are between the ages of 35 and 44. As you would expect, there is a direct correlation between income and check size. Married people spend more per person than single people. And, in general, the size of the check seems to be higher in the West than in any other part of the country (this could be because of the high cost of living in this region, however).

A dynamic force behind the food service industry's growth is modern marketing techniques. Even institutions that have traditionally been content with non-profit food service programs have begun to market their food service differently in order to turn non-profit centers into revenue producers. For example, many hospitals now have the equivalent of a hotel's food and beverage manager in charge of their food service. Gourmet meals and wine are available to patients at extra cost. Hospitals also run employee cafeterias, special dining rooms for doctors, and coffee shops for visitors. Some hospitals have gone into off-premises catering as well to maximize kitchen use. Many university food service programs now employ marketing techniques such as theme meals (Italian nights, for example), tent cards, and more attractive food presentation and displays to keep students eating on campus instead of at the nearest Pizza Hut or Kentucky Fried Chicken.

Characteristics

All service businesses have characteristics that substantially affect the way their products and services are delivered to consumers. These characteristics include:

- Intangibility

- Inseparability

- Perishability

- Repetitiveness

- Labor-intensiveness

Intangibility. Although hotels and restaurants sell service—that is, an intangible—we tend to think of them in terms of their tangible products—rooms and meals. This can be a costly error. Although it is common in the industry to speak of "selling" rooms, guests do not buy rooms—they buy safe, comfortable, and clean accommodations. Restaurants do not simply sell food. They sell convenience, atmosphere, and special occasions as well.

Restaurants do not simply sell food. They also sell the intangibles of convenience, atmosphere, and special occasions.

Peter Drucker, the well-known management consultant, has pointed out that people almost never buy a tangible product; rather, they buy the intangible utility they expect to receive from that product.

Many successful hospitality marketers understand this very well. One good example is McDonald's. Think about some of its memorable advertising slogans: "You deserve a break today," or "We do it all for you." If McDonald's thought it was primarily in the business of selling tangible products—hamburgers—its slogan might have been, "You deserve a hamburger today." McDonald's understands that it is in the business of selling the intangibles of convenience and a pleasant experience, of which the food is certainly an important, but not the only, part. Equally important is the restaurant's decor, cleanliness, and smiling crew.

As previously mentioned, hotels do not sell rooms, although the room plays a role in what guests actually purchase. What a hotel sells is the experience of staying there. The hotel experience starts the moment a guest makes a reservation. A long wait on the telephone for a reservation or an inattentive front desk agent* can set the whole tone for what is to follow. When the guest enters the lobby, is he or she greeted with respect and warmth or simply like another body to fill an empty bed? Does a bellperson help with the luggage? Is the guestroom clean? Does the mattress sag? Is there a restaurant on the premises, and is a table available? The answers to these and a hundred other questions are what constitute the intangible product a hotel sells.

Inseparability. In the industrial sector, tangible goods are produced in a factory and then transported to distribution points, where they are sold to consumers who take them somewhere else for consumption. This is true whether we are talking about personal computers or canned soup. In the service sector, however, the consumer comes to a service "factory" and consumes the product on the premises. Production and consumption are simultaneous.

Hotels and restaurants are perfect examples of service businesses. Their services are purchased, produced, delivered, and consumed on-site. This puts unique pressure on hotels, restaurants, and other businesses that provide service. When you buy a couch for your living room, you don't care whether the workers who put your couch together were unfriendly or indifferent, and it doesn't matter what the factory looked like because you didn't visit it to watch your couch being made. At a hotel or restaurant, however, you do visit the "factory" where your "product" is being "manufactured"—and you want the factory to be attractive and clean, and the workers to be friendly and attentive.

Another factor is introduced when production and consumption are simultaneous: the consumer becomes a part of the production process. The company that manufactured your couch did not have to deal with you while your couch was being made. In a hotel or restaurant, however, employees must try to provide the product—consistent services and goods

---

*There are many different terms in the hospitality industry for the employees who check guests in and out at the front desk. "Front desk clerk," "room clerk," "guest service agent," and "front desk agent" are some examples. The industry has not agreed on which term is most appropriate, but for the sake of consistency we will use "front desk agent" in this text when referring to these employees.

delivered in a hospitable way—despite the fact that some guests are unfriendly, uncooperative, or have unreasonable expectations. Quality control is also more difficult. You can thoroughly test and inspect a couch before shipping it to a consumer; a service cannot be inspected before the guest receives it.

Another facet of inseparability in the service industry is that every hotel, restaurant, and club is a microcosm of the entire industry. Each is a financial entity, a marketing entity, and a production and distribution entity. Having all of these functions under one roof means that service managers must be specialists as well as generalists. Besides having good general management skills, they must possess some basic technical skills in such areas as finance and accounting, marketing, and operations. Technical skills in the operations area include food production techniques, plant management, and human resources management.

Perishability. Services are more perishable than any tangible product. Unsold artificial Christmas trees can be stored until next year. Yesterday's unused hotel room and empty restaurant seat represent lost sales opportunities that can never be recovered.

A service does not exist until it is delivered to and experienced by the guest. You cannot create an inventory of services and store them for later use when they are needed. This puts pressure on service providers. Because a service cannot be stored, providers of services must be prepared to (1) create services on demand and (2) price them to sell. The longer a guest has to wait for a service, the less real or perceived value it has. A hotel room that is priced too high to sell is worthless.

Repetitiveness. Many people find the hospitality industry exciting because each day brings new guests and new situations. But some service activities are standardized and repetitive. During an eight-hour shift, a front desk agent will register many guests by asking the same questions and performing the same functions over and over again. A food server or bartender's day consists of taking orders, recording guest checks, and serving in a prescribed manner. The repetitive nature of the work can adversely affect the consistency of goods and services. Workers tend to get tired, or want to do things differently for a change of pace. Quality control therefore can become a problem.

Labor-Intensiveness. Service businesses are labor-intensive. They depend on personal interaction between employees and guests and complicated physical tasks. While many manufacturers of tangible goods have turned to automation and/or robots on a large scale, the service industries still rely mainly on people.

Careers in the Hospitality Industry

Why do people go into the hospitality industry? If you were to ask people who have spent their careers in this business what they like most about it, you would get a wide variety of answers. Some of the most popular are:

- *The industry offers more career options than most.* No matter what kind of work you enjoy doing, and wherever your aptitudes lie, there is an organization that can use your talents.

- *The work is interesting.* Because hotels, restaurants, and clubs are complete production, distribution, and service units, managers are involved in a broad array of activities.

- *There are many opportunities to be creative.* Hotel and restaurant managers have a chance to design new products to meet the needs of their guests; to produce training programs for employees; and to implement challenging advertising, sales promotion, and marketing plans.

- *This is a "people" business.* Managers and supervisors spend their workdays satisfying guests, motivating employees, and negotiating with vendors and others.

- *Hospitality jobs are not nine-to-five jobs.* Hours are highly flexible in many positions. (Some see this as a disadvantage, however.)

- *There are opportunities for long-term career growth.* If you have ambition, you are unlikely to find yourself trapped in a dead-end job.

Despite these advantages, there are some aspects of the business that many people find disagreeable:

- *Long hours.* In most hospitality businesses the hours are long. The 40-hour workweek is not the norm, and 50- to 60-hour workweeks are not unusual.

- *Non-traditional schedules.* Hospitality managers do not work a Monday through Friday schedule. In the hospitality field you will probably find yourself working at many times, including weekends, when your friends are relaxing. As one manager told his employees, "If you can't come to work Saturday or Sunday, don't bother to come in on Monday."

- *Pressure.* There are busy periods when managers are likely to be under intense pressure to perform.

- *Low beginning salaries.* Entry-level jobs for management trainees tend to be low-paying compared to some other industries.

Selecting an Industry Segment

As we have pointed out, one of the attributes that prompts many people to enter the hospitality industry is its diversity. It is difficult to imagine another business in which there are as many different kinds of work you can do. Before a hotel, restaurant, or club is built, for example, a feasibility study is made by a management consulting firm. Research-oriented hospitality graduates often join consulting firms because of the opportunity to combine their interest in collecting and analyzing data with their interest in hotels and restaurants.

Management positions abound in every conceivable area within the industry. Although hotels and restaurants may represent the largest sectors, they are by no means the only ones. There is a need for hospitality managers in clubs, hospitals, nursing homes, universities and schools,

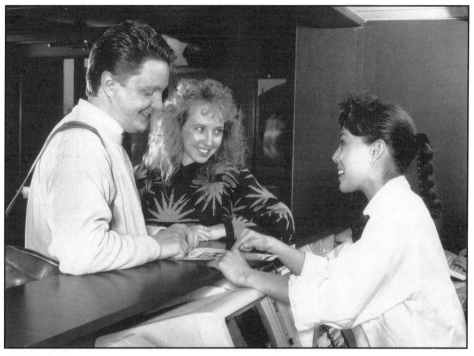

There are plenty of opportunities in the hospitality industry for individuals with people skills.

cafeterias, prisons, corporate dining rooms, snack bars, management companies, airlines, cruise ships, and many other organizations. Even the royal palace of the Sultan of Brunei is run by the Hyatt organization!

Within these organizations you can go into marketing and sales, rooms management, housekeeping, cooking, engineering, dining-room management, menu planning, security, accounting, food technology, forecasting and planning, recreation, entertainment, guest relations, and so on. Moreover, you have an almost unlimited choice of where you want to live—you can choose between warm climates and cold; cities, suburbs, and even rural areas; the East, South, Midwest, West, and foreign countries. There simply is no other industry that offers more diverse career opportunities.

Skills Inventory. One of the best ways to select a career niche you will be happy with is to start by making an inventory or list of your own skills. What are the tasks you do best? Most skills fall into one of three areas:

- Skills dealing with data

- Skills dealing with people

- Skills dealing with things

You will probably find that the majority of your skills will fall into one or two of these areas.

People whose skills fall into the data group are good in subjects such as math and science and enjoy working with computers. They like analyzing information, comparing figures, working with graphs, and solving abstract problems. Such individuals would enjoy doing feasibility studies for a hospitality management consulting firm such as Pannell Kerr Forster. They would also probably be happy in corporate planning departments of large hotel and restaurant chains where data is analyzed and demand is forecast. Most auditors and accountants fall into the data-skills group.

If you are good at dealing with people, you most likely enjoy helping them and taking care of their needs. You can take and give advice and instructions. You probably also enjoy supervising and motivating other people, and you have found that they respond to your leadership. Individuals with people skills are good at negotiating and selling—they like to bargain and are not afraid to make decisions. In the hospitality industry, general managers and marketing and sales managers of hotels often fall into this category. So do independent restaurant owners, catering managers, and club managers.

The third group of skills are those dealing with things. If you excel in this area, you may be good at building or fixing things. You like to work with your hands and use tools and gadgets of all kinds. You enjoy setting up things—when there is a party in your house you like to put up the decorations, for example. If your skills lie here you may be attracted to food production jobs. Chefs, bakers, and cooks all like working with things. So do the engineers who manage the hotel's physical plant.

Most of us have skills in more than one area. What is important is to identify your skills and rank them according to how much you enjoy using them. That will help you find a career niche that suits you.

Career Options

The type of business you choose for your first job puts you into a definite career slot. While skills and experience are usually transferable within a particular industry segment, such as resort hotels, generally you cannot jump from one kind of industry segment to another very easily. For example, it's unlikely you would progress from managing a Taco Bell to managing food service in a hospital, or from managing a Motel 6 to managing a Ritz-Carlton. However, it's important to note that owners and operators of motels and fast-food restaurants often have incomes that are as high as, or higher than, those of hotel managers at some deluxe hotels. With this in mind, let's take a close look at the career options open to you.

Hotels. There are many types of hotels to choose from. There are luxury commercial properties such as the Stanford Court in San Francisco or the Plaza in New York. There are mid-market properties—the Marriott and Hilton chains operate many hotels in this industry segment. Then there are economy properties like Days Inn and Best Western. In recent years, further segmentation has occurred. One fast-growing segment is all-suite hotels in luxury and mid-market versions. Embassy Suites and Comfort Inns are contenders in this field.

Extended-stay properties are also growing rapidly. Residence Inn by Marriott caters to people who stay for an average of five to seven days. Guests have kitchens and conversation/reading areas in rooms that are about twenty percent larger than ordinary hotel rooms.

Resort hotels are another type of hotel. Some of these, like the Boca Raton Hotel and Beach Club in Florida and the Arizona Biltmore, are geared to convention groups. Others, such as the Williamsburg Inn in

Virginia and the Trapp Family Lodge in Vermont, cater to individuals and small meetings. Finally, there are casino hotels like Caesars Palace in Las Vegas and Trump's Castle Hotel and Casino in Atlantic City. These are specialized operations that are organized and managed differently from other properties.

People who choose the hotel business as a career often do so because they enjoy traveling and living in different places. Hotel management personnel are in great demand, and since most hotels are part of chains, managers are often offered opportunities to move into new positions in different geographic locations. Some people enjoy working in large metropolitan areas and in the course of their careers may live in New York, Chicago, and San Francisco. Others like warm weather resorts and may start in Miami, then move to a better position in Puerto Rico, then on to Hawaii, and so forth. Managers who like to ski or climb mountains often opt for hotels in the Rocky Mountains of Colorado, the Cascades of Washington and Oregon, or even the Berkshires of New England. Some people enjoy quiet suburban life and move their families to communities where there are independent inns or conference centers. At an independent hotel you are not as likely to be uprooted from your home and community by a transfer.

Another way of thinking about hotel career options is to consider whether you would rather be part of a large national or international hotel chain or work for an independent operation. There are a multitude of opportunities in both areas. The arguments for working for a large hotel chain include:

- *Better training.* Companies such as Marriott and Hyatt have very sophisticated training programs. In many cases, you will get up to a year of education in one of their management training programs and get paid at the same time.

- *More opportunities for advancement.* Suppose your goal is to be a food and beverage director. If you work for an independent hotel, you will usually have to wait until the person holding that position is promoted or leaves the hotel before you have a chance of moving up. But a large chain is always developing new properties; thus there are usually more opportunities to get ahead faster without switching companies.

- *Better benefits.* If you want superior life and health insurance benefits, vacation and sick time, use of a company car, moving expenses, stock purchase options, and so forth, you are more likely to get these from a large chain.

A career with independent hotels also offers some advantages, however:

- *More chances to be creative.* You will have a chance to set standards and initiate change instead of just adhering to company programs and rules.

- *More control.* You are more likely to be in control of your own destiny. In large chains, decisions that involve your salary, advancement, and place of residence are often made by persons in corporate headquarters thousands of miles away. In an independent hotel, however, you deal with the people who will be deciding your fate on a regular basis. And, as mentioned earlier, with an independent hotel you are not as likely to be transferred.

- *Better learning environments.* Independent hotels offer better learning environments for entrepreneurs. Because all the financial and operating decisions are made on the property, you will have a better opportunity to understand how and why things are done the way they are. If you intend to buy your own hotel some day, you will learn more at an independent operation than at a chain operation where data is forwarded to headquarters for analysis.

Positions within hotels. Whether the hotel is a chain or an independent operation, as a hospitality student you have a wide variety of hotel positions open to you. Many people enjoy aiming for the top administrative job of general manager, but others prefer to specialize in certain areas. These include:

- Catering

- Engineering

- Food and beverage

- Finance and accounting

- Human resources

- Marketing and sales

- Rooms management

- Systems management

Let's take a look at management positions in these areas.

The *general manager* is the chief operating officer of the hotel. He or she is responsible for attracting guests and making sure that they are safe and well served while visiting. The general manager supervises, coordinates, and administers policies established by the owners or chain operators. Chains such as Holiday Inn and Marriott have very specific service, operating, and decorating guidelines. For example, the arrangement of furniture and room amenities is usually standardized by corporate headquarters. It is the general manager's job to see that all departments adhere to those standards.

Most general managers hold frequent meetings with their department heads. If a convention is about to arrive, for instance, the general manager will want to make sure that the staff is on top of all the details necessary to make the conventioneers' stays pleasant: limousine service, check-in procedures, banquets, meeting rooms, audiovisual facilities, entertainment, and so on.

The financial performance of the business is the general manager's main responsibility. The compensation a general manager receives is often tied to the profitability of the business he or she manages. Hiring and firing when necessary is also part of a general manager's job. The general manager can be involved in union negotiations as well.

Good general managers are skilled at getting along with people. They are able to forge positive relationships with employees, guests, and the community at large. They believe in team effort and know how to get things done through other people. Effective general managers are also technically proficient. They do not subscribe to "seat of the pants" managing but instead study problems and carefully formulate short- and long-term solutions.

A *catering manager* promotes and sells a hotel's banquet facilities and uses his or her expertise to plan, organize, and perform the hotel's banquets, which can range from fine dining to picnic buffets. Knowledge of food costs, preparation techniques, and pricing is essential. Good catering managers are also aware of social customs and etiquette. Creativity and imagination are useful qualities as well.

Chief engineers are responsible for the hotel's physical operation and maintenance. This includes the electrical, heating, air conditioning, refrigeration, and plumbing systems. Chief engineers must have extensive background in mechanical and electrical equipment and may need numerous licenses.

Food and beverage managers direct the production and service of food and beverages. They are responsible for training the dining room and kitchen staffs and ensuring quality control. Food and beverage managers at large properties work with their head chefs to plan menus, and with their beverage managers to select wines and brands of liquor. At small properties the food and beverage manager has sole responsibility for these tasks. Menu pricing and cost control are also the province of the food and beverage manager.

This job requires a keen interest in food and wines and an up-to-date knowledge of food trends and guests' tastes. Because food and beverage service is offered from 15 to 24 hours a day, managers in this field must be prepared to work long shifts and endure periods of pressure—dealing with unexpectedly large dinner crowds, getting a banquet served, and so on.

The *controller* is in charge of the accounting department and all of its functions, such as the management of credit, payroll, guest accounts, and all cashiering activities. The controller also prepares budgets and daily, weekly, and monthly reports showing revenues, expenses, and other statistics that managers may require. Controllers are detail-oriented people and favor an analytical approach to business problems.

Human resources managers are in charge of employee relations within a hotel. This includes counseling employees, developing and administering programs to maintain and improve employee morale, monitoring the work environment, and so on. Human resources managers are also responsible for recruiting and training the majority of the hotel's employees. An important part of their job is to oversee compliance with equal employment opportunity and affirmative action laws and policies. People who choose human resources as a career usually have a good deal of empathy and are excellent negotiators.

The marketing and sales function at a hotel consists of several different activities. Sometimes a large hotel will have two managers overseeing marketing and sales. In that case, the *marketing and sales manager* develops and implements a marketing plan and budget. This plan lays out the ways in which the hotel intends to attract business. It includes sections on meeting and convention sales, as well as local sales, advertising, and promotion plans. The marketing and sales manager is also in charge of corporate accounts and may work with an advertising and public relations agency. The *director of sales* conducts sales programs and makes sales calls on prospects for group and individual business. He or she usually reports to the marketing and sales manager. Marketing and sales people tend to be service-oriented and possess good communications skills.

Resident managers are often the executives in charge of the rooms division of a hotel. Their areas of responsibility include the front office, reservations, and housekeeping, as well as sources of revenue other than the food and beverage department, such as gift shops or recreational facilities. In small hotels, resident managers are also in charge of security. They report directly to the general manager and share responsibility for compliance with budgets and forecasts. Resident managers are good leaders and have many of the same qualities that general managers have.

Systems managers are the computer experts in a hotel. They are in charge of computerized management information systems—the computers used for reservations, room assignments, telephones, housekeeping, accounting functions, and labor and productivity reports. They often know how to write simple computer programs and easy-to-follow instructions for using computers. They have good problem-solving aptitudes and verbal and written communication skills.

The salaries for the hotel management positions just described vary according to the area of the country you are in, the size of the property, and your own experience. However, a survey done in southern Florida gives a good indication of average management salaries at various levels (see Exhibit 2.3).

Restaurants. There is also a wide variety of job opportunities and geographic locations to choose from within the restaurant industry. Those who are interested in restaurants often choose between chain operations and

Exhibit 2.3 Average Hotel Management Salaries

	Entry	Midpoint	High
General Manager	$60,400	$77,100	$93,800
Resident Manager	44,500	56,800	69,100
Food & Beverage Dir.	49,300	62,600	76,500
Marketing Dir.	40,200	51,300	62,400
Controller	40,200	51,300	62,400
Executive Chef	40,200	51,300	62,400
Human Resources Dir.	33,700	42,100	50,500
Chief Engineer	33,700	42,100	50,500
Reservations Manager	24,100	30,100	36,100

Source: *Miami Herald*, February 13, 1989, "Business" section.

independent operations in the commercial sector. But the institutional sector holds more interest for some. The hours for institutional food service managers are usually more regular than for commercial food service managers, and there may be better job security. Institutions with food service facilities include businesses, schools, hospitals, nursing homes, and prisons.

General types of commercial restaurants you can choose from include:

- Luxury

- Family

- Chain

- Limited-menu

Luxury. At the top of the restaurant spectrum are luxury restaurants in which the check per person can easily approach $100. Within the trade, these are sometimes called "white tablecloth" restaurants. Most of their patrons are on expense accounts. Lutece and the Four Seasons in Manhattan are perennial favorites in this class.

Guests at luxury restaurants usually enjoy superior service. Some luxury restaurants, for example, feature French service, in which meals are served from a cart or guéridon by formally dressed personnel. Tables are waited on by servers, a *chef du rang,* and an apprentice called a *commis du rang.* In the back of the house there is a classic kitchen in the tradition of Escoffier, with an executive chef and a brigade of cooks organized into departments headed by a *chef du partie.*

Contrary to popular belief, luxury restaurants are not necessarily high-profit ventures. Often, their rent and labor costs are excessive, and there is intense competition for a limited number of guests. These restaurants are usually open for both lunch and dinner (some only offer dinner), but the work starts early in the morning, when much of the food is purchased fresh and delivered for cooking that day, and runs until midnight or even later.

Many hospitality students aspire to run and eventually own a luxury restaurant. The top restaurants have a substantial volume and are very sophisticated operations. The Tavern on the Green in New York City sells $27 million in food and beverages annually, for example. Most do considerably less: $5 million to $6 million is a more typical figure for this kind of establishment. The best way to the top is to work in a luxury restaurant and learn the ropes. Many of these restaurants are owned by an individual. They are usually sold to an employee or another entrepreneur who can get financing when the owner retires. Banks and other lending institutions look to see what experience the prospective owner has before approving loans, so a good track record in management positions at similar restaurants is your best ticket for getting the financing you need to buy your "dream" restaurant.

Family. Family restaurants are found in suburban neighborhoods all over America and are generally patronized by people who live close by. Because their target market is families, many of these establishments do not serve alcohol, or serve only beer and wine. They often have a children's menu. Most family restaurants are independently owned.

Some luxury restaurants feature French service—an elegant service style in which all or part of the guests' orders are prepared or finished tableside.

Family restaurants are coming under increasing pressure from chain operations such as Red Lobster, The Olive Garden, and TGI Friday's.

Chain. Chain restaurants recruit the majority of their managers from universities such as Florida International, Michigan State, and Cornell. Entry-level jobs for graduates with hospitality degrees are often on the assistant-manager level, with progression to manager, then district manager responsible for a group of restaurants, and then regional manager.

Limited-menu. The limited-menu segment is the fastest growing part of the restaurant business today. Many of these establishments are fast-food

Exhibit 2.4 Average Food Service Manager Salaries

Vice President of Operations	$55,000
Marketing Manager (Regional)	51,900
F&B Manager (Regional)	46,500
F&B Manager (Property)	34,650
Executive Chef	34,041
Unit Manager	28,000
Manager Trainee	16,800

Source: National Restaurant Association, *Survey of Wages & Benefits: 1987–1988.*

restaurants or, as they prefer to be called, "quick service" restaurants. Menus hardly ever change in these restaurants. Their strategy calls for delivering a large number of meals at fairly low prices. The free-standing buildings they occupy are usually specially built food production factories filled with specially designed equipment. Minimum-wage employees turn out a standardized product. Successful fast-food chains depend on a large number of units so that they can engage in regional and national marketing and advertising programs. Expansion is usually accomplished through franchising, although some of the largest fast-food chains own as many as 30% of their units. Small fast-food chains such as A&W do as little as $300,000 annually per unit, but large chains like McDonald's average more than $1,500,000 per unit.

Hospitality students often bypass fast-food management opportunities. This is usually a mistake. To begin with, these jobs often pay very well and offer security and excellent benefit packages. Many McDonald's managers of single stores make as much as $40,000 annually; regional and district managers make considerably more (see Exhibit 2.4 for salaries of various food service personnel). Second, if you dream of owning your own franchise, the franchise company may help you if you've worked hard and well in one of their franchises. Domino's Pizza recruits all of its franchisees from its store managers and helps them arrange financing. Burger King and McDonald's have leasing programs that allow successful managers to lease units from them and pay the rent out of sales until they can afford to buy their unit.

Clubs. Clubs are another career option open to you. Clubs are very different from other types of hospitality businesses because the "guests"—the club members—are also the owners in many cases. There are country clubs, city clubs, luncheon clubs, yacht and sailing clubs, military clubs, tennis clubs, even polo clubs—all with clubhouses and other facilities that need to be managed. Some, like the Yale Club in New York City, offer complete hotel services. Large clubs have many of the same positions found in hotels and restaurants: a general manager, a food and beverage director, a catering director (weddings, bar mitzvahs, and other parties are an important part of club operations), and a controller.

Today it's estimated that there are more than 10,000 recreational and social clubs in the United States that lease or own their facilities and have them run by professional managers. Most clubs are non-profit organizations that

Exhibit 2.5 The 1989 Country Club Income Dollar

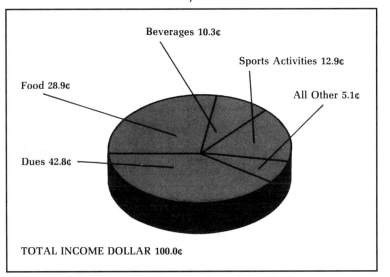

Source: *Clubs in Town and Country, 1989,* Pannell Kerr Forster.

are owned by and run for the benefit of the members. Some clubs are built by developers as part of housing developments and are proprietary, for-profit enterprises.

Most clubs are country clubs. Country clubs usually have a golf course for use by the club's members and their visitors. Many country clubs also have tennis, swimming, and dining facilities. The Westchester Country Club in Harrison, New York, has three golf courses, stables, a trap and skeet club, a beach club, tennis courts, rooms for members to stay overnight, and private homes. According to a 1990 report by Pannell Kerr Forster, in 1989 the average club received 42.8 cents from dues, 39.2 cents from food and beverage sales, and the rest from sports activities and other sources (see Exhibit 2.5).[13]

City clubs are the next biggest category of clubs. Some of these offer mainly dining and lounge facilities where members can socialize and entertain at lunch and dinner. Others have athletic facilities, overnight accommodations, libraries, and meeting rooms.

Many hospitality managers enjoy working in clubs. As Ted White, author of *Club Operations and Management,* points out, "In a private club the manager generally knows more about the business than the owners (the members). Therefore the manager has an opportunity to use all of his own ideas and imagination to develop a different club from the one down the street."[14] Since the nature of clubs requires specialized training and knowledge (such as golf course maintenance), club managers often come up through the ranks of other clubs.

Catering. Social catering is another part of the food service industry that many hospitality graduates become interested in. It is a business that requires very little capital to get into—facilities and equipment can usually be leased on a short-term basis from restaurant supply houses. Food servers can be hired as needed. In some cases, caterers provide only food; in others, they are responsible for tables, chairs, utensils, tents, servers, and decorations.

Contract Food Companies. Contract food companies are generally hired by organizations whose major business purpose is not food service, but they must for some reason provide it. The biggest users of contract food services are large manufacturing and industrial concerns in which workers have a short lunch period. Contractors such as ARA and Marriott establish cafeterias and executive dining rooms in these companies. The service is often subsidized by the contracting company, which may supply the space and utilities and, in some cases, underwrite some or all of the food costs. Schools and colleges, hospitals, sports arenas, airlines, cruise ships, and even prisons use contract food companies. In the case of airlines, meals are cooked and prepackaged in central commissaries and then delivered to the airplanes for preparation and service as needed.

Contract food management is somewhat unique because the manager must please two sets of employers. First there is the home office, then there is the client that has contracted for the service. Many contract food programs, such as those at schools and hospitals, have strong nutritional requirements as well. Others, such as airline programs, require a knowledge of advanced food technology.

Careers in contract food service are considered attractive by many hospitality majors. Contract food managers work more regular hours and are under less pressure than restaurant managers. Why? Because contract food managers are able to predict with certainty how many people they are going to feed, what they will feed them, and when the meals will be served.

Because of the large volume of meals involved, contract food managers must be highly skilled in professional management techniques and cost control. For this reason, contract food companies tend to hire people with experience within their industry and recruit from professional hospitality schools.

Institutional Food Service. Although contract food companies can supply food for schools and hospitals, the majority of these institutions handle their own food service programs. Most public schools, for example, belong to the National School Lunch Program established by the federal government in 1946. The purpose of this program is twofold: (1) to create a market for agricultural products produced by America's farmers, and (2) to serve a nutritious lunch to schoolchildren at a low cost. Public elementary schools, on the whole, tend to offer only those menu items that qualify for government support, but high schools often add items such as hamburgers, french fries, and even diet sodas. High school food managers are coming up with more creative and innovative menu plans to keep students in school cafeterias rather than in fast-food restaurants. Even the look of school cafeterias has changed as managers have tried to develop new methods of merchandising food.

Colleges and universities have also experienced changes in their food service programs. With more students living off campus, there has been a trend toward flexible meal plans in which students have a choice of how many meals they wish to purchase from the institution. To compete successfully, many universities have opened special table-service restaurants in addition to their traditional cafeterias. Another move has been to offer a more varied cafeteria menu with salad bars; croissant sandwiches; and even bagels, lox and cream cheese, and belgian waffles for breakfast.

Hospital programs are usually administered by trained dietitians or professional food service managers working with one. Menus are generally simple and nourishing. In the past, most hospitals had a central kitchen where all foods were prepared and then sent in insulated carts or trays to the patients' rooms. Recently, however, some hospitals have been decentralizing their food service. Under this system the hospital purchases frozen and portion-packed entrées and salads and keeps them in small pantries in various parts of the hospital. The meals are then plated and heated in microwave ovens as needed. As mentioned previously, another recent trend has been the attempt to turn hospital food service from a cost center into a revenue center. Some hospitals sell take-home food to doctors and employees and even do outside catering.

As you can see, institutions are beginning to compete with commercial food service operations for consumers. This means that there are more opportunities than ever before for hospitality students to enter what is clearly a growing field.

Your First Moves

Many students enter the hospitality field with a preconceived idea of what they want to do. Their parents, someone they admire, or a family friend may have been in the business and advised them to take a particular position. Or they may have had an enjoyable summer or part-time job in a restaurant or hotel. In the view of career counselors, however, it's better to keep an open mind. If you don't explore other career possibilities, there is a danger that you will overlook opportunities that might be more appealing to you in the long run. A sound understanding of your own goals and lifestyle, and a thorough knowledge of the companies that might be interested in what you offer, is an important foundation for your career search.

Every job you take should help you on your way to your final goal. If you look at jobs as stepping-stones on a career path, there are several questions you should answer before you decide whether a job is right for you:

- What can I learn from this job that will contribute to my career goals?

- What are the long-term opportunities for growth in this company?

- What is this company's reputation among the people I know? Is it a good place to work? Do they deliver on their promises to employees?

- How good is their training program? Do they really make an effort to educate me?

- What is the starting salary? What about other benefits? Do they add up to a competitive package?

- How do I feel about the location? Will I be living in a place I can be happy in? What about proximity to friends and relatives?

Management Training Programs

If you decide to start your career with a large company, be prepared for more studying. Most large hospitality organizations will want you to join their management training program. The best programs have two objectives: (1) to teach the technical skills that you will need to do your job well, and

(2) to teach you general management skills—planning, organizing, communicating, supervising, motivating, and so on. They will teach you how to deal effectively with employees and help you build on your strengths and minimize your weaknesses.

Every company's program is unique, but there are some similarities. Westin Hotels and Resorts has a program that is representative of the good ones. The first phase of Westin's program is a comprehensive introduction to Westin, from engineering to security to marketing. The second phase is skill-specific. Tasks and training formats depend on the training program selected—restaurants, human resources, the front office, food and beverage operations analysis, accounting, reservations, or housekeeping. Hyatt International has a similar 12-month training program in which trainees gain experience in every department of a hotel operation. After they've completed the program, the trainees are assigned to key supervisory positions in their chosen discipline.

The objective of Sheraton's management training programs is to "provide [Sheraton with] qualified management personnel who are skilled in the technical, human relations, and conceptual aspects of hospitality management." Sheraton states that its management programs are designed for "hotel/restaurant school graduates, Sheraton employees, and others who demonstrate exceptional potential for growth and advancement." The five programs Sheraton offers are general management, controllership, food and beverage management, personnel management, and systems management. All of these programs give trainees an opportunity to develop their skills. For example, systems management trainees are encouraged to develop new computer-system capabilities, and human resources trainees are given the opportunity to deal with personnel problems. These Sheraton programs run from 9 to 12 months.

Some companies offer shorter and more specific programs. The Marriott Hotels and Resorts ID (Individual Development) program provides training in sales and marketing, food and beverage, front desk, housekeeping, or gift shop management. These programs run from 8 to 24 weeks.

Many companies with management training programs also have sample career paths (see Exhibit 2.6). For example, Marriott trainees in catering typically start as catering service managers in hotels. Their next position might be executive meeting manager, catering manager, or catering sales manager. After a satisfactory performance at one of these posts, they would be promoted to director of catering. Someone on the sales and marketing career path typically starts with a position as convention service floor manager. The next promotion is to convention service manager or executive meeting planner. Successful managers then move on to catering or sales manager, then to director of sales or director of catering, and finally to director of marketing.

If you are interested in a career in club management, there are many independent clubs, as well as a chain operation that manages 200 clubs nationwide—the Club Corporation of America, headquartered in Dallas, Texas. This chain offers some management training. To apply for a club management position, in most cases you apply directly to the club(s) you are interested in. You will probably be trained on the job.

Exhibit 2.6 Sample Career Path—McDonald's

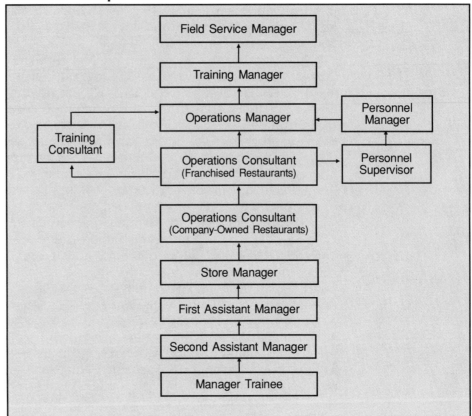

Courtesy of McDonald's Corporation, Oak Brook, Illinois.

Chapter Summary

Ellsworth Statler was the first modern American hotelier, followed by Conrad Hilton, Ernest Henderson, and finally Kemmons Wilson, who founded Holiday Inns—now one of the largest hotel chains in the world. Howard Johnson brought standardization to the roadside restaurant business. Ray Kroc pioneered the franchising concept. All of these men set standards and paved the way for hospitality innovators and developers in the latter part of the twentieth century.

One driving force behind the growth of the hospitality industry has been the development of transportation. As people were able to travel farther away from their homes, there was an increasing demand for transient lodging and eating establishments.

In recent years the hospitality industry's growth has been due in part to the average individual's higher standard of living, higher level of education, increased leisure time, and longer life span. The greater opportunities available in a rapidly developing society have also contributed to industry growth.

There is no doubt that growth in the lodging segment of the hospitality industry is slowing down when compared to the period of rapid building and expansion it enjoyed in the early 1980s. Today, many hotels, after years of comfortable success, are showing red ink for the first time. This has led to a renewed emphasis on making hotels profitable. The food service industry is experiencing a healthier growth pattern.

Most Americans are employed in service industries. Service industries have unique qualities. They include:

- *Intangibility.* The intangible service "product" is the total experience a guest has at a hotel or restaurant. Consumers are not sold simply a room or a meal.

- *Inseparability.* The consumer comes to the service "factory" to consume the service product. This makes quality control especially difficult.

- *Perishability.* Services are perishable. Yesterday's unsold hotel room or empty restaurant seat is a lost sales opportunity that can never be recovered.

  A service does not exist until it is delivered to and experienced by a guest. Since services cannot be stored, providers of services must create services on demand.

- *Repetitiveness.* Service procedures often tend to be standardized and repetitive.

- *Labor-intensiveness.* Service businesses are labor-intensive. Supervision and training programs are of paramount importance.

The hospitality industry offers many more career options than most. The work is interesting, and there are numerous opportunities for advancement. But some people don't like the occasional pressures and long hours that go along with many hospitality positions. Management positions in a hotel include general manager, catering manager, chief engineer, food and beverage manager, controller, human resources manager, marketing and sales manager, sales manager, resident manager, and systems manager.

It's important to select the segment of the industry that will best suit you. To do this you must understand your skills: whether you work best with data, people, or things. Once you have considered your strengths and weaknesses, you are in a position to evaluate areas of specialization. Your choices include hotels, restaurants, clubs, catering, contract food companies, institutional food service, and more.

In deciding on your first career move, you need to evaluate your own personal goals, the reputation of the companies you are considering, and, finally, the quality and depth of each company's training programs. Different companies offer management training programs of varying lengths and purposes.

Endnotes

1. David Hughes Farmer, *Oxford Dictionary of Saints* (Oxford: Oxford University Press, 1987), pp. 243–244.

2. "The Evolution of the Hospitality Industry," *The Cornell Quarterly,* May 1985, p. 36.

3. *Les Misérables* by Alan Boubil and Claude-Michel Schonberg, based on the novel by Victor Hugo. Lyrics by Herbert Kretzmer. Copyright 1985 Exallshow Ltd.

4. Samuel Johnson, March 21, 1776, in *Boswell's Life of Johnson* (L. F. Powell's revision of G. Hill's edition), Vol. 2, p. 452.

5. Clifton Fadiman, *The Little, Brown Book of Anecdotes* (Boston: Little, Brown and Company, 1985), p. 536.

6. Donald A. Lundberg, *The Hotel and Restaurant Business,* 4th ed. (New York: VNR, 1984), p. 21.

7. Daniel J. Boorstin, *The Americans: The National Experience* (New York: Vintage Books, 1965), p. 135.

8. Boorstin, p. 139.

9. Reary Tannahill, *Food in History* (Granada Publishing Ltd.: Paladin, Frogmore, St. Albans, Hertz, England, 1975), pp. 173–174.

10. Tannahill, p. 141.

11. Larry Littman, "Despite Its Rocky Start, Hotel Industry Continues to Flourish into the 1990s," *Travel Agent Magazine,* February 26, 1990, p. 62.

12. Richard Turner, ed., *1990 Directory of Hotel & Motel Systems,* 59th ed. (New York: American Hotel Association Directory Corporation, 1990), p. 288.

13. *Clubs in Town and Country* (Houston, Tex.: Pannell Kerr Forster, 1990), p. 8.

14. Ted E. White, *Club Operations and Management* (Boston: CBI Publishing, 1979).

Key Terms

career path

catering manager

chief engineer

controller

food and beverage manager

general manager

Henderson, Ernest

Hilton, Conrad

hospitality industry

hospitia

human resources manager

Johnson, Howard

Kroc, Ray

management training programs

marketing and sales manager

resident manager

Rogers, Isaiah

Saint Julian the Hospitaller

Saint Notburga

sales manager

Statler, Ellsworth

systems manager

Wilson, Kemmons

Discussion Questions

1. What role did early American hotels play that distinguished them from European hotels?

2. How did early railroads affect the hospitality industry?

3. Who are some of the early hotel-chain pioneers? restaurant-chain pioneers?

4. What has the growth pattern for the hotel industry been like in the last few decades? Why?

5. Are there any unique characteristics that separate service businesses from businesses that deal with tangible products? If so, what are they?

6. What are some of the advantages and disadvantages of a career in hospitality?

7. What are some of the career options in the hospitality industry?

8. What are the advantages of working for a large hotel chain? for an independent operation?

9. Should a hospitality student bypass fast-food management opportunities? Why or why not?

10. What are some of the questions you should ask yourself before you decide that a job is right for you?

Part II

Hotels, Restaurants, and Clubs

Chapter Outline

Hotel Categories
    Location
    Price
    Guests
    Other Hotel Categories
Chains versus Independents
    The Major Players
Developing and Planning New Hotels
    Site Selection
    The Feasibility Study
    Financing
Chapter Summary

3 Types of Hotels

In Chapter 3 we will discuss various types of hotels and how hotels are classified. You will learn about emerging hotel concepts and some of the differences between chain and independent hotels. Major players will be identified so you can become familiar with the business philosophies of the most successful hotel companies. Finally, there is a section on developing and planning new hotels. Included in this section is information on the use and structure of feasibility studies.

Hotel Categories

It's important that you understand the ways in which hotels are categorized. Hotels can be categorized by location, price, guests, and other factors.

Location Many hospitality publications and consulting firms categorize hotels by location. Some of the most generally recognized hotel location categories are:

- Center city

- Resort

- Suburban

- Highway

- Airport

Center City. After the Depression, there was a considerable amount of rebuilding and construction in the United States as part of President Franklin Roosevelt's New Deal. One result of that program was that by 1941, when America entered World War II, most cities had at least one downtown hotel built to create jobs and stimulate the economy. Major cities like New York, Chicago, and Los Angeles had many downtown hotels, some of which were internationally famous. Typically these hotels were built near railroad stations, for at that time railroad stations were located at or near the center of a city's business district. In New York City, the

Commodore (which is now the Grand Hyatt Hotel) was built right over Grand Central Station. In St. Louis, the Head House (now an Omni Hotel) was part of Union Station.

Other popular downtown locations for hotels were near centers of government such as city halls and courts, and in financial districts like merchandise marts and stock exchanges. In those days virtually all of the important business of the nation took place near these downtown areas.

After World War II the face of America began to change. Automobiles and airplanes replaced trains as the favored means of transportation for most Americans. Automobiles and good road systems made suburbs possible. Soon the suburbs began attracting office parks, shopping centers, airports, and other businesses. Downtown areas in many parts of the country began to decline.

The Plaza Hotel, overlooking Central Park in New York City.

How the Government Categorizes Lodging Properties

The U.S. government has its own way of categorizing hotels and other lodging properties. The basis of government classification of all businesses in the United States is the Standard Industrial Classification code (SIC). This code is based on the U.S. census reports. Businesses covered by the census were assigned kind-of-business classifications. Most hotels, rooming houses, camps, and other lodging places are listed together in this classification system's SIC Major Group 70. Tourist homes and hotels that provide accommodations for permanent residents are classified in Major Group 65, which covers real estate.

Within these two major groups, there are smaller classifications for census purposes. For instance, all hotels, motor hotels, and motels within Major Group 70 are classified together under Industry Group 701. In some government reports the data within this group is broken down even further into subdivisions such as:

- Hotels, 25 guestrooms or more

- Hotels, less than 25 guestrooms

- Motels and tourist courts

- Motor hotels

Rooming and boarding houses (including bed and breakfast establishments) are in Industry Group 702. Establishments renting rooms, with or without board, on a fee basis to permanent or transient guests are covered by this classification. However, nursing homes and homes for the aged and handicapped have different code numbers entirely.

Sporting and recreational camps that provide lodging and meals or lodging only are in Industry Group 702. Dude ranches, fishing camps, hunting camps, and children's camps also fall into this classification. Trailer parks and camp sites that provide overnight or short-term sites for trailers, campers, and tents have a different classification number—Industry Group 703.

Finally, Industry Group 704 covers hotels and lodging houses that are operated by membership organizations for the benefit of their members and guests and are not open to the public. Some of these groups operate commercial hotels, which are classified as hotels, motels, and motor hotels (Group 701).

Knowing these government classifications can help you should you need to look at government data when conducting research. Developers or hoteliers contemplating building a new hotel can consult government data to find out the number and type of hotels that are located near the site of the proposed hotel.

But most Americans were not ready to let their downtown metropolitan areas die. In the mid-1960s a trend began (which is still continuing today) to restore and rebuild downtown areas. This included building new hotels and refurbishing many of the old ones. In 1969 the Parker House was bought by the Dunfey hotel chain and a total renovation took place. In Seattle the Four Seasons purchased the historic Olympic Hotel from Westin. In 1986 Washington D.C.'s Willard Hotel—the hotel of choice for foreign dignitaries, several presidents-elect, and other notables in the nineteenth century—was reopened as an Inter-Continental Hotel after

$113 million was invested in her restoration. And in Chicago, the 3,000-room Conrad Hilton Hotel, built in 1927, was closed in 1984 and reopened in 1988 as the Chicago Hilton and Towers after a $180 million renovation.

The story of downtown hotels can be illustrated by examining *Lodging Hospitality's* analysis of the age of the top 100 center city hotels:

More than 50 years	16%
26–50 years	2%
11–25 years	28%
5–10 years	26%
Less than 5 years	28%

As you can see, 54% of center city hotels are 10 years old or less. But a surprising 18% are more than 25 years old.

The growth of downtown hotels is just one part of the rebirth of downtown areas. Along with new hotels have come new skyscrapers such as the Sears Tower and the John Hancock Building in Chicago, Columbia Center in Seattle, and the World Trade Center in Manhattan. These buildings have kept corporate headquarters in town and attracted new businesses as well. As you would expect, the hotels that surround them mostly attract business travelers. The profile of guests for center city hotels is 74%

The Palace Hotel in Beijing is a full-service center city hotel, with five hotel restaurants; 24-hour room service; six meeting rooms and a 700-person capacity ballroom; a fully equipped gymnasium; a heated swimming pool; two executive floors for business travelers that feature express check-in/check-out services, complimentary Continental breakfasts, and dry cleaning and laundry services; and a business center open 24 hours a day. Courtesy of The Peninsula Group, Hong Kong.

commercial and convention guests, and only 26% leisure guests. The majority of center city hotels (57%) are chain operated or managed.

Center city hotels achieved the highest average room rate of all the non-resort hotel categories—$70.69—but with an occupancy rate that fell below those of airport and resort properties.[1]

Modern center city hotels are, for the most part, full-service facilities. Their guests demand it. In addition to rooms, center city hotels may have a coffee shop as well as other restaurants, at least one bar or cocktail lounge, room service, laundry and valet services, a newsstand and gift shop, and a health club. Many of the older properties have no parking facilities and must offer valet service to park guests' cars off-site. In some cases hotels have acquired their own parking facilities or contracted with independent garages away from the property. Parking fees can be high. For example, overnight parking for guests at the Grand Hyatt Hotel in New York City costs $27 per day, with no in or out privileges. On Sundays the car must be out of the parking facilities by 1 p.m. to avoid additional parking charges! On the other hand, the Chicago Hilton and Towers is able to charge a lower fee—$14—because nearby parking space is available.

Resort. Resort hotels are generally found in destinations that are desirable vacation spots because of their climate, scenery, recreational attractions, or historic interest. Mountains and seashores are favorite locales. It is not unusual for resorts to have elaborately landscaped grounds with hiking trails and gardens, as well as extensive sports facilities such as golf courses and tennis courts.

The Romans were the first to build hotels for recreational purposes—generally around hot springs. Famous spas dating back to the Roman Empire still exist, though in modern form, in Baden-Baden, Germany; Bath, England; and other countries such as Switzerland and Turkey. In the United States early resorts were linked to the transportation system—the highways, rivers, and railroads. Reputedly, the first American resort advertisement appeared in 1789 for Gray's Ferry, Pennsylvania. Guests were offered fishing tackle and free weekly concerts. Transportation to and from nearby cities was provided by "a handsome State Wagon mounted on steel springs with two good horses."[2]

Early American resorts were also built around hot or mineral springs. The Greenbriar in White Sulphur Springs, West Virginia; the nearby Homestead in Hot Springs, Virginia (which owns 15,000 acres of Allegheny mountain forests); and the many facilities in Saratoga Springs, New York, all survive today as popular vacation destinations.

Major growth in U.S. resorts came in the nineteenth century with the development of railroads and steamships. The Mountain View House in Whitefield, New Hampshire, opened in 1865. The Del Coronado (still in operation today) opened its doors in 1888. That was the same year Henry Flagler opened the Ponce de Leon in St. Augustine, followed by the Royal Poinciana in Palm Beach in 1893 and the Royal Palm Hotel in Miami in 1896. Another great resort, the Grand Hotel on Mackinac Island in northern Michigan, opened in 1879 and has preserved its original turn-of-the-century atmosphere to this day—helped greatly by the island's ban on all automobiles.

The Mena House Oberoi in Cairo, Egypt, is a luxury resort featuring 40 acres of ornamental gardens; seven deluxe restaurants (including a night club and a disco-theque); 24-hour room service; and recreational attractions that include a casino, a golf course, lighted tennis courts, and horse or camel riding. Courtesy of Oberoi Hotels International, Delhi, India.

The first resorts were summer retreats only. In the winter, fashionable people stayed in the cities to work and attend the opera, theater, and other cultural events. One went to the mountains and seashore in the hot summer months to escape the heat of the city. California resorts were the first to solicit winter vacation business, followed by Florida hoteliers who recognized the potential profit in offering those in northern cities a way to get out of the cold.

The trend today is for resorts to stay open year-round. Even resorts that used to stay open only part of the year have concluded, for the most part, that this policy is no longer economically feasible in today's business climate. Moreover, it is often more practical to stay open all year because if you close your property and lay off employees it may be difficult to get them back when you wish to reopen. In a service industry, and especially at resorts where services are expected to be at a high level, a trained staff is essential and can only be achieved with full-time employees who have job security on a 12-month basis. Nevertheless, many year-round resorts let part of their staff go, curtail some services in the off season (such as 24-hour room service), and train the permanent personnel to do double duty.

A resort's guest base may vary greatly according to the season. For example, in Palm Springs, California, the winter months are the peak season. That is when movie stars and other celebrities are in town and rates are at their highest. In the summer, when temperatures often approach 100 degrees in the shade, the same resorts offer bargain prices to tour operators, conventioneers, and individual guests who could never afford to come during the cooler months.

Early resorts did not have extensive entertainment or recreational facilities. The principal activities consisted of dining, walking, climbing, horseback riding, swimming, and lawn games. These resorts all featured large verandas with comfortable chairs for sitting, reading, and enjoying the scenery. Dinner was served early, and many guests retired to their rooms by 10 p.m. On weekends there might be a dinner dance. Contemporary resorts offer much more to their guests. In Las Vegas resorts, for example, there are nightly shows featuring star entertainment, all-night casinos, discos, elaborate health spas, two or even three golf courses, tennis courts, boating, arts and crafts classes, and children's programs. Fine dining is an important part of all resort operations. Guests expect it and are not willing to pay high room prices unless the resort has a superior restaurant.

Some resorts—like those at Opryland in Nashville, Tennessee, and the Grand Floridian at Walt Disney World—are in theme parks. In Hawaii, Hyatt spent $360 million to build the Hyatt Regency Waikoloa, the most expensive resort in the world thus far, which some observers have said is a hotel that *is* a theme park.

Resorts remain largely independent from chains, compared to other segments of the industry. Today it is estimated that there are 450,000 resort hotel rooms in the United States. Most new resorts are being built in the sun states of California, Florida, Hawaii, and Nevada, as well as in the

The Grand Hotel, Mackinac Island, Michigan.

Most resorts are expensive to build because of the high cost of desirable land and the expenses involved in constructing golf courses, swimming pools, and tennis courts. Courtesy of Rancho Las Palmas, near Palm Springs, California, and the Marriott Corporation.

sun and ski areas of Colorado, Utah, and the Carolinas. Most resorts require a good deal of capital to develop—desirable land in scenic locations or on the waterfront has appreciated greatly in recent years, and the necessary amenities are costly to build and maintain. An 18-hole golf course, for example, can easily cost $11 million or more to build, not including the cost of the land. In California the 393-room Ritz-Carlton Laguna Niguel cost $100 million to build in 1984—a cost of approximately $250,000 per room.

Lodging Hospitality provides us with a profile of successful resorts from their 1988 list of top performers (see Exhibit 3.1). Top resorts achieve 70% occupancy and high sales per room. However, resorts are the most expensive properties to operate—they average 160 employees for every 100 rooms, and thus their payrolls are much higher than those of other kinds of hotels.

Resorts are attracting more business guests these days than ever before. In 1987 business travelers made up nearly 40 percent of the resort lodging market, an increase of 25 percent over the previous year. Three-quarters of the business guests were attending conventions or conferences. It is interesting to note how the mix of guests is related to property size (see Exhibit 3.2).[3]

Because of the increase in business guests, many resorts are adding or increasing amenities that are important to this market segment, such as facsimile machines, secretarial services, and on-site travel agencies (see Exhibit 3.3).

Some resort operators see the combination resort/business property as the wave of the future. At the 1989 conference of the Institute of Certified

Exhibit 3.1 Profile of Successful Resorts

Guest Composition	Years in Operation
• 64% Leisure	• 10% More than 50 years
• 36% Commercial and conventions	• 15% 26 to 50 years
	• 33% 11 to 25 years
Type of Property	• 24% 5 to 10 years
• 69% Independent	• 18% Less than 5 years
• 7% Franchised	
• 10% Chain operated	
• 14% Chain managed	

Source: *Lodging Hospitality,* 1988.

Exhibit 3.2 Guest Mix for Resorts of Various Sizes

Mix of Guests	Less than 150 Rooms	150–299 Rooms	300–600 Rooms	More than 600 Rooms
Leisure	77.9%	48.1%	46.5%	39.5%
Business/ Government	6.4	15.2	8.7	4.6
Conference Participants	14.5	32.4	41.1	52.4
Other	1.2	4.3	3.6	3.5

Source: Laventhol & Horwath, *The U.S. Resort and Lodging Industry 1988.*

Exhibit 3.3 Percentage of Resorts with a Particular Business Amenity

Barber/Beauty Salon	74%	Newsstand	27%
Game Room	68	Secretarial Services	21
Health Club Facilities	67	24-Hour Door Attendant	18
Audiovisual Equipment	63	Concierge Services	15
Auto Rental	62	Airport Transportation	13
Gift Shop	56	24-Hour Room Service	12
Free Parking	46	Travel Agent on Premises	11
Overnight Dry Cleaning	43	Retail Outlets	10
Executive Floors	43	Multilingual Staff	9
Personal Bathroom Amenities	28		

Source: Laventhol & Horwath, *Business Travel News,* February 8, 1988.

Travel Agents in San Antonio, W. Craig Parsons, assistant vice-president of international sales for Hyatt Hotels, told delegates, "You will see the rise of the resort conference center, with meeting space and full recreational facilities, particularly golf, in resort-like cities, as American companies increasingly realize that doing business and having fun are not incompatible."

According to Michael Butler, chairman and CEO of Midland International Resort Realty Inc., more and more resorts of the future will be "mixed use," which he defines as a resort development that includes most or all of the following spectrum of possibilities:

- Convention and meeting facilities, shops and boutiques, food and beverage services, and extensive recreational and entertainment opportunities.

- Hotel rooms or suites in which the consumer has no ownership interest.

- Time sharing, a form of interval ownership, in which the consumer buys a one-week-per-year interest in a leisure lodging unit (sometimes a hotel room or suite, but more often a condominium apartment or villa) in a popular vacation locale.[4]

Suburban. With the rebirth of American cities in the two decades after World War II, the U.S. economy expanded rapidly, and construction of major office buildings in downtown areas reached a new peak of activity. Landowners soon realized that new buildings commanded a much higher rent than older ones, and real-estate prices in many downtown areas doubled and tripled.

Many corporations that did not want to pay the higher downtown rents moved to the suburbs. Land there was available at a much more reasonable price and, with improved highway systems, proliferating suburban housing developments, and gigantic shopping centers, it made sense to relocate. IBM, for example, moved from Manhattan to Armonk, New York, and set up entire new divisions in places like Boca Raton, Florida. Many of the other large business tenants in Manhattan moved to Connecticut, New Jersey, and upstate New York.

Inevitably, a strong demand arose for building new hotels near these suburban businesses. Land developers recognized this need and found meeting it particularly attractive. Unlike suburban townhouses and rental apartments, a hotel seemed to be a more profitable investment. After all, when you rented out a new apartment you were tied into a lease at a set price for a year or more. Inflation could easily erode your profits because you couldn't raise the rent whenever you wanted to cover increased costs. A hotel was different. You were not locked into fixed rates at all. If prices went up, you could raise rates accordingly in less than 24 hours. While many land developers didn't know the first thing about running a hotel, a solution was readily available. Large hotel chains were selling franchises, and management companies were available to completely take over the new hotels from those developers who were not really interested in hotelkeeping.

In addition to the new businesses, there were other reasons for locating new hotels in the suburbs. Newer and larger hotels offering parking space and other amenities could be built much more economically in suburban locations than downtown. Moreover, the growth of motels (which were on their way to being called motor hotels), combined with the need for suburban accommodations, further eroded the desirability of building hotels downtown.

Today it is difficult to distinguish between a suburban hotel and any other kind of hotel. It is the location that makes the difference. Nevertheless, there are some characteristics that suburban hotels have in common:

- As a group, they tend to be somewhat smaller than downtown hotels. Many suburban properties have 250 to 500 rooms and limited banquet facilities.

- They are primarily chain affiliated; 70% belong to national chains or referral organizations. Just about every major chain operates several suburban properties.

- Their major source of revenue is from business meeting and convention attendees and from individual business travelers. In 1988 *Lodging Hospitality* reported that, as a group, 75% of suburban hotels' business was commercial, 25% leisure.

- They have all of the facilities that center city hotels offer. Because they depend heavily on local patronage, restaurants in suburban hotels frequently offer superior dining experiences. Hotel services such as laundry, valet, and room service are on a par with center city standards.

- Many of these properties have sports and health facilities as well as swimming pools.

- Suburban hotels are often cornerstones of their communities. They frequently host the weekly meetings of such major service clubs as Rotary and Kiwanis.

Suburban hotels that have consistently achieved a high level of sales per room include the Grand Bay Hotel in Coconut Grove, Florida; the Sheraton Valley Forge in King of Prussia, Pennsylvania; and the Boston Marriott Hotel Newton in Newton, Massachusetts.

Highway. As soon as America began to develop its highway system in the 1920s and 1930s, small tourist courts began to spring up along major roads such as the Boston Post Road (U.S. Highway 1) from Maine to Florida. At first these tourist courts were a row of simple cabins with direct access to the outside. Many of them did not even have private baths. In 1925 Arthur S. Heineman opened the Milestone Motel in San Luis Obispo, California. Heineman proceeded to claim a copyright on the word "motel" and thus he is often credited with creating the concept. These early motels averaged 20 rooms and were usually owned by a couple who lived on the premises and handled all of the work. No effort was made to provide food or any other services. Because rooms were often rented for just a few hours with no questions asked, early highway motels in some communities developed an unsavory reputation.

It was not until after World War II, when the pent-up demand for automobiles and travel was finally released, that the highway motel business really grew. With the new interstate highways came a need for families and businesspeople to have a safe and comfortable place to stay en route to their destination. As mentioned in Chapter 2, one of the first to recognize this need was Kemmons Wilson, whose Holiday Inn chain was launched

Motels provided informal accommodations in which travelers could relax and get a good night's sleep before hitting the road the next day. Courtesy of the State of Michigan Archives.

in 1952 in Memphis, Tennessee. One of Wilson's major innovations was to put a restaurant in his motel so that travelers could eat a meal without leaving the property. This upgraded the status of these properties considerably, making them more like hotels. Soon the evolution from tourist court to motel to motor hotel was complete. Today's highway hotels offer all of the same facilities found in downtown and suburban hotels, but with a distinct identity of their own.

Most highway hotels feature a large sign that can be seen from the highway and an entrance where travelers can leave their automobiles while they check in. Parking space is plentiful and the atmosphere is informal. Just about all highway hotels offer ice machines, vending machines with snacks and sodas, and a swimming pool to relax in after a long drive. Beyond that, the distinction blurs—a highway hotel can be just like any other hotel except that it is on the highway.

According to *Lodging Hospitality,* 61% of highway hotels are franchised, compared to 16% of center city hotels and 44% of suburban hotels. This is undoubtedly because the companies that are most involved in selling franchises—Holiday, Ramada, and Quality—started with highway products because of the lower cost of entry for prospective franchisees. Moreover, the nature of highway hotels—often located away from urban centers—presents management and quality control problems that can best be solved by independent entrepreneurs operating with a franchise.

Highway hotels have the lowest number of employees per 100 rooms: 30, as compared to 41 in suburban hotels and 56 in center city properties. This is because highway hotels generally provide fewer services. Guests spend less time at this kind of hotel than in other kinds of hotels; consequently, total sales per room, which in 1988 averaged $13,405, were the lowest of any of the industry's hotel groups. Like most other types of hotels, highway properties depend mainly on commercial traffic—73% of their guests are there for business reasons. Many highway hotels are older properties—50% of them are between 11 and 25 years old. But a strong 23% are relatively new—less than 5 years old. This disparity is causing an interesting phenomenon in the business—an increasing number of franchise conversions. Rather than upgrading and modernizing their properties to keep up with new standards, many franchise owners have elected to convert their hotels to franchises that offer fewer services and a lower-price product. For instance, many older full-service Holiday Inns have been converted to Days Inns.

Airport. It did not take long for the chains to identify another growing need for hotel space in the United States—rooms on or adjacent to airports. Eighty-five percent of airport hotels today are affiliated with chains. Even though airport hotels tend to have difficulty attracting weekend guests because most airline travel occurs on weekdays, airport hotels enjoy some of the highest occupancy rates in the lodging industry. In 1988 airport properties averaged 67% occupancy—more than center city, suburban, or highway hotels and equal to resorts.

Airport hotels are full-service hotels, but some services are more important than others because of the hotels' location. For instance, more airport hotels (88%) offer in-room movies than any other kind of hotel. Because airport hotels have a very high guest turnover every day, they are more likely than other hotels to have computerized property management systems and call accounting systems. Another problem that airport hotels face is the need to respond to a high demand almost immediately. A severe snow storm or an airline strike can fill up an airport hotel instantly and put a severe strain on the rooms division and food service facilities.

Price

Another way of categorizing hotels (or segmenting them, a marketing term we will increasingly use here) is by the prices they charge. Market segmentation of product by price is a fairly recent development in the hotel business, although it has been common in other fields for decades. For example, General Motors manufactures budget automobiles like Chevrolets, mid-price automobiles like Oldsmobiles, and luxury cars such as Cadillacs. The idea is that different segments of the consumer market are attracted to different price levels, and if you want to sell a car to everyone you need to have different kinds of cars with different prices. When Henry Ford first pioneered the business, his intention was to offer only one kind of car—a basic black Model T that he could sell for $500. It was not until General Motors demonstrated that it could sell more cars by having a range of products at different price levels that Ford decided to change his strategy of offering only one very good product at a rock-bottom price.

Similarly, in the lodging industry the major hotel chains started by offering one kind of product only. Initially these were mid-price products introduced by Sheraton, Hilton, and Marriott. They were priced to appeal to the largest segment of the traveling public—mid-level business executives. Top executives in those days wouldn't dream of staying at a chain hotel—they stayed at independent properties or properties that may have been part of a group but were perceived to be unique or independent, such as the Plaza Hotel in New York City (now the Trump Plaza) or the Drake in Chicago (now a Hilton International property).

Today, chains have properties in one or more of three basic price categories:

- Economy/limited service
- Mid-price/extended stay
- Full-service/luxury

Economy/Limited Service. The first chain to go after a low-price consumer market was Holiday Inn. Holiday Inns were not budget properties, however. Their construction costs were relatively high because they contained restaurants, and their aim was to provide a better product than what had previously been available on the highway.

It was not until the 1960s that the first budget motels were introduced—Motel 6 in California, Days Inn in Georgia, and La Quinta in Texas. Sam Barshop, founder of La Quinta, explained his idea this way: "We have a very simple concept. What we're doing is selling beds. Not operating restaurants, not running conventions—just selling beds." By eliminating the restaurants and the lobby and meeting space that Holiday Inns offered, La Quinta and other budget properties were able to offer Holiday Inn-type rooms at 25% less. Some chains, like Motel 6, sold rooms for as low as $6. They were able to achieve that price by using modular and pre-fabricated construction materials and choosing less-than-ideal locations where land costs were lower. These chains offered hardly any amenities at all. In the early days, some had a coin slot in their guestroom television sets for pay-as-you-view TV!

The early budget motel segment has evolved into what is today called the economy/limited service segment. According to the Economy Lodging Council, a budget or economy hotel is one with an average daily rate of less than $40. However, since pricing varies among market areas and changes with the rate of inflation, it is more realistic to define the category as one in which rooms are offered at 20% to 50% below prevailing mid-market rates. Of course, hotel rates are continually changing. Days Inn, where the average room cost is $38 and discounts range from 10% to 50% for corporations, government workers, and senior citizens, no longer defines itself as a budget property and is now building a new chain called DayStop where the average room rate will be under $30. DayStop hopes to compete in the low end of the economy market, which Motel 6 currently dominates with rooms averaging $24 a night. Hampton Inns, owned by the Holiday Corporation, is at the high end of this same market and offers more elaborate budget rooms that average around $45 a night before discounts.

The economy/limited service hotel category is the star performing segment of the lodging industry. According to a 1989 study, in 1988 hotels with an average room rate of under $40 achieved an operating ratio of income before fixed charges to room sales of 43.5%, higher than any other segment. In the early 1980s, after a period of stagnation, they represented about 7.5% of the total hotel rooms in the United States. It is estimated that their share will grow to more than 20% by the early 1990s. In 1988, for example, the number of rooms in this segment was estimated to have grown by an additional 102,200 rooms from a base of 498,800 rooms, an increase of 20.5%.[5]

Mid-Price/Extended Stay. In the 1960s Sheraton, Hilton, Ramada, Quality, and Holiday used the term "inn" to designate their mid-price products. At that time the mid-price hotel segment was the fastest-growing segment of the industry. Fueled by the growth of the economy and the development of automobile and commercial air traffic, a strong need existed for mid-price lodging facilities with restaurants and some other amenities previously found only in higher-price establishments. Today, however, the term "inn" no longer identifies this category. For example, Hampton Inns and Days Inns are both economy products.

Although many consider mid-price properties to be those with average prices from $60 to $90, there is considerable variance by market. In Manhattan a mid-price hotel could easily average $150 a night. In Sacramento, California, a room in a similar hotel might cost as little as $50.

The mid-price segment has lost its attractiveness to many consumers. Squeezed by rising costs, the middle class has lost much of its spending power and so, in many cases, has traded down to economy properties that offer a similar room with a restaurant nearby. However, innovative new mid-price hotels have been able to hold on to some of this business by offering what is perceived as a better value. Marriott, for example, has pioneered Marriott Courtyard hotels, which offer a residential atmosphere in a low-rise, limited-size property. Another Marriott property, Residence Inn, is somewhat similar, except that all rooms contain kitchen facilities and comfortable chairs arranged for watching television or reading. These properties are designed for extended stays.

Full-Service/Luxury. At the top of the price scale there is a range of products, from the full-service hotels of Hyatt, Hilton, Stouffer, and Marriott to the luxury properties of Four Seasons, Ritz-Carlton, and Inter-Continental. Before these chains offered successful luxury hotels, "luxury chain hotel" was considered a contradiction in terms. By definition, a luxury hotel used to be an independent property in which the owner/manager was present to greet guests and see that their every need was satisfied. A perfect example of this kind of property was the Ritz Hotel in Paris on the Place Vendome. Its founder, the legendary Caesar Ritz, set unusually high standards for facilities and services. But Ritz also recognized the marketing advantages that could accrue from having more than one Ritz Hotel and so, with his partner Auguste Escoffier, he acquired an equity interest in the Carlton Hotel in London and then formed the Ritz-Carlton chain. Other luxury chains followed. One highly successful example is the Canadian-based Four Seasons hotel company. The company's strategy is to operate only mid-size hotels of exceptional quality and have the finest hotel or resort in each destination where it locates. At the Four Seasons in Washington, D.C., the 1990 room rates ranged from $175 to $275 per night.

Price Segmentation Strategies. Some chains, like Marriott, have chosen to build hotels in every price category so as to maximize market share. Their philosophy is that, if it is no longer possible to appeal to everyone with one kind of hotel, they will build as many kinds of hotels as are necessary

The Willard Inter-Continental Hotel, a luxury property renovated in 1986. Courtesy of Inter-Continental Hotels.

to ensure that as many people as possible who stay in hotels will stay in a Marriott. On the other hand, Four Seasons and Hyatt feel that their expertise lies not in managing hotels in general but in managing a particular kind of hotel, so they've decided to offer only products that appeal to their current guest base.

Exhibit 3.4 shows how the market looks now for the leading chains that have decided to follow a segmentation strategy and offer different products for different price categories.

Guests   Up to this point we have categorized hotels in terms of location (city center, suburban, etc.) and prices (from economy to luxury). Another way

Exhibit 3.4 Segmentation Strategy of Selected Hotel Chains

Chain	Economy/ Limited Service	Mid-Price/ Extended Stay	Full Service/ Luxury
Marriott	Fairfield Inn	Courtyard Residence Inn	Marriott Suites Marriott Hotels & Resorts
Promus	Hampton Inn	Homewood Suites	Embassy Suites Harrah's
Choice	Comfort Inn Comfort Inn Suites	Quality Inn Quality Inn Suites	Clarion Clarion Suites
Ramada		Ramada Inn	Ramada Renaissance

of categorizing hotels, and by far the most useful from a marketing standpoint, is by the type of guests who patronize them.

In his book *Hospitality in Transition*, Albert J. Gomes describes the "most important demand segments that constitute the market for the hotel industry today."[6] They are:

- Corporate—individuals

- Corporate groups

- Convention and association groups

- Leisure travelers

- Long-term stay/relocation guests

- Airline-related guests

- Government and military travelers

- Regional get-away guests

Corporate—Individuals. These guests are persons who are traveling for business purposes. They are not part of any group. They usually stay one or two nights and pay rack (non-discounted) rates. Corporate guests are the most frequent users of lodging services—typically staying in hotels 15 to 20 times annually. While they are not price sensitive, they care about recognition and special treatment. Frequent-stay programs, such as Hilton Honors and Hyatt's Golden Passport, have proved particularly effective with this market segment. Individual corporate travelers are often members of airline frequent-flyer programs and may choose hotels tied in with them. They also respond to concierge floors, upgraded rooms at standard prices, and express check-in and check-out services.

Corporate Groups. Corporate group travelers also travel purely for business purposes but, unlike individual corporate travelers, they are usually attending a small conference or meeting at the hotel or at another facility in the area, and their rooms are booked in blocks by their company or a travel agency. These travelers usually stay from two to four days. While top managers are typically assigned single rooms, middle- and lower-level managers often have to share rooms.

Hotels that offer intimate meeting rooms and private dining facilities are often favored by this type of traveler. In recent years several conference center hotels with these features have been constructed in suburban locations conveniently located near major cities and airports. The idea is to do away with big-city distractions and give participants a chance to interact not only during meetings but between them as well.

Convention and Association Groups. Generally, what distinguishes these groups from other corporate groups is their size. The number of people in a convention or association group can run well into the thousands. A world congress of the American Society of Travel Agents typically attracts between 5,000 to 7,000 delegates, for example, and every year the National Restaurant Show in Chicago attracts approximately 90,000 visitors. Delegates tend to stay in large convention hotels where a negotiated package price covers rooms, meals, functions, and often athletic events. Regular transient hotels, which have fewer rooms and limited function space and cater primarily to the individual traveler, often compete for group business in slow periods by offering extremely competitive rates. Convention delegates often share rooms and stay three to four days. Large convention groups choose their venues several years in advance, so a hotel's selling efforts are often sustained and intensive and may involve cooperation from airlines and local convention and visitors' bureaus.

Leisure Travelers. These travelers are often with their families and sightseeing or visiting friends and relatives. Except at resorts, they typically spend only one night at the same hotel, and a room may be occupied by a couple as well as one or more children. Because they travel during peak season, they usually pay full rack rates unless they are members of such organizations as the American Automobile Association or the American Association of Retired Persons, which have been able to negotiate discounts with many hotel chains.

Long-Term Stay/Relocation Guests. These guests consist primarily of individuals or families relocating to an area and requiring lodging until permanent housing can be found. Often they are government or military personnel. Their needs include limited cooking facilities and more living space than is available in a typical hotel room. Residence Inns by Marriott is an example of a product designed specifically for the needs of this group. A Residence Inn room has a small kitchenette with counter space and stools for eating meals, a sofa and side chair in front of a television set, and extra closet space.

Airline-Related Guests. Airlines negotiate rates with hotels for airplane crew members and for passengers who need emergency accommodations because they are stranded by the weather, for example. These rooms are usually booked in blocks at rock-bottom prices. Rooms that are reserved for these purposes are often the least favorable a property has to offer.

Government and Military Travelers. Travelers in these groups are reimbursed on fixed per diem allowances, which means they only receive a certain amount for lodging expenses no matter what they have to pay for a room. Therefore, as a general rule these guests stay only in places that have negotiated acceptable rates with their organizations or offer very low rates.

Regional Get-Away Guests. Originally this guest segment developed when hotels that normally catered to commercial and convention groups on weekdays put together special weekend packages designed to entice nearby residents to leave the kids at home, check into a hotel for Friday and Saturday nights, and enjoy a night or two "on the town." Rates are discounted substantially and often include some meals and/or entertainment.

Guest Mix. "Guest mix" refers to the variety or mixture of guests who stay at a hotel. A hotel's guest mix might consist of 60% individual business travelers, 20% conventioneers, and 20% leisure travelers, for example. Guest mix is very carefully managed in successful hotels.

With few exceptions, hotels, no matter where they are located or what their price structure is, strive to capture multiple market segments. A hotel's guest mix depends on its location, size, facilities, and operating philosophy. Transient hotels cater to groups as well as to single business travelers. To fill up rooms not booked by convention groups, hotels geared to convention sales seek individual business travelers and vacationers willing to pay non-discounted rates. At any one time, a hotel such as the 2,000-room New York Hilton in Manhattan will have several groups, some individual business travelers, families visiting New York City on vacation, as well as airline crews and government employees. By diversifying their guest base, hotels hope to minimize the effect of seasonality, economic recessions, and changing market dynamics.

In recent years, however, some properties have recognized that there are dangers inherent in this strategy. Sometimes different kinds of clientele do not mix well together. For instance, business executives paying a top rate for a room may be annoyed to find a noisy tour group blocking their way to the coffee shop in the morning. Some luxury hotels control their mix very carefully, only allowing groups on weekends and, even then, supplying special facilities for registration and dining so as not to interfere with their regular guests.

Other Hotel Categories

Other hotel categories reported on by trade periodicals and consulting firms include:

- All-suite hotels
- Casino hotels
- Conference centers
- Time-share condominiums and condominium hotels
- Cruise ships
- Continuing-care retirement communities

All-Suite Hotels. All-suite hotels are the newest entry into the price-segmentation field. Although all-suite hotels can be viewed as a different kind of product, they are also a way the traditional mid-price hotel chains have been able to enter the low end of the luxury market.

When the all-suite hotel was first introduced, the concept was simple—two connected hotel rooms for approximately the price of one, at a price much lower than that for a traditional hotel suite. One room was furnished as a typical hotel guestroom with a bed; the other, with a fold-out sofa (or a table and chairs) in place of the bed. The first all-suite hotel was built in 1961—the Lexington Apartments and Motor Inn in Grand Prairie, Texas. It took 11 years for one of the major chains to embrace the idea— Guest Quarters Suite Hotels opened its first property in Atlanta in 1972. The product was originally positioned to attract extended-stay travelers, but it proved popular to other kinds of travelers as well. An all-suite hotel gave guests more private space, but the trade-off was that much of the hotel's public space—the lobby, meeting rooms, health club, and (most important) restaurant and kitchen—was eliminated.

Residence Inns developed an all-suite concept in the early 1980s and had more than 100 hotels when it was acquired by the Marriott Corporation in 1987. All-suites continued to develop and be embellished; today there are all-suite hotels that are upscale, mid-price, extended stay, and resort. Some of these hotels still embrace the original concept, but others have added back the lobbies, restaurants, health clubs, and more.

On the whole, all-suite hotels are very appealing to several kinds of travelers. Business travelers are still the primary target and account for two-thirds of the users. Executives find all-suites particularly attractive because they can hold private meetings outside of a bedroom setting. Families also like all-suites. The kids can sleep on the convertible sofa in the living room, leaving the parents with the master bedroom. And the ranges and microwave ovens are great for preparing meals or popping popcorn while watching the latest episode of *Cheers* or *America's Funniest Home Videos.*

All-suites still constitute only 4% of the lodging industry's room inventory, but they are increasing rapidly. The top 16 all-suite lodging chains had a combined total of 375 properties with approximately 61,800 suites at the end of 1988. One industry expert predicts a 33% annual growth in the years ahead.[7]

The largest chain of all-suite hotels today is Embassy (operated by the Holiday Corporation), with 21,866 suites in 89 establishments. However, Marriott has more properties in its Residence Inn chain—139 properties with 16,353 rooms.[8]

Casino Hotels. Casinos are a special kind of hotel. The best way to understand casino hotels is to think of them not as hotels with casinos attached but rather as casinos with some rooms and food and beverage facilities attached for the gamblers' convenience. Although there is legal gambling in various forms in most of the 50 states and in many European and Asian nations as well, only two U.S. states—Nevada and New Jersey—have legalized full casino gambling. The major casino hotels in the United States are located in Atlantic City, New Jersey, or in Las Vegas, Reno, or Lake Tahoe in Nevada.

The most striking difference between a casino hotel and other types of hotels can be seen in the organization and management of the facility. In casino hotels the hotel operation is subordinate to the gambling operation. The hotel manager reports to a higher resident authority who usually holds the title of president. There may also be a casino manager whose rank may be equivalent to, if not greater than, the hotel manager's.

Another major difference in casino hotels is the control system. Because of the high volume of cash and credit transactions, controls must be much more stringent and complex than in other hotels. In addition to the usual system of checks and balances supervised by accounting personnel, there are greater numbers of on-site inspectors as well as sophisticated electronic surveillance systems that monitor areas and individual tables in the casino.

Casinos are also carefully monitored by the governments that sanction them. This is necessary to ensure that the government collects its share of the proceeds, as well as to discourage organized crime activities. Legislation usually dictates a casino's size, types of games permitted, investigation and licensing of employees, hours and days of operation, marketing activities, and type and size of public space.

Service operations in casino hotels are unique as well. Entertainment and food are important components of the gambling experience. They provide opportunities for winners to celebrate and losers to console themselves. This means that casino hotels are even more labor-intensive than other kinds of properties. The elaborate and extensive entertainment and the multiple dining facilities with all-night service mean that the number of employees per hotel room may be three or four times higher than that in conventional hotels and resorts.

Despite the complexity of operating casino hotels, they are considered to be tremendously attractive "cash cows" to knowledgeable operators who have experience in handling them. Although not all casino hotels have been financially successful, those that are generate profits far in excess of other hotels. Therefore it was no surprise to industry observers when

Casino hotels in Las Vegas.

Ramada, a large operator of hotels and casinos, decided to sell off its hotel division in 1988 and concentrate on casino operations. The largest hotel in the world at present is the Excalibur Hotel-Casino in Las Vegas, which opened in June 1990 and cost $290 million to build. The Excalibur, owned by Circus Circus Enterprises, has 4,032 rooms and a casino the size of four football fields.

Conference Centers. Although all hotels with meeting facilities compete for conferences, there are specialized hotels called conference centers that almost exclusively book conferences, executive meetings, and training seminars. While they provide most of the facilities found at conventional hotels, conference centers are built to provide living and conference facilities without any of the outside distractions that might cloud or detract from meetings held in ordinary hotels. Conference centers almost always have more audiovisual equipment on-site than is available at other hotels. Theaters, videotaping facilities, closed-circuit television, secretarial services, and translation facilities are common amenities. Conference centers are usually accessible to major market areas but in less busy locations. They generally have fewer than 200 rooms.

As with other kinds of hotels and resorts, conference centers can be classified according to usage. There are four general classifications:

- *Executive conference centers*, which cater to high-level meetings and seminars.

- *Corporate-owned conference centers*, used primarily for in-house training.

- *Resort conference centers*, which provide extensive recreation and social facilities in addition to conference facilities.

- *College and university conference centers*, which tend to be used mostly by academic groups. These facilities range from dormitory accommodations to modern hotels.

Time-Share Condominiums and Condominium Hotels. In an age of inflation, time sharing—which first started in the French Alps in the 1960s—seemed like an idea whose time had come. Many people enjoyed taking their vacation every year at the same time and at the same place. Many Californians, for example, went to Hawaii every winter for a week or two, rented a hotel room at the same property, played the same golf course, and had a group of friends who would go at the same time. The more affluent Californians bought condominiums, but for most people it didn't make sense to own and pay off the mortgage on a $50,000 to $100,000 condominium that they might use for only a few weeks a year.

Time sharing seemed the perfect answer. Instead of selling an individual an entire condominium, developers reasoned, why not sell them only one-twelfth of one, which would give them the use of it for 30 days—or even one-fiftieth of one, which would allow buyers to use their condo for one week every year? You could pick your own month or week and actually own the condo for that period of time. If you couldn't go on your designated week, you could trade with another owner. By buying a block of time in a time-share condominium you would not only be assured of getting the accommodations you wanted when you wanted them, but over the years your rate would stay the same even if hotel room rates doubled or tripled.

Problems with the first time-share condominiums occurred when unscrupulous developers made no provisions for maintaining the properties, and when some properties were oversold (that is, more than 52 weeks of the same condo were sold). Fortunately, the federal government cracked down on these practices and today time sharing is a successful concept. According to one survey there were 1,100 time-share condominium resorts in the United States with sales of just under $2 billion in 1988. It is estimated that 1.3 million Americans now own time-share units.[9] Owners pay an average of $8,500 for one week and maintenance fees of about $250 a year. Florida and California are the major locations for time-share condominiums.[10] Companies such as Marriott, Sheraton, Walt Disney, and Sonesta manage many of these operations, which continue to gain in popularity.

Condominium hotels, also known as condo hotels or even condotels, first surfaced in the 1960s and weathered some difficult early years as a result of dishonest practices by some developers. A condo hotel is one in which investors take title to specific hotel rooms. Investors stay in their rooms whenever they wish, and inform management of the times during the year when they will not be using their rooms. When an investor does not occupy his or her hotel room, it is placed in the pool of hotel rooms available to be rented to transient guests. The investor expects to receive a gain from the increase in value of the condominium hotel over time, as well as receive ongoing income from the rental of his or her room. According to a *Forbes* magazine report, in 1985 $800 million in hotel condos were either in the process of entering the market or already available to potential investors.[11]

There are some significant differences between managing traditional hotels and managing time-share condominiums and condominium hotels. To begin with, time-share properties are tougher to manage because owners are always present and concerned about their investment. Managers must deal with numerous owners, all of whom have their own ideas about what kind of improvements should be made. Many condominium hotels only rent rooms for 50 weeks of the year because if rooms are rented for 52 weeks, refurbishment becomes a serious problem.

With time-share properties, selling must be handled more aggressively, and sales costs are considerably higher than for traditional hotels. After all, you are selling a piece of property, not simply an overnight stay. Different types of salespersons with strong closing techniques are required for the initial sell-out period.

Cruise Ships. The astounding fact about the cruise industry is that only about five percent of Americans have ever taken a cruise. For members of the cruise industry, that statistic has become a driving force in what is certainly one of the most dynamic segments of the travel and tourism industry. According to the research department of the consulting firm Morgan Stanley, "The cruise industry has been expanding much more rapidly than the vacation market as a whole. In fact, travel sources believe it may be the fastest growing segment of the industry."[12]

A 1988 study by Cruise Lines International Association (CLIA) shows that over 30 million Americans expressed an interest in taking a cruise—a 122% increase over 1986. Of the nearly nine million Americans who have

Carnival Cruise Lines' SuperLiner *Fantasy* is a 70,367-ton, $225 million ship that can accommodate 2,600 passengers. Courtesy of Carnival Cruise Lines.

already taken a cruise, nine out of ten expressed very high satisfaction with the experience, and most indicated an interest in taking another cruise vacation. The average age of cruisers has been dropping steadily. The average cruiser today is between 40 and 59 years old. CLIA projects that the largest group of new cruisers (12.3 million of them) will come from the 25–39 age group.[13]

Some financial analysts feel that most of this growth is coming, and will continue to come, at the expense of the traditional land-based resort. A report by Alex Brown & Sons, Inc., a consulting firm, states that "historically, cruise industry capacity additions have been absorbed by means of market share gains from land-based resort and sightseeing vacations; we believe these share gains have resulted in part from the introduction of shorter cruises, the offering of more varied activities and services, increasingly sophisticated marketing efforts and in some instances lower fares and/or fare discounting."[14]

Although you may have been surprised to find cruise ships listed as a hotel category, cruise ships today can be thought of as floating resort hotels. While there are vast differences between land-based resorts and cruise ships, there are also great similarities. More and more hospitality companies are recognizing this fact. The Cunard Line, owner and operator of the *Queen Elizabeth II* and other cruise ships, also operates Le Toc resort in the Caribbean as well as other hotels. The Pritzger family, which owns Hyatt Hotels, bought a 25% interest in Royal Caribbean Cruise Lines in 1988. In the same year, Carnival Cruises opened the Crystal Palace Resort and Casino in the Bahamas in partnership with The Continental Companies, a hotel company based in Miami. Carnival also acquired Westours, which operates almost two dozen hotels in Alaska.

Club Med, a resort operator up until 1988, has launched its first cruise ship and has more under construction. Even Radisson Hotels has announced it is taking a look at the cruise industry.

A modern cruise ship may have fancy dining rooms and à la carte restaurants; a health and fitness club; a professional theater for presenting Las Vegas-style entertainment; a casino; a cinema showing first-run movies; several bands and cabaret acts, along with an entertainment director; and a full-time social staff that organizes activities both on shore and at sea, with special programs for toddlers and teenagers. Many cruise ships even hire golf pros. The Royal Caribbean Cruise Line is the official cruise line of the Professional Golfers Association, and passengers can play golf at every port.

On today's cruise ships the ship's purser has been replaced by a hotel manager. Like hotels, cruise ships have a front desk, food and beverage facilities (many times with 24-hour room service), a housekeeping department, and a maintenance department. The latter is the only part of the ship run by the ship's crew—traditional sailors who are under the direct command of the ship's captain. The rest of the staff works for the hotel manager. He or she performs every function that a hotel manager on shore does. Food servers and room attendants are paid very little and they receive the majority of their income from tips.

Most cruise ships are registered in foreign countries such as Bermuda and Liberia and carry an international hotel staff. However, the deck and engine crew usually reflect the true country of origin of the line—for instance, Kloster Cruise Lines and Royal Caribbean Cruises both use Norwegians in these posts. Cunard's sailors are British, but the hotel crew is international.

Cruise-ship job opportunities for American hospitality students have in the past been limited, except in the areas of reservations and marketing and sales. With the industry's growth, however, many more jobs will become available. Jonathan Booth, a graduate of a hotel school in Bristol, England, and hotel manager of the Royal Caribbean Cruise Line's 37,000-ton, 1,500-passenger ship *Song of America*, claims that his job aboard ship is very similar to that of a hotel manager ashore, but notes some dissimilarities: "Sometimes my duties are considerably more varied. I need diplomatic skills to deal with foreign officials in all of the ports we call at, my knowledge of foreign currencies and how to convert them must be current on a daily basis, and on some sad occasions I have had to handle notifying next of kin and arranging for shipment of bodies."[15]

There is a good deal of consolidation and merging going on in the cruise industry. In recent years the Princess and Sitmar Lines have merged; Carnival acquired Holland American; Royal Caribbean Cruise Line bought Admiral; and Home Lines discontinued passenger service. The clear industry leader today is Carnival. Other major lines are Kloster (which owns both Norwegian Cruise Lines and the Royal Viking Line), Princess, Cunard, and Chandris.

Continuing-Care Retirement Communities. Continuing-care retirement communities (CCRCs) are new types of facilities for retired Americans. CCRCs are very much like residential hotels, except that they offer special safety features, structured group activities, meals that conform to special dietary needs, and readily available medical care.

CCRCs are getting the attention of hotel corporations, as well as major real-estate developers with hotel interests. The reason for the growing interest is the "graying of America," which so many marketing people have commented on and written about. Although in 1980 only 11.3% of America's population was over 60 years of age, that figure is projected to reach 12.2% by the turn of the century, and 18.3% by 2030. In sheer numbers, the size of America's elderly population will more than double—from 25.5 million to 55 million—in just 50 years.[16]

In the past, many elderly Americans moved in with their children; retired to states like Florida, Arizona, or California; or ended up in nursing homes. However, today's senior citizens are a different breed. For example, the very term "senior" is rejected by many older citizens. They prefer to think of themselves as active, mature people with distinct needs. They are, on the whole, more educated and affluent than their parents. And many of them prefer the new CCRCs.

There is no doubt that CCRCs, or "life-care" centers (as they are sometimes called to distinguish them from "health-care" facilities like nursing homes), are targeted at affluent Americans. Residents can buy apartments or rent them, but many cost over $100,000 to buy, and rents of $1,500 or more per month are common. Buyers or renters typically get small studios, or one- or two-bedroom apartments with utility kitchens where they can prepare their own meals, although usually at least two meals a day are included in the rent or maintenance plans. Often there are activities every day, including daily trips to shopping malls and grocery stores, movies, and fitness centers. Market studies show that CCRCs appeal mostly to women (approximately 75% of residents), especially widows. Married couples account for most of the other residents.[17]

The Marriott Corporation was one of the first hospitality companies to enter this new market. In 1988 it opened its first two developments: the Fairfax in Ft. Belvoir, Virginia, and the Quadrangle, outside of Philadelphia. Each had more than 80% of its units spoken for the day it opened.[18] A new complex in the Washington D.C. area, the Jefferson, is scheduled to open in 1992; its units (condominiums) are priced from $106,000 to $260,000. The Jefferson will offer such expected amenities as housekeeping services, a pool, and a health club. In addition, it will also feature 24-hour emergency call buttons in all bathrooms, a communal dining room, and two special floors—an "assisted-living" floor for people who, for example, need help dressing themselves, and a floor with skilled nursing care. Marriott's plans call for spending more than $1 billion by 1994 to develop 150 retirement centers.[19] Marriott wants to rent rather than sell units in most of its projects, in order to appeal to a wider market of elderly citizens who wish to conserve their capital. These units will be similar to other CCRCs in amenities but will offer only one meal a day. Rents should run from $900 to $2,000 per month. The Hyatt Corporation is also developing a chain of CCRCs.

Chains versus Independents

There are six different ways in which hotels are owned and operated. It is important that you clearly understand the differences because the management goals of the different owners are not always congruent and it is the job of the hotel manager to integrate these different viewpoints.

Hotels can be:

- Independently owned and operated.

- Independently owned but leased to an operator.

- Owned by a single entity or group that has hired a hotel management company to operate the property.

- Owned and operated by a chain.

- Owned by an independent investor or group and operated by a chain.

- Owned by an individual or group and operated as a franchise of a chain. The franchise holder may be an individual or a management company.

In order to understand these various forms of operation we need to first define some terms. Chapters 12 and 13 deal with franchising and management contracts in depth, but for the purpose of this discussion it will be helpful for you to understand these basic definitions:

- An *independent hotel* is not connected with any established hotel company and is owned by an individual or group of investors.

- A *management company* contracts with hotel owners to operate their hotel for them. The management company may or may not have any of its own funds invested. It is usually paid by a combination of fees plus a share of revenues, and profits.

- A *chain* is a group of affiliated hotels.

- A *franchise* is the authorization granted by a hotel chain to an individual hotel to use the chain's trademark, operating systems, and reservation system in return for a percentage of the hotel's revenues plus certain other fees, such as advertising fees.

A franchisor is the party granting the franchise. Holiday Corporation is an example of a franchisor. A franchisee is the party granted the franchise. A franchisee can be a hotel management company—The Continental Companies, for example—or an individual who has applied and been granted a license to do business under the franchisor's name.

There are also referral systems. Referral systems tend to be independent properties or small chains that have grouped together for common marketing purposes. Best Western is the largest of these. Its properties have no common designs or standard amenities, but a room at a Best Western can be reserved anywhere in the United States through a central reservations number.

Chain hotels represent by far the largest share of the lodging industry. According to a 1989 study, 62.7% of all U.S. hotels were chain owned, leased, managed, or franchised. Only 37.3% were independent.[20]

There is no significant difference in the occupancy rates of chain and independent hotels. Overall annual occupancy for all establishments in 1989 was 66.3%—independent hotels scored 64%, while chain-owned hotels achieved 64.9%. People did seem willing to pay more for a room in a good chain hotel however. The average annual room rate for all hotels was $55.26, while for chain-owned properties the figure rose to $63.59. Independents rented their rooms for an average rate of $72.62.[21]

According to an article in *Hotel & Motel Management*, "the two main advantages that chains have over individual properties are deeper pockets for the purchase of goods, services, and talent—and economies of scale that institute substantial cost savings when supplies and advertising are acquired in bulk." However, the same article points out that experts in the field believe that sharp negotiators for independent hotels are often able to minimize this discrepancy.[22] In addition, independent hoteliers have an inherent advantage in that they are often more flexible and thus able to respond to changing conditions and local promotions much faster than a chain operator. They are also freer to use their own creative abilities in solving problems, rather than having to check with corporate headquarters. Managers who prefer to run their own show often prefer independent hotels, while those who are more comfortable with team decision-making processes or doing things by the book feel more secure with chains.

The Major Players

Every summer *Lodging Hospitality* magazine publishes an annual survey entitled "The Top 400 Performers." The 400 most successful hotels in the United States are ranked on such criteria as occupancy, total sales per room, payroll expense per room, employees per one hundred rooms, and total sales per employee. Figures are given for the industry as a whole and then for each hotel. The survey also shows the percentage of the top 400 hotels that are independent, franchised, chain owned, chain managed, or part of a referral system, as well as the percentage that offer room service, valet service, and even electronic door locks. You should familiarize yourself with the most recent version of this study since it is a good barometer of trends as well as an excellent career guide tool.

The following list provides a group profile of the types of properties that make up the top 400 performers:

Independent	42%
Franchise	29%
Chain owned	14%
Chain managed	13%
Referral group	2%

As you can see, despite the proliferation of chains and management companies, independent hotels remain by a healthy margin the top performers in America today.[23]

One of the most important and telling criteria that *Lodging Hospitality* ranks hotels by is total sales per room. In other words, how many dollars does a hotel generate per room each year? These figures include money spent not only on the room itself but also on food, telephone, laundry, and other services. Exhibit 3.5 ranks the leading hotels by location category in terms of total sales per room.

Chains. Let's begin by considering the leading chain operators in America. Exhibit 3.6 ranks the top 26 chains in terms of total number of rooms they operate in the United States.

It should be noted that the figures in Exhibit 3.6 can be somewhat misleading without a more complete understanding of these organizations. For example, how many of the properties listed are company owned, fran-

Exhibit 3.5 Leading Hotels by Location Category in Total Sales Per Room

Location	Hotel	Sales per Room
Center City:	The Pierre Hotel, New York, New York	$212,699
Resort:	Trump Plaza Hotel & Casino, Atlantic City, New Jersey	$168,020
Suburban:	Sheraton Valley Forge Hotel, King of Prussia, Pennsylvania	$ 82,337
Highway:	Hanover Inn at Dartmouth College, Hanover, New Hampshire	$ 57,119
Airport:	Red Lion Hotel, San Jose, California	$ 51,282

Source: *Lodging Hospitality,* August 1990.

chised, under management contracts, or simply marketing organizations in which independent hotels have banded together solely to advertise and set up a common reservation system? For instance, Best Western (ranked second on the list) does not own, franchise, or manage a single property. The only affiliation any of its properties have is that all of them are part of a common reservation and marketing system. The same is true for Preferred Hotels (#26). On the other hand, Hyatt Hotels (#11) are operated under management contracts, although Hyatt has recently expressed an interest in possibly taking an equity position in some future properties. Companies like Rodeway Inns International (#25) and Hospitality International (#18) franchise all of their properties, while Red Roof (#19) owns everything it puts its name on. Most companies have a mix. Marriott Hotels, Resorts & Suites (#3) owns 162 properties, franchises 57, and has 256 under a management contract.

Independents. Most hotels that are classified as independent are independently owned and managed but are allied with a referral or marketing association. Three such associations are Preferred Hotels, The Leading Hotels of the World, and Best Western. The Breakers Hotel in Palm Beach, Florida, and the Hotel DuPont in Wilmington, Delaware, are Preferred Hotels. The famous Hotel Bristol in Paris is a member of both Preferred Hotels and The Leading Hotels of the World. Best Western has over 3,300 members, located in 2,400 cities in 34 different countries. It is sometimes difficult to differentiate hotels that are independent from those that are actually managed or owned by chains. For example, the Pierre Hotel in New York City, which many consider to be a fine independent hotel, is actually managed by the Four Seasons chain. The Watergate Hotel in Washington, D.C., is a Cunard Hotel.

As mentioned earlier, an important measure of a hotel's success is its total sales per room. Some examples of how top independent hotels fare using this measure are shown in Exhibit 3.7.

Developing and Planning New Hotels

Before a new hotel is built (1) a site is selected, (2) a feasibility study is conducted to determine the potential success of the planned hotel, and (3) financing is arranged.

Exhibit 3.6   The Top 26 Hotel Chains

CHAIN	NUMBER OF ROOMS	NUMBER OF PROPERTIES
1. Holiday Inn Worldwide	264,523	1,365
2. Best Western International	163,797	1,782
3. Marriott Hotels, Resorts & Suites	140,634	575
4. Days Inns of America	134,204	1,017
5. Quality International	112,845	1,011
6. Hilton Hotels Corp.	92,513	260
7. ITT Sheraton Corp.	90,551	321
8. Ramada Franchise Systems	79,209	483
9. Radisson Hotels International	65,700	242
10. Motel 6	61,525	536
11. Hyatt Hotels Corp.	55,486	105
12. Howard Johnson Franchise Systems, Inc.	54,795	443
13. Promus Companies, Inc.	52,615	330
14. Econo Lodges of America	46,000	592
15. Super 8 Motels	44,884	714
16. Travelodge Inns, Hotels & Suites	35,641	438
17. La Quinta Motor Inns	26,332	206
18. Hospitality International	25,346	297
19. Red Roof Inns	22,803	205
20. Westin Hotels & Resorts	20,903	34
21. Knights Lodging System	20,745	197
22. Treadway Inns Partners	18,000	450
23. MetHotels	16,782	64
24. Park Inns International	16,400	88
25. Rodeway Inns International	15,673	140
26. Preferred Hotels & Resorts Worldwide	14,000	57

Source: *Lodging Hospitality,* August 1990.

Site Selection   According to the American Hotel & Motel Association, "Choosing the geographic region or area and [the] specific site for development is usually first in the series of critical decisions affecting the eventual success of the [hotel] project."[24] The site must be accessible to the market it hopes to attract.

Exhibit 3.7   Leading Independent Hotels in Total Sales Per Room

HOTEL	SALES PER ROOM
Royalton, New York, N.Y.	$156,962
Boston Harbour Hotel, Boston, Mass.	126,087
The Hay-Adams Hotel, Washington, DC	83,916
Hotel DuPont, Wilmington, Del.	74,576

Source: *Lodging Hospitality,* August 1990.

If the location is downtown, for example, it should be convenient to either the central business district, the financial district, the entertainment district, or a major convention hall. It also needs to be accessible by public transportation. If it is a highway location, whether or not the highway is a major route and will continue to be one needs to be established. Many of the old "ma and pa" tourist courts and motels were put out of business when new freeways and turnpikes bypassed their locations.

The site must be adaptable to the type and size of the proposed hotel. A 400-room commercial hotel with meeting space can't be built on a site where zoning laws prohibit a building of that size. Zoning ordinances could also limit the type and size of ancillary facilities that would make the property more attractive and marketable, such as restaurants and lounges. Parking requirements are another consideration. Many cities have ordinances that dictate the number of spaces that must be available to employees and guests. That requirement must be satisfied before a hotel can be constructed.

The Feasibility Study

After the site is selected, a market study and financial analysis, called a feasibility study, is conducted to determine the economic viability of the hotel project. Among other things, a feasibility study determines the size and scope of the potential guest market for the new hotel. It would be imprudent to construct a hotel without first making sure that a market for it exists and learning about the market's size and characteristics. The kinds of questions the study needs to address include: What kind of hotel is most likely to succeed in this location? What types of guests is it likely to attract? How much will these guests be willing to pay? What occupancy rate can be expected? How many competitors are there and where are they located?

A feasibility study helps prospective owners in a number of ways. They can use feasibility studies to help them obtain financing and negotiate contracts for a franchise, lease, or management contract. A feasibility study can guide planners and architects of the facility. A study also helps the new hotel's management team formulate operating and marketing plans and prepare the initial capital and operating budget.[25]

Feasibility studies are conducted at the request of lenders, investors, franchisors, and management companies. Usually the person or persons conducting the study are independent consultants, although it is not uncommon for developers, management companies, or institutional investors to conduct their own study as well.

Construction of a new hotel should not begin until a thorough feasibility study has been conducted.

The person or consulting firm commissioned to conduct a feasibility study should have both expertise and prior experience. That expertise should be in the areas of hotel marketing, operations, and finance. There are a number of domestic and international companies that are considered to be experts in these disciplines. Most are firms of certified public accountants that have developed special consulting divisions for the hospitality industry. These include Pannell Kerr Forster, Coopers and Lybrand, Deloitte Haskins & Sells, Ernst & Whinney, and Peat Marwick Main. Personnel in the consulting divisions of these and other accounting firms are often graduates of hospitality management schools rather than accounting schools.

Most feasibility studies are performed to determine the suitability of a location for a hotel-chain property. Hotel chains already have brand-name recognition, tested hotel concepts, and established markets. Consumers have definite expectations as far as these hotels are concerned. Therefore, an important purpose of a feasibility study is to ascertain whether the proposed site and hotel can meet these consumer expectations.

The Report. When a feasibility study is conducted the final product is always a written report. This report typically includes the following sections.

Market area characteristics. This section contains a review of demographic and other relevant economic data for the area surrounding the site. The purpose is not to provide an in-depth economic evaluation but to obtain a sampling of those factors that support or reject the need for the proposed hotel. For example, a profile of the commercial and industrial sectors of the area can indicate the degree of economic stability and strength of the market. Population statistics, along with growth trends and income levels, are valuable in helping to determine the potential demand for food, beverage, and catering facilities. Employment statistics are helpful as well. Not only are they another indicator of economic strength, but they also may be useful in forecasting potential employment problems or opportunities in operating the hotel. Highway traffic counts, air arrivals and departures, and tourism statistics often are included and analyzed in relation to their potential impact on the proposed project.

Site and area evaluation. The father of the modern American hotel, Ellsworth Statler, was reputed to have said that there were three reasons for a hotel's success: location, location, and location. That maxim may be as true today as it ever was. As pointed out earlier, convenience and accessibility are key components to a new hotel's success. There may be a real demand, but if the proposed hotel is not easily accessible to the source of that demand, it cannot succeed. Moreover, ideally the proposed hotel should be *more* accessible than existing or proposed competing hotels.

Accessibility is a relative concept, of course, which varies according to the kind of facility proposed. Club Med has built one of the largest hospitality organizations in the world by going into areas that are by definition inaccessible—except to its own guests. To make sure that guests can get to its hotels, Club Med often charters aircraft and buses, and it has even developed airports in partnership with local governments (as was necessary in Mexico). In general, resort hotels may not need to be accessible by automobile as long as they are convenient by air, train, bus, or even ferry (as is Nantucket Island in Massachusetts). On the other hand, highways are the lifelines of motels.

Finally, the reputation of the area may well be an important factor in

Club Med properties are usually built in remote areas. Courtesy of Club Med, Ixtapa, Mexico.

determining the feasibility of the proposed site. Travelers tend to avoid areas with high crime rates, blatant poverty, and/or political unrest. Unless there is an overriding reason for building a hotel in these kinds of areas, they are best avoided.

Competition analysis. A good feasibility study carefully details all of the competition in the area in order to reveal the size and nature of the market as it currently exists. Facilities, services, and price levels of competitors need to be carefully noted. This section of the report is a good place to look for opportunities that may have been overlooked or simply not taken advantage of by competitors. There may be a lack of fine dining in the area, for example. The Sonesta Beach Hotel on Key Biscayne in Florida does a land-office business with its Two Dragons Chinese and Japanese Restaurant—among other reasons because there are no other Chinese or Japanese restaurants in the area. Hyatt often puts revolving restaurants on top of its properties for a similar reason—both the height and the concept are unique.

Demand analysis. The feasibility study must answer a number of questions about potential guests. Who are they and where are they going to come from? How many are there? Is this number likely to grow or decline in the future? Which hotels are they going to now? How are we going to take these guests away from them? A detailed approach to demand analysis is a vital part of any sound marketing plan (there is much more on this subject in Chapter 10).

If demand is expected to be generated from local industry and commercial activity in the area, then surveys of potential guests in the area are one of the best ways to confirm that demand. On the other hand, if the potential market is anticipated to come from incoming travelers such as conventioneers and sightseers, then the market survey needs to be extended to cover those groups. The market as a whole needs to be quantified, then the potential for the proposed property to gain a fair share of that market must be appraised. Generally, through a series of interviews with potential guests, a profile of the needed facilities and services can be formulated.

Proposed facilities and services. After analyzing market area characteristics, evaluating the site, reviewing the competition, and preparing a demand analysis, the next step in a feasibility study is the proposal of facilities and services. At this stage analysts conducting the study are expected to recommend the size and type of facilities the proposed hotel should have, as well as the services that should be provided. The purpose here is to establish a market difference that gives the hotel a competitive advantage. Recommendations may cover architectural and design considerations as well as overall concept and ambience.

Financial estimates. The last section of the study contains estimates of revenues and expenses, based on (1) the type of the proposed hotel and the services it will offer, and (2) the size of the projected guest demand.

Studies often vary at this point. Some will present estimates of operating results only, while others, at the request of those commissioning the study, provide additional information such as (1) the fixed charges that can be anticipated—for example, property taxes, insurance on building and contents, and interest on borrowed capital and depreciation; and (2) an analysis of the expected return on investment (ROI). A study that includes ROI is a true feasibility study. Most studies end at the point of forecasting income before fixed charges—that is, they estimate only operating revenues and expenses. Those studies are known as market studies with estimates of operating revenues and expenses.

Financing   When investors are asked to participate in the financing of a new hotel there are several components of that investment that they look at carefully:

- *The land on which the hotel will be built.* How large is it? What condition is it in? What is its appraised value? What is its market value? What has comparable land sold for in the last year?

- *The building.* What construction costs are involved? How long will it take to construct the hotel?

- *Furniture and fixtures.* What is needed to decorate rooms and public areas? How much will it cost?

In addition to these hard costs there are some soft costs as well that need to be factored into any financing package:

- *Architectural fees.* These include site elevations, final blueprints from which contractors will work, and sometimes models.

- *Pre-opening expenses.* Certain members of the management team will be on board months before opening day. New managers and employees must be trained. Security guards will be needed to protect the property. There will be an advertising campaign that will appear several months before opening day. Working capital will also be needed until the hotel is open and generating its own.

There are two general types of hotel financing—permanent financing loans and construction loans.

Permanent financing is a long-term mortgage loan—traditionally 25 to 30 years. Long-term mortgage loans are obtained from institutions such as insurance companies, pension funds, and banks.

The lending institutions provide the financing and charge interest at what the going rate is when the loan is made. In addition, they often take an equity position in the property—that is, they become part-owners of the hotel as well. Typically these institutions put up as much as 75% of the cost of the entire project. The developer, either alone or with partners, is expected to provide the other 25%, as lenders do not wish to loan money to projects if the developer is unwilling or unable to risk any of his or her own funds.

A construction loan is obtained from a bank or a group of banks. This is a short-term loan to be used while the hotel is being built, with repayment to be made in three years or less. In most cases the construction loan is approved only after permanent financing, known as "take-out," has already been granted, since once the hotel opens and the permanent financing is in place, part of the permanent financing will be used to pay off the construction loan.

Chapter Summary

Hotels can be categorized by location. Center city hotels have been experiencing new growth in recent years with the rebirth of downtown areas. More than half of downtown hotels today are 10 years old or less. The majority are chain operated or managed and serve business guests.

Resorts are built in destinations that are desirable because of climate, scenery, recreational facilities, or historic interest. Many resorts such as spas are patronized for health reasons. While early resorts were seasonal operations, today there is a year-round demand in many locations. Most resort business comes from leisure travelers, but resort use by businesses for meetings and incentive programs is increasing. Most resorts are still independent operations. They are expensive to build and operate.

Suburban hotels followed corporations and factories that relocated from downtown to the suburbs because of land costs. These hotels tend to be somewhat smaller than downtown properties and are primarily chain affiliated. Individual business travelers represent their single largest market, although their food and beverage operations are often patronized by the local community.

Highway hotels have evolved from early tourist courts. Large signs, easy access, motor entrances, and ample parking facilities are distinguishing characteristics. Many are franchised by companies like Holiday and Quality and are relatively new structures. They require the least number of employees per room to operate. Like downtown and suburban properties, business travelers are their main source of revenue.

Airport hotels are for the most part affiliated with chains and enjoy some of the highest occupancy rates in the lodging industry. Their biggest operating problem is the need to respond to high demand instantly when weather or other conditions delay flight arrivals and departures.

Hotels can also be categorized by price. The most important classifications are: economy/limited service, mid-price/extended stay, and full-service/luxury.

Another way of classifying hotels is by consumer. The major classifications here are:

- Corporate—individuals
- Corporate groups
- Convention and association groups
- Leisure travelers
- Long-term stay/relocation guests
- Airline-related guests
- Government and military travelers
- Regional get-away guests

A fairly recent development in the lodging industry has been the growth of segmentation strategies. In order to capture more guest markets, companies like Quality International, Holiday, and Marriott now offer a complete line of properties that range from economy to luxury.

Other hotel classifications include all-suite hotels, casino hotels, conference centers, time-share condominiums and condominium hotels, cruise ships, and continuing-care retirement communities (CCRCs).

Most hotels today are chain owned, leased, managed, or franchised. Nevertheless, many independent hotels have overcome the chains' economies of scale with other business strategies that allow them to compete effectively.

Business philosophies vary from chain to chain. Some hotel chains prefer to own, others to franchise, and others to manage. Many have a mix of the three. In addition, there are some very successful management companies that operate and manage chain properties.

Feasibility studies are conducted as part of the process of developing and planning new hotels. They help prospective owners obtain financing and help managers prepare marketing plans. Location is a key consideration in all new hotel projects.

Feasibility studies usually include the following sections:

- Market area characteristics
- Project, site, and area evaluation
- Competition analysis
- Demand analysis
- Proposed facilities and services
- Financial estimates

Financing covers the land, building, furniture and fixtures, and equipment, as well as architectural fees and pre-opening expenses. Financing for new hotels is usually provided in two types of loans—long-term permanent financing loans (mortgage loans) and short-term construction loans.

Endnotes

1. *U.S. Lodging Industry 1988*, Laventhol & Horwath.
2. Donald E. Lundberg, *The Hotel & Restaurant Business* (New York: CBI Books).
3. *U.S. Lodging Industry 1988*, Laventhol & Horwath.
4. Michael J. Butler, "Mixed Use to Dominate Resorts of the Future," *Lodging*, February 1990, p. 12.
5. *U.S. Lodging Industry 1988*, Laventhol & Horwath.
6. Albert J. Gomes, *Hospitality in Transition* (Houston, Texas: Pannell Kerr Forster, 1985), pp. 32–34.
7. Daniel Daniele, "Forecast Is Sweet for All-Suite Segment," *Hotel & Motel Management*, March 13, 1989, p. 52.
8. *1990 Directory of Hotel & Motel Systems*, 59th ed. (Washington, D.C.: American Hotel Association Directory Corporation, 1990).
9. Kenneth Miller, Miller Marketing Network, quoted in the *New York Post*, "Timeshares for Fun but Not for Profit," August 31, 1989, pp. 39–40.
10. *Lodging Hospitality*, "Timeshare Becomes Big Business," February 1989, p. 87.
11. "Turkey of the Year," *Forbes*, September 9, 1985, p. 32.

12. Investment Research Report, Morgan Stanley, Carnival Cruise Lines, New York, N.Y., October 28, 1987, p. 7.

13. Highlights 1988 CLIA Cruise Market Profile Study, Cruise Lines International Association, 500 Fifth Ave., Suite 1407, New York, N.Y. 10110

14. Transportation Group Research Report, Carnival Cruise Lines, Alex Brown & Sons Inc., 135 E. Baltimore Street, Baltimore, Md. 21202, Nov. 6, 1987, p. 5.

15. Jonathan Booth, hotel manager on the cruise ship *Song of America.* Interview with Andrew Vladimir aboard ship, June 24, 1989.

16. Robert Meyer, "The Hospitality Industry Entering the Life Care Market: Implications for Hotel Restaurant and Institutional Management Curricula," *Hospitality Education and Restaurant Journal,* 1988, p. 242.

17. Robert L. Roher & Robert Bibb, CCRC, Contemporary LTC, May 1986, p. 51.

18. Janet Novack, "Tea, Sympathy, and Direct Mail," *Forbes,* September 18, 1989, p. 210.

19. Novack, p. 210.

20. *U.S. Lodging Industry 1988,* p. 15.

21. *U.S. Lodging Industry 1989,* p. 42.

22. Russel Shaw, "Independent vs. Chain Properties," *Hotel & Motel Management,* October 17, 1988, p. 46.

23. Rocco M. Angelo, *A Practical Guide to Understanding Feasibility Studies* (East Lansing, Mich.: Educational Institute of the American Hotel & Motel Association, 1985), p. 17.

24. Angelo, pp. 5–6.

25. Angelo, p. 25.

Key Terms

airline-related guests
airport hotels
all-suite hotels
casino hotels
center city hotels
condominium hotels
conference centers
construction loan
continuing-care retirement communities (CCRCs)
convention and association group
corporate groups
corporate—individuals
cruise ships
economy/limited service hotels
feasibility study
franchise
franchisee
franchisor

full-service/luxury hotels
government and military travelers
guest mix
highway hotels
hotel chain
independent hotel
leisure travelers
long-term stay/relocation guests
management company
referral systems
regional get-away guests
resort hotels
Standard Industrial Classification code
suburban hotels
take-out
time-share condominiums
tourist courts

Discussion Questions

1. What are some of the differences between a center city hotel and a resort hotel?

2. What are some characteristics of suburban hotels? highway hotels?

3. Airport hotels possess what unique characteristics?

4. What are some hotel price categories?

5. How can economy/limited service hotels offer such low rates?

6. What are some important guest categories?

7. How do casino hotels differ from other types of hotels?

8. What do cruise ships and land-based resorts have in common?

9. What are the differences between chain and independent hotels?

10. How many sections are in a typical feasibility study and what do they cover?

Chapter Outline

How Is a Hotel Organized?
    Revenue Centers versus Cost Centers
Revenue Centers
    Rooms Division
        Organization of the Rooms Division
    Food and Beverage Division
        Selecting Food and Beverage Outlets
        Organization of the Food and Beverage Division
        Why Food and Beverage Divisions Fail
    Other Revenue Centers
        Telephone Department
        Concessions, Rentals, and Commissions
        Fitness and Recreation Facilities
Cost Centers
    Marketing Division
    Engineering Division
        Controlling Energy Costs
    Accounting Division
    Human Resources Division
    Security Division
Control Systems
    Financial Controls
        Uniform System of Accounts
    Quality Controls
        Establishing Standards of Operation
Chapter Summary

4 Hotel Organization

In order to gain a perspective on the ways in which hotels are organized, there are a few hotel characteristics that need to be noted at the outset:

- All hotels are in the business of renting rooms.

- Hotels vary in size from under 100 rooms to over 3,000.

- Hotels vary in type. As pointed out in the previous chapter, hotels can be suburban, airport, all-suite, and so on.

- Hotels vary in the nature and extent of their facilities. Some hotels offer only rooms, while others have coffee shops, gourmet restaurants, swimming pools, golf courses, and other facilities.

- Hotels vary in the level of service they offer. For example, some offer 24-hour room service, others offer room service only from 7 a.m. to 10 p.m., and some do not offer room service at all.

As you can see, hotels are not all alike. Nevertheless, no matter what category a hotel falls into, it needs to be organized in order to: (1) coordinate the many specialized tasks and activities necessary to attract and serve guests, and (2) produce a reasonable profit consistent with the amount of money and time invested in the enterprise. Organizing is one of the principal jobs of management.

How Is a Hotel Organized?

In order to attract and serve guests and make a reasonable profit, hotels are organized into functional areas or divisions* based on the services the hotel provides. For instance, all hotels have a rooms division to manage

---

*The use of the terms "division" and "department" is not standardized in the industry. Some properties call their main functional areas (rooms, food and beverage, etc.) departments; the smaller functional areas within departments (e.g., room service) may be called sub-departments. Large properties often call their main functional areas divisions and units within divisions, departments. Neither option is better than the other. For consistency, however, throughout this chapter we will call the main functional areas "divisions" and the smaller areas "departments."

the guestrooms rented to overnight guests. If the hotel operates a restaurant or lounge, it is likely to have a food and beverage division as well. Within each division there are specialized functions. The rooms division handles reservations, check-in and check-out activities, housekeeping, uniformed service, and telephone service. At a small hotel, these functions are performed by personnel who report to and take their instructions from the general manager. At a large hotel, rooms personnel report to a rooms division manager. The tasks each employee is responsible for also vary with the size of the hotel. For example, in a small hotel, one person behind the front desk may act as a receptionist, a cashier, and the hotel operator. In a large hotel, these jobs would be handled by different individuals.

Revenue Centers versus Cost Centers

The divisions in a hotel can be categorized as revenue centers or cost centers. Revenue centers generate income for the hotel through the sale of services or products to guests. Cost centers, also known as support centers, do not generate revenue directly. Instead, they provide the necessary support for the proper functioning of revenue centers.

Probably the easiest way to understand revenue and cost centers is to take a look at hotel organization charts. Exhibit 4.1 shows a typical organization chart for a small hotel. As you can see, this hotel has four divisions. The general manager has four people working under him or her, each of whom has the responsibility and the authority to take care of one of the four principal areas in this hotel. Each of these individuals may or may not have a number of other employees reporting to him or her, depending on the size of the property.

Let's examine a much larger hotel that has a more complex organization (see Exhibit 4.2). The divisions and departments shown in Exhibit 4.2 can be categorized thus:

REVENUE CENTERS	COST CENTERS
Rooms	Marketing
Food and Beverage	Engineering
Telephone	Accounting
Concessions, Commissions, Rentals	Human Resources
Fitness and Recreation Facilities	Security

Now let's take a closer look at each revenue and cost center.

Revenue Centers

Rooms Division

In most hotels, the rooms division is the major division and the central reason for the business entity. Casino hotels are an exception to this, since their rooms are occupied by guests whose primary reason for being at the hotel is to gamble, not spend the night. However, most of any hotel's square footage is devoted to guestrooms and areas that support the operation of those rooms. Therefore, the major segment of the building investment and, in most cases, the land cost is related to the rooms division.

Exhibit 4.1 Sample Organization Chart—Small Hotel

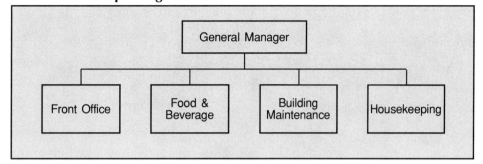

For all hotels except casino hotels, guestroom rentals are the single largest source of revenue. Here are the way the figures broke down for American hotels in 1989:[1]

Guestroom Rentals	55.2%
Food Revenue	20.3
Minor Operated Departments	9.4
Beverage Revenue	7.1
Rentals and Other Income	4.9
Telephone Sales	1.9
Other F&B Income	1.2

Not only do rooms occupy the most space in a hotel and produce the most revenue; they generate the most profit. In a study done by Pannell Kerr Forster, rooms division income (which is defined as room revenues or sales less room operating expenses) amounted to 73.4% of rooms revenue. In other words, for every dollar spent on guestrooms, 73.4 cents was available for general overhead after deducting the direct rooms division expenses.[2]

Organization of the Rooms Division. No matter what the size or category of hotel, rooms divisions are organized and function in a similar manner. Large hotels have more departments and personnel within the division, but this does not change the basic tasks that have to be performed.

In a small hotel, the general manager or owner directly oversees the rooms division because of its paramount importance. In a mid-size to large hotel (300 rooms or more), there is likely to be a rooms manager or an executive assistant manager in charge of rooms. In either case, the rooms division is usually organized like the sample division shown in Exhibit 4.3. As you can see, the rooms division has four departments:

- Front office

- Reservations

- Housekeeping

- Uniformed service

Exhibit 4.2 Sample Organization Chart—Large Hotel

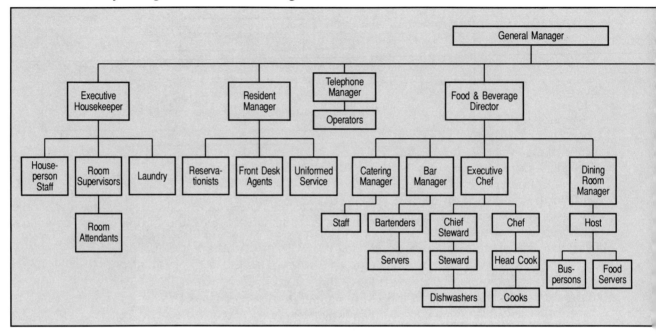

Front office. The front office is the command post for the processing of reservations, the registration of guests, the settling of guest accounts (cashiering), and check-out. Front desk agents also handle the distribution of guestroom keys and mail, messages, or other information for guests.

The most visible part of the front office area is of course the front desk. The front desk can be a counter or, in some luxury hotels, an actual desk where a guest can sit down and register. Traditionally, the front desk was placed so that the person behind it had a view of both the front door and the elevator. This was so front desk agents could discourage unwelcome guests from entering, and keep non-paying guests from departing. Because of modern credit and security procedures, this is no longer necessary.

The duties of front desk agents include:

- Greeting guests

- Registering guests

- Establishing a method of payment for the guestroom—credit card, cash, or direct billing

- Assigning guestrooms that are unoccupied and have been cleaned

- Assigning guestroom keys to guests

- Informing guests about their room location and special hotel facilities and answering questions about the property and the surrounding community

- Calling a bellperson to assist guests with their luggage if such service is normally provided

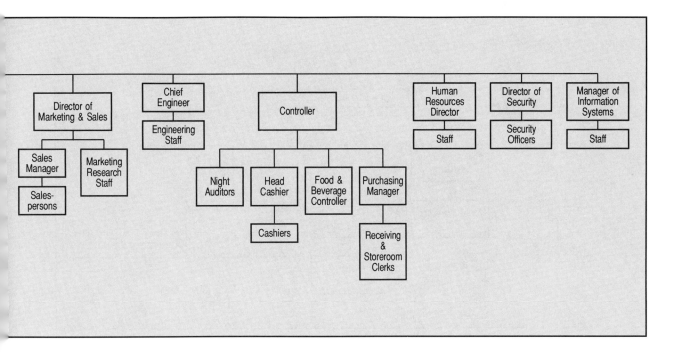

In small and mid-size hotels the front desk agent is also the cashier. Although the front desk station and cashier's station are usually separated in large hotels, employees are often cross-trained to be able to handle both jobs. One main duty of a cashier (or a front desk agent performing cashier duties) is to post charges to the guest's account. This means that the cashier must make sure that any expenses the guest may have incurred, such as restaurant bills and telephone calls that were charged to the room, are added to the bill before it is presented. This task is not necessary in hotels that have a computerized property management system (PMS) where electronic cash registers at points of sale (dining rooms, bars, and gift shops, for example) automatically post charges to guest accounts. Once the posting has been accomplished (either manually or electronically), guests can settle their account when they check out. Checking guests out requires tact and diplomacy because guests often have questions about their charges and, in some cases, may not even be aware that they incurred a charge when using a particular service (such as making telephone calls).

With computerized property management systems, checking out has become greatly simplified. Some hotels have these systems connected to guestroom television sets so that guests can view their account and then send a signal through the channel selector to acknowledge that their account is in order and authorize payment. The bill is then charged to their credit card. A copy of the bill can be mailed directly to them or picked up in the lobby upon departure. Since most hotels do not yet have this system, another common procedure is to place a copy of the final bill under the door of the guestroom during the night, while the guest is sleeping. This system saves time because the bill does not need to be requested and because it allows the guest to study the bill beforehand. If guests have no questions, they can simply phone the front desk and tell the front desk

Exhibit 4.3 Sample Organization Chart—Rooms Division

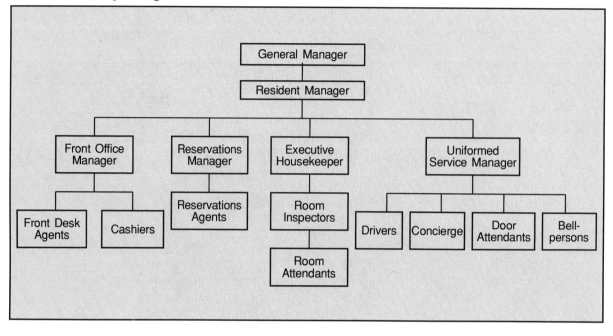

agent that they agree with the charges as posted. Any charges incurred between the time the bill is okayed and the time check out actually occurs are added to the guest's final account. The total amount of guest charges will appear on their personal or corporate credit card statement.

This system presumes that the guest has used a credit card and that an imprint of that card was taken at registration. Usually, approval of the card and the guestroom charges is obtained from the credit card company at check-in, not check-out. If a credit card is not used, then the cashier must handle payment by cash or check according to the hotel's policies.

Another important duty performed at the front desk is the night audit. This is usually done at the quietest times—between 11 p.m. and 6 a.m., when there are few other distracting duties. In a small hotel, the night audit is performed by the front desk agent on duty. In a larger property, an auditor from the accounting division usually is assigned the task. If the hotel does not have a computerized property management system, the night auditor's job can be a tough task since it involves a lot of detail. The night auditor must verify that guest charges have been accurately posted to each guest's account (or "folio") and that the income is properly credited to the division that earned it. This can be tedious work, especially since it involves checking for errors.

Another function of the front desk staff, that of relaying messages to guests, is undergoing a change in some hotels because of new technology. For instance, Boston's Park Plaza has a voice-mail system. Each guest's electronic mailbox is capable of holding as many as 25 phone messages, each one of which can be up to five minutes in length. By dialing a three-digit number on the phone in their room, guests can retrieve these messages. If they wish, the messages can be repeated, saved, or deleted with the touch of a button. The hotel estimates that this automated system, which releases front desk personnel from handling this chore, will save them $50,000 annually.[3] Other hotels have systems that allow guests to display incoming phone messages on their TV screen after being alerted by a light on the phone.

Voice mail is just one of the new electronic amenities hotels are installing that save staff time and upgrade services to guests. Some hotels are considering offering flight-reservation services, restaurant reservations, and even shopping services from the hotel's gift shop to guests via their guestroom television. Several companies are developing keyboards that, when attached to a TV set, turn the television into a computer terminal that is capable of these new functions.

Even the typical metal guestroom keys and locks are being slowly replaced by electronic locking systems that operate with disposable plastic card keys. An electronic connection between guestroom door locks and a console at the front desk makes it possible to code a card key with each check-in, matching the card key's code with a code programmed into the console for the guest's room. When the guest inserts his or her card key into a slot in the guestroom doorknob assembly, the door is unlocked. The door will stay locked if someone tries to use a card key whose code does not match the electronic code for the lock that was programmed at the front desk console. These new card keys generally do not carry the name of the hotel or the room number on them, so if lost they are of no use to whoever finds them. In some of these new card key systems, guestroom locks are connected to a central computer so that the hotel has a record of everyone who has entered the room (each housekeeping and maintenance employee's key registers its owner's code), along with the time of entry.

Friendly, attentive front desk agents help set the right tone for a guest's lodging experience. Courtesy of The Dusit Thani, Bangkok, Thailand.

In addition to all of their other duties, front desk employees represent the first and last (and often the only) contact the guest has with hotel personnel. Thus, the front desk agents' success or failure at making the guest feel welcome and special can have a tremendous impact on the quality of a guest's experience. It's essential, therefore, that the front desk staff be well trained and that morale be kept high so that interactions with guests and among staff members are always positive.[4]

Reservations. Another part of the rooms division is the reservations department or office. A reservations department should be managed by skilled telemarketing personnel who are able to accept reservations over the phone, answer questions about the facilities, and quote guestroom rates and available dates. Since some callers are shopping around, reservationists should be trained in how to make a sale as well as simply accept reservations. Reservationists also process reservations that may arrive through central computer reservation systems or through third parties such as travel agents and hotel representatives.

When travel agents and hotel representatives call in a reservation, they are often very professional in their approach and need to be handled with skill and efficiency if they are to be served properly. They require immediate and correct information on current room status. These travel professionals are compensated by commissions that the hotel sends to them after guest stays are completed. Naturally, a major concern of theirs is that the hotel will keep accurate records so that they will be paid promptly.

Here are how advance reservations come into hotels:[5]

Direct Inquiry	45.9%
Own Reservation System	22.1
Travel Agents	12.6
Hotel Representatives	8.9
Tour Operators	5.6
Independent Reservation System	3.8
Transportation Company	1.1

Many industry observers expect that the number of hotel reservations made by travel agents will increase dramatically in the next decade—some chains are projecting by as high as 50%.

Housekeeping. Housekeeping is another department of the rooms division. Housekeeping is responsible for cleaning the hotel's guestrooms and public areas. In many hotels, this department has the largest staff, consisting of an assistant housekeeper, room inspectors, room attendants, a houseperson crew (which cleans the public areas and handles the logistics of moving housekeeping supplies throughout the hotel), linen room attendants, and personnel in charge of employee uniforms (see Exhibit 4.4). Many hotels also have their own laundry and valet service. Hotels with laundry and valet equipment may use it only for hotel linens and uniforms and send guest clothing to an outside service where it is likely to be handled with greater care and specialized equipment.

The department is directed by an executive housekeeper. The executive housekeeper has an enormous amount of responsibility not only for cleaning and maintenance, but also for training staff and controlling

Exhibit 4.4   Sample Organization Chart—Housekeeping Department

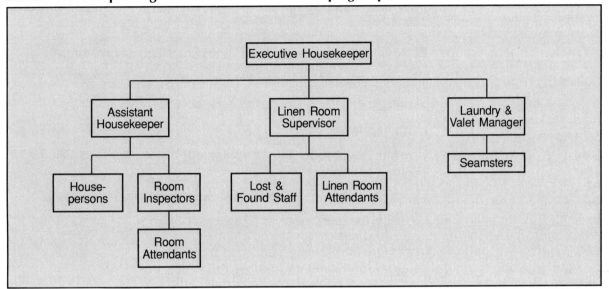

large inventories of linens, supplies, and equipment.[6] Room inspectors supervise room attendants. Room attendants are responsible for cleaning guestrooms according to specified procedures and for maintaining a predetermined level of supplies in the linen closets located on each floor. They are usually assigned a quota of rooms to clean in a given number of hours. Fifteen guestrooms per shift is average, although this figure may vary considerably because of such conditions as geographic location, union contracts, the size of the property, and the wage scale. In most hotels, room attendants are paid relatively low wages.

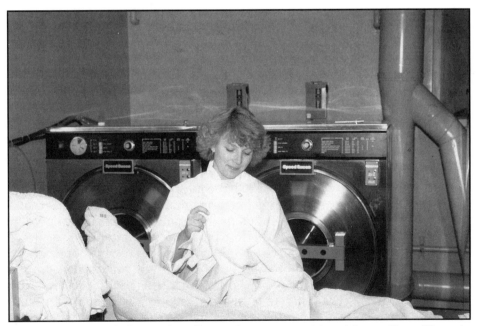

Many hotels have their own laundry service. Courtesy of Speed Queen, Ripon, Wisconsin.

When guests check out, it is the room attendants' responsibility to clean guests' rooms so that they are available again for rental. This includes such duties as:

- Removing soiled linen and towels and replacing them withfresh ones
- Checking the bed and blankets for damage
- Making the beds
- Emptying trash
- Checking the guestroom for broken appliances, damaged shades or blinds, and leaky faucets
- Checking closets and drawers for items forgotten by guests
- Cleaning the guestroom and bathroom
- Replacing bathroom towels and amenities

Some hotels contract with outside cleaning services to handle the hotel's lobbies, restaurants, restrooms, and windows. With the exception of windows, much of this cleaning needs to be done late at night, and hotels often find it difficult to find supervisors and employees willing to work at those hours. Contract cleaning firms, many of whom handle offices and airline terminals as well, are geared to handle these cleaning tasks and unusual hours efficiently.

Uniformed service. The uniformed service department is sometimes referred to as the guest service department. Employees in this department include bellpersons (so called because originally they were summoned by a bell), a concierge, and transportation or valet-parking employees.

Bellpersons move guest luggage to and from guestrooms. Some large hotels have door attendants who move luggage from cars or taxicabs into the hotel. Bellpersons have other duties as well:

- Escorting guests to their rooms
- Inspecting guestrooms while rooming the guest
- Explaining the features of the room and the hotel to guests

Good bellpersons possess a detailed knowledge of the hotel, including the hours of operation of the hotel's restaurants, lounges, and other facilities. They also know the local community.

Some hotels have adopted the European system of concierge service. The concierge performs many of the functions that a host might perform for guests in his or her home. The idea is to give guests the feeling that they are receiving personal and attentive service. The concierge is the main source of information about the hotel. He or she is not only familiar with the hotel's facilities and services but also has a thorough knowledge of the local area. A good concierge knows what's going on in town. He or she can recommend a romantic candlelight bistro within walking distance or the best steak house in the city. The concierge can make reservations and get theater tickets or suggest who can. He or she can also recommend secretarial services and copying centers, order limousines, and perform many other services that give guests the feeling that they are important and being well cared for.

Transportation services include valet parking, which may utilize either the hotel's own garage or a nearby facility. If there are other transportation services provided, such as airport vans, these are normally handled by the same department. In most large hotels, garages and limousines are handled by outside contractors.

Food and Beverage Division

Although in most hotels the rooms division generates the greatest amount of revenue, this is not always the case. In a few hotels, most often resorts and convention properties with extensive banquet sales, food and beverage operations may produce more revenue than does the rooms division. This is because guests in resorts tend to stay on the premises and may be less price-sensitive because they are on vacation. In convention hotels, the added food sales come from the multitude of restaurants, banquet rooms, and bars.

Whether the food and beverage operation is large or small, most hotel managers have found that their food and beverage facilities are of paramount importance to the reputation and profitability of the hotel. There

The Caxton Grill in London's Stakis Ermins Hotel. Courtesy of Stakis Hotels, Glasgow, Scotland.

Exhibit 4.5 Types of Hotel Food and Beverage Outlets

Food Service	Beverage Service
Dining Room	Cocktail Lounge
Specialty Restaurant	Public Bar (for guests)
Coffee Shop (mid-price restaurant)	Service Bar (for servers)
Supper Club	Banquets
Snack Bar	Discotheques
Take-Out	Mini-Bars (in guestrooms)
Cafeteria	
Room Service	
Banquets	
Employee Food Service	

is no doubt that in many cases the quality of a hotel's food and beverages powerfully affects the opinion a guest forms of a particular property and influences his or her willingness to return.

Successful hotel operators no longer consider dining facilities merely a convenience for guests. A hotel's food and beverage outlet(s) must attract members of the local community, convince hotel guests to dine on the premises, and return a fair profit. The "capture rate"—that is, the percentage of meals consumed by hotel guests—is measured regularly by some chains.

Except for many of the economy-class hotels and motels (which achieve that status partially by staying out of the restaurant business), virtually all lodging facilities offer some level of food and beverage service. Large hotels usually have a wide array of facilities, while small properties may have just one dining room which serves breakfast, lunch, and dinner. Exhibit 4.5 lists the types of food and beverage outlets that may be found in a hotel.[7]

Selecting Food and Beverage Outlets. There are several criteria that are used in deciding what type of food and beverage service should be offered in any given hotel. It is worthwhile to think about these carefully both in the initial planning stages of a new hotel and as a hotel matures and the market it appeals to changes.

The first of these is the type of hotel. Does this property primarily serve transient businesspeople or conventioneers? Is the property a resort? Business clientele are more interested in private dining, while convention hotels need ballrooms for large gatherings. Resorts often do well with specialty restaurants.

Next is the class of hotel. Five-star hotels need five-star restaurants. Moderate-price hotels could not sustain this kind of restaurant quality, nor would their guests expect it.

Competition is another consideration. What kinds of restaurants are already available in the area? If you are surrounded by Italian restaurants,

Meal Plans

There are several meal plans that hotel food and beverage divisions offer, among them the Full American Plan, the Modified American Plan, the Continental Plan, and the European Plan.

The Full American Plan and the Modified American Plan are usually seen in resort hotels. Under the Full American Plan, the room rate quoted includes all major meals—breakfast, lunch, and dinner. In effect, guests are offered a package price that includes their room and all three meals for as long as they stay. This has great appeal to guests who are concerned with the total cost of their resort vacation and like to budget for it ahead of time. The Modified American Plan provides two meals only—usually breakfast and dinner.

The Continental Plan includes a continental breakfast with the room rate. This plan is also called a Breakfast Plan, and in Bermuda it's known as the Bermuda Plan. With the European Plan, no meals are included in the room rate.

Isolated resorts with few or no restaurants in the surrounding area and no centers of population nearby are more likely to offer an American Plan. These were especially popular in the early 1900s, when travelers stayed at resorts for two weeks or more. Most guests today don't want to be locked into a meal plan—they prefer the freedom to try other restaurants in the area. As a result, offering a meal plan is not a growing hotel service since demand for it, on the whole, is decreasing. Hotels can be sympathized with for wishing this were not so. From the hotels' standpoint, there is much better control over purchasing, preparation, and staffing when the number of meals that will be served is known in advance. Moreover, both American plans guarantee food revenue and, to a great degree, beverage revenue as well since guests often order cocktails before dinner, wine with dinner, or after-dinner drinks.

putting another one in your hotel would probably not be a good idea. It might be wiser to try something completely different.

Product availability also counts. A fresh-fish restaurant might have a difficult time making it unless it limited itself to the kind of fish that could be caught in local lakes and rivers. The cost of flying in Alaska Salmon, Maine Lobster, and Dover Sole could easily price it out of the market.

Availability of labor is another important consideration. A menu that requires a lot of employees—for example, one that features tableside cooking with dishes like Steak Diane and desserts such as Crepes Suzette—might not be practical in a tight labor market.

Finally, there is the question of demand. Certain kinds of food are more popular in some areas of the country than others. Mexican restaurants are more in demand in the Southwest than the Northeast, for example. Is the type of restaurant in the hotel one that the hotel's guests will want to patronize?

Organization of the Food and Beverage Division. Clearly, the food and beverage division of a major hotel can be very complex, offering a variety of different kinds of restaurants and bars, each with its own unique decor, menu, and style of service. Such a division requires well-trained employees and highly skilled and versatile managers in the kitchen, bar, and service areas.

Exhibit 4.6 Sample Organization Chart—Food and Beverage Division in a Mid-Size Hotel

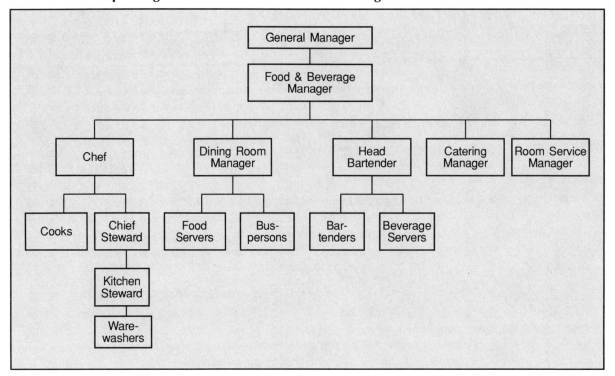

We can examine an organization chart of a typical food and beverage operation in a mid-size hotel to get a clear picture of how a food and beverage division works (see Exhibit 4.6). As can be seen from the exhibit, the person who is in charge of the food and beverage division reports to the general manager and is known as the food and beverage manager. Since this job entails responsibility for a major business entity of the hotel staffed by persons with specialized technical skills, the food and beverage manager needs to have a thorough knowledge of general business and management practices. He or she should also be well versed in the technical aspects of food and beverage preparation and service.

Reporting to the food and beverage manager is the chef, sometimes called the executive chef or head chef, who is in charge of the kitchen staff. An important member of the chef's team is the chief steward, whose job is to direct the kitchen steward and warewashers and to arrange to have sufficient inventories of clean china, glass, and silverware available for all dining rooms, bars, and banquet rooms.

The dining room manager must see that guest service goes smoothly, that there is a sufficient number of food servers and buspersons on duty, and that all dining room employees are well trained and are meeting the property's service standards. The job may also include training new employees.

In mid-size hotels with a lounge, a head bartender oversees the lounge's operation. He or she supervises bartenders and beverage servers.

Catering. The catering department's importance is twofold. Not only is it an image-maker for the hotel, but it also can be the most profitable segment of the food and beverage division. Catering arranges and plans food and beverage functions for (1) conventions and smaller hotel groups, and (2) local banquets booked by the sales department. Catering sales, in many instances, represent as much as 50% of a hotel's total food and beverage sales.

Catering is a highly competitive business in most market areas. To succeed, a catering department must have employees with a broad range of abilities and knowledge. Good catering departments excel in sales, menu planning, food and beverage service (including wines), food production, product knowledge, cost control, and, last but not least, artistic talent and a sense of theater. All of this requires sound technical knowledge as well as skillful use of the hotel's facilities and equipment.

The catering manager generally reports to the food and beverage manager. There are some exceptions to this rule, however. In some instances, the catering manager reports to the director of sales or directly to the hotel's general manager. When hotels are organized in this manner, the banquet head server usually reports to the food and beverage manager. Such a division of labor separates the selling function from the production and service function.

Room service. Most hotels with a food and beverage division provide some type of food service to guests in their rooms. Room service—or "private dining," as the highly marketing-oriented Walt Disney Corporation refers to it—is one of the most difficult areas of hotel food service to manage and has the greatest potential for losing money.

There are two main difficulties with room service. First, food and beverages are served at great distances from production areas. In resorts where there are cabins for guests, electric carts are often used to transport food, and several stops are frequently made. There is a real likelihood of hot items arriving cold and cold items becoming tepid. Second, and again because of distance, the productivity of food servers is low—they can take care of fewer guests in a given amount of time. The revenue generated, therefore, is often not sufficient to cover costs. These problems are made worse by the fact that the greatest demand for room service is at breakfast and the most popular type of morning meal is the continental breakfast (juice or fruit, roll with butter and jam, and a beverage). This meal has a low check average compared to room service items served the rest of the day.

In order to deal with room service costs, many hotels charge higher prices for room service food, as well as an additional charge per order (or per person) for the service. The cost problem can be further alleviated by limiting (1) the number of items on the room service menu, and (2) the hours of service. This does not solve the problem of potentially inferior food quality, however.

To retain food quality, the food must be delivered to the room as quickly as possible and at the appropriate temperature. This requires proper equipment and a highly efficient organization in the room service area. Many hotels use a doorknob menu that invites guests to order their breakfast the night before, indicating the items they want and the time they would like to be served. The menus are then placed on the outside doorknobs of the room, for collection during the night. This allows the hotel to do a much better job because the hotel can plan the number of breakfasts to be served in each time period and organize delivery to the rooms. Another innovative approach to room service can be found at the Palmer House & Towers hotel in Chicago. They have a special large elevator equipped with a telephone, food service equipment, and limited breakfast food items. A guest's room service call is routed directly to the elevator, so service is provided within minutes of the call. Since most hotels do not have this luxury, they must tightly manage their service elevators—which means room service personnel get top priority during peak serving hours.

Because of the problems associated with delivering a satisfactory room service experience, hotels have been cutting back on offering room service in recent years. Only 14% of hotels offered 24-hour room service in 1989, down from 18% in 1988. "You'll see less of it," predicts one management consultant. "Only luxury hotels will need it."[8]

Support and control services. Support and control services related to the food and beverage division include the purchasing department and the accounting division. Large hotels have a purchasing manager who is responsible for buying all of the products used in the hotel, including food and beverage items. Usually, orders are given to the purchasing department by the chef, by the bar manager (or head bartender), and often by the food and beverage manager directly. The purchasing department then receives competitive bids on the basis of precise specifications for each of the food and beverage items.

The control aspect of food and beverage is generally under the supervision of the hotel's controller. Reporting to the controller are:

- Receiving clerks who verify the number and quality of food and beverage items received

- Storeroom clerks who are responsible for properly storing and issuing items from the food and beverage storeroom

- Cashiers in restaurants, coffee shops, and other food and beverage outlets who handle the settlement of guest checks

Some properties also have a food and beverage controller who reports to the hotel's controller. This individual is the food and beverage expert in the controller's office and is responsible for ensuring that optimum value is attained in the food and beverage division. A food and beverage controller's duties include:

- Tracking food and beverage costs

- Monitoring ordering and receiving procedures, including adherence to purchasing specifications

- Costing and pricing menu items

- Conducting monthly storeroom inventories

- Keeping management informed of costs and, when necessary, recommending actions to lower costs

• Creating monthly and daily reports on food and beverage costs

In some hotels, the food and beverage controller reports to the food and beverage manager. From a control standpoint, this arrangement is not desirable because the food and beverage controller, in effect, is the watchdog over the food and beverage division, with his or her reports serving as an evaluation of the division. However, the food and beverage controller is sometimes positioned that way because the job is often an early step in the career path toward food and beverage manager.

Why Food and Beverage Divisions Fail. Although many hotels show a substantial profit in all of their food and beverage operations, not all food and beverage divisions are profitable. Some lose money in all areas, while others lose money in their food operations but make a profit with their beverage operations. Sometimes losses are attributed to bad management alone, but there are a number of other reasons that have been identified and can often be corrected.

Long hours of operation. Hotel restaurants must maintain an adequate level of service even during slow periods in order to satisfy the needs of hotel guests. But the low volume of business during slow times is not always sufficient to cover the cost of operation. Tightly managed employee scheduling can help alleviate this problem.

Low check averages. Low-priced breakfasts and inexpensive snacks served at odd hours are frequently cited as reasons for unprofitability. Clever marketing of more profitable items can often overcome this obstacle.

Too many facilities. Trying to satisfy a wide variety of hotel guests by having several different types of food and beverage facilities tends to be inefficient from a cost standpoint. However, sometimes proper planning, using central kitchens, and coordinating menus so that different recipes use many of the same ingredients can help solve this problem.

High turnover. Because of the increasing complexity of the food and beverage division, there is a greater need for highly paid personnel. This labor cost cannot be avoided. What can be avoided is a high turnover rate among this group, which increases recruiting and training costs. Good human resources management can make a real difference here.

Costly entertainment. Hotels with several restaurants and bars face the possibility of high entertainment costs to entice guests into a night out. Although entertainment is a specialized business, prices charged by entertainers are negotiable. Hotels that utilize experienced booking agents often have lower entertainment costs and get better entertainers.

Insufficient marketing. In the past, few hotels marketed their food and beverage outlets. Some are still guilty of that omission today. But one of the most significant changes in most hotels in recent years is their emergence as aggressive marketers of their restaurants and lounges. Now many hotels compete successfully with free-standing restaurants by employing some of the same techniques that these independents have used so successfully: exciting themes and decor, interesting and dramatic menus, and quality entertainment.

Other Revenue Centers

Telephone Department. Hotel managers know that good telephone service adds to a guest's positive evaluation of the hotel, while poor service, like misplaced telephone messages or mishandled telephone requests, causes frustration and a negative perception of the hotel. This can result in lost repeat business.

The use of modern telephone systems and equipment has lessened the guest's dependence on the hotel's telephone operators. Many hotel services can be accessed directly by dialing a given extension. Guests can retrieve their own phone messages, if they are taken (or recorded) correctly, by dialing a digital code. Wake-up calls can be automated, although clock radios in guestrooms often eliminate the need for these calls completely. Local and long-distance calls no longer require the assistance of the hotel's operator.

As a result of these advances, the telephone department in a modern hotel not only provides better service than ever before, but has a greater potential for profit than previously realized. According to a 1989 study of the U.S. lodging industry, telephone department income—that is, sales less direct expenses—was at 12% of sales.[9] This is a far cry from the losses that this department incurred before deregulation.

There is no doubt that good phone service is appreciated, and guests may be willing to pay extra for it. Writing in the *Miami Herald*, travel columnist Peter Greenberg praised hotels that featured phones with two lines and a "hold" button, such as the Four Seasons Hotel in Beverly Hills, whose telephones also include a special port for personal computers. Greenberg also singled out the Hilton Hotel in Lake Buena Vista, Florida, where telephones in each room have buttons to turn on heat and air conditioning and to regulate fan speed. Other buttons serve as a remote control for the TV set. In the Drake Hotel in New York, touch-tone phones are placed on the desk as well as on the bedside table of guestrooms, and every phone has a call-waiting feature to let you know that someone else is trying to reach you. New technology soon available at many hotels will provide registered guests with telephone beeper service throughout the city and "Phone Mail," which will allow guests to leave and receive recorded messages.[10]

Concessions, Rentals, and Commissions. If there is enough guest demand, a hotel has the potential to sell more than rooms, food, and beverages. Concessions, commissions, and other income amounted to almost five percent of hotel sales in 1989. Gift shops, newsstands, flower shops, beauty salons, jewelry stores, secretarial services, and even office space are just a few of the types of services that can be made available within the hotel and accessible through the lobby or a separate street entrance. Hotel management has the choice of either operating these services themselves or bringing in others to do it for them. Either way, some hotels have an opportunity to raise their sales significantly.

A concession is a facility that might well be operated by the hotel directly, such as a beauty salon or fitness club, but instead is turned over to an independent operator who is responsible for the concession's equipment, personnel, and marketing. The hotel's income from concessions is

Telephone Deregulation—What It Has Meant to Hotels

In the United States, as in most countries, major forms of mass communication, including telephone service, are regulated by the government. The Federal Communications Commission regulates interstate communications, while public service commissions in individual states regulate communications within the state's borders.

Prior to 1968, all hotels were required to lease their telephone equipment from the American Telephone and Telegraph Company (AT&T) which had been given its authority by the federal government. As a result of the *Carterfone* decision in a Texas court, private companies other than AT&T were allowed to manufacture and sell telephone equipment to hotels and other businesses. This meant that hotels could avoid paying an often expensive monthly rental fee to AT&T by buying their own equipment. However, governmental authorities continued to define how a hotel could be compensated for providing telephone service to guests. The Federal Communications Commission prohibited hotels from charging guests for interstate calls (long-distance calls between states), but hotels could receive commissions from AT&T. For intrastate calls (calls within the same state), the procedures established by the public service commissions of the different states varied. In some states, the telephone company was permitted to pay commissions to hotels for each call placed by guests, and the amount of that commission was regulated by law. Other states instituted a fee system, and still others used a combination of guest fees and commissions. Some states, however, simply avoided the problem by not giving any clear direction.

In 1981, as a result of far-reaching telephone deregulation, other telephone companies were allowed to compete with AT&T. Companies such as Sprint and MCI installed their own long-distance lines or rented AT&T's lines and resold them. They solicited hotels and other private concerns on a competitive basis to provide long-distance service to their guests.

Also, hotels were no longer required to use costly operator-assisted long-distance service. Hotels could purchase long-distance service at the lower direct-dial rate and charge their guests the operator-assisted rates they were used to paying. The equipment that enabled them to accomplish this is known as a call accounting system. Call accounting systems gave hotels the capability of keeping track of their guests' long-distance time and charges rather than relying on phone company operators.

Another piece of equipment that hotels were able to purchase was a least-cost router. This equipment allowed the hotel to connect with telephone systems other than AT&T so that they could route calls the least expensive way. This provided greater flexibility and profitability for hotels.

It should be noted, however, that there have been some abuses of the system. The Federal Communications Commission has issued warnings to some alternative operator systems that when their facilities are involved they are responsible for identifying themselves to callers, supplying them with rate information, and—should the callers desire—providing access to other carriers. Some hotels that initially imposed surcharge fees on certain types of calls, such as credit card calls and collect calls, have decided to drop these as a result of consumer resistance.

Today there exists a considerable divergence in the way hotels charge and are charged for calls. Not every hotel has purchased a call accounting system or a least-cost router, and some still have their long-distance calls handled by AT&T operators. Some hotels levy surcharges on local calls; others do not. What hotels charge for long-distance calls depends on the telephone company and equipment the hotel uses and on what policy it has adopted in charging for telephone service.

A hotel gift shop. Courtesy of the Hyatt Regency Grand Cypress, Orlando, Florida.

determined in several ways. It can be a flat fee, a minimum fee plus a percentage of the gross receipts over a specific amount, or simply a percentage of total gross sales.

Rentals are common in many properties. Here the hotel simply rents space to an enterprise such as an office or a store. The rent charged is usually spelled out in a lease, usually on a long-term basis with options to renew and annual rent adjustments specified.

Commissions are fees paid to the hotel by suppliers that are located outside the hotel but provide services for hotel guests. Some examples are car rental agencies, photographers, and dry-cleaning services. They pay a commission to the hotel based on a percentage of their gross sales to guests.

One important aspect of these kinds of arrangements is that unless the company or individual providing the service within the hotel is recognized in its own right (such as Scandinavian Fitness Centers), as far as most guests are concerned their relationship is not with the vendor but with the hotel. Therefore, the quality and service standards of vendors must conform to the rest of the hotel's operation, or they can affect the guest's perception of the hotel itself. For example, if a gift shop sells tasteless novelties, guests are likely to conclude that the hotel itself has those same tastes and standards. An agreement with a vendor therefore needs to explicitly spell out standards of cleanliness, personnel dress codes, and other "image" issues, as well as more practical matters such as hours of operation.

Fitness and Recreation Facilities. Until just a few years ago, gymnasiums, saunas, and swimming pools were common at resort properties, but certainly not in commercial hotels. After all, that was why many people went away to resorts—not only to relax but to get back in shape.

However, the American consumer has changed. More and more people have learned that it is not enough to get back in shape once a year on vacation—you have to exercise all year long if you wish to reduce the risk of heart attacks and other debilitating conditions. Today's businessperson may well travel with a pair of running shoes and feel that a daily run or workout of some kind is important. Hotels that have recognized this and provided workout facilities and indoor swimming pools have been able to capitalize on this new demand and increase their guest base. Other hotels have not kept up with the times and have lost guests that insist on some provision for exercising while they are away from home.

Usually guests are not charged for the use of basic exercise facilities, although there may be a fee for extras like massages or rental bicycles. Some hotels have recognized the potential to sell health-club access to office workers and residents near the hotel and have sold health club memberships, thus turning what started out as a cost center into a revenue producer.

Another growing trend in travel is to combine business with pleasure. It is not uncommon to see businesspeople traveling with their spouses and children. As a result, some properties have installed video game rooms, which have turned out to be exceedingly popular. Such rooms can gross more than $500 per week, with approximately half of that ending up on the bottom line as profit to the hotel.

A major source of recreation revenue comes from pay TV in guestrooms. There are many systems for delivering television programming to hotel guestrooms and lounges. In addition to regular broadcast channels, there are cable channels such as HBO, Showtime, ESPN, and MTV. First-run movies are also available on a pay-as-you-view basis. This is one service that a deluxe or even middle-market hotel can hardly afford not to offer. It has reached the point where many guests expect to be able to watch movies in their room—often with pizza or popcorn delivered by room service—and are disappointed when this is not available.

Cost Centers

As mentioned earlier, cost or support centers are hotel divisions that do not directly generate revenues. These divisions include:

- Marketing

- Engineering

- Accounting

- Human resources

- Security

Marketing Division

The mission of a hotel's marketing division is to (1) identify prospective guests for the hotel, (2) conform the products and services of the hotel as much as possible to meet the needs of those prospects, and (3) persuade prospects to become guests. This task begins before the first brick is laid.

One way to understand marketing is to look at what it is not. Marketing is not selling. It has been said that the difference between marketing and selling is that selling is getting rid of what you have, while marketing is having what people want. If you have what people want and you tell them about it, sales will come easily—assuming that not too many others have it at the same place for the same price at the same time! If you don't have what people want and you are forced to get rid of what you have, you may have to discount it or promote it heavily, and even then it might not sell.

Marketing a hotel is not an activity confined to the marketing division; every employee is involved in providing what guests want. It is part of the job of the marketing division to understand what the needs and wants of the hotel's guests are and to advise management so that it can train employees in how to meet those needs and wants.

The marketing division is charged with the responsibility of keeping the rooms in the hotel occupied at the right price and with the right mix of guests. It accomplishes this through many activities, including:

- Contacting groups and individuals

- Advertising in print and on radio and television

- Creating direct mail and public relations campaigns

- Participating in trade shows

- Visiting travel agents

- Arranging familiarization tours (free or reduced-rate travel programs designed to acquaint travel agents and others with the hotel and stimulate sales)

- Participating in community activities that raise the community's awareness of the hotel

On average, hotels spend approximately five percent of sales on such efforts. This figure is misleading, however, and should be considered very cautiously. For example, marketing a new hotel is much more expensive than marketing an established one. The marketing expenses involved in opening a new hotel, such as parties for community leaders and familiarization tours for travel agents, are often capitalized and charged off over a period of time. Hotels that are members of chains contribute fixed percentages of room sales to national marketing budgets, but independent properties often have to spend considerably more to establish an identity and personality for themselves. Moreover, the cost of reservation systems is often charged to the rooms division, although it could be argued that such a system is a marketing tool and ought to be treated as a marketing expense.

In most large hotels, the marketing division is headed by a director of marketing and sales. Reporting to the director is a sales manager, an advertising and public relations director, and a convention sales manager (see Exhibit 4.7). Each of these individuals heads a department that is responsible for a distinct and separate activity within the overall marketing mission.

The sales department is responsible for prospecting for business and making sales calls on individuals and companies. The advertising and public relations department attempts to attract guests through advertising and create a positive image of the hotel. Commonly used public relations

Exhibit 4.7 Sample Organization Chart—Marketing and Sales Division

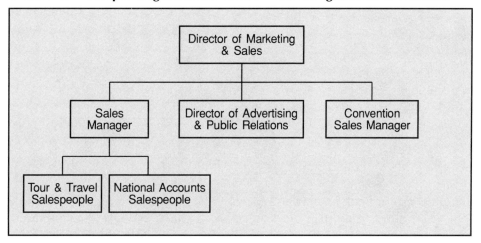

techniques are news releases about the hotel and its employees or guests, and involvement by managers and employees in community service. The convention sales manager specializes in finding and booking group and convention business.

In many ways, the marketing and sales function of a hotel can be considered the very essence of the operation. A frequently quoted remark by management consultant Peter Drucker puts it this way: "There is only one valid definition of business purpose: to create a customer."[11] For this reason, Chapter 10 is devoted to a detailed discussion of the marketing concept and effective marketing practices and principles.

Engineering Division

Taking care of the hotel's physical plant and controlling energy costs are the responsibilities of the engineering division.[12] The physical upkeep of the building, furniture, fixtures, and equipment is essential for a number of reasons:

- Deterring a hotel's physical deterioration

- Preserving the original hotel image established by management

- Keeping revenue-producing areas operational

- Keeping the property comfortable for guests and employees

- Preserving the safety of the property for guests and employees

- Creating savings by keeping repairs and equipment replacements to a minimum

The engineering division is also responsible for heating and air-conditioning systems and the systems that distribute electricity, steam, and water throughout the property.

In order to accomplish the many tasks of the engineering division, several types of technicians are employed: electricians, plumbers, carpenters, painters, refrigeration and air-conditioning engineers, and others. The division is headed by a chief engineer. In a large hotel, the chief engineer may be called a plant manager. When the size of the hotel warrants, there is also a secretary

Exhibit 4.8 Sample Organization Chart—Engineering Division

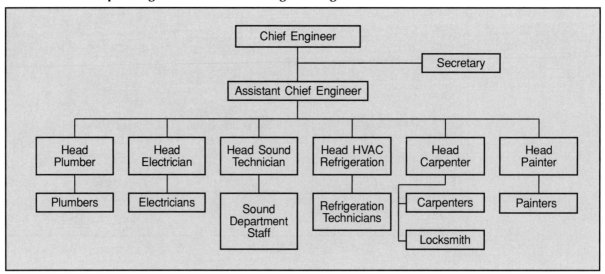

Courtesy of Professor Fritz Hagenmeyer, Florida International University.

or administrative assistant to deal with the logistics of handling repair requests and scheduling service. Exhibit 4.8 shows a sample organization chart for the engineering division of a 700-room convention/resort hotel.

The maintenance and repair work performed by the engineering staff is one of two kinds: preventive or as needed. Preventive maintenance is a planned program of ongoing servicing of the building and equipment in order to maintain operations and prolong the life of the facility. Outside contractors may be hired for some jobs either on an as-needed basis or through a service contract. An important aspect of maintenance work is that in all areas there should be documentation to track labor and material costs. A master checklist groups the work to be done on a daily, weekly, and monthly schedule. Detailed equipment checklists outlining tasks to be performed and how long it should take to perform them assist managers in scheduling employees.

In addition to preventive maintenance, the engineering staff performs routine repairs. Repair logs should be used to keep track of the start and finish of each repair assignment. Major projects that require the purchase of building materials may also be undertaken by the engineering division. Management usually determines whether extensive repairs or replacement of equipment not covered by service contracts is to be done by the hotel's own staff or given to an outside contractor.

In its annual study of 1,000 hotels and motels in the United States, Pannell Kerr Forster reports that its sample spent 5% of total sales on maintenance, including administrative costs. Energy cost was 4.6%.[13]

Controlling Energy Costs. Controlling energy and utility costs while continuing to maintain guest comfort and operational efficiency is one of the functions of the engineering division.[14] A sound cost-control program must begin with an understanding of how energy is used. This requires a careful analysis of energy-consuming equipment and electricity, water, and fuel bills.

Water. According to Robert E. Aulbach, president of RoBach Inc. and an energy consultant to major hotel chains and independent hotels, over a period of three months a single dripping faucet can waste about 2,000 gallons of water.[15] When you think of the potential for costly water loss in a hotel, with all its toilets and sink, bath tub, and shower faucets, it is clear that diligence is important if costs are to be managed at all. Moreover, environmental concerns are causing more and more hotels to conserve water because of its scarcity in some areas.

Aulbach recommends some steps that can be taken to improve water management (see Exhibit 4.9). It should be noted that some of these steps might affect guest perceptions of the hotel. Although visitors are not likely to be concerned about whether the boiler is metered or the rinse cycles in the laundry are reduced, serving water in the dining room only on request or lowering the water pressure in the hotel and restricting the flow of shower heads may be noticed and disapproved of by some guests. These measures, therefore, should be tempered with a firm understanding of the business strategy of the hotel and the needs and expectations of the guests it is trying to attract.

Electricity and fuel. While saving water is important, heating and air-conditioning systems are the major users of energy. The cost of energy varies depending on both consumption and time of day. Utility companies commonly charge premium rates for peak periods, when demand is greatest.

Many hotels have adopted energy control systems that allow front desk personnel to turn off or reduce energy when a room is vacated. An even more efficient system is one in which individual units, placed in each guestroom, are equipped with motion detectors. The unit is activated by

Engineering division employees perform routine repairs as well as other duties.

Exhibit 4.9 Tips for Conserving Water

- Reduce toilet flush quantities by installing water dams and bottles
- Adjust flushometers to the minimum required flow
- Install shower restrictors to reduce flow
- Install a meter on the boiler makeup
- Inspect the boiler system for leaks and open steam traps
- Review laundry operations and reduce rinse cycles to a minimum
- Reduce watering landscaping to once a week
- Turn off swimming pool system when not in use at night
- Inspect kitchen operations and turn off running water used for soup cooling, vegetable cleaning, and so on
- Control dishwashing by running the dishwasher only with full loads
- Serve water only to guests who request it
- Reduce water pressure within the hotel

Source: Robert Aulbach, "Water and Energy: Limited Commodities," *Lodging*, December 1988, p. 43.

the opening and closing of guestroom doors. If no motion is detected, the unit shuts down air-conditioning and heating systems; when motion is detected, the guestroom's systems are turned on to predetermined levels set by management.

Computerized property management systems can control peak demand by leveling off consumption. This is accomplished by automatically reducing non-essential energy requirements at times of greatest energy demand. Many hotels without sufficient budgets for computerized property management systems rely on well-trained and energy-conscious employees who manually monitor heating and air-conditioning systems and make periodic adjustments as needed.

Cogeneration. Cogeneration is a fairly new concept in the lodging industry. It refers to the construction and operation of small on-site power plants.

Large hotels are often described as being self-contained communities in that they have their own living, eating, and recreational facilities. It also makes economic sense for some hotels to have their own supply of energy. This is not a new idea—many manufacturing companies have their own power plants. Energy is not a cheap commodity, and the long-term outlook is that it is likely to get more expensive.

Most cogeneration systems consist of a simple generator to which heat recovery equipment has been added to increase the efficiency of the system. Often they are gas-powered and supplement the hotel's normal electric service. Alternatively, the system may be dedicated to some specific purpose such as providing hot water for the hotel. In some cases, it is possible to sell surplus electricity produced by the cogeneration system to the local utility system and thus reduce costs even further.

One constraint that has deterred owners from installing a cogeneration system is that these systems are most efficient in producing thermal energy.

Exhibit 4.10 Sample Organization Chart—Accounting Division

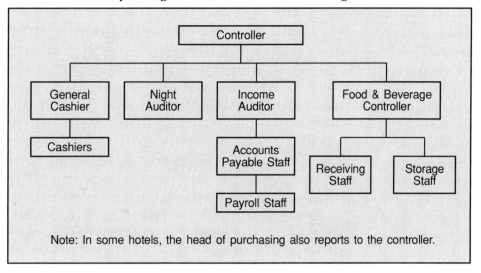

If heating is not required on a year-round basis, it may be difficult to recover the costs associated with cogeneration, which can run as high as $500,000 or more.[16]

Accounting Division

The accounting division is responsible for keeping track of the many business transactions that occur in a hotel. The accounting division does more than simply keep the books—financial management is perhaps a more appropriate description of what the accounting division does. An organization chart of an accounting division might look like the one shown in Exhibit 4.10.

The responsibilities of the accounting division include:

- Forecasting and budgeting

- Managing what the hotel owns and what money is due from guests

- Controlling cash

- Controlling costs in all areas of the hotel—revenue centers as well as cost centers and payroll

- Purchasing, receiving, and issuing operating and capital inventory such as food and beverages, housekeeping supplies, and furniture

- Keeping records, preparing financial statements and daily operating reports, and interpreting these statements and reports for management

In order to accomplish these diverse functions, the head of accounting—the controller—relies on a staff of auditors, cashiers, and other accounting employees. Not all of the controller's staff works in the hotel's accounting office. Accounting functions are performed throughout the hotel. For example, credit staff, front office cashiers, and night auditors work in the front desk area. Cashiers work in the restaurant and bar. The food and beverage controller is sometimes located in the receiving area, and others responsible for control functions, such as receiving clerks, are in close proximity to the hotel's service entrances.

The accounting division bridges and interacts with all of a hotel's revenue and cost divisions. In many cases, the controller reports directly to the corporate controller of the parent company (if the hotel is part of a chain or some other corporation). Nevertheless, he or she is responsible for all of the control functions within the hotel and, in that capacity, also reports to the hotel's general manager.

Human Resources Division

Human resources is a relatively new term in management. It has emerged from an expanded definition of a manager's job. Managers are not simply directors of people but are also facilitators. Today's managers see themselves as developers of people, as trainers, as mentors, and as guardians of their company's most important asset—its employees. Thus, the traditional personnel division is slowly going the way of the dinosaur. In the old days the personnel manager of a company was little more than a clerk. His or her job was to accept applications, check references, and keep records of who was hired, fired, and promoted.

Today's human resources division does much more. Modern human resources managers are concerned with the whole equation of people and productivity. Their job description includes recruiting, orienting, training, evaluating, motivating, rewarding, disciplining, developing, promoting, and communicating with all of the employees of the hotel. How this is accomplished is discussed in detail in Chapter 9.

Security Division

The security of guests, employees, personal property, and the hotel itself is an overriding concern for hotel managers these days. In the past, most security precautions concentrated on the prevention of theft from guests and the hotel. However, today such violent crimes as murder and rape have become a problem for some hotels. Unfortunately, crime rates in most major cities are going up. Hotel owners and operators are concerned about their ethical and legal responsibility to protect guests and their property. Not giving security the attention it deserves can be costly. Courts have awarded plaintiffs thousands (or, in some cases, millions) of dollars as a result of judgments against hotels for not exercising reasonable care in protecting guests.[17]

A hotel security program should be pro-active—that is, preventive in nature. While ultimate responsibility for security remains with the general manager, most hotels have one or more security officers on staff who are professionally trained in crime prevention, detection, and handling.

Traditionally, security has been the responsibility of the front office. The trend today is to give security the status of an independent division or department reporting directly to the general manager or resident manager. In large hotels, the head of the security division may be called the chief of security. This person usually has an extensive background in law enforcement.

Those involved in security should have specialized training in civil and criminal law because they must work closely with local police and fire departments to ensure that all regulations pertaining to hotels are enforced. Applicants for security positions should be trained in self-defense.

A comprehensive security program includes all of the following elements:

- *Security officers.* These people make regular rounds of the hotel premises, including guest floors, corridors, public and private function rooms, parking areas, and offices. Their duties involve observing suspicious people and taking appropriate action, investigating incidents, and cooperating with local law enforcement officials.

- *Equipment.* Security equipment includes communications equipment such as two-way radios; closed-circuit television (CCT) to monitor entrances, elevators, and corridors; smoke detectors and fire-alarm systems; fire-fighting equipment including extinguishers, hoses, and fire axes; and adequate lighting in areas where the potential for violence exists.

- *Master keys.* Security officers should be able to gain access to guestrooms, storerooms, and offices at all times.

- *Safety procedures.* A well-designed security program includes evacuation plans in case of fire, bomb threats, terrorism, or some other emergency. These plans should be communicated to all employees. Employee training and procedure manuals should be part of safety-procedure training.

- *Identification procedures.* Identification cards with photographs should be issued to all employees. Name tags for employees who are likely to have contact with guests not only project a friendly image for the property but are also useful for security reasons.

Control Systems

An important part of managing is to measure performance levels and take corrective action if they do not meet the goals of the enterprise. In order to maintain control over all aspects of an organization, managers and owners must first establish goals against which results can be measured. For example, an organization may establish a payroll goal of 30% of revenues—that is, the operating plan is to spend 30% or less of sales on salaries and other payroll expenses. The plan may also provide that a variance of 2% is acceptable, but that anything above that is not. If payroll expenses exceed 32%, management must take action.

The ideal control system allows managers to quickly recognize and correct deviations from the operating budget or some other management standard before they become major problems. One way hotel managers accomplish this is to have very accurate forecasting systems. To continue with our payroll example: By being able to forecast with a high degree of accuracy what sales are likely to be in a given period, it becomes possible for managers to adjust staffing levels accordingly to meet the payroll goal. For instance, if the dining room manager knows from sales history records that on Monday evenings in February the dining room is likely to serve only 100 meals, then the number of food servers and cooks that will be required is no longer a matter of guesswork but can be carefully planned.

In too many cases, corrections are made long after the problem started. The longer the period between the variation from property goals and the correction, the weaker the control system and the greater the potential for lost revenue, increased costs, and disappointed guests.

Training also plays a key role in control systems. A certain number of errors by front desk personnel and food servers is inevitable. No human system is perfect. But careful training can minimize errors and bring performance levels up to standard.

Many of management's goals can be quantified. The more specific the goal and the easier it is to quantify, the more likely it is that the goal will be met. Guestroom occupancy levels, guest counts in restaurants, and revenue and expense targets are examples of quantifiable goals. Not all goals are easy to measure. For instance, an operating plan might have a goal of increasing guest satisfaction or employee morale. However, even there it is possible to be more specific and measure the results accordingly. In Chapter 8 we will discuss this in more detail.

Two of the most important types of controls for managers are financial controls and quality controls.

Financial Controls

One of the most useful financial control tools is financial statements. Investors use them to monitor profitability. Lenders read them as a measure of financial stability. Managers base their planning on them and monitor the success of their planning with them.

In order to understand a hotel financial statement, it is necessary to be familiar with the hotel industry's financial terminology and to understand the manner in which revenues and expenses are grouped by division.

Uniform System of Accounts. In March 1926 the American Hotel & Motel Association (at that time it was called the American Hotel Association of the United States and Canada) adopted a manual called the *Uniform System of Accounts for Hotels*. The system was formulated by a committee of accountants and hoteliers in New York City.

The *Uniform System of Accounts for Hotels* classifies the different types of hotel revenues and expenses and groups them in the statement of income by division or department. The statement of income is one of management's major control tools. It shows the total sales by product or service category (rooms, food, beverage, and so on) for a stated period of time, the expenses incurred in generating those sales, and the profit earned or the loss incurred as a result of those activities (see Exhibit 4.11).

There are three types of hotel expenses: divisional expenses, overhead expenses, and fixed charges or capital costs. Divisional expenses include such items as rooms division payroll expenses, restaurant laundry, and telephone supplies like message pads and pencils. Overhead expenses are costs such as marketing and energy—costs that relate to the entire hotel and not to one specific department. Fixed charges or capital costs are expenses related to the investment, such as insurance on the building and contents, and interest on the mortgage loan.

The uniform system also classifies assets (something of value that is owned) and liabilities (what is owed to creditors). Examples of assets might be the hotel building itself, furniture and equipment, and courtesy vans to transport guests to and from airports. Liabilities include items such as

Exhibit 4.11 Sample Hotel Statement of Income

Hotel DORO, Inc.
Statement of Income
For the year ended December 31, 19X2

NET REVENUE		
Rooms	$ 897,500	**56.3%**
Food and Beverage	524,570	32.8
Telephone	51,140	3.2
Other Operated Departments	63,000	3.9
Rentals and Other Income	61,283	3.8
Total Departmental Revenue	1,597,493	100.0
COSTS AND EXPENSES		
Rooms	205,239	12.8
Food and Beverage	437,193	27.4
Telephone	78,763	4.9
Other Operated Departments	50,354	3.2
Administrative and General	164,181	10.3
Marketing	67,868	4.2
Property Operation and Maintenance	61,554	3.9
Energy Costs	47,312	3.0
Rent, Property Taxes, and Insurance	80,738	5.1
Interest Expense	192,153	12.0
Depreciation and Amortization	146,000	9.1
Total Costs and Expenses	1,531,355	95.9
INCOME BEFORE GAIN ON SALE OF PROPERTY	66,138	4.1
Gain on Sale of Property	10,500	.7
INCOME BEFORE INCOME TAXES	76,638	4.8
Income Taxes	16,094	1.0
NET INCOME	$ 60,544	3.8%

food purchases for which payment is due, the mortgage loan, and the owner's (or owners') equity. All of these items are grouped together in the financial statement known as the balance sheet (see Exhibit 4.12). A balance sheet reports the financial position of a business by presenting its assets; liabilities; and owner's, owners', or shareholders' equity on a given date.

Quality Controls

It is a relatively simple task to standardize the quality and cost of a manufactured product. This is because products, whether they be toasters or skis, are produced in a factory under strictly controlled conditions. Some assembly lines are computerized, and many use robots to perform some functions. Moreover, quality control inspectors not only monitor all operations but inspect each finished item before it leaves the plant and a consumer sees it.

As mentioned in Chapter 2, service businesses such as hotels operate under an entirely different set of circumstances. The "product" that a hotel produces—the experience of staying there—is manufactured and consumed in the hotel "factory" in front of the consumer's very eyes. For example, a guest enters a hotel, goes into the lounge, sits down at a table, and orders

Exhibit 4.12 Sample Hotel Balance Sheet

<table>
<tr><td colspan="3" align="center">Hotel DORO, Inc.
Balance Sheet
December 31, 19X2</td></tr>
<tr><td colspan="3" align="center">ASSETS</td></tr>
<tr><td colspan="3">CURRENT ASSETS</td></tr>
<tr><td>Cash</td><td>$ 58,500</td><td>1.9%</td></tr>
<tr><td>Marketable Securities</td><td>25,000</td><td>.8</td></tr>
<tr><td>Accounts Receivable (net)</td><td>40,196</td><td>1.2</td></tr>
<tr><td>Inventories</td><td>11,000</td><td>.3</td></tr>
<tr><td>Prepaid Expenses</td><td>13,192</td><td>.4</td></tr>
<tr><td>Total Current Assets</td><td>147,888</td><td>4.6</td></tr>
<tr><td colspan="3">PROPERTY AND EQUIPMENT</td></tr>
<tr><td>Land</td><td>850,000</td><td>26.2</td></tr>
<tr><td>Building</td><td>2,500,000</td><td>77.0</td></tr>
<tr><td>Furniture and Equipment</td><td>475,000</td><td>14.6</td></tr>
<tr><td>Total</td><td>3,825,000</td><td>117.8</td></tr>
<tr><td>Less Accumulated Depreciation</td><td>775,000</td><td>23.9</td></tr>
<tr><td>Total</td><td>3,050,000</td><td>93.9</td></tr>
<tr><td>Leasehold Improvements</td><td>9,000</td><td>.3</td></tr>
<tr><td>China, Glassware, and Silver (net)</td><td>36,524</td><td>1.1</td></tr>
<tr><td>Total Property and Equipment</td><td>3,095,524</td><td>95.3</td></tr>
<tr><td colspan="3">OTHER NONCURRENT ASSETS</td></tr>
<tr><td>Security Deposits</td><td>1,000</td><td>—</td></tr>
<tr><td>Preopening Expenses (net)</td><td>3,000</td><td>.1</td></tr>
<tr><td>Total Other Assets</td><td>4,000</td><td>.1</td></tr>
<tr><td>TOTAL ASSETS</td><td>$3,247,412</td><td>100.0%</td></tr>
<tr><td colspan="3" align="center">LIABILITIES</td></tr>
<tr><td colspan="3">CURRENT LIABILITIES</td></tr>
<tr><td>Accounts Payable</td><td>$13,861</td><td>.4%</td></tr>
<tr><td>Current Portion of Long-Term Debt</td><td>70,000</td><td>2.2</td></tr>
<tr><td>Federal and State Income Taxes Payable</td><td>16,545</td><td>.5</td></tr>
<tr><td>Accrued Payroll</td><td>11,617</td><td>.4</td></tr>
<tr><td>Other Accrued Items</td><td>7,963</td><td>.2</td></tr>
<tr><td>Unearned Revenue</td><td>3,764</td><td>.1</td></tr>
<tr><td>Total Current Liabilities</td><td>123,750</td><td>3.8</td></tr>
<tr><td colspan="3">LONG-TERM DEBT</td></tr>
<tr><td>Mortgage Payable, less current portion</td><td>2,055,000</td><td>63.3</td></tr>
<tr><td>TOTAL LIABILITIES</td><td>2,178,750</td><td>67.1</td></tr>
<tr><td colspan="3" align="center">SHAREHOLDERS' EQUITY</td></tr>
<tr><td>Common Stock, par value $1, authorized and
   issued 50,000 shares</td><td>50,000</td><td>1.5</td></tr>
<tr><td>Additional Paid-In Capital</td><td>700,000</td><td>21.6</td></tr>
<tr><td>Retained Earnings</td><td>318,662</td><td>9.8</td></tr>
<tr><td>Total Shareholders' Equity</td><td>1,068,662</td><td>32.9</td></tr>
<tr><td>TOTAL LIABILITIES AND SHAREHOLDERS' EQUITY</td><td>$3,247,412</td><td>100.0%</td></tr>
</table>

a strawberry daiquiri. The product in this case is not simply the daiquiri—it also includes the lounge, the server, and the bartender who mixes the drink. It is this total experience that the guest pays for. If the guest had just wanted a strawberry daiquiri, he or she could have made one at home or bought a bottled one at the corner liquor store.

Because of the nature of a service business, it is extremely difficult to standardize or even control the service that guests receive. There are too many variables that can interfere with the process, including the guests, who, for example, can be rude and insensitive and may encourage service that is the same.

The opportunities for dissatisfaction abound. Take our guest who ordered the strawberry daiquiri. Possibly the guest had to wait for a table because none was available or the host was out of the room temporarily.

Maybe the seating was prompt, but the guest had to wait longer than expected for the order because the ice machine or the drink mixer was broken. Perhaps the bartender was preoccupied with a personal problem instead of concentrating on fixing a perfect strawberry daiquiri. Even if everything else goes well, it can all be spoiled if the guest has to wait too long for the check or if there is a mistake on it. All of these possibilities exist whenever a guest enters the lounge. Any of them can affect the quality of the experience (the product) and thus the guest's perception of the lounge and the hotel. This one transaction is a single example of the many kinds of things that can go wrong in a hotel that is open 24-hours a day, where guests interact regularly with, and receive service from, front desk agents, food servers, room attendants, bellpersons, concierges, valets, maintenance people, and gift shop employees.

Product and service consistency is of primary importance and can only be achieved on a continuing basis by establishing superior standards, training employees how to achieve those standards, and then inspecting their performance regularly.

Establishing Standards of Operation. Quality is an overriding concern in the hotel industry, but what does "quality" mean? There is no universal industry agreement on what quality is, nor should there be. Quality has to do with expectations versus reality. When guests check into a $29-a-night budget hotel, they expect a certain standard of service and no more. If they get what they expect (or a little more), they can be said to have enjoyed a quality experience from their point of view. If they get less than what they expected or thought they were paying for, then they will think they received poor-quality service. The formula is the same for a hotel room that costs $200 a night. A guest who pays that amount has certain expectations. His or her perception of quality depends to a large degree on whether those expectations are met or exceeded. All hotels strive for quality for their type of product and target market. Quality, then, means that the guest experience in terms of the cleanliness of the rooms, the taste and presentation of the food, and the physical condition of the hotel is consistent with what the management has promised and is striving to deliver.

Quality assurance. In 1982 a committee of leading hoteliers was formed and consultants were hired by the American Hotel & Motel Association (AH&MA) to develop a quality assurance (QA) program for the association. This QA program, which any hotel could adopt, included the following elements:

- A quality committee
- An initial quality audit
- The establishment of quality improvement teams made up of management and staff
- A quality assurance plan
- A training program for employee trainers
- An evaluation program for measuring and reporting results

- A program of rewards and recognition for employees

One noteworthy feature of AH&MA's program is that it recognized that good quality depends not only on guest satisfaction, but on employee satisfaction. In a service business you cannot expect satisfied guests unless you also have satisfied employees. Satisfied employees usually give good service; dissatisfied employees usually do not.[18]

Quality standards are achieved by setting forth procedures to be followed. For example, when a room attendant has completed cleaning a room so that it is ready for guest occupancy, the position of the furniture, the number of towels as well as other guest supplies and amenities, and, most important, the overall cleanliness of the room must be exactly the same every day for every room. How many towels to leave in the bathroom or what constitutes "clean" should not be left to the discretion of the person doing the cleaning. Procedures must be established for each task to be performed. At the same time, a standard of what is acceptable and what is not must be spelled out for each procedure. It is not reasonable to set standards without specifically detailing the procedures that must be followed in order to achieve those standards. The function of a hotel's quality committee therefore is twofold—first, to establish the standards that are necessary to ensure guest satisfaction and, second, to lay out the procedures that will be followed to reach those standards.

Examples of this are the kind of food service standards and procedures that are set forth by the Boca Raton Hotel and Club in Florida as part of their QA program. Here is one concerning the task of greeting guests at a table:

> *Procedure:* After table is seated greet the table: "Good morning. May I offer you some coffee?" Be pleasant, unhurried. Pour coffee/Sanka with cup on table, and to right of guest. If tea is served, the tea pot is served on a butter plate with a doily, lemon on top of tea pot with logo facing up.

> *Standard:* Make guest feel comfortable. Strike positive note in your "beginning" with guest.[19]

In 1983 fifteen Bermuda hotels joined together under the leadership of the Bermuda Hotel Association to institute a QA program. With the support of the Department of Tourism and Bermuda College's Department of Hotel Technology, the program was launched with the objective of enlisting everyone's cooperation in the industry in assessing errors in hotel operations that had a negative effect on guest satisfaction. The program, which is still active, has had positive results not only on guest levels of satisfaction (as measured by the Department of Tourism), but on overall employee morale at the hotels involved, decreasing absenteeism and employee turnover, reducing grievances, and boosting productivity. The bottom line was more profits and a much more positive image for the island as a quality vacation spot.

Training. It is not enough to establish standards and procedures. Employees need to be shown how to perform the procedures. It is not reasonable to expect someone who has never cleaned a guestroom or waited on a table to know what to do simply by being given a manual.

Exhibit 4.13 Sample Guest Comment Card

Please Tell Us About Your Visit!
At Sheraton, little things mean a lot.
So, if during your stay, you need anything attended to, any little thing at all,
don't hesitate to call extension 7000.

This is the cover of one of Sheraton's guest comment cards. Inside, guests are invited to rate their guestroom as well as the hotel's front desk, telephone service, restaurants, lounges, and recreational facilities. Courtesy of ITT Sheraton Corporation, Boston, Massachusetts.

To succeed, training needs to be ongoing and have the full commitment of management. No matter how good the hotel's QA program is, the nature of the industry means that high turnover can be anticipated; therefore, unless training is a continual process, the program cannot succeed.

Inspection. Management must verify the consistency of product and service quality in order to evaluate the success of its QA efforts. One of the simplest methods of verification is "management by walking around." Successful hotel managers have found that periodic tours of the hotel and alertness to what is going on around them is one of the best ways of ensuring that the program is working. There is a saying in the United States Navy that also applies to the hotel business: "You get what you inspect, not what you expect."

Guest comment cards are another important tool for verification (see Exhibit 4.13). Although many feel these cards encourage negative comments, they are nevertheless a valuable tool. Cards typically are placed in guestrooms on the dresser or desk. Some hotels require front desk agents to ask departing guests if they have completed a card. Experience has shown that open-ended questions that ask guests to write a description of their experiences do not work as well as simple rating scales from 1 to 10 where guests can indicate their level of satisfaction with various components of the hotel's service and facilities. There should be room, however, for guests to add some comments if they choose and to identify employees whom they wish to single out either positively or negatively.

Another method of inspection involves hiring outside inspectors, usually referred to as "mystery shoppers." These inspectors, who are not known to hotel employees, make reservations, stay in a guestroom, eat in the dining room, check out, and then prepare elaborate reports on the level of service they received. Some hotels announce inspections in advance and the inspectors are known. While employees often favor this system, the level of management confidence in the results of such inspections tends to be much lower.

Chapter Summary

Managers manage by organizing hotels into various functional areas and then delegating responsibility and authority. The functional areas are divided into revenue and cost (or support) centers. Divisions such as rooms and food and beverage are revenue centers; others, like engineering and accounting, are cost centers. The number of such centers (or divisions) depends on the size of the hotel.

In most hotels, the rooms division is the largest and generates the most revenue and profit. It generally consists of four departments; front office, reservations, housekeeping, and uniformed service. Front office duties include checking guests in and out, posting charges to their accounts, and collecting payments. In small hotels, front desk agents may also accept reservations, relay messages to guests, and handle the telephone switchboard.

The housekeeping department is responsible for cleaning guestrooms and public areas. Often it is the largest department in terms of employees. Besides cleaning, the housekeeping department also takes care of laundry and valet services.

Uniformed service employees deal with guest luggage and transportation, as well as provide concierge services.

The food and beverage division is of paramount importance to a hotel's profitability and reputation. There may be many different types of food and beverage outlets in a hotel. Factors that influence the level of food and beverage service that is offered include the type of hotel, the class of hotel, the competition, product availability, availability of labor, and guest demand. The food and beverage manager typically has restaurant managers, beverage managers, and a catering director reporting to him or her. Support and control personnel for the food and beverage division include purchasing managers, receiving clerks, storeroom clerks, cashiers, and a food and beverage controller.

The overall profitability of food and beverage operations is dependent on several factors, including hours of operation, guest check averages, the number and kind of facilities, employee turnover, entertainment costs, and marketing.

A well-managed telephone department can also contribute to a hotel's profits. Modern telephone systems have made a big difference in the way hotel telephone departments function and have helped increase guest satisfaction with telephone service. Deregulation, call accounting systems, and the choice of alternative operator systems all have influenced telephone department operations.

Concessions, rentals, and commissions are other sources of hotel revenue. However, managers need to be careful that the standards of concessionaires are compatible with the hotel's.

Guests' changing lifestyles have made hotel health spas, cable movies, and video game rooms important parts in satisfying today's guests.

The marketing division is charged with identifying prospective guests, seeing that management understands and responds to their needs and wants, and persuading prospective guests to stay at the hotel. To accomplish these tasks, the marketing division usually has a director of marketing and sales, a sales manager, a director of advertising and public relations, and a convention sales manager.

Engineering takes care of the hotel's physical plant and the hotel's utility systems. The division is headed by a chief engineer, assisted by his or her own staff and outside contractors. Preventive maintenance duties as well as repairs are performed. One important aspect of the engineering division's mission is the conservation of energy and water. Cogeneration is one of the newer techniques for conserving energy.

The accounting division is charged with the financial management of the hotel. It is headed by a controller who oversees personnel such as the general cashier, the night auditor, the income auditor, and the food and beverage controller.

The human resources division is responsible for recruiting, orienting, training, evaluating, motivating, rewarding, disciplining, developing, promoting, and communicating with hotel employees.

Security of hotel employees and guests is of overriding importance today. Hotel security programs are pro-active and should be under the direction of a person with law enforcement experience.

Hotel managers have two major kinds of controls: financial controls and quality controls. Important financial controls are the hotel's financial statements. These statements are generated using the *Uniform System of Accounts for Hotels.* In this accounting system, hotel expenses are classified as divisional, overhead, and fixed. Assets and liabilities are also classified.

Quality controls are essential in order to ensure that standards established by management are adhered to. Quality assurance (QA) programs include a quality committee, a quality audit, the establishment of teams to identify and correct errors, a quality assurance plan, a training program, an evaluation program, and a system of employee rewards and incentives.

Endnotes

1. Laventhol & Horwath, *U.S. Lodging Industry 1989.*

2. Pannell Kerr Forster, *Trends in the Hotel Industry 1988, USA Edition.*

3. "Park Plaza Adds Voice Mail," *Lodging Hospitality,* August 1989, p. 15.

4. Front office operations are covered in detail in Charles E. Steadmon and Michael L. Kasavana, *Managing Front Office Operations,* 2d ed. (East Lansing, Mich.: Educational Institute of the American Hotel & Motel Association, 1988).

5. Laventhol & Horwath, *U.S. Lodging Industry 1989.*

6. The housekeeping department, from an executive housekeeper's perspective, is the subject of Margaret M. Kappa, Aleta Nitschke, and Patricia B. Schappert, *Managing Housekeeping Operations* (East Lansing, Mich.: Educational Institute of the American Hotel & Motel Association, 1990).

7. For students desiring a good introductory text to food and beverage operations, see Jack D. Ninemeier, *Management of Food and Beverage Operations,* 2d ed. (East Lansing, Mich.: Educational Institute of the American Hotel & Motel Association, 1990).

8. Jonathan Dahl, "Tracking Travel—Room Service Goes Out the Door at More Hotels," *Wall Street Journal,* February 27, 1990, p. B-1.

9. Laventhol & Horwath, *U.S. Lodging Industry 1989.*

10. Peter S. Greenberg, "Hotels Dialing Into Better Service," *Miami Herald,* November 20, 1988, p. J-6.

11. Peter E. Drucker, *Management: Tasks, Responsibilities, Practices* (New York: Harper & Row, 1974), p. 61.

12. For more information on the responsibilities of a hotel's engineering division, see Michael H. Redlin and David M. Stipanuk, *Managing Hospitality Engineering Systems* (East Lansing, Mich.: Educational Institute of the American Hotel & Motel Association, 1987).

13. Pannell Kerr Forster, *Trends in the Hotel Industry 1988, USA Edition.*

14. For more information on controlling energy costs, see Robert E. Aulbach, *Energy and Water Resource Management,* 2d ed. (East Lansing, Mich.: Educational Institute of the American Hotel & Motel Association, 1988).

15. Robert E. Aulbach, "Water and Energy: Limited Commodities," *Lodging,* December 1988, p. 43.

16. The information on cogeneration has been drawn from an article by Donald W. Lystra, "Cogeneration: Introduction to Hotel/Motel Technology," *Lodging* Reprints Series, pp. 18–20.

17. Legal ramifications of hotel security are covered in Part Three of Jack P. Jefferies, *Understanding Hospitality Law,* 2d ed. (East Lansing, Mich.: Educational Institute of the American Hotel & Motel Association, 1990). The security responsibilities of hotel managers and hotel security programs are the subjects of Raymond C. Ellis, Jr., and the Security Committee of AH&MA, *Security and Loss Prevention Management* (East Lansing, Mich.: Educational Institute of the American Hotel & Motel Association, 1986).

18. Quality assurance programs are discussed in detail in Stephen J. Shriver, *Managing Quality Services* (East Lansing, Mich.: Educational Institute of the American Hotel & Motel Association, 1988).

19. Jim Pearson, "Quality Assurance Case Study III, The Boca Raton Hotel and Club," *Lodging* Reprints Series, Quality Assurance Educational Institute of the AH&MA, p. 29.

Key Terms

accounting division	human resources division
balance sheet	marketing division
card keys	night audit
catering	purchasing department
cogeneration system	quality controls
commissions	rentals
concessions	reservations office
cost centers	revenue centers
engineering division	rooms division
familiarization tour	room service
financial controls	security division
food and beverage division	statement of income
front office	telephone department
housekeeping	uniformed service

Discussion Questions

1. What is the difference between a revenue center and a cost center?
2. Which division provides the largest source of revenue for most hotels?
3. What are some of the duties of a front desk agent?
4. How is a typical housekeeping department organized?
5. Why do some food and beverage divisions lose money?
6. What changes have occurred in hotel telephone departments?
7. What are the marketing division's challenges and responsibilities? the engineering division's?
8. How have the new human resources divisions changed from the old personnel divisions?
9. Why have hotel security programs increased in importance in recent years, and what are the elements of a good security program?
10. What are two of the most important types of controls for managers and how are they used?

Chapter Outline

Food Service Industry Segments
    Eating and Drinking Places
        Full-Menu Restaurants
        Limited-Menu Restaurants
        Commercial Cafeterias
    Lodging Places
    Transportation Market
    Leisure Market
    Retail Market
    Business and Industry Market
    Student Market
    Health Care Market
    Prison Food Service
    Military Food Service
Starting a New Restaurant
    Why Do Restaurants Fail?
    The Cost of Starting a New Restaurant
    Building a Successful Restaurant
        The Concept
        Site Selection
Chapter Summary

5 Types of Restaurants

This chapter describes the diversity and complexity of all of the various segments of the restaurant business. We will take a look at eating and drinking establishments; hotel food and beverage operations; food service for airlines, trains, and cruise lines; and the leisure, retail, business and industry, student, and health care markets. The chapter also covers how new restaurants are started.

The food service industry runs the gamut from gourmet restaurants to hot dog stands. According to the National Restaurant Association, in 1989 food service sales reached $227.3 billion dollars. The industry employed eight million people in 626,000 different establishments. The industry is expected to employ 11.4 million workers by the year 2000.

Food service industry sales equal nearly five percent of the U.S. gross national product. The proportion of the food dollar spent away from home has risen dramatically, from 25% in 1950 to 41.1% in 1986. Americans eat out an average of 3.7 times a week, or 192 times a year. Lunch is still the main meal eaten away from home. Over half of all consumers eat out once a week—49% at dinner and 18% at breakfast. Obviously, some consumers eat out more than once a week and some eat more than one meal a day at a restaurant. Over 50 percent of all consumers visit a restaurant on their birthday—the most popular day to eat at a restaurant. Mother's Day and Valentine's Day are second and third, respectively.

The food service industry is truly an equal opportunity employer. The industry employs more minority managers than any other retail industry. Over half of all food service managerial and administrative personnel are women.

From a career standpoint, a person who enters the food service field can work for small independent operators who run fine-dining restaurants, pizza parlors, or ice cream stands. Working at an independent operation is good training for future entrepreneurs.

As mentioned in Chapter 2, another career track might begin in the management training program of a large corporation such as Gilbert and Robinson, which operates such full-menu restaurants as Houlihan's, Darryl's, and Charley's Place. There are also contract food companies such as ARA and the Marriott Corporation where future managers are placed in executive or employee dining facilities, schools, colleges and universities, and specialty restaurants like the 95th in the Sears Tower in Chicago.

Working at an independent pizzeria can be good training for future entrepreneurs. Courtesy of Bakers Pride Oven Co., Inc., New Rochelle, New York.

Another student might find his or her niche with a small company that operates unique concept restaurants such as Lettuce Entertain You, run by Richard Mellman in Chicago.

There are many opportunities in the fast-food field with companies like McDonald's, Kentucky Fried Chicken, and Pizza Hut (the latter two are part of PepsiCo). The Walt Disney Corporation runs a huge number of diverse food operations and actively recruits hospitality graduates to manage its theme park restaurants and snack bars.

Airlines are supplied meals by in-flight catering operators such as Dobbs International Services. Even many large banks, insurance companies, and advertising agencies have executive dining rooms run by professional food service managers. There are many career choices available to you in the food service industry.

Food Service Industry Segments

As you can see, the food service industry is very large, with many different types of food service facilities and markets. For reporting and other purposes the industry has been divided into various industry segments.

Eating and Drinking Places

Eating and drinking places constitute the largest segment of the food service industry. Included in this segment are:

- Full-menu restaurants

- Limited-menu restaurants

- Commercial cafeterias

- Social caterers

- Ice cream and frozen custard stands

- Bars and taverns

Over ninety percent of this segment's sales come from the first three groups on the list. That is where the most opportunities for hospitality students lie. For this reason most of this section deals with full-menu restaurants, limited-menu restaurants, and cafeterias.

Full-Menu Restaurants. There is a wide variety of full-menu restaurants. According to Mike Hurst, a past president of the National Restaurant Association, full-menu restaurants are restaurants that (1) have more than a dozen or so main-course items on the menu, and (2) cook to order. Full-menu restaurants can be casual or formal. They are generally categorized in terms of price, menu, or atmosphere. These categories are not mutually exclusive, however. Many full-menu restaurants can be placed in more than one category.

Price. An example of a high-price or luxury restaurant is the Four Seasons in New York City, where dinner for two consisting of an appetizer, entrée, dessert, coffee, and an accompanying bottle of wine could cost $100 per person.

Luxury restaurants are generally small and independently operated. They usually feature well-trained, creative chefs and skilled dining room service headed by a maitre d'. Some have tableside cooking. In order to provide the expected high level of service, luxury restaurants employ more kitchen and dining room staff per guest than other restaurant types.

Some luxury restaurants are famous tourist attractions the world over, such as New York's Russian Tea Room. Others, such as Lutece in Manhattan and Spago in Los Angeles, cater to a crowd of regulars: members of the jet set, movie stars, and others who lead the lifestyle of the rich and famous. These establishments are generally owned by a chef who supervises the cooking in the kitchen every evening. While luxury restaurants in the past generally featured French cuisine, this is no longer the case. Today's top cuisine often consists of regional specialties from all over the world and is created by innovative young chefs, many of whom have been trained in the United States at places such as the Culinary Institute of America in Hyde Park, New York.

Mid-price restaurants such as cafeterias and low-price limited-menu restaurants are discussed later in this section.

Menu. Steak houses and seafood restaurants are examples of full-menu restaurants defined in terms of menu. For example, Ponderosa restaurants specialize in beef. The 400-unit Red Lobster chain features shrimp, crab, and lobster.

A restaurant with a strong architectural and decorating theme may become known primarily for its atmosphere. Courtesy of the Kohler Co.

Atmosphere. An example of a restaurant known primarily for its atmosphere might be a place where the architecture, decor, or setting is unique. For example, a famous Los Angeles landmark for many years was the Brown Derby Restaurant, built in the shape of a giant derby in 1926 on Wilshire Boulevard in Hollywood. The cafe quickly gained popularity among movie stars because proprietor Herbert K. Somborn honored his famous guests by creating Derby's Wall of Fame—a collection on the restaurant's walls of caricatures of Charlie Chaplin, Bette Davis, John Wayne, Shirley Temple, and hundreds of other guests. Three years later the Original Brown Derby opened in Hollywood, and this second restaurant in Somborn's chain became known all over the world. There Clark Gable proposed to Carole Lombard in booth 5, and Lucille Ball and Jack Haley fought a duel with flying dinner rolls. The world's first Cobb salad was created when one-time Derby owner Robert Cobb raided his refrigerator to make a midnight snack for Sid Grauman (who owned Grauman's Chinese Theater in Hollywood, where all of the top movie openings took place). Today the Original Brown Derby is still a popular Hollywood restaurant, guided by its current owner Walter P. Scharfe. Walt Disney World recreated the Original Brown Derby as its premier restaurant for its new Disney-MGM Movie Studio Park.

Restaurants that rely primarily on atmosphere for their appeal also include the old-fashioned stainless steel and formica diners that are currently enjoying a revival. After almost disappearing from the American scene, diners have made a comeback, largely inspired by "The Diner Man," American architect Richard Gutman. Gutman wrote his college thesis on diners and has spent most of his life since then "writing, lecturing, and consulting on diners—their design, materials, and decor; their music, prices, and menu."[1] As a result of his efforts several enterprising restaurateurs began to design and build new old-style diners. There is already one thriving chain of diners called Ed Debevic's, based in Chicago, that even has a licensed diner in Japan. Debevic's diners are dedicated to traditional diner fare, including breakfast all day and perennial favorites like meat loaf. Even the food servers are a throwback to the 1950s—they chew bubble gum and pop bubbles in guests' faces. At another 1950s revival spot, the American City Diner in Washington, D.C., servers wear buttons that say "Eat and Get Out."[2] However, other new old-style diners are quite elegant and expensive. For instance, the Flash in the Pan Diner in Danvers, Massachusetts, accepts reservations and has a menu that includes marinated duckling and French wines. Tables are covered with white linen tablecloths.[3]

Other categories. In addition to these three basic types of full-menu restaurants there are some variations and combinations. For instance, there are "theme" restaurants. These restaurants are distinguished by their combination of decor, atmosphere, and menu. Many of them are chain restaurants. TGI Friday's, Houlihan's, and Bennigan's are all casual theme restaurants. Seafood restaurants typically combine decor, atmosphere, and menu by decorating with fishing nets, captain's wheels, and other nautical items and being located (whenever possible) on or near the water.

Ethnic restaurants are restaurants that use a specific kind of food as their distinctive theme. Chi Chi's and Garcia's feature Mexican food, for example. Other ethnic restaurants include Chinese, Italian, Greek, Japanese, Polynesian, Scandinavian, Korean, and Indian.

There are also restaurants that have been identified by the media as "mega restaurants." One such establishment is Weylu's Chinese restaurant in Saugus, Massachusetts, a 60,000-square-foot replica of the Imperial Palace in Beijing complete with a 28-foot gold-plated dragon and solid brass doors. Weylu's cost a reputed $20 million to build and seats 1,500 patrons. Right down the road in the same town is the Hilltop Steak House, which in 1990 was ranked as the largest restaurant in America in terms of sales.[4] This restaurant has plastic cattle and a 68-foot neon cactus out front. In 1990 the Hilltop's sales were $32.1 million, with an average dinner check of only $10 per person.

Every year *Restaurants & Institutions* picks the top 100 independent full-menu restaurants in America, ranked in order of total sales in dollars. Exhibit 5.1 shows the top 25.

Limited-Menu Restaurants. The distinguishing features of limited-menu restaurants is that they offer a much smaller selection of food, provide limited service, and consider speed of preparation and delivery of the essence. Convenience is what these restaurants focus on. In this group are fast-food restaurants such as Wendy's, Pizza Hut, and Taco Bell, as well as local coffee shops and restaurant chains like Waffle House.

Because convenience is such an important element from the consumer's point of view, many limited-menu restaurants stay open from early morning until late at night; some are open 24 hours a day. However,

Exhibit 5.1   Top 25 Independent Full-Menu Restaurants

1990 Rank	Restaurant/city/opened/owner	Sales (in $ millions)	Seats	Dinner check (w/bev.)	People served/ year
1	**Hilltop Steak House** Saugus, Mass., 1951 Frank Giuffrida & Jack Swansburg	$32.130*	1,300	$10.00	2,427,600
2	**Rainbow Room** New York, 1934 Joe Baum, Michael Whiteman, Dennis Sweeny	26.700+	1,200	100.00	450,000
3	**Tavern on the Green** New York, 1976 Warner LeRoy	25.550	1,197	46.00	560,000
4	**Smith & Wollensky** New York, 1977 Alan Stillman	17.500	420	50.00	369,200
5	**Phillips Harborplace** Baltimore, 1982 B. Phillips, S. Phillips, S. Phillips, P. Wall	15.884	700	16.25	990,000
6	**Anthony's Pier 4** Boston, 1963 Anthony Athanas & Family	15.096	650	23.00	663,000
7	**The Manor** West Orange, N.J., 1957 Harry Knowles & Family	14.600	1,500	47.00	433,500
8	**Sparks Steakhouse** New York, 1964 Pat & Mike Cetta	13.617*	300	60.00	266,100
9	**Legal Sea Foods** Boston (Park Plaza), 1980 The Berkowitz Family	13.318	380	24.00	546,000
10	**The Kapok Tree** Clearwater, Fla., 1957 Aaron R. Fodiman	12.864	1,750	14.68	1,019,397
11	**Spenger's Fish Grotto** Berkeley, Calif., 1890 Frank L. Spenger & Frank Spenger Jr.	12.500	700	17.00	910,000
12	**The Four Seasons** New York, 1959 Paul Kovi & Tom Margittai	12.374**	400	80.00	164,100
13	**The Waterfront** Covington, Ky., 1986 J. Ruby, C. Collinsworth, B. Esiason	12.130	290	39.80	166,400
14	**The "21" Club** New York, 1923 Knoll Intl. Holdings (Marshall Cogan)	12.000	650	65.00	162,000
15	**Scoma's** San Francisco, 1965 Al Scoma	11.865	300	23.90	475,211
16	**Old San Francisco Steakhouse** Dallas, 1974 Henry Reed & Partners	11.220*	750	18.00	514,000
17	**Old Original Bookbinders** Philadelphia, 1865 John & Albert Taxin	11.000	950	35.00	300,000
18	**Bob Chinn's Crabhouse** Wheeling, Ill., 1982 Robert & Marilyn Chinn	10.819	630	22.91	592,000
19	**Jerry's Famous Deli** Los Angeles, 1978 Issac Starkman	10.200**	350	20.00	525,000
20	**Joe's Stone Crab** Miami, 1913 JoAnn Sawitz-Bass	10.000++	400	32.00	325,000
21	**Le Cirque** New York, 1974 Sirio Maccioni	10.000	125	70.00	80,000

Exhibit 5.1 *(continued)*

1990 Rank	Restaurant/city/opened/owner	Sales (in $ millions)	Seats	Dinner check (w/bev.)	People served/ year
22	**The Cheesecake Factory** Marina del Rey, Calif., 1983 Cheesecake Corp. of America (David Overton)	9.900	250	12.60	550,000
23	**Jimmy's Harborside** Boston, 1924 Charles Doulos	9.870**	460	25.00	394,000
24	**Hard Rock Cafe** Honolulu, 1987 Peter Morton	9.750	248	13.45	719,000
25	**Gallagher's Steak House** New York, 1937 Jerome Brody	9.500	240	32.00	296,875
R&I estimate; +includes entertainment charge; **owner estimate; ++open 214 days a year.					

Source: *Restaurants & Institutions*, March 7, 1990, p. 50.

some 24-hour operations are reassessing that position. Late-night business is not always profitable, and in many areas labor and security problems have become more severe in recent years. Some 24-hour restaurants have had to hire security guards, install extra lighting, and pay higher wages to workers and managers who work the late shifts. Moreover, there is a growing realization that (1) equipment and personnel can get over-stressed in a restaurant that never closes, and (2) there are trade-offs in quality and service standards when convenience is the overriding issue. Nevertheless, in today's competitive environment 24-hour service remains a powerful marketing position that many companies have opted to continue while looking for ways to solve their late-night problems.

Exhibit 5.2 shows the top ten restaurant chains in 1989. Note that all of them are limited-menu restaurants. The largest group of limited-menu restaurants by far specializes in hamburgers, and the leader of the pack is McDonald's. McDonald's has more than 10,000 units worldwide, and annual sales per unit average $1.5 million.

McDonald's is a leader in innovative approaches to marketing its product to new market segments such as the business-lunch market. In Manhattan, for instance, an electronic ticker tape has been installed in a McDonald's located 3½ blocks from Wall Street. The restaurant also has a host, a pianist who plays in an atrium above the eating area, and a fax machine for accepting orders for delivery to nearby offices. The largest McDonald's in Texas (10,000 square feet) is in Houston in the upscale Galleria area. It also has an electronic ticker tape as well as fax machines patrons can use and business publications available for reading. Some tables even have telephone jacks.

McDonald's also leads limited-menu restaurants in new product development and in designing new equipment intended to increase food and service quality and reduce labor costs. In 1988 new equipment introduced in McDonald's units included a clamshell grill that reduces cooking times, a mini-computer that reduces the time managers must spend in the office,

Exhibit 5.2   Top Ten Restaurant Chains Ranked by System-Wide Sales

		U.S. System Sales (000)	U.S. System Units	Avg. Unit Volume (000)	Unit Rank
1	**McDonald's**	$12,011,739 5.5%	8,270 4.6%	$1,621 1.3%	1
2	**Burger King**	$5,036,000 1.9%	5,387 3.4%	$1,000 1.6%	3
3	**Pizza Hut**	$3,300,000 17.9%	6,243 9.4%	$570 9.6%	2
4	**Kentucky Fried Chicken**	$3,000,000 3.4%	4,961 1.3%	$607 1.7%	5
5	**Hardee's**	$2,900,000 6.4%	3,291 5.8%	$923 0.3%	9
6	**Wendy's**	$2,760,000 2.6%	3,490 (0.9%)	$789 4.0%	8
7	**Domino's Pizza**	$2,500,000 8.7%	5,185 12.8%	$485 0.0%	4
8	**Taco Bell**	$2,000,000 25.0%	3,082 7.1%	$686 16.5%	10
9	**Dairy Queen**	$1,965,000 3.4%	4,627 1.6%	$425 4.2%	6
10	**Denny's**	$1,300,000 2.5%	1,274 3.2%	$1,120 1.8%	17

Note: The percentages above represent the change in sales, units, and average unit volume from 1988 to 1989.

Source: "The Top 100 Chains," *Restaurant Business*, November 20, 1990, pp. 144, 146.

and a high-speed toaster. Currently they're giving robots that make french fries a try!

Other limited-menu restaurants are also using innovation to increase their share of the market. Arby's is testing the use of credit cards in its units. It's involved in a pilot program with Visa International and has found that credit cards (in units where cards are accepted) account for up to 5% of orders. Moreover, the average credit card purchase is significantly higher than the average cash purchase—about $5.50 compared to $3.20. Arby's is also experimenting with computerized screens from which customers can order directly to cut down service time. Burger King and Wendy's are also conducting credit card tests.[5]

However, trends in the business show that major growth in limited-menu restaurants is coming not from hamburger chains but from other types of menu items such as pizza and Mexican food. The leaders in both of these categories—Pizza Hut and Taco Bell—are owned by marketing giant PepsiCo, and it is likely that the battle for consumers will heat up further in years to come. McDonald's is now trying out pizza on a national basis. Pizza Hut's carry-out business has been seriously eroded by Domino's, so it has been developing a home delivery system that eventually will be available nationwide. Pizza Hut is also trying an entirely new format that will allow consumers to order and pick up a pizza in approximately 30 seconds at a

"And would the gentlemen like a table with a fax or without?"

Drawing by Mort Gerberg; © 1989, The New Yorker Magazine, Inc.

drive-through facility. Kentucky Fried Chicken is also testing home delivery in several cities.

Hospitality-school graduates tend to look at careers in limited-menu or fast-food restaurants last, according to Phil Belanger, the employment manager for Marriott's food service management division.[6] They prefer to work for major fine-dining restaurants. But, as mentioned in Chapter 2, fast-food companies offer graduates a chance to get into positions of great responsibility very rapidly, and pay very well because of liberal bonus and incentive plans.

Commercial Cafeterias. One of the main advantages that a cafeteria holds for consumers is that they are able to see the menu items before they choose them and thus have more control over getting their money's worth—a primary consideration for many of today's consumers. Total sales of commercial cafeterias were $3.7 billion in 1987. The typical cafeteria serves between 1,000 and 1,200 meals a day, with an average check of $4.50. Cafeterias gross approximately $1.6 million a year per unit. The industry estimates that today it takes at least $2 million and 100 employees to open a cafeteria.[7] Exhibit 5.3 shows the top ten cafeteria chains in the United States in 1989.

Many of today's cafeterias feature hidden cafeteria lines, tablecloths, and even limited table service so that the experience is like that of a full-service restaurant once the food has initially been picked up by guests.

The cafeteria industry is continuing to explore new concepts. According to Don Fritz, president and chief operating officer of Furr's/Bishop's Cafeteria, one popular idea the company has been exploring is an innovative concept where the guest chooses between an à la carte price and

Exhibit 5.3 Top Ten Cafeteria Chains

RANK	NAME	NO. of UNITS	VOLUME ($ MILLIONS)
1	**Morrison's,** Mobile, Alabama	165	$295
2	**Furr's/Bishop's,** Lubbock, Texas	154	270
3	**Luby's,** San Antonio, Texas	118	254
4	**Piccadilly,** Baton Rouge, Louisiana	119	235
5	**Wyatt's,** Dallas, Texas	121	190
6	**Old Country Buffet,** Eden Prairie, Minnesota	51	75
7	**K&W,** Winston-Salem, North Carolina	21	50
8	**MCL,** Indianapolis, Indiana	27	48
9	**S&S Cafeterias,** Macon, Georgia	22	45
10	**Blue Boar Cafeterias,** Louisville, Kentucky	15	20

Source: *Nation's Restaurant News,* February 6, 1989, p. F-14.

an "all you can eat" price at the start of the serving line. There is a station in the dining room where guests who have paid the all-you-can-eat price can get seconds. Furr's/Bishop's is also expanding into full-service specialty restaurants such as Furr's Pie Kitchen and Rio's Authentic Mexican Restaurant and Cantina.[8]

Another area cafeterias are exploring is take-out service. All of the top five cafeteria chains are increasing their operations in this area by building drive-though windows and adding separate take-out entrances.

Cafeterias are most popular in the southern region of the United States, although major chains are optimistic about growth opportunities in other parts of the country. Piccadilly, for instance, has announced that it is looking at California for new growth. Like Furr's/Bishop's, Piccadilly is trying to move away from having all of its eggs in the cafeteria basket. In 1989 it purchased six Ralph & Kacoos family-style seafood restaurants and plans to expand the chain. Morrison's Custom Management, based in Mobile, Alabama, has found that cafeterias have been hard to establish outside the Sun Belt and hopes its specialty restaurants—such as Ruby Tuesday, L&N Seafood Grill, and Silver Spoon—are more universal in appeal.[9] Recently some cafeteria chains have explored television advertising as a means of reaching more of the 30- to 45-year-old market.

Like fast-food restaurants, cafeterias offer managers the opportunity to gain responsibility and substantial salaries early in their careers. According to its recruiting literature, Piccadilly starts its management trainees at $20,000 and estimates that they will be earning $48,000 (on average) in three to four years, $68,000 in six to seven years.

Lodging Places   Food and beverage operations in hotels and other lodging facilities were discussed in Chapter 4. No matter how you look at them, the amount of lodging food service sales is tremendous. Lodging establishments enjoyed more than $15 billion in food service sales in 1990.[10]

As mentioned in Chapter 4, in recent years hotels and motels have become more aggressive in marketing their food service outlets. "Not so long ago," said Astef Mankarios, president of the Rosewood Hotel Group, "many hotels viewed the hotel restaurant as a necessary evil. This approach resulted in a half-hearted effort with boring and predictable food served with neither flair nor care."[11] Mankarios's Rosewood Hotel Group, which operates the Mansion on Turtle Creek in Dallas as well as other hotels in Hawaii and California, goes out of its way to hire chefs who are recognized as leaders within the industry. Menus are distinctive and feature products indigenous to the hotel's particular region. "A restaurant is not just a service that a hotel must provide," says Mankarios. "It can be a powerful marketing tool. A first-class restaurant helps build a national reputation for a hotel, while at the same time helping to build close ties with the local community by attracting its residents."[12] Rosewood's philosophy pays off. In 1989 the Mansion on Turtle Creek's restaurant was the highest grossing restaurant per square foot in America.

Transportation Market

Travelers are eating at highway stops; on airplanes, ships, and trains; at airport terminals and train stations; and at other facilities in the transportation market. United Airlines maintains its own in-flight kitchens. Other airlines buy their meals from Caterair (formerly Marriott's in-flight service division, sold in 1989), Ogden Food Service, Sky Chef, and Dobbs International Services. Many airlines today are trying hard to differentiate themselves by serving more distinctive and higher-quality food. There is a tendency to use more fresh food instead of frozen items when possible. Even the selection of wines available on board has been greatly upgraded in some instances. In addition, the trend toward more nutritious meals has become an integral part of many airline food programs. For example, Delta passengers are served oat bran muffins and natural grain bread.

Cruise lines such as Carnival and Cunard run their own completely staffed kitchens, while others like Premier hire contract food companies. Most cruise lines offer reduced calorie and low-fat menu items as part of their standard menu fare.

Food service in airport and train terminals is often provided by restaurants—frequently limited-menu restaurants—and contract food companies such as ARA that bid for the opportunity to sell food in the terminals.

Leisure Market

The leisure market includes recreational food service facilities located at sports arenas, stadiums, race tracks, movie theaters, bowling lanes, amusement parks and other attractions, municipal convention centers, and hunting facilities. Altogether this amounts to a $6.8 billion market.[13] In many cases leisure market food service facilities are concessions run by contract food companies.

The foods served at these facilities vary greatly. For example, amusement parks tend to sell novelty foods such as elephant ears and cotton candy. Large municipal convention centers may have a variety of food service outlets, ranging from snack bars to full-service restaurants and even private clubs. The largest contract food company in this area is Sportservice, whose system-wide sales in 1989 amounted to $209 million.

Another operator specializing in the leisure market is the Fine Host Corporation. Typical of its operations is Arlington International Race Course, Arlington Heights, Illinois. At Arlington, Fine Host provides an extensive array of food services. Dining facilities at the track include:

- The Turf Club—a private club offering fine food for members in a rich setting reminiscent of an English social club

- Private suites—29 luxury suites providing housekeeping and butler service

- The Million Room—a 1,000-seat clubhouse dining room

- International Buffet—a 400-seat buffet

- Mr. D's—a 300-seat casual theme restaurant

- Silks—a posh saloon featuring international dishes

In addition to these dining facilities, Fine Host also operates 14 bars, and all of the concessions run from 17 permanent stands. Concessions serve everything from popcorn to "designer ice cream" made on site. The concession stands include delis, charbroiling hearths, bake shops, ice cream parlors, pasta bars, Oriental stands, Mexican-theme stands, fried chicken stands, and hot dog stands. Private catering facilities are also available for parties of 12 to 2,000.

At the new $100 million Joe Robbie football stadium where the Miami Dolphins play, Fine Host not only runs the food and beverage concessions but also is in charge of gifts, novelties, and programs sold at the stadium or through a mail order catalog developed by Fine Host. Valet parking, cleaning, and equipment maintenance services are also provided by the company. Fine Host provides many similar services for Texas Stadium, home of the Dallas Cowboys.

One of the most important companies in the leisure market is Canteen Corporation. Canteen operates concessions for the New York Yankees and the Oakland Athletics as well as other teams. It also operates in national parks such as Grand Canyon, Bryce, and Zion.

Retail Market

Two major trends in food service have surfaced in recent years. The first is the increasing tendency for Americans to eat food prepared outside of the home—as evidenced by the dramatic growth in restaurant food sales. The second trend, which is developing even more rapidly, is the growth in the take-out and delivery segment of the fast-food market. It is evident that Americans are cooking less. It is also evident that there is a growing tendency to buy food prepared outside the home and bring it home to consume it. This last development is in line with marketing trends in other areas such as home electronics and furniture, where research has shown that people are increasingly looking at their homes as recreational and entertainment centers.

Major beneficiaries of these trends have been retail businesses that sell take-out food—convenience stores and supermarkets, department stores, drug stores, gasoline stations, and specialized retail outlets such as gourmet delicatessens. These retail stores have been increasing their share of the take-out market rapidly, and most industry observers think this trend will continue at an accelerating pace. A 1987 national survey by the Food Marketing Institute and Campbell Soup Company showed that 36% of consumers' take-out food dollars were spent in supermarkets and other food stores such as 7–Eleven, Circle K, and various gourmet food shops. This translates into sales of $22.5 billion.

There is no doubt that a good part of these take-out sales are at the expense of traditional restaurants and fast-food outlets. This is due, among other reasons, to increased marketing by convenience stores and supermarkets of their prepared take-out foods. Circle K, for instance, reports that it spends 85% of its marketing dollars on prepared foods. In some cases, stores have formed alliances rather than compete with each other. For example, in some areas 7–Eleven stores sell Hardee's hamburgers, and Circle K has a joint agreement to sell Dunkin' Donuts from special display cases that are stocked twice daily with fresh donuts.

Supermarkets are increasing the size and scope of their take-out food operations. Some industry observers expect the average supermarket to increase in size from its present 30,000-50,000 square feet to 200,000 square feet by the mid to late 1990s. Much of that space will be devoted to pre-cooked take-out dishes and sit-down food service areas. Many supermarkets already offer take-out salad bars in addition to their traditional deli sections. By using ovens installed in their bakeries, approximately 15% of today's supermarkets have small restaurants and cafeterias featuring their complete line of prepared products. Research done by supermarkets has shown that people perceive produce in a supermarket to be fresher than that sold in most restaurants, and some stores are exploiting this advantage by selling a wide range of freshly prepared salad and vegetable dishes. Some supermarkets have hired chefs who work in open kitchens so that customers can see the dishes being prepared and thus be convinced that pre-packaged menu items have not been brought in.

Business and Industry Market

The business and industry market consists of non-food-service businesses that offer on-site food service to their employees. The National Restaurant Association (NRA) estimated total 1990 sales in this market to be almost $7.2 billion.[14] Most businesses employ contract food companies to provide employee meals. Large companies that offer contract food service include Marriott, Greyhound, ARA Services, Morrison's, and Canteen Corporation.

Contract food companies have been facing increasing competition from fast-food and limited-menu restaurants and are responding by entering into agreements with some of these companies to operate franchises. Marriott's agreement with Pizza Hut, for instance, allows Marriott to operate 900 Pizza Hut mobile food carts in business locations and other types of facilities such as airports. Morrison's is testing Baskin-Robbins ice cream products.

A number of companies operate their own employee food programs. Some of these are quite innovative. At Eastman Kodak in Rochester, New York, company employees can even purchase fresh baked goods to take home from bakery outlets around the plant.

Student Market

Recently one of the biggest changes in college food service programs has been the gradual shifting away from mandated meal plans to an à la carte

Employee cafeterias. Top: Detroit Edison Company, circa 1950. Courtesy of State of Michigan Archives. **Bottom: Amway Grand Plaza Hotel, 1988.** Courtesy of Amway Grand Plaza Hotel, Grand Rapids, Michigan.

operation. "College food service operators are now beginning to perceive themselves as revenue producers instead of revenue consumers," according to Clark DeHaven, director of the National Association of College and University Food Service.[15] DeHaven also points out that as colleges see more older students returning to pursue advanced degrees, dining directors have had to accommodate preferences that are somewhat different from those of the typical 18-year-old.

The Marriott Corporation, which has 450 college food program accounts, has developed the "Grand Marketplace," a collection of small food boutiques including La Cuisine, which serves steak and lobster, and Greenstuffs, a salad and health food section. ARA's School Nutrition and Dining Services have also introduced some new concepts to capture the

Exhibit 5.4 Top College Contract Food Companies

Name	No. of College Contracts	Major Accounts	Estimated Annual College Food Service Revenues
Marriott Corp.	450	Marquette, Texas Christian, Harvard Business School, Washington University, Georgetown	$345 million
ARA Services	250	University of Virginia, Clemson	$300 million
Service America Corp.	81	University of Florida, University of Alabama	$143 million
Seiler Corp.	115	Johns Hopkins, De Paul, Fairleigh Dickinson, Colby, University of Maryland	$60 million
Morrison Custom Management	112	University of Illinois, University of Chicago, Swarthmore	$55 million
Canteen Corp.	53	University of California, Irvine; University of Kentucky	$40 million

Source: *Nation's Restaurant News*, March 20, 1989, p. F-15.

changing student market. These include Deli Corner, Itza Pizza, and Gretel's Bake Shop. At Ohio State, McDonald's runs the food service concession in the student union.

Contract food companies controlled 41.3% of the $6.5 billion college and university food service programs in America in 1990 (see Exhibit 5.4).[16] Typically a contract food company guarantees a college or university a profit of 6% to 10% of sales in return for a five- to ten-year operating contract. Small colleges in particular are attracted to companies that can offer a higher level of expertise and professionalism than the school itself can supply. "If you're a small school, you're almost forced to investigate the possibility of using a contractor," observes Karl Oldag, vice president of college and university food service sales for Morrison's.[17]

However, many universities still believe that contract food companies cannot always do it better. Some universities that have used contractors in the past, such as Notre Dame and the University of Pennsylvania, are now once again running their own programs. The University of Pennsylvania's program is unusually complex. It consists of three residence dining halls, the Faculty and Alumni Club, the Penn Tower Hotel, and a full banquet and catering division. The university also does a brisk take-out business with off-campus students as well as student residents. "Within four years of self-operation we went into the black and have been there ever since," says Bill Canney, Penn's dining services director.[18]

Health Care Market

The health care market consists of three principal segments: hospitals; nursing homes; and retirement communities, including congregate food sites (community-sponsored meal centers for senior citizens). The total estimated 1990 food and beverage sales in this market were $14,315,828.[19] Charles Bernstein, editor of *Nation's Restaurant News*, calls the health care market "one of the largest untapped markets for food service management companies . . . a real sleeper, in reality a rapidly awakening giant."[20] Bernstein attributes this to a combination of factors: rapidly changing lifestyles, an aging population, skyrocketing medical costs, restricted federal funds, and a lack of family support systems. Typical of the large contract food companies in this field is Morrison's. With over 400 health care accounts, Morrison's provides everything from bedside meals for patients to non-patient food service in cafeterias, fine-dining facilities for health care employees, and catering for special events. The company also offers nutrition expertise and consulting services.

The majority of health care facilities have traditionally run their own food service departments. Some of these can be quite extensive. Many hospitals operate vending machines, a coffee shop for visitors, an employee cafeteria, a special dining facility for doctors, a day-care food program for employees' children, a regular patient food program, and a special patient food program that can include gourmet meals with accompanying wines served in patients' rooms by a special staff. Some hospitals have even gone into the catering business to fully utilize their extensive (and expensive) commercial kitchen facilities.

There are a number of trends in hospital food service that are expected to have a positive impact on the future of this market segment:

- Hospitals are serving more non-patient meals than ever before. Baptist Hospital in Miami estimates that less than 50% of its food is served to patients.

- Hospitals are serving better and more varied food. Some hospital menus include meals such as this one: an appetizer; freshly grilled

Patient food programs vary from hospital to hospital. Room service is popular with patients at Baptist Hospital in Miami. Patients and their visitors can order from a room service menu that includes milk shakes, salads, deli and grilled sandwiches, and desserts. Courtesy of Baptist Hospital, Miami, Florida.

filet mignon, lobster, or stuffed shrimp; a dessert; and a beverage served on a tray with fresh flowers—all for $15. Guests visiting patients can order trays of their own, as well as fruit and gourmet food baskets.

- Many hospitals are adding VIP suites that have carpeting, mini-refrigerators, a room for a family member to stay in, and an amenity package that includes gourmet meals.

- Off-premises catering is adding to hospital food service revenues. One franchise company that specializes in helping hospitals turn their kitchens into money-making facilities even holds a one-week cooking school to teach hospital chefs how to prepare more inviting food for catering.[21]

- Hospitals have begun to market their food services.

Prison Food Service

Correctional institutions—state and federal prisons—are another segment of the food service industry. Correctional institutions often have a hard time attracting and retaining food service staff because they cannot offer much professional career growth. However, the unique challenge they offer is attractive to some people. A prison needs to offer a cyclical menu that is not overly repetitive and has the flexibility to meet special religious and medical dietary needs, while still offering a bit of creativity in both preparation and presentation. Some institutions prepare a variety of special dishes every meal to meet special dietary requirements—medical diets such as low sodium, diabetic, and low fat, for example, or religious diets such as Muslim and kosher. Another problem encountered by prison food service systems is inventory control and shrinkage. Very stringent controls need to be applied. Food costs are a further constraint on operations. Correctional institutions often have limited budgets for food service; economies of scale can thus make a substantial difference in the menus offered inmates. For this reason, contract food companies are now successfully competing in this area because their professional expertise and buying power make it possible for them to solve some of the problems that prison administrators have had little experience with.

Military Food Service

Military food service is a very specialized area and not within the scope of this text. Nevertheless, it deserves mention because of its size and diversity, both geographically and in terms of types of facilities. Within the continental United States alone, military food service sales were projected to reach $1.1 billion in 1990.[22] Careers in military food service can include everything from preparing food for space shuttle astronauts to running the mess on a nuclear submarine or aircraft carrier to managing officers' clubs in army, navy, air force, marine, and coast guard bases all over the world. Both civilians and military personnel are employed in many of these facilities.

Starting a New Restaurant

Many students dream of someday owning their own restaurant. To be sure, huge fortunes have been made in the restaurant business. The entire

Marriott empire grew from a single Hot Shoppe Restaurant opened in 1927 in Washington, D.C., by J. Willard Marriott, a 27-year-old sheep herder from Salt Lake City, Utah. (In 1989 the Marriott Corporation decided to abandon its restaurant businesses with the exception of its Hot Shoppe chain, which it kept for sentimental as well as business reasons.) Frank Giuffrida, who owns the largest independent restaurant in America—the previously mentioned Hilltop Steak House in Saugus, Massachusetts—started as a meat manager in a butcher store (which he still owns) next door to his restaurant. America's second largest independent restaurant, the Tavern on the Green in Manhattan, is the creation of Warner LeRoy, whose father, Mervyn LeRoy, produced the movie "The Wizard of Oz." LeRoy made his fortune by understanding the meaning of showmanship in the restaurant business—his employees often refer to him as a "food impresario." Anthony Athanas, who opened Anthony's Pier 4 in Boston in 1963, is an Albanian immigrant who came to America at age 13 and with no formal education became a multi-millionaire.

Another legendary name in the restaurant business is Joseph H. Baum, one of the most important restaurateurs of our time. Among the well-known establishments Baum created and opened are the Four Seasons, Windows on the World, and the newly refurbished Rainbow Room at Rockefeller Center. Many people call him the father of the theme restaurant.

Some entrepreneurs never go beyond a single restaurant, nurturing it to perfection. The Four Seasons on Park Avenue in New York is a good example. Owners Paul Kovi and Tom Margittai personally manage every aspect of their $12-million-a-year 400-seat restaurant. Mike Hurst, past NRA president and creator and owner of Fort Lauderdale's 15th Street Fisheries (with food sales of more than $7 million in 1990 from a mere 320 seats[23]), is a master of food and beverage merchandising. While managing the kitchen and other back-of-the-house areas is important, his basic philosophy is to emphasize the front-of-the-house and give his guests "recognition, recommendations, and reassurance."

According to a 1990 survey of the leading 500 independent restaurants, in 1989 average annual sales for these leaders were $3,021,000.[24] Not all restaurants do this well, of course. According to the NRA there are 454,000 commercial food service units in the United States, and 70% of them gross less than $500,000 annually.

The restaurant business is one of the easiest businesses to enter, requiring comparatively little capital and virtually no experience. To novices, there seem few barriers to entry—used commercial ovens, stoves, and other fixtures are readily available; almost any location will do, they think; and no special skills or technology are required—anyone can cook, right? Moreover, most of the labor (if any is needed besides that of the owner's) can be obtained at minimum wage.

Staying in business is much harder, however. Being a good cook, a popular host, and a creative promoter is not enough when it comes to running a successful restaurant. The business is in fact a good deal more complicated than it looks on the surface. That is why those who have studied it at colleges and universities have a much better chance of succeeding. Without that knowledge, prospects can be bleak. Fifty percent of all restaurants close within a year, and half of the other 50% fail in their second year. By their fifth year, 85% are no longer in business. The figures may be higher since they are based on bankruptcy, and not all restaurant failures result in recorded bankruptcies. Many restaurants simply close their doors when they have exhausted their capital and end up as unrecorded failures.

Why Do Restaurants Fail?

There are several reasons why so many restaurants fail every year.

Lack of Business Knowledge. The first and most important reason restaurants fail is a simple lack of business knowledge. Successful restaurant operators have a working knowledge of marketing, accounting, finance, law, engineering, and human resources. Knowing and loving food is not enough to operate a thriving food service operation.

Lack of Technical Knowledge. A second reason is a lack of technical knowledge. Attorneys, accountants, movie stars, and sports figures have all tried their hand in the restaurant business. While some have succeeded, they tend to be the ones who have invested capital in or simply lent their name to the enterprise in return for a share of the profits. They have left the planning and operations to professional restaurateurs. Successful restaurant operators must understand site selection, menu planning, recipe development, purchasing, production techniques, and sophisticated service procedures that make it possible to deliver a consistent and reliable experience that meets guest expectations.

Lack of Sufficient Working Capital. A third reason for restaurant failure is a lack of sufficient working capital. In the restaurant business, where word-of-mouth recommendations play such an important part, it takes a good deal of time to develop a solid guest base. During that time new restaurants can expect to lose money. Many new operators badly underestimate the amount of capital they will need to pay for food, labor, and fixed operating expenses until they reach the break-even point—which can often be six months to a year down the road.

The Cost of Starting a New Restaurant

Some restaurants fail before they ever get off the ground because their operators underestimate the cost of opening a new restaurant. *Changing Times* magazine asked Stephen Zagon, a food service consulting manager, and Doyle Wayman, president of Index, a restaurant consultant and design firm in Houston, to estimate the probable start-up costs for two hypothetical restaurants, both in major metropolitan areas (see Exhibit 5.5).[25] The first example is for a 5,940-square-foot fine-dining restaurant with 150 seats in the dining room and 30 in the bar. It has a contemporary decor and a new state-of-the-art kitchen. The second is for a more modest bistro cafe with 75 seats, 15 in the bar, and a total of 2,430 square feet. The menu choices are more limited and the decor and kitchen less expensive. Both lease rather than buy space and would have to convert the property.

As you can see, while opening a restaurant is inexpensive compared to starting other businesses, opening costs can be substantial. It should be noted that these figures are based on doing a first-class job and buying new equipment. Costs can be reduced considerably by purchasing used equipment.

Exhibit 5.5 Restaurant Start-Up Costs

	FINE DINING	CAFE / BISTRO
HARD CAPITAL COSTS		
Kitchen & other non-public areas	$247,500	$60,750
Dining room & other public areas Plumbing, electrical, decorating, furnishing	297,000	72,900
SOFT CAPITAL COSTS Pots, pans, linens, silverware, china & some promotional & marketing costs	31,500	6,750
PROFESSIONAL FEES Licenses (except liquor), lawyer, accountant, interior designer, etc.	115,200	28,080
ADDITIONAL WORKING CAPITAL		
Beverage & food inventory;	25,000	10,000
three-month payroll	65,790	22,430
TOTAL	$781,990	$200,910

It should be noted that these figures are based on doing a first-class job and buying new equipment. Costs can be reduced considerably by purchasing used equipment.

Building a Successful Restaurant

Let's assume that you have enough business knowledge, technical knowledge, and capital to start a restaurant and keep it going until you reach the break-even point. What's the first step? How do you go about deciding what kind of a restaurant it is going to be and where it should be located?

Many would-be restaurateurs approach this issue by first deciding what kind of a restaurant they would like to have and then picking a location they're comfortable with. A person might conclude, for example, that they would like to operate an Italian restaurant in the neighborhood where they live. The next step would be to negotiate a lease in a nearby shopping center where some space is available, come up with a name, then hire a contractor to "build out"—do the interior construction needed to add finishing touches to the restaurant such as roman columns, trellises from which grapes can be hung, or other details suggesting an Italian setting.

While this approach might succeed, modern management theory suggests that this is putting the proverbial cart before the horse. In the situation we have just described, the concept and location have been decided on without any regard to who the guests are likely to be for this new restaurant and what other restaurants will be competing for those same guests. Fred Turner, former president of McDonald's, was quoted as saying "we lead the industry because we follow the customers."[26] Part of what makes McDonald's successful is that its product and service concepts are based on listening to customers and potential customers. For example, breakfast was introduced by McDonald's not because it wanted to keep its stores open longer hours (although that was a consideration) but because it recognized a demand among its customers for earlier hours and breakfast items. Similarly, pizza is McDonald's response to customer demand for other items besides hamburgers, salads, and chicken at dinner time.

Before selecting a concept and a site for your restaurant, you should first ask yourself:

- Who are the people I hope to attract? Are they families, business-people, tourists, or some other guest groups?

- What needs of theirs am I trying to satisfy? Do these people want convenient fast-food or fine dining?

- Where do these people live and work? Are they located near my proposed location?

- When do they buy? Are they in the habit of eating out at lunch and dinner, or only at dinner? What are their peak hours and days?

- How do they buy? Do they dine in, take out, or want delivery?

- How much competition is there now and is there likely to be in the near future? If the neighborhood for your proposed Italian restaurant already contains a half-dozen of them, you need to be sure that there is room for another one—and that your restaurant will offer something that is clearly better from the point of view of your potential guests. Smart marketers do a thorough competition analysis that takes into account all the restaurants in the neighborhood—their menus, prices, and hours of operation.

The Concept. Once you have answered these questions you are ready to develop a concept. The concept consists not only of the products and services that your proposed restaurant will offer but also the manner in which they will be presented. The restaurant's name, atmosphere, location, and menu prices are all elements of the concept. In other words, the concept is the physical embodiment of the answers to the questions you have just finished asking—it is your idea of a restaurant that will attract the customers you have decided to go after.

How does one arrive at a concept? A new restaurant's concept can come from an already developed concept, as happens when a restaurant chain expands, or from individuals who have created fresh concepts—usually after asking themselves the questions we have posed above. In either case the foundation of the concept is the menu. Will it be ethnic, regional American, eclectic Californian, traditional, or limited? One way to address this question is to study overall market trends in terms of the popularity of various menu items. Much of this information is available from studies done by trade media (e.g., magazines such as *Restaurant Hospitality* and *Nation's Restaurant News*) as well as from trade associations such as the NRA. For example, in March 1989 the NRA conducted a study of the fast-growing demand for ethnic foods in restaurants. It wanted to find out which ethnic foods were the most popular, what kinds of people ordered ethnic foods and how frequently, consumption patterns (take-out versus eat-in), and consumer attitudes in general toward ethnic food. Exhibit 5.6, extracted from that study, shows the popularity of various ethnic foods.

Once the menu has been decided on, many other aspects of the concept can be put into place. These include decor, number of seats, type of service, hours of operation, pricing structure, and, finally, the level of investment required.

Exhibit 5.6 Ethnic Food Popularity

RANK	ETHNIC FOOD	PROPORTION OF RESPONDENTS*
1	Chinese	88.1%
2	Italian (excludes pizza)	78.9
3	Mexican	72.6
4	Greek	36.8
5	Latin American	32.7
6	Spanish	26.8
7	French	23.7
8	Caribbean	21.9
9	Japanese	21.0
10	Vietnamese	19.0
11	Russian	17.4
12	German	16.1
13	African	16.0
14	Indian	14.9
15	Middle Eastern	13.1
16	Thai	13.1
17	Scandinavian	11.7
18	Korean	10.8
19	Eastern European	9.8

*Meals were eaten on or off the premises sometime in the past month.

Source: "The Market for Ethnic Foods in Restaurants, 1989," the National Restaurant Association.

The final investment figure may be modified several times in the course of creating the restaurant. To begin with, market research is likely to influence some of the elements of the concept—remember that the focus must be on the potential guests' needs and wants. Another constraint is one of limited resources. Most restaurateurs do not have unlimited funds. Even large restaurant chains must be concerned with how long it will take them to break even and make a profit with a new restaurant. This means that the amount of capital available for investment may be established early on, and that in turn may determine many of the elements of the concept.

Site Selection. One important decision that needs to be made about any proposed restaurant is its location. A restaurant site can be an undeveloped lot where a new building must be constructed, or an existing building that is already a restaurant or can be converted to one. There is of course no such thing as a universally ideal restaurant site. Some restaurants need to be in areas where there is a substantial amount of foot traffic; others should be near a busy highway intersection. Still others rely on neighborhoods with certain predetermined characteristics. In any case, the site of a restaurant has a tremendous influence on its success.

Expanding restaurant chains like Bonanza and Shoney's provide examples of how the site selection process works. Most chains start by selecting cities or metropolitan areas with a certain-size population whose average disposable income is within a certain range. For instance, one chain's criterion might be that "we will locate our new restaurants in cities of more than 250,000 where the average household income is $20,000 or more annually." Domino's pizza units generally serve population bases of 40,000 or more, although Domino's believes it is possible to be profitable in a location with only half that number. Often, rather than thinking in terms of cities or metropolitan areas, sites are selected in specific ADI areas. ADI stands for "Areas of Dominant Influence" and describes the areas covered by the signals of major television stations as measured by Arbitron, a national TV rating service. By selecting a site in this manner, the chain knows in advance that it will be able to advertise economically using television.

Restaurant sites often fall into one of four areas:

- *Central city business and shopping districts.* These are near office buildings, downtown department stores, and/or major commercial hotels.

- *Shopping centers.* Modern shopping centers serve as the central community focus in suburban areas. City government offices, churches, recreational facilities such as movie theaters and fitness centers, and restaurants usually are nearby or in the centers.

- *Planned communities.* Planned communities are often projects of large developers or may be urban renewal projects.

- *Highway intersections.*

Large restaurant chains usually carefully analyze market data from locations where their restaurants already exist to make sure that the kinds of people who live in, work in, and travel through the proposed new restaurant's community match the profile of their typical restaurant guests in other communities.

In order to be desirable, a site needs to possess certain characteristics. First, it must be easily visible. If the proposed site is off a highway, it should be near a clearly marked or well-known exit. It should also be possible to put up a sign that can be seen far enough in advance from either direction so that a driver can slow down and exit safely. If the restaurant is in a major shopping complex, the site cannot be off in a corner where no one will see it. It should be visible from the parking lot where shoppers entering the mall or movie theater are bound to notice it.

Second, a site must be easily accessible. Some otherwise favorable sites are rejected because they are on side streets or one-way streets that are inconvenient for customers or simply hard to find. Moreover, the restaurant must be accessible to the market it intends to serve. Depending on the type of restaurant, "accessible" can range from a few minutes' walk to a one-hour drive. Restaurants that serve upscale markets or have unique themes may have a large geographic range, while limited-menu or fast-food restaurants tend to serve markets no more than five square miles in size.

The third consideration is availability. Can the property be rented or purchased? When? Are there any zoning restrictions?

A fourth factor to consider is affordability. A restaurant built on an undeveloped lot may require extensive site preparation costs. Are power and other utilities readily available or are they going to have to be brought in? What are the terms of the purchase? If you are buying an already existing building, is the seller willing to help in the financing? Are the taxes reasonable? If an already existing building can be leased, both the length of the lease and the terms are important. Is the landlord going to pay for remodeling costs and other improvements, or is that cost to be borne by the new operator? Since under-capitalization is a major cause of restaurant failure, operators must be careful not to commit themselves to higher rent or remodeling costs than they can afford to pay. When deciding what they can afford to pay, operators should be conservative because business may not go as well as they expect.

The feasibility study. Before they decide on a site, restaurateurs usually have a feasibility study done. These studies are very similar to the feasibility studies that are done for new hotels (described in Chapter 3). The major difference is that the demand for hotel rooms is usually generated by travelers or others coming from outside of the hotel's immediate area, while the demand for restaurants is mostly local. Therefore, different market characteristics need to be examined.

In addition to information on population characteristics of the local area, a good deal more information is available from various sources. The NRA hires the Gallup organization to conduct a monthly poll, called the Food Service Market Measure, which asks a nationally representative sample of adults questions such as:

- Which of the following did you do yesterday?

  a. Ate on the premises of a restaurant, fast-food place, cafeteria, or any other place where you purchased a meal or snack.

  b. Purchased take-out food "to go" or had it delivered.

- Was the food you ate on the premises for breakfast, lunch, dinner, or a snack?

- Was the take-out food you had delivered for breakfast, lunch, dinner, or a snack?

With the answers to these and other questions, it is possible to forecast seasonal trends by region of the country.

The Bureau of Labor Statistics publishes an annual Consumer Expenditure Survey based on interviews and diaries that consumers keep of their purchases. This survey is available from the Government Printing Office in Washington, D.C. According to a recent survey, the average American household allocated 37% of its annual food budget to food purchased away from home. Households headed by an individual less than 25 years old and those with an annual income of more than $50,000 allocated the highest portion of their annual food budgets to food purchased away from home. Families with children spent the least on food purchased away from home.

Several other research services, using the Consumer Expenditure Survey as well as data collected from other sources, are able to take specific zip codes in the United States and report exactly how often the people in areas with that zip code eat out, which meals they eat out, what they like to eat, and how much they spend.

People with personal computers who subscribe to Compuserve Information Service can access a database called "Supersite." Supersite demographic information is available for the entire United States, broken down by state, county, Arbitron's areas of dominant influence (ADIs), Nielsen TV market areas, and zip code. Fourteen different demographic reports for any given area are available from Supersite, including income, housing, education, and employment reports. In addition, sales-potential reports for restaurants and other services are available.

Information on the buying habits of restaurant patrons is available through ACORN Target Marketing, which can be accessed through the Supersite data base. ACORN is an acronym for "A Classification of Residential Neighborhoods," which classifies all households in the United States according to demographic, socio-economic, and housing characteristics of the neighborhoods. A similar service called PRIZM is available for every zip code in America from the Claritas Corporation.

As you can see, there are many sources of information that writers of feasibility studies can draw on to make a qualitative and quantitative analysis of a proposed restaurant operation. A feasibility study identifies possible guest market(s) for the proposed restaurant, evaluates the proposed site, and, finally, analyzes the financial prospects of the restaurant.

The financial analysis portion of the study also contains a capital investment budget. The purpose of a capital investment budget is to make certain that enough capital will be available for the following items:

- Land and construction costs (or for an extended lease on an existing building)
- Equipment
- Furniture and fixtures
- Working capital
- Pre-opening expenses for inventory
- Pre-opening staff salaries, including necessary training
- Pre-opening advertising and promotion

Finally, the study should contain a proposed operating budget for the restaurant's first year. This budget should include a forecast of sales based on expected market share and the estimated average expenditure per guest, as well as estimated payroll, utility, supply, and food and beverage costs; rent or mortgage payments; and taxes.

Chapter Summary

Food service is a huge industry with over $200 billion in annual sales, 626,000 units, and eight million employees. Career opportunities abound because of the diversity to be found within the industry. Some students are attracted by the many opportunities to climb the corporate ladder at companies ranging from McDonald's to Marriott. Others look forward to the chance to play host to movie stars and other celebrities at their own unique restaurants. Compared to other businesses, the opportunities for entrepreneurship are unmatched.

Food service establishments can be classified in the following ways:

A. Eating and Drinking Places
 1. Full-Menu Restaurants
 2. Limited-Menu Restaurants

3. Commercial Cafeterias
4. Social Caterers
5. Ice Cream and Frozen Custard Stands
6. Bars and Taverns

B. Lodging Places

C. Transportation Market

D. Leisure Market

E. Retail Market

F. Business and Industry Market

G. Student Market

H. Health Care Market

I. Prison Food Service

J. Military Food Service

Entrepreneurs who have started their own restaurants have followed various paths. Approximately 85 percent of new restaurants that open in a given year will be out of business within five years. Restaurants often fail for three reasons: a lack of business knowledge, a lack of technical knowledge, and/or a lack of sufficient working capital.

Successful restaurateurs start by focusing on the needs and wants of their potential guests. From this they develop a restaurant concept. Next, a site is selected. This step is generally part of a feasibility study that also analyzes the market in which the site is located and includes a financial analysis and capital operating budget.

Endnotes

1. "For an Aficionado, a Diner Is More Than a Food Joint," *Wall Street Journal*, December 13, 1989, p. A-1.

2. "A Diner Is More Than a Food Joint," p. A-4.

3. "A Diner Is More Than a Food Joint," p. A-4.

4. Monica Kass, "R&I's Top 100 Independents: America's Highest-Grossing Restaurants," *Restaurants & Institutions*, March 7, 1990, p. 50

5. "Fast Food Industry Increases Tests of Sales on Credit," *Wall Street Journal*, November 30, 1988, p. B-1.

6. "Foodservice Offers Diverse Opportunities," *Nation's Restaurant News*, Career Paths Supplement, January 1988, p. 5.

7. "Cafeterias Slip into New Wardrobe," *Nation's Restaurant News*, February 6, 1989, p. F-14.

8. "Cafeterias Explore New Turf," *Nation's Restaurant News*, August 7, 1989, p. F-46.

9. Christy Fisher, "Cafeteria Chains Try Full-Service Side Dish," *Advertising Age*, March 26, 1990, p. 10.

10. 1990 National Restaurant Association Foodservice Industry Forecast, *Restaurants USA*, December 1989.

11. Astef Mankarios, "Great Hotels: Restaurants with Rooms," *Restaurants & Institutions*, October 30, 1989, p. 16.

12. Mankarios, p. 16.
13. 1990 National Restaurant Association Foodservice Industry Forecast.
14. 1990 National Restaurant Association Foodservice Industry Forecast, p. 38.
15. "Focus—College Feeding," *Nation's Restaurant News,* March 20, 1989, p. F-15.
16. 1990 National Restaurant Association Foodservice Industry Forecast, p. 37.
17. "Focus—College Feeding," p. F-16.
18. "Focus—College Feeding," p. F-16.
19. 1990 National Restaurant Association Foodservice Industry Forecast, p. 39.
20. "Health Care Foodservice Up-Close," *Nation's Restaurant News,* Career Paths Supplement, January 1988.
21. "Hospitals Try Franchising to Cut Costs, Add Services," *Wall Street Journal,* October 14, 1988, pp. B-1, B-9.
22. 1990 National Restaurant Association Foodservice Industry Forecast, p. 38.
23. Kass, p. 60.
24. "Last Words," *Restaurant Hospitality,* June 1990, p. 139.
25. "The High Cost of Starting a Restaurant," *Changing Times,* March 1990, p. 72.
26. Ronald Zemke and Dick Schaat, *The Service Edge* (New York: New American Library, 1989), p. 297.

Key Terms

areas of dominant influence (ADI)	limited-menu restaurant
cafeteria	luxury restaurant
ethnic restaurant	mega restaurant
full-menu restaurant	theme restaurant

Discussion Questions

1. What are the three most important food service facilities within the food industry segment called "Eating and Drinking Places"?

2. What characterizes a full-menu restaurant? a limited-menu restaurant?

3. The cafeteria industry is exploring what new concepts and directions?

4. What two major trends in food service have surfaced in recent years, and how have they benefited certain retail businesses?

5. What changes have been seen in the student food service market?

6. What are some positive trends in hospital food service?

7. Why do restaurants fail?

8. What are some strategies for building a successful restaurant?

9. Most restaurant sites fall into which four classifications?

10. What are some desirable characteristics any restaurant site should have?

Chapter Outline

Organizing for Success
    Guests
    Ambience
    Menu
        Basic Rules
        Menu Preferences
        Menu Categories
        Menu Design
    Menu Prices
Financial and Operational Controls
    Financial Controls
        Accounting Systems
    Operational Controls
        Budgeting
        Controlling Food Costs
        Controlling Labor Costs
        Controlling Beverage Costs
Chapter Summary

6 Restaurant Organization

In this chapter we will focus first on organizing a restaurant for success. We will discuss the importance of the guest, ambience, menu, and menu prices. Then we will describe financial and operational controls for restaurants, including menu planning, purchasing, receiving, storing and issuing, producing, serving, guest payment, and food cost analysis procedures. We will briefly consider labor costs (more material on this subject appears in Chapter 9). The chapter ends with a discussion of beverage control.

Organizing for Success

In order to attract guests and earn income, restaurant managers must have a broad base of skills. These include marketing (to bring guests in) and quality control and service (to satisfy them so they will want to return). Of course, having guests does not guarantee a profit. Restaurants have gone bankrupt even when running at capacity every night. Often, the difference between successful food service operations and unsucessful ones is that the successful ones are more organized. Well-organized restaurants are able to budget and control expenses so that they maximize profits. Even the success of non-profit or subsidized operations, such as school food programs, is measured in financial terms—in their cases, by their ability to minimize expenses and thus operate within their budget limitations.

All types of food service operations have the same mission—to prepare and serve food while staying within financial guidelines. Because their mission is the same, they all operate under similar principles of management and control.

Four elements crucial to the success of any restaurant are a restaurant's guests, ambience, menu, and menu prices.

Guests   Everything starts with the guest or consumer. Indeed, finding and holding on to this elusive creature is the most important factor in the success of any business. In the previous chapter, the discussion of starting a new restaurant centered on understanding where guests will come from and what needs they will have. With this understanding, you can determine the feasibility and optimal location of any food service operation. But a thorough knowledge of the guest tells us a good deal more than simply where to put the restaurant. Guests' wants and needs guide new restaurateurs in formulating menus, determining ambience, setting the level and style of service, and creating advertising and marketing plans.

The marketing research that goes into a feasibility study for a new restaurant is only the beginning. Guest research needs to be updated continually because we live in a dynamic society where markets change quickly. Continual research makes it possible not only to measure current guest preferences but discover trends—how those preferences are changing and how fast.

Restaurants with long, successful track records and loyal guests have sometimes lost their guests' allegiance virtually overnight. According to management consultants Albrecht and Zemke, guest loyalty "must be based on a continuously satisfying level of service."[1]

The key word is "continuously." It is not hard to find examples of restaurants that lost touch with their guests and either failed or fell under the control of new companies with new concepts. For example, Sambo's, a popular limited-menu chain for many years, derived its name and decor from the children's story "Little Black Sambo." The civil rights movement focused attention on the racial aspects of Sambo's concept, and the chain died a painful death. The Royal Castle hamburger chain started during the Depression, offering 24-hour service and five-cent hamburgers. Over the years, the units became too small, old-fashioned, and limited in their menu choices. Soon the land on which the 175 restaurants rested was worth more than the company, and the company was liquidated. Then there was Victoria Station. Here was an attractive concept—restaurants in the form of a cluster of railroad cars that served extraordinarily good roast beef and generous drinks at reasonable prices. But beef consumption began to decrease and the restaurant's concept became less popular. The owners tried many new concepts, one after the other, leaving customers guessing about what they might find on their next visit. Eventually, most customers went elsewhere.

Guest attitudes and desires change constantly. Years ago few people thought about nutrition or the environment. But a 1988 Gallup survey shows that there has been a dramatic change in our feelings about these subjects. Respondents were asked to identify amenities that they looked for in table-service restaurants. Exhibit 6.1 lists these amenities in order of popularity. The top two issues in this survey—smoking and nutrition—probably would have scarcely received mention 20 years ago. That is why modern managers regard market research as a continual process and why they look for new studies supplying new information about changing guest preferences.

A word of caution, however. The fact that a new trend appears to be taking hold or an old one losing ground is not a reason in itself to make dramatic changes in methods of operation. Few trends are universal. Different regions of the country and different countries have their own values, and what is true in California may be less true or not true at all in Vermont. Restaurateurs should use national surveys and studies only as guides. Whether they apply to your city and your restaurant can only be determined by asking your guests.

Exhibit 6.1 Table-Service Restaurant Amenities

Amenity	Percentage of Survey Respondents Interested in the Amenity
Separate smoking/no-smoking sections	78%
Nutritious menu items	76
Food or salad bar	71
Children's menu	67
On-premises baking	65
Seasonal menu features	62
Daily menu changes	60
Display cooking	53
Dessert display	52
Live entertainment	48

Source: National Restaurant Association Gallup Survey, 1988.

Ambience   In successful food service operations of all types, ambience plays a key role. The decor, lighting, furnishings, service methods, and other elements combine to create a feeling about or an identity for a restaurant—that is, they create the restaurant's ambience. Consider One Hudson Cafe, which is close to Wall Street in Lower Manhattan. The restaurant is named after its address and attracts a variety of stockbrokers, artists, and municipal officials who live or work in the area. Here is the way *Gourmet* magazine described the restaurant's ambience in an October 1988 review:

> One of the things that draws . . . crowds is the cafe's greenery. Southern exposure and large expanses of glass permit a veritable grove of braided ficus trees to thrive in the middle of the dining room. Bay laurels (harvested by the kitchen) climb along the front windows, and pots of herbs are usually found sunning nearby. There are often enough herbs on hand for every table to have its own pot of rosemary, savory, lemon thyme, or sweet myrtle. The room is set with comfortably separated tables and flawless white napery. Looming from the back wall is a grand Flemish tapestry from the late seventeenth century, with classically clothed figures and a cheerful border of garlands and fruit. One Hudson Cafe is among the rare restaurants in New York City that somehow persuade their customers to linger awhile and soak up the peaceful atmosphere, which is enhanced on Wednesday and Fridays by an unobtrusive classical guitarist.[2]

Clearly, One Hudson Place was designed to attract a specific type of clientele in a neighborhood where tall buildings and narrow streets close out nature.

A legendary industry story about designing the ambience to satisfy the clientele comes from the early days of McDonald's. Founder Ray Kroc decided to concentrate on reaching families with young children. Why? Research showed that this was a large and growing market segment. The research also showed that the children often cast the deciding vote on which restaurant a family visited. With that in mind, Kroc and his associates designed a restaurant that not only served food children would like, but served it in a setting that small children would feel comfortable in. Kroc ordered cameras mounted on three-foot-high tripods to photograph a prototype McDonald's restaurant. Looking at the restaurant through the eyes of a child made the necessity for some changes immediately evident. Counters, for example, were lowered so a child could order without having to strain or stand on tiptoe. Seats and tables were also lowered. The interior was accented with bright yellow and red—the same colors used on many toys at the time.

Benihana of Tokyo is another restaurant chain in which ambience played an important part in the success of the venture. Japanese immigrant Rocky Aoiki, the chain's founder, was a stickler for authentic detail. Not only did he train his chefs at a special school in Tokyo before bringing them to the United States, he imported wooden beams from Japan at great expense to create the atmosphere of an authentic Japanese inn. Many of Aoiki's advisors told him that this was an unnecessary expense since the same look could be produced with American materials, but Aoiki refused to compromise.

Restaurant designers today talk about "fusing the decor with the region." Colonial-style furnishings and fabrics are often used in New England inns. Nautical themes are popular at restaurants located in seaports, and Southwest native decor predominates in cities like Santa Fe, New Mexico. The Spanish Mediterranean style Addison Mizner developed for his buildings in Palm Beach, Florida, is still characteristic of that region.

The ambience of a restaurant's building often dictates the restaurant's concept. Many restaurants are housed in old warehouses (the Old Spaghetti Warehouse in Seattle, Washington, for example), historic railroad stations, and even former ocean liners (the *Queen Mary*, which is now docked permanently in Long Beach, California, has an excellent restaurant on board). In Europe, castles, country houses, and châteaus are favored locales for restaurants because of their distinctive character.

Menu   A restaurant's menu is much more than a list of items for sale. The menu helps define and explain what the restaurant is all about. It represents (or should represent) what the guests expect and want. And there is a more subtle dimension. The menu states (or should state) what the restaurant does best. Unfortunately, what a restaurant does best sometimes changes. This is often the case with independent restaurants. Cooking is a creative process; dishes conceived by one chef are not always as deftly executed by assistants and successors. This is one of the main reasons menus should and do change—so that the restaurants they represent can put their best foot forward.

Basic Rules. There are some basic rules that good restaurateurs follow when creating menus.

Give guests what they want. Offer your guests what they are looking for at your restaurant. If your restaurant emphasizes convenience and speed of service, then be certain that menu items that take a long time to prepare are not on the menu. If Italian specialties are what you promise, you must offer more then just spaghetti and lasagna.

Exhibit 6.2 Sample Standard Recipe

	Fish Fillet Amandine	**IX. MAIN DISHES—FISH 2**	
Yield:_____ **Size:**_____		**Yield: 60** **Size: 6 oz**	**Baking Temperature: 450°F** **Baking Time: 14–15 min**

Amount	Ingredients	Amount	Procedure
_____	Fish fillets, fresh or frozen 6 oz portion	22 1/2 lb	1. Defrost fillets if frozen fish is used. 2. Arrange defrosted or fresh fillets in single layers on greased sheet pans.
_____	Almonds, toasted, chopped or slivered	1 lb	3. To toast almonds: a. Spread on sheet pans. b. Place in 350°F oven until lightly toasted. *Approximate time:* 15 min
_____	Margarine or butter, softened	2 lb 8 oz	4. Add almonds, lemon juice, lemon peel, salt, and pepper to softened margarine or butter.
_____ _____ _____ _____ _____	Lemon juice Lemon peel, grated Salt Pepper, white Weight: Margarine-almond mixture	1/2 cup 2 3/4 oz 4 tbsp 1 tbsp 4 lb	5. Mix thoroughly. 6. Spread margarine mixture on fillets as uniformly as possible. *Amount per fillet:* #60 scoop 7. Bake at 450°F for approx. 15 min or until fish flakes when tested with fork. 8. Sprinkle lightly with chopped parsley or sprigs of parsley when served.

Use standard recipes. Standard recipes are formulas for producing a food or beverage item that specify ingredients, the required quantity of each ingredient, preparation procedures, portion size and portioning equipment, garnish, and any other information necessary to prepare the item (see Exhibit 6.2). Standard recipes are an essential part of quality control. Guests who come for your Dover sole *à la meunière* expect it to look and taste the same every time they come back for it.

Match the menu to the staff's abilities. Make certain that all of the items on the menu can be correctly prepared and served by your staff. Servers' abilities are especially important when the menu includes items that are prepared tableside.

Take equipment into account. Take into account the limitations of your kitchen and dining room equipment. Menu items that call for grilling should not be broiled. Grilled items do not taste the same as broiled items. Dishes that should have authentic wood-smoke flavors require a hickory or mesquite grill.

Provide variety and balance. Present a variety of items, colors, and textures in your menu. Much of any restaurant's business is repeat, especially at lunchtime. Daily or weekly specials ensure that there are always new

Exhibit 6.3   The Five Least Popular Menu Items by Region*

	New England	Mid-Atlantic	East North Central	West North Central	South Atlantic	East South Central	West South Central	Mountain	Pacific
1.	Enchiladas	Burritos	Enchiladas	Veal	Enchiladas	Wine	Hot tea	BBQ chicken	Spicy fried chicken
2.	Tacos	Enchiladas	Vegetable platter	Spicy fried chicken	Other Mexican	Omelets	Decaf Coffee	Veal	Coleslaw
3.	Other Mexican	Other Mexican	Iced tea	Heros/subs	Burritos	Veal	Cheese	Spicy fried chicken	Breakfast sandwich
4.	Burritos	Tacos	Boiled/ steamed/ raw seafood	Boiled/ steamed/ raw seafood	Tacos	Alcholic beverages	Soup	Breakfast sandwich	Iced tea
5.	Taco salad	Taco salad	Broiled/ baked/grilled seafood	Wine	Donuts/ sweet rolls	Hot tea	BLT/ club sandwich	Boiled/ steamed/ raw seafood	Pan pizza

*Relative to national average.

Source: NPD CREST.

choices for guests. Strive for balance so that foods complement each other or contrast nicely. Cream soups should not be followed by main courses with cream sauces. Some items should be heavy, others light. Since poultry and meat are white or brown, liven up their presentation with colorful vegetables.

Pay attention to the season. Food costs are higher and quality is lower when you use fresh fruit or vegetables that are out of season. Recipes calling for fresh ingredients that are not readily available should perhaps be dropped from the menu until the ingredients are in season again.

Keep nutrition in mind. Probably a certain number of your guests are committed to eating nutritious meals. Many of today's consumers try to eat a balanced diet. They may also be interested in reducing their intake of salt, fat, or sugar. Don't make that difficult to do in your restaurant.

Use food wisely. Strive for a menu that will produce profits. Carefully plan how to use perishable items and make full use of leftovers. Throwing food away is the same as throwing money away. Smart chefs use meat and vegetable scraps for stews and soups. Day-old bread can be used for stuffings and croutons. Good menu planners automatically think of daily specials that chefs can prepare using leftovers from the previous day's production.

Menu Preferences. Menu preferences vary significantly by region. Fortunately, there are studies available that assist restaurateurs in determining what their guests want. For example, the National Restaurant Association's 1989 CREST study listed the five least popular menu items by region and compared them to the national average (see Exhibit 6.3). Careful study of

Exhibit 6.3 reveals some interesting facts. Look at the West North Central part of the country. Veal, seafood, and wine—all items one would expect to find in sophisticated or upscale restaurants—rank among the least popular items. This part of the country clearly favors more modest establishments. This exhibit also shows that New England and the Mid-Atlantic states are tough markets for Mexican restaurants. All five of the least favorite items in these areas are Mexican foods! The South Atlantic is not much different in this regard: the top four most disliked items are Mexican.

Studies of what people like to eat and drink are available from many sources. Restaurant owners and managers need to be alert to all reports concerning restaurant and food trends. For example, at the end of 1989 the *Miami Herald* published a special section devoted to food trends in the eighties and nineties and listed "What's Hot" and "What's Cold." Among the new hot items, according to the *Herald*, were game (particularly venison), chicken, Eastern European food, and risotto. Among the foods losing popularity were blackened fish, which the *Herald* called "a no taste item that was only an excuse to drink beer to cool off the mouth." The *Herald* threw similar brickbats at wine coolers and mesquite.[3] A recent U.S. Department of Agriculture report showed that between 1985 and 1989 per capita consumption of red meat declined from 144 pounds to 135.4. And the *Wall Street Journal*, citing a report from the National Centers for Disease Control, said that U.S. consumption of distilled spirits (liquors and liqueurs) continues to decline. According to the article, the average

"All our vegetables are well done. It's a return to the old values."

Drawing by Weber; © 1988, The New Yorker Magazine, Inc.

American consumed only .85 gallons of distilled spirits in 1989, the lowest rate in 27 years.[4]

Menu Categories. There are two menu categories based on how the menu is scheduled: fixed menus and cycle menus. Menus can be further categorized as breakfast, lunch, dinner, or specialty menus.

Fixed menus. A fixed menu, also known as a static menu, is typically used for several months or longer before it is changed. Daily specials may be offered, but a set list of items forms the basic menu.

Fast-food operations are examples of restaurants with fixed menus. Fast-food restaurants can get away with offering the same menu items every day in part because the items they serve—typically hamburgers, chicken, pizza, or Mexican foods—appeal to a broad market. Many chain-operated full-service restaurants also feature fixed menus.

One of the principal advantages of a fixed menu is its simplicity. Operational procedures such as purchasing, staffing, and inventory control are straightforward and uncomplicated. Even the equipment requirements are minimal and less complex. But there are disadvantages. A fixed menu provides no variety and few options for coping with increased costs other than raising menu prices. One solution to these problems is to expand the fixed menu from time to time by adding new menu items on a temporary or permanent basis. Burger King's Bundles of Burgers and McDonald's Shamrock Shakes are both examples of temporary items. Both chains added salads and desserts on a permanent basis to provide more variety and achieve a higher average check per customer.

As mentioned earlier, some restaurants, such as independent family restaurants, may offer daily specials to put a little variety in their fixed menus. The specials are usually printed on a separate sheet and inserted into the regular menu. Adding daily specials to an otherwise fixed menu may satisfy a broader market by attracting new guests seeking the restaurant's specialties as well as keeping regulars who occasionally want to try something different.

Cycle menus. A cycle menu is a menu that changes every day for a certain number of days before the cycle is repeated. Modern desktop publishing using personal computers has made changing menus easy and inexpensive compared to a few years ago, when any major change required a costly reprinting job.

Institutional food service operations, and commercial operations that are likely to serve guests for an extended period of time, use cycle menus. A cruise ship where guests typically stay for a week needs a seven-day cycle menu so that different menus can be offered each day. Menus can be numbered and may run from #1 to #7 before starting with #1 again. Hospitals where patients are sometimes confined for long periods sometimes use longer cycles. Nursing homes may use a very long cycle menu.

Specialty menus. Specialty menus differ from typical breakfast, lunch, and dinner menus. They are usually designed for holidays and other special events or for specific guest groups. Most restaurants offer a specialty menu featuring turkey and ham at Thanksgiving and Christmas, for

Exhibit 6.4 Sample Restaurant Menu

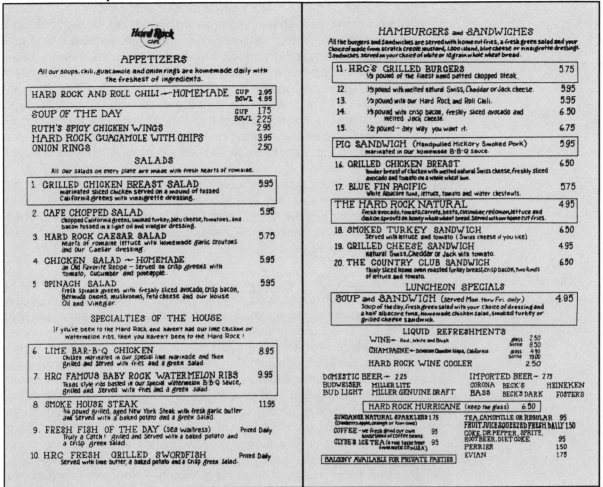

This menu's hand-lettering is in keeping with the restaurant's informal personality. Courtesy of the Hard Rock Café, Chicago, Illinois. Lettering by B. Perry White.

example. Catered events such as birthdays, weddings, bar mitzvahs, and other social occasions may call for specialty menus. In some cases, specialty banquet menus may be created. There are many other kinds of specialty menus used by restaurants, such as children's, early-bird, beverage, senior citizens', dessert, and take-out menus.

Specialty menus are marketing tools—extra incentives to bring patrons in. Their only limit is the menu planner's imagination.

Menu Design. Like a brochure for a hotel, a menu is a sales tool and motivational device for a restaurant. A menu's design can affect what guests order and how much they spend. The paper, colors, artwork, and copy all can influence guest decisions, while helping establish a restaurant's ambience or image. William Doerfler, considered the leader in menu design by many of the best-known restaurateurs in America, feels that while menus should not mislead or misidentify the origin and presentation of an item, imaginative embellishment in menu descriptions is often appropriate. "French onion soup may be an eternal favorite of the

American public, but its description is not immutable. Why not designate it as 'tureen of French onion soup with toasted croutons'?"[5]

Other menu designers stress the importance of tying in the look and language of the menu with the restaurant's concept (see Exhibit 6.4). Tutto Bene, a northern Italian restaurant in San Francisco, uses menu covers inspired by the three huge pastel murals on its back wall.[6] Guaymas, a Mexican seafood restaurant in Tiburon, California, uses durable, leather-like synthetic paper for the menu cover and paper resembling tortilla chips for the insert containing the menu items and wine list. The insert is preserved with book lacquer. According to Judi Radice, the design director of Spectrum Foods in San Francisco, this menu fits in well with the concept and look of the restaurant.[7]

Remember that when guests sit down at a restaurant table, there is no question about whether they are going to buy something; the question is how much they are going to spend. Blackboards, tent cards, well-trained food servers, and—most important—a well-designed menu can all influence that decision and, ultimately, affect the restaurant's bottom line.

Menu Prices

The goal in establishing menu prices is to bring in sufficient revenue to cover operating costs and overhead, and to provide a reasonable return on the owner's (or owners') investment. In other words, price is related to costs and investment. Clearly, a restaurant with a low investment and low operating costs should be able to charge less than one with high costs and a larger investment. Fast-food restaurants use computer-designed standard facilities and specialized equipment to prepare their menu items. The result is a relatively low investment cost plus low operating costs since the menu and the equipment are designed with unskilled labor and a limited menu in mind. Other operating costs are also kept to a minimum because nothing is added to the system that is not absolutely necessary for the smooth functioning of the unit. Therefore, prices in fast-food restaurants can be kept low.

On the other hand, restaurants such as Nikolai's Roof, on the top floor of the Atlanta Hilton, are designed to offer extraordinary dining. These restaurants have lavish appointments, are located on valuable real estate, and provide luxury service with a classically oriented menu requiring highly skilled chefs, cooks, dining room captains, and servers. Luxury restaurants charge high prices to cover their high food costs, operating costs, and overhead. They can do this because their guests are willing to pay for their fine-dining experience.

There are a number of mathematical models and other methods that are used to set menu prices. Most of them involve a markup over food and/or labor costs. Whatever method is used, there are some basic questions to ask after pricing menu items:

- Are these prices appropriate for my type of operation? Obviously cafeterias should be able to charge less than table-service restaurants for the same items.

- Will my guests feel that I am offering a good price/value relationship? In other words, will they feel they're getting a good deal for their dollars?

- Are my prices competitive? What do similar restaurants in this same locale charge?

"We use the cheapest ingredients and pass the savings on to you."

Drawing by Weber; © 1988, The New Yorker Magazine, Inc.

- Do these prices deliver a fair profit? Profit, of course, depends on many factors, but, generally, people who invest in restaurants expect to be able to generate enough profit to pay back their original investment in three to five years. After that, since restaurants are considered risky investments, the return should be higher than the same funds could earn in a safer investment, such as a bank certificate of deposit.

Financial and Operational Controls

Control is one of management's fundamental responsibilities. In Chapter 4, we pointed out that in hotels effective control is a result of establishing standards based on the needs of guests and the goals of the business. This principle holds true for restaurants and other food service operations. In this respect, there is little difference between fine-dining restaurants, fast-food outlets, and even institutional food service operations. Managers must establish standards for financial performance, operations, and quality control. Without standards, there can be no real management, only organized confusion.

Financial Controls   Financial controls are tools managers use to measure the worth of the business and its level of sales, costs, and profitability. They include such documents as balance sheets and statements of income. Managers use an accounting system to gather the financial information that makes control possible.

Accounting Systems. An accounting system that provides usable and sufficient information for management decisions is the basis for sound financial control. One such accounting system is the *Uniform System of Accounts for Restaurants.* The system in this manual is similar to the *Uniform System of Accounts for Hotels* in that it establishes categories of revenues and expenses, as well as formats for financial statements. The advantages, too, are similar. The *Uniform System of Accounts for Restaurants* provides a common language for the industry, so operators can compare the performance of their restaurant with other restaurants in the same chain, with similar establishments in different chains, or with industry performance as a whole.

Within the *Uniform System of Accounts for Restaurants,* there are two important components that need to be understood: the balance sheet and the statement of income.

The balance sheet. A restaurant's balance sheet shows the restaurant's financial condition on a given day. It is similar in many ways to a hotel's balance sheet (in fact, to any business's balance sheet); but there are differences.

For example, although many restaurants accept credit cards as well as cash, they are, in fact, cash businesses since the credit card companies rapidly redeem the charges. Therefore, unlike many other kinds of businesses, restaurants do not have high levels of accounts receivable—that is, money due them from guests. And since restaurants deal mostly with perishable products that are delivered frequently, inventory levels are relatively low. Suppliers usually extend credit to regular customers, so a restaurant's need for cash to pay for inventory tends to be less acute than that of other businesses. Indeed, cash taken in on any given day can be used immediately to pay for purchases.

The statement of income. A statement of income shows the results of operations—the sales, expenses, and net income of a business—for a stated period of time. Whereas a hotel has a number of services for sale, a restaurant basically sells only food and, in some cases, alcoholic beverages. Hence the statement of income is uncomplicated and relatively easy to understand.

Exhibit 6.5 shows an income statement for the fictional Brandywine Restaurant. Note the division of sales into "food" and "beverage" sales. (Food sales include sales of non-alcoholic beverages.) The cost of sales is also divided into "food" and "beverage" categories, representing the cost of the food and beverages sold to guests. "Other income" includes income derived from service charges, cover and minimum charges, banquet room rentals, and gift and sundry shop sales. Although this other income can be profitable, it is not very significant in food service operations. "Controllable expenses" relate to the entire operation, with "payroll" the largest single controllable expense.

"Occupation costs" relate to the financial structure of the restaurant. The levels of these expenses do not vary with sales, as operating expenses do—with the exception of rent on the land or building(s), which may

Exhibit 6.5   Sample Statement of Income

Brandywine Restaurant Income Statement Month Ended January 31, 19XX		
Sales	Amount ($)	Percent
Food	533,250	71.9
Beverages	208,500	28.1
Total Food and Beverage Sales	741,750	100.0
Cost of Sales		
Food	217,033	40.7
Beverages	58,172	27.9
Total Cost of Sales	275,205	37.1
Gross Profit		
Food	316,217	59.3
Beverages	150,328	72.1
Total Gross Profit	466,545	62.9
Other Income	8,250	1.1
Total Income	474,795	64.0
Controllable Expenses		
Payroll	203,981	27.5
Employee Benefits	35,604	4.8
Direct Operating Expenses	48,214	6.5
Music and Entertainment	6,676	0.9
Advertising and Promotion	14,093	1.9
Utilities	18,544	2.5
Administrative and General	40,055	5.4
Repairs and Maintenance	12,610	1.7
Total Controllable Expenses	379,777	51.2
Profit Before Occupation Costs	95,018	12.8
Occupation Costs		
Rent, Property Taxes and Insurance	35,604	4.8
Interest	6,676	0.9
Depreciation	17,060	2.3
	59,340	8.0
Net Income Before Tax	41,612	5.6

contain a percentage clause related to sales. For example, the rent may be $20,000 a year plus 2% of gross sales.

Operational Controls

Budgeting. Budgeting—the forecasting of revenues, expenses, and profits—is another tool management must use to track actual performance and make necessary adjustments. Many chain restaurants use telephone/computer hookups to collect sales figures on a daily basis. This process is called "polling." Management then compares actual sales with forecasted sales and takes appropriate action. If sales are down, management can increase advertising or change the advertising campaign. Without standards and budgeting procedures, operators can (and do) allow difficult situations to develop

Exhibit 6.6   Prime Costs—Ratio to Sales

	Full-Menu Table Service	Limited-Menu Table Service	Limited-Menu No Table Service	Cafeteria
Cost of Food Sold[1]	29.5%	28.3%	31.1%	36.9%
Payroll[2]	26.9	28.9	23.5	25.4
Employee Benefits[2]	2.6	4.5	3.1	4.1

[1]Weighted average ratio to food sales.
[2]Weighted average ratio to total sales (food, beverage, other).

Source: National Restaurant Association and Laventhol & Horwath, *Restaurant Industry Operations Report 1989.*

past the point where anything can be done about them and financial disaster becomes almost a certainty.

Many management experts feel that budgeting for the first year of operation for any food service enterprise is as much an art as a science. The reason, of course, is that the venture is new—there are no sales history records on which to base forecasts. That means that estimates of the number of guests to expect and the expenses that are likely to be incurred ought to be made by persons with experience or at least a solid understanding of what goals are reasonable in terms of revenues and costs. Once the business has been running for a year or more and has a track record, the forecaster's work becomes easier.

Since food is the primary tangible item for sale in a restaurant, the procedures related to menu planning, the acquisition of food products, and the processing of food through storage, production, and service are important elements of a restaurant's control system. Equally important is control over labor costs. The cost of food sold plus payroll cost and employee benefits (such as paid vacation, sick leave, employee meals, and bonuses), constitute the largest costs of operation. Together they are known as prime costs, representing approximately 60 percent of sales. A survey of prime-cost levels for different types of food service operations is presented in Exhibit 6.6. While all expenses must be controlled, prime costs are management's major concern.

Controlling Food Costs. Food cost is defined as the cost of food used in the production of a menu item. To control food costs, most restaurants use a system of control points that are linked in a cycle similar to the one shown in Exhibit 6.7. A problem anywhere in the food cost control cycle can weaken the operation's control over food costs. Let's take a closer look at each of the control points.

Menu planning. Once a restaurant is in operation, ongoing market research is needed to update the existing menu or develop a new one. Such research includes periodic analyses of menu items sold. The computerized point-of-sale (POS) systems available today make this analysis easy. Sales of menu items can be tracked by meal period or, if necessary, by the hour. This information can guide the menu planner in developing a menu guests

Exhibit 6.7 Food Cost Control Cycle

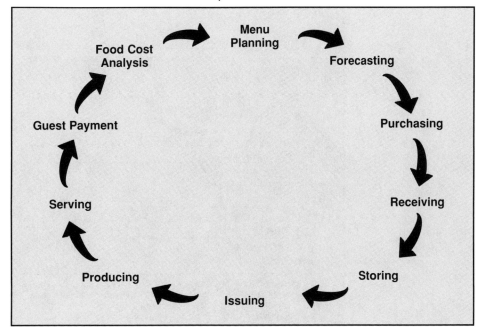

will like and can help him or her keep food costs down as well. With such an analysis in hand, the planner can remove menu items that are not selling and replace them with more popular ones, while keeping in mind that each menu item provides a different contribution margin. (Contribution margin is the menu item's selling price minus the cost of the food that went into preparing the item.) Trying to achieve an optimal mix of popular and profitable menu items is referred to as menu engineering.

The Boston Consulting Group did a study that placed all menu items into a chart consisting of four sections. Items were classified as "stars," "plowhorses," "puzzles," or "dogs." Stars are popular menu items with a high contribution margin. Plowhorses are popular items with a low contribution margin. Puzzles are items that are low in popularity but have a high contribution margin, while dogs are unpopular items with a low contribution margin. The idea of menu engineering is to feature the stars, include but not highlight the plowhorses, keep a few puzzles on the menu and creatively merchandise them, and eliminate the dogs if possible.[8] Such a finely tuned menu means that an operation orders and prepares only what it truly needs, which cuts down on unnecessary food costs and waste through spoilage.

Forecasting. Once the menu is fixed and a sales pattern is established, management should forecast total expected business by meal period, as well as by menu item, in order to determine purchasing needs and production planning. Accurate forecasting keeps food costs down because food is not purchased only to be left sitting in a storeroom, perhaps to spoil before it is needed.

Purchasing. In any food service operation, the goal in purchasing is to keep food costs down by obtaining the right product for the best

Exhibit 6.8 Sample Purchase Specification Format

```
                    _____
                       (name of food and beverage operation)

1.  Product name:_____

2.  Product used for:
    ┌──────────────────────────────────────────────────────────────────────┐
    │ Clearly  indicate product use (such as olive garnish for beverage, hamburger patty or grill-fry for │
    │ sandwich, etc.)                                                        │
    └──────────────────────────────────────────────────────────────────────┘

3.  Product general description:
    ┌──────────────────────────────────────────────────────────────────────┐
    │ Provide general quality information about desired product. For example, "Iceberg lettuce: heads to │
    │ be green and firm without spoilage, excessive dirt, or damage. No more than 10 outer leaves. Packed │
    │ 24 heads per case."                                                    │
    └──────────────────────────────────────────────────────────────────────┘

4.  Detailed description:
    ┌──────────────────────────────────────────────────────────────────────┐
    │ Purchaser should state other factors that help to clearly identify desired product. Examples of │
    │ specific factors, which vary by product being described, may include:  │
    │                                                                        │
    │  • Geographic origin        • Grade              • Density             │
    │  • Variety                  • Product size       • Specific gravity    │
    │  • Type                     • Portion size       • Container size      │
    │  • Style                    • Brand name         • Edible yield, trim   │
    └──────────────────────────────────────────────────────────────────────┘

5.  Product test procedures:
    ┌──────────────────────────────────────────────────────────────────────┐
    │ Test procedures can occur at the time the product is received and/or after the product is pre- │
    │ pared/used. For example, products that should be at a refrigerated temperature upon delivery can │
    │ be tested with a thermometer. Portion-cut meat patties can be randomly weighed. Lettuce packed │
    │ 24 heads per case can be counted.                                      │
    └──────────────────────────────────────────────────────────────────────┘

6.  Special instructions and requirements:
    ┌──────────────────────────────────────────────────────────────────────┐
    │ Any additional information needed to clearly indicate quality expectations can be included here. │
    │ Examples include bidding procedures, if applicable, labeling and/or packaging requirements, and │
    │ special delivery and service requirements.                             │
    └──────────────────────────────────────────────────────────────────────┘
```

Source: Adapted from Jack D. Ninemeier, *Purchasing, Receiving, and Storage: A Systems Manual for Restaurants, Hotels and Clubs* (Boston: CBI, 1983), p. 60.

price. To accomplish this, purchase specifications must be developed for all food items ordered, so that bids based on those specifications can be obtained from suppliers. A purchase specification is a detailed description of a food item for ordering purposes (see Exhibit 6.8). The description might include size by weight ("3 lb. chicken") or by dimension ("#2 can"); grade ("Rib of Beef—USDA Prime" or "Peaches—Fancy"); and packaging ("Iceberg lettuce—24 count" or "Eggs—30 dozen").

Lendal H. Kotschevar, author of *Management by Menu* and other food service industry texts, writes that most food specifications should include the following:

• Name of the item

• Grade of the item, brand, or other quality information

- Packaging method, package size, and special requirements

- Basis for price—by the pound, case, piece, or dozen

- Miscellaneous factors required to get the right item, such as the number of days beef should be aged, the region in which the item is produced, and the requirement that all items be inspected for wholesomeness[9]

Purchase specifications enable the purchaser to communicate to the supplier an exact description of what is needed to meet the restaurant's standards. Veteran operators are able to establish these specifications based on need and personal experience. Beginners and others who would like assistance can turn to sources such as the National Association of Meat Purveyors in Chicago, which publishes the "Meat Buyers Guide to Portion Control Meat Cuts" and the "Meat Buyers Guide to Standardized Meat Cuts." The U.S. Department of Agriculture offers a variety of helpful publications, including the *Agriculture Handbook* (#341), covering the purchase of produce, milk, and fresh and processed food products.

Once purchase specifications are developed, the next task is determining quantities of items to be purchased. As explained earlier, the best way to accomplish this is to forecast the number of guests expected and identify the menu items they are most likely to order. Delivery schedules also play a part in determining how much to order. Delivery schedules depend in part on the restaurant's location in relation to its suppliers; the greater the distance, the costlier the deliveries. Many restaurants order large quantities of what items they can stock up on (such as non-perishable items) so less frequent deliveries are needed. Many restaurants like to receive fresh fish and produce daily; meats, twice weekly; canned and frozen items, weekly or bi-weekly; and non-perishable items, such as napkins or sugar packets, quarterly or even semiannually. The level of inventory already on hand is another obvious factor in determining how much to order. Computer technology makes it easier to track inventory levels closely and makes rate-of-consumption information on individual items readily available.

Recent years have seen a major trend developing in food purchasing—not unlike the revolution that overtook home shopping when supermarkets replaced traditional grocery stores. The new concept is known as one-stop purchasing. Some food distributors have broadened and expanded their product lines so that it is now possible to find one supplier who sells everything from produce and dairy products to fresh meat and poultry to non-food supplies and even kitchen equipment. One-stop purchasing helps food service operations streamline their ordering, receiving, and accounting procedures.

Receiving. Acceptable receiving procedures mandate that the people receiving the food items clearly understand the food specifications adopted by the restaurant. Receiving clerks help keep food costs down by verifying that:

- The items delivered are the ones ordered and correspond to the amount on the supplier's invoice

- The quoted price and the invoice price are the same

- The quality and size of the items delivered match the restaurant's specifications

In addition, receiving clerks handle initial processing of invoices and deliver the food to the kitchen or to storage areas. Some operators favor "blind receiving" systems in which suppliers give the receiving clerk a list of items being delivered but not the quantities or weights. This forces the clerk to count or weigh the incoming products and record his or her findings on the invoice. Later these figures are compared with (1) the supplier's invoice received by the accounting office, and (2) the restaurant's purchase order.

In designing the interior of any food service operation it is important to make sure there is sufficient space in the receiving area to accomplish receiving tasks. Clerks must check large shipments on a random basis for quality and count. Items that do not meet the restaurant's standards are generally returned and a credit is recorded on the invoice. Those items that are acceptable are placed in storage, ready to be used as needed.

Controlling the receiving process is an important part of keeping food costs down because receiving is an area in which dishonest employees and/or suppliers can take advantage of employers. For example, suppliers may deliver a lower-grade product than ordered, with the hope that it will pass unnoticed; or use extra packing material to increase the weight of goods delivered.

Storing. Food storage facilities consist of dry storerooms, refrigerators, and freezers. Ideally, food storage areas should:

- Have adequate capacity

- Be close to receiving and food preparation areas

- Have suitable temperature and humidity levels

- Be secure from unauthorized personnel

- Be protected from vermin and insects

In addition, careful consideration should be given to storage shelves and the arrangement of items within the storage facility. Obviously, the items used most frequently should be stored near the entrance. Sometimes goods are stored on shelves by groups and then alphabetically within those groups.

A standard inventory system of first-in, first-out (FIFO) is almost always adopted. With this system, the older products (those received first) are stored in front so that they will be the first to be used, and the newer shipments are stored behind them so that they will be used later. Proper storage reduces spoilage and waste.

Issuing. Formal procedures for getting food from storage to production or service areas are an essential part of any control system. The purpose of such procedures is to keep track of inventory usage, making sure only authorized employees take food from storage.

In some instances, a small amount of food goes directly from the receiving area to the kitchen or dining room, bypassing the issuing system used to requisition food from storage areas. This is known as a direct purchase. Most direct purchases consist of items that will be used that day, such as fresh baked goods and fresh fish. Food service operations are able to calculate their daily food costs by adding together direct purchases and storeroom issues.

The bulk of the inventory received in each shipment goes to various storage areas. Items from storage are issued using a requisition system. A requisition form indicates the person who ordered the items and the type, amount, and price of each item. Sometimes the area the items are going to—for example, the pantry or kitchen range area—is identified. Although many operations calculate the cost of food requisitioned by hand, the trend is toward computerized systems that provide a faster method of pricing and tabulating the total value of the requisitions. Some operators track food by categories such as meat, fish, fresh produce, or staples. This enhances control by showing how the restaurant uses specific food categories and, within each category, specific food items.

Modern food service operations with relatively uncomplicated menus have been the first to adopt computerized issuing. For computerized issuing to work, standard recipes must be used. When food is requisitioned for a specific menu item, the computer determines the quantity to be issued based on the standard recipe. Computerized issuing systems work best in hospitals, schools, and other institutional food service operations which prepare large numbers of the same types of meals. Few hotels—with their many different restaurant concepts and menus—have adopted the system. But as new software becomes available this technology is expected to spread.

Producing. Standard recipes are essential in controlling food costs. With a standard recipe, managers can figure out exactly how much it should cost to produce each menu item. As a result, managers have something to compare actual costs with, and can take into consideration the cost of producing menu items when setting menu prices. Standard recipes are also important in controlling labor costs, since employees using such recipes require less training and supervision.

Standard recipes play a major role in guest satisfaction. By using standard recipes, operators are able to provide consistency in quality and quantity no matter who is in the kitchen. Standard recipes enable restaurants to ensure that every time a repeat guest orders a particular item, he or she will receive the same product and portion.

Serving. If service is not friendly and efficient, all other efforts in the control cycle are in vain because most guests will stop going to a restaurant where they receive poor service. A well-trained staff that knows the menu and has good people skills can help overcome production problems. However, if servers are not attentive to the needs of guests, the best efforts of the chef and others in the kitchen will not be enough to produce a satisfactory experience. It is a mistake to assume that operations that do not offer table service need not be concerned with their level of service. Even

Servers have a tremendous impact on the guests' experience—and on the bottom line.

the food servers in a cafeteria serving line help set the mood for guests and can affect the bottom line more than the quality of the food.

Guest payment. Obviously, a restaurant can't recoup its food costs if guest payments are not collected. There is no one universal payment system—systems vary from operation to operation. Here are some of the ways guest payment can be settled:

- The guest pays a cashier who tabulates the food order (as in a cafeteria).

- The guest pays an order taker/cashier who rings up the order on a cash register before the food is delivered (as in fast-food operations.)

- The server writes the order and prices on a guest check, or the order is machine-printed and priced on a guest check. The check is then settled in one of the following ways: (1) the guest pays the cashier; (2) the guest pays the server, who pays the cashier; or (3) the guest pays the server, who maintains a bank.

The goal of any cash control system is to ensure that what comes out of the kitchen is in fact served to the guest and recorded as a sale. In those establishments where the server takes the guest's order, the server writes the order on a guest check. The original is kept for presentation to the guest for payment at the end of the meal, and will eventually be placed in the cash register. A duplicate of the check is carried to the kitchen so that production personnel know what to prepare. Modern computerized point-of-sale systems can help servers perform this process faster and with

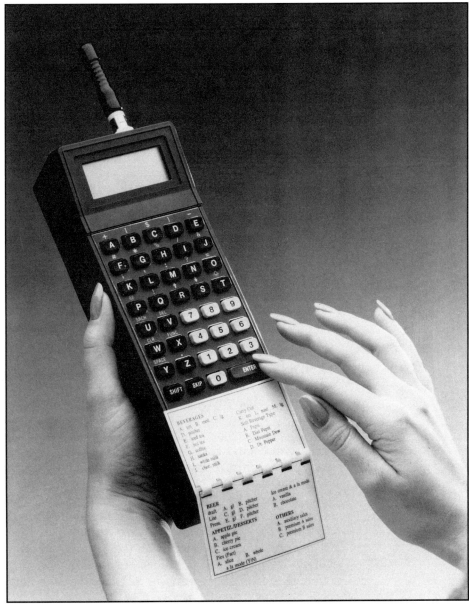

Hand-held server terminals not only speed ordering but help with control. Courtesy of Norand Corporation, Cedar Rapids, Iowa.

less legwork. Servers input the guest's order into a hand-held or stationary point-of-sale terminal in the dining room. The order is electronically transmitted to the kitchen where it is (1) shown on a kitchen video display monitor and/or (2) printed by a small work station printer. Whether guest checks are recorded manually or by computer, control records (i.e., the machine data, the guest check, and the duplicate guest check) are established that can be reconciled at the end of the meal.

Food cost analysis. A common statistic used throughout the food service industry is the food cost percentage. This number represents the cost of food sold to guests in a given period (the month of June, for example), divided by food sales for the same period.

To reach the cost of food sold, one must deduct meals that are consumed but not sold to guests, such as employee meals and complimentary meals to guests. The cost of food sold is based on beginning and closing inventories and food purchases for the period between the two inventories, minus free meals. The following figures from June illustrate how this works:

Beginning Inventory	$20,000
Add Food Purchases	+ 15,000
Total	$35,000
Deduct Closing Inventory	− 4,000
Cost of Food Consumed	$31,000
Deduct Employee meals ($1,500)	
and Complimentary meals ($500)	− 2,000
Cost of Food Sold	$29,000

Assume food sales for June were $100,000. To compute the food cost percentage, the formula is:

$$\frac{\$29,000 \text{ (cost of food sold)}}{\$100,000 \text{ (food sales)}} = .29 \times 100 = 29\%$$

In this example, 29% reflects the actual cost of food sold (expressed as a percentage of food sales) during June. This percentage has little value unless it can be compared to a goal or an acceptable food cost percentage range established by management.

How do managers come up with a food cost goal or an acceptable range within which food costs should fall? Often by using a standard cost system based on standard recipes. Since each standard recipe is an exact formula for making X number of menu items, the exact or standard cost of preparing a menu item can be computed. Managers can total the standard costs for all the menu items sold during June, divide this figure by the total menu item sales for June, multiply by 100, and come up with the standard food cost percentage—which would match the actual food cost percentage for June if everything worked exactly as it should have. Assuming the manager assessed standard food costs in June at $27,000, the standard food cost percentage would be calculated as follows:

$$\frac{\$27,000 \text{ (standard food costs)}}{\$100,000 \text{ (food sales)}} = .27 \times 100 = 27\%$$

In this case, the standard food cost percentage for June is 27%. The actual food cost percentage for June was 29%—2% higher than the standard. Since a standard food cost represents the ideal cost that management can expect if everything goes exactly as planned, the actual food cost percentage is almost always higher than the standard food cost percentage. Management at each property must determine an acceptable limit for actual food costs. One property may set a limit of 7% over standard food cost, for example, which means if the standard food cost percentage for a period of time is 22%, an actual food cost percentage of 29% or below is acceptable.

Each individual menu item has a standard food cost percentage and, of course, some menu items have a higher food cost percentage than others.

Exhibit 6.9   Breakdown of Payroll by Function

	Full-Menu Table Service	Limited-Menu Table Service
Service	34.3%	36.3%
Preparation	34.0	27.8
Sanitation	6.8	6.0
Administrative & General	19.6	25.0
Other	5.3	4.9
Total Payroll	100%	100%

Source: National Restaurant Association and Laventhol & Horwath, *Restaurant Industry Operations Report 1989.*

However, it is unwise to decide whether to keep an item on the menu or add a new one by looking at the item's food cost percentage alone. The following comparison between two menu items shows why:

	Lamb Chops	Deluxe Omelet
Menu Price	$18.00	$8.00
Food Cost %	52.8%	25%
Gross Profit	$8.50	$6.00

The deluxe omelet has a lower food cost percentage, which is desirable, but the lamb chops provide a higher gross profit. Obviously, it's preferable to sell the lamb chops, despite the higher costs associated with them, because their gross profit gives the operation $2.50 more ($8.50 − $6.00) to cover other costs and add to profits.

Controlling Labor Costs. The cost of payroll and employee benefits is about 30 percent of sales for most of the food service industry. This is a high figure when you consider that the industry has more entry-level and minimum-wage employees than most other industries. The fact is that food service is highly labor-intensive and quality service on any level demands that employees be well trained, efficient, and productive. Fast-food restaurants and cafeterias have lower payroll costs primarily because of their method of service and, in the case of fast-food restaurants, their limited menu and production-line system of food preparation. The percentage of total payroll spent on service is significant for restaurants with table service (see Exhibit 6.9).

Commercial food service establishments have a unique problem in controlling payroll. The amount of money an operation must allocate to payroll depends on two factors: (1) the rates of pay for employees, and (2) the time required to do a given job—that is, productivity. While payroll costs escalate every year, productivity does not. Indeed, we prepare and serve food today, in many cases, with the same type of equipment and in the same way as did restaurateurs 50 years ago. As a result, the industry, for the most part, has responded to higher payroll costs by raising menu prices rather than employee productivity, adhering to the conventional wisdom that you cannot raise productivity when you are dealing with low-paid, inexperienced personnel. However, as we shall see in Chapter 9, there is a new school of managers that feels you get what you pay for and that it is possible to increase productivity by paying higher wages to more skilled and responsible workers.

However, you can't raise productivity if there aren't enough guests in the restaurant. Even the hardest-working employees can't be productive if there is no one to serve. And the best managers can only trim payroll costs to a certain point because a minimum number of employees always has to be on hand when a restaurant opens, even when business is projected to be terrible. Therefore, keeping payroll costs in line depends in part on having a concept and menu that appeal to the target market and having a marketing program strong enough to keep guest demand high.

Controlling Beverage Costs. The drinking of fermented beverages made from fruits, grains, and other substances is a practice that predates recorded history. Alcohol, with its perceived benefits and dangers, has long been a part of civilization. But in recent years the dangers of the excessive use of alcohol have gained greater recognition in the United States and elsewhere, and consumption of all kinds of fermented and distilled spirits has dropped dramatically.

Nevertheless, wine, malt beverages (beer, ale, stout), and distilled spirits—the major categories of alcoholic beverages—are still an important part of restaurant revenue. Alcoholic beverages account for approximately 22 percent of restaurant sales. These sales are highly profitable because of the high markup on beverages. In fine restaurants a markup of 100% for a bottle of inexpensive wine is not unusual. Most drinks are easy to pour or mix, and the labor and beverage costs combined represent a small part of the sales price.

Purchasing alcoholic beverages is relatively uncomplicated compared to purchasing food. Purchase specifications are limited to brand (Dewars White Label scotch, Budweiser beer, Robert Mondavi wine); size (liters, quarts, fifths, kegs); and, in the case of wine, vintages. Competitive bidding is usually not necessary. Beverage prices are set by some states, known as monopoly or control states, and beverage purchases can be made only from state-owned stores. Most states are license states. In these, operators can buy from private wholesalers licensed by the state. Even in these states, state laws are typically designed to limit price wars, and prices do not vary a great deal among wholesalers. Most license states publish each month a master list of wholesalers in the state, the beverages they carry, and the prices they charge.

Receiving is also straightforward. For example, weighing or checking for wholesomeness is not necessary. The receiving clerk simply verifies that what was ordered—brand, size, amount, and vintage—is what has been delivered and billed on the invoice.

Secure storage is of prime importance. Access to beverage storage areas must be limited to authorized personnel. All items should be grouped by brand. Wine bottles should be stored on their side or bottom-up to keep the cork moist. For the same reason, temperature control during storage is crucial. The ideal storage temperature for red wines is 65°F (18.3°C), and for white wines 45°F to 50°F (7.2°C to 10°C).

Issuing is generally done by requisition. If there is more than one bar, separate requisitions are written by personnel at each bar. Some operations stamp their liquor bottles with their name or logo to prevent unscrupulous bartenders from bringing in their own bottles, pouring drinks from them, and pocketing the money.

In most operations, a perpetual inventory of beverage items is maintained either manually or by computer. A perpetual inventory is a record that shows what should be on hand in the storeroom at any one time. It is compiled from daily invoices and requisitions by adding each day's purchases and subtracting each day's issues. Of course, inventory levels should be checked by a physical count on a regular basis, usually monthly. The perpetual inventory system is particularly valuable in deciding purchasing levels since it tracks inventory usage on a daily, weekly, and monthly basis.

Control over individual drink sales may take one or more forms. Many operators have employed automated systems with electronic or mechanical devices attached to each bottle that record every drink poured. The advantages are obvious. The manager or owner can easily determine how many drinks have been sold and thus what the receipts should be. The system reduces loss from spillage and overpouring and prevents a bartender from underpouring or offering complimentary drinks to friends. The disadvantage of an automated system is that it eliminates the personal touch of the bartender handling bottles and providing a theatrical presentation.

Managers can control the amount of beverages on hand at a bar by establishing a "par." A bar's par is the amount of each type of beverage that managers want to be available behind the bar. A bar's par is based largely on expected consumption. Levels are set high enough so that the bar will not run out of an item during a bartender's shift, but not so high that theft is encouraged. At the end of each shift, empty bottles are replaced so that the bar's beverage stock is at par for the next shift.

Beverage control is crucial to running any establishment that sells beverages to guests. Product consistency and the threat of theft are key areas of concern. Only through proper controls can these concerns be addressed and guest satisfaction and profitability be ensured.

Chapter Summary

Food service operations that are organized for success focus on their guests. Since preferences and tastes constantly change, a restaurant's management team needs to keep track of national trends and conduct ongoing research of its own guests to make sure that the restaurant's concept and menu reflect current guest preferences.

A restaurant's ambience is also important. Decor, lighting, furnishings, and other features should all be a natural extension of a restaurant's concept.

A third important element of a successful restaurant is its menu. A good menu offers guests what they want; is based on standard recipes that can be prepared and served by the staff of the establishment; takes into account equipment limitations; and lists a variety of items. Menus can be categorized as either fixed menus or cycle menus. Menus can be further categorized as breakfast, lunch, dinner, or specialty menus. It should be remembered that the menu is primarily a sales tool and should be constructed and presented with that in mind.

Pricing menu items correctly is also a key element of being organized for success. Menu prices are related to costs and investment. Basic considerations when setting menu prices include the type of operation, the guests' perception of the price/value relationship, the competition, and the desired level of profit.

Sound financial management is achieved through efficient budgeting, using a system such as the *Uniform System of Accounts for Restaurants*. Components of this system include a balance sheet and a statement of income.

A successful operation keeps its costs within budgeted levels. Prime costs are the most important costs for management to keep under control. Prime costs consist of the cost of food plus payroll and related employee benefits.

There are many control points in the food cost control cycle that help restaurant managers keep food costs down. The first is menu planning. A correctly planned menu has few, if any, unpopular menu items. This helps control food costs by reducing or eliminating the need to purchase food for unpopular menu items. Such food may spoil and have to be thrown away before it is used. Accurate forecasting also helps to reduce food costs because unnecessary food is not ordered. A restaurant's purchaser can minimize food costs by obtaining the right products for the best price. Purchase specifications play an important role in this. If various suppliers have a restaurant's purchase specifications in hand as they're formulating a bid, their bids are more likely to be truly comparable, since they are all basing their bids on the same criteria. One trend in purchasing that helps keep food costs down is one-stop purchasing.

Receiving procedures can also affect food cost. What is received must be verified and compared with what was ordered.

Storage and issuing also require attention if food cost is to be adequately controlled. Storage must protect the operation's inventory from deterioration or theft. Issuing procedures allow the operator to keep track of inventory and calculate a daily food cost figure. Daily food cost is calculated by adding together direct purchases and storeroom issues.

Standard recipes that yield standard portions cut back on waste in production. Standard recipes also reduce food and labor costs. The cost of preparing menu items can only be calculated accurately when standard recipes are used.

Service and cash control concerns include the manner in which guest payments are handled. This varies by type of establishment, but the goal of all cash control systems is to ensure that what comes out of the kitchen is in fact served, recorded, and paid for.

Food cost calculation is essential if one is to operate a successful and profitable establishment. A restaurant's overall food cost percentage for a given period is calculated by dividing the cost of food sold during the period by total food sales during the same period. Each menu item has a unique food cost percentage and contribution margin. Although, as a rule, a low food cost percentage is desirable because a high contribution margin results, some menu items with high food cost percentages also have high contribution margins. Therefore, operators should keep contribution margins as well as food cost percentages in mind when making decisions about whether to drop or add menu items.

Payroll expenses, including employee benefits, represent about 30 percent of sales in the food service industry, but payroll costs vary considerably by type of establishment. Many of the problems associated with controlling labor costs stem from the low-paying nature of the work.

The drinking of alcoholic beverages predates recorded history and has become an integral part of society. Today, alcoholic beverages account for approximately 22 percent of restaurant sales—sales that have a high profit margin. Purchasing beverages is fairly uncomplicated since (1) purchase specifications are largely limited to brands and size, and (2) competitive bidding is not necessary. Receiving is also straightforward. Issuing is usually tracked by a perpetual inventory system that shows what ought to be on hand in the beverage storeroom. These records should be checked by taking a physical inventory on a regular basis, usually monthly. Finally, a bar par based mostly on expected consumption is established at each bar.

Endnotes

1. Ken Albrecht and Ron Zemke, *Service America* (Homewood, Ill: Dow Jones-Irwin, 1985), p. 49.

2. Andy Birsh, "Specialties de la Maison: One Hudson Cafe," *Gourmet*, October 1989, pp. 44, 48.

3. Geoffrey Tomb, *The Miami Herald*, December 28, 1989, pp. E-1, E-10.

4. *The Wall Street Journal*, November 27, 1989, p. B-9.

5. "Menu Design for Effective Merchandising," *Cornell Quarterly*, November 1978.

6. Judi Radice, "The Menu as Star," *Restaurants USA*, June/July 1989, p. 32.

7. Radice, p. 35.

8. James Keiser, *Controlling and Analyzing Costs in Foodservice Operations*, 2d ed. (New York: Macmillan, 1989), pp. 63–64.

9. Lendal H. Kotschevar, *Management by Menu*, 2d ed. (National Institute for the Foodservice Industry/William C. Brown, 1987), p. 261.

Key Terms

ambience
bar par
blind receiving
contribution margin
cycle menu
direct purchase
dogs
first-in, first-out (FIFO)
fixed menu
food cost
food cost percentage
menu engineering

one-stop purchasing
perpetual inventory system
plowhorses
prime costs
purchase specifications
puzzles
return on investment (ROI)
requisition
specialty menu
standard recipe
stars

Discussion Questions

1. What is the most important success factor for any business?
2. Why is keeping up with guest preferences so important?
3. What contributes to a restaurant's success?
4. What are some basic rules to keep in mind when creating menus?
5. How do fixed menus differ from cycle menus?
6. What is a balance sheet? a statement of income?
7. What control points make up the food cost control loop?
8. A purchase specification should include what kinds of information?
9. What is a food cost percentage and how is it calculated?
10. In what ways does beverage management differ from food management? In what ways is it similar?

Chapter Outline

Background on Clubs
Types of Clubs
    City Clubs
        Athletic
        Dining
        Professional
        Social
        University
    Country Clubs
    Other Clubs
        Yacht
        Fraternal
        Military
Club Ownership
    Equity Clubs
    Proprietary Clubs
Club Organization
Club Operations
    Revenue
        Membership Dues
        Initiation Fees
        Assessments
        Sports Activities Fees
        Food and Beverage Sales
        Other Sources of Revenue
    Expenses
    Control
Chapter Summary

Clubs

In this chapter we will discuss the organization and management of private clubs. While they are in many ways similar to hotels (especially resorts), there are some distinct differences. The chapter explains the different kinds of clubs and their membership composition. It also describes how clubs are owned, organized, and managed. We then examine the unique aspects of clubs, including sources of revenue, and profile several prominent clubs and their memberships.

Background on Clubs

Private clubs are gathering places for members only. They bring together people of like interests. Those interests could be recreational, social, fraternal, or professional. Private clubs can be found in many communities in the United States—but they are not an invention of modern society.

Wealthy citizens of ancient Greece and Rome formed clubs. Clubs have been an integral part of the social fabric of upper-class English society for centuries. As the English colonized the world, they established clubs. English social clubs and the golf club of St. Andrews in Scotland are the forerunners of city clubs and country clubs in the United States. Some U.S. city clubs, such as the Somerset Club in Boston, the San Francisco Commercial Club, and the Wilmington Club in Delaware, date back to the mid-nineteenth century. Perhaps the oldest country club—founded in 1882—is located in Brookline, Massachusetts.

In many parts of the world the club you belong to is an indication of your position in society. Comedian Groucho Marx sent a telegram to the Friar's Club in Hollywood to which he belonged: "Please accept my resignation. I don't want to belong to any club that will accept me as a member." Marx was commenting on the fact that many people join clubs to enhance their own social status. While some clubs continue to be vestiges of the class system, by and large the exclusionary aspect of private clubs in the United States has changed due to equal rights legislation and society's increased social consciousness.

Today there are about 14,000 private clubs in America, providing diverse opportunities in management.[1] Private club management is closely related to hotel and food service management. Many of a club manager's responsibilities in the areas of control, human resource management, guest relations, marketing, and maintenance are very similar to those of a hotel manager's. Most clubs have dining facilities of some sort. In fact, some have multiple dining rooms and lounges as well as extensive private meeting rooms for catering. In addition to these facilities, many city clubs have gymnasiums, racquetball courts, and guestrooms for overnight guests. Country clubs may have dining rooms, meeting rooms, one or more golf courses, a tennis club, a beach club, and even a skeet- and trap-shooting club. Such country clubs are very much like resort hotels, except that they are not open to the public.

There are many similarities in the organization of clubs and hotels. A basic difference between clubs and hotels is that the club's "guest" is a dues-paying member with a financial and emotional attachment to the club, whereas hotels are open to the public and the relationship between the guest and the hotel is less personal.

Types of Clubs

There are two basic types of private clubs: city clubs and country clubs. There are also some private clubs that do not easily fit into either of these classifications, which we will discuss under a third classification called "other private clubs."

City Clubs

City clubs vary in size, type, facilities, and membership. Some clubs own their own real estate; others lease space in office buildings or hotels. What they have in common is that food service is generally offered and a manager is hired to oversee the entire operation. The basic types of city clubs are:

- Athletic
- Dining
- Professional
- Social
- University

Athletic. Athletic clubs are as varied as the club industry itself. The Downtown Athletic Club, known for its annual award of the Heisman Trophy, occupies an entire building in downtown Manhattan in New York City. Its 35 stories plus a sun deck contain 136 guestrooms; dining rooms with a total capacity of 1,000; conference rooms; and extensive health club facilities, including squash and handball courts and an indoor swimming pool. It also sponsors many social programs. The Dayton Racquet Club in Dayton, Ohio, is a more modest facility located on the top floor of a 29-story office building. Squash is the main athletic activity, but a running track and fitness equipment are available. The club also has dining facilities.

Dining. The number of dining clubs located in office buildings proliferated in the 1960s. Building owners offered them mainly to induce companies to lease office space. Many dining clubs are only open for lunch—these

Some clubs are very much like resort hotels. In fact, some clubs become resort hotels. The Jekyll Island Clubhouse on Jekyll Island, Georgia, was built in 1887 and was the nucleus for many of the private club's activities. A large clubhouse annex was built around the turn of the century. Following a $17 million restoration, the clubhouse opened in December 1986 as a world-class hotel—The Jekyll Island Club, a Radisson Resort. Courtesy of the Jekyll Island Authority, Jekyll Island, Georgia.

clubs are usually referred to as luncheon clubs. In some instances, facilities that are used exclusively as private luncheon clubs in the day are open to the public for dinner in the evening. Some dining clubs located in downtown office buildings remain open for cocktails after work, and a few even serve dinner, but most shut down quite early unless they have some lodging facilities.

The Marco Polo Club, located in the Waldorf Astoria, is a dining club that leases space from the hotel. Although the club is operated as a separate entity open only to club members and their guests, the food served in the club is made in the Waldorf Astoria's kitchens, with production supervised by the club's manager.

Professional. Professional clubs are dining and social clubs for people in the same profession. Clubs of this nature include the Press Club in Washington, D.C., for journalists, the Lawyers' Club in New York City for attorneys, and the Friars Club in Manhattan for actors and other theater people.

The Downtown Athletic Club. Courtesy of the Downtown Athletic Club, New York, New York.

One famous professional club located on Gramercy Park in New York City is the National Arts Club, founded in 1898 by Charles de Kay, at that time the literary and art critic for the *New York Times*. De Kay's aim was to unite all the arts—painting, sculpture, music, and literature—and allow serious patrons to mingle with the men and women whose works they admired and collected.[2] Mark Twain was one of the early members of this club, as was the American painter George Bellows.

Social. Members of a social club may have no affiliation except that they enjoy being in each other's company. These clubs were modeled originally after men's social clubs in London such as Boodle's, St. James, and White's, where persons from similar backgrounds could meet with each other at the end of a day for cocktails and general companionship or entertainment unrelated to business. Indeed, in some social clubs it was considered bad manners to talk about business.

The oldest social club in America is said to be the Fish House in Philadelphia, founded in 1832. To ensure that the Fish House would always be socially oriented rather than business-oriented, it was formed as a men's cooking club, with each member taking turns preparing meals for the membership.[3] Social clubs in Manhattan include the Union League Club, founded in 1863; the Knickerbocker Club, started by author Washington Irving for gentlemen with New York roots; and the Links Club, which was originally established "to promote and conserve throughout the United States the best interests and true spirit of the game of golf." Links Club members include business leaders and politicians from all over the country, such as former President Nixon, the Minneapolis Pillsbury family, the Dohenys of Beverly Hills, the Dorrances from Philadelphia, and the Kleenex-making Kimberlys from Neenah, Wisconsin.[4] In New Orleans there's the Louisiana Club, and on the West Coast the most famous social club is San Francisco's Bohemian Club, founded in 1847. This club, which occupies a handsome red brick Georgian clubhouse on the side of Nob Hill,

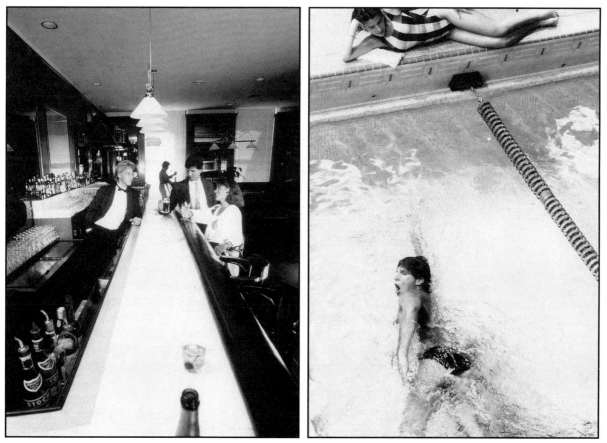

Some city clubs offer facilities such as lounges and swimming pools to their members. Photos courtesy of the Downtown Athletic Club, New York, New York.

The University Club of Michigan State University. Photos courtesy of the University Club, East Lansing, Michigan.

has a 750-seat theater where members perform amateur theatricals. The club also owns a 280-acre estate in the Sierra Mountains where members gather every summer for a two-week "encampment," during which there are poetry readings, musical productions, and concerts presented by the club's own 70-piece orchestra.[5]

In recent years social clubs have been founded for other purposes besides leisure, recreation, and camaraderie. One such club is the Commerce Club in Atlanta, Georgia, whose stated purpose is "to provide, for the political, business, and civic leadership of metropolitan Atlanta, club facilities and programs designed to stimulate and maintain vigorous and healthy communication and discourse on issues of common interest affecting metropolitan Atlanta, in an environment offering comfortable surroundings, modern meeting facilities, and the finest food and service."

University. University clubs are private clubs for university graduates. Some clubs of this nature are quite open. For instance, the University Club in Seattle is not affiliated with any university, and to be eligible to join you only have to be a university graduate. Other university clubs are for graduates of specific schools and exist in cities where there may be a large concentration of alumni who either live there or visit often. In New York City, for example, Harvard, Princeton, Yale, and Cornell have their own clubs with restaurants, health clubs, guestrooms, and regular activities such as lectures and concerts. The largest of these clubs is the Yale Club. Guestrooms, dining facilities, meeting and banquet rooms, an indoor swimming pool, and a gymnasium are provided for Yale (and Dartmouth) alumni. The club stands on the exact spot where one of Yale's most celebrated sons, Nathan Hale, uttered the famous phrase, "I regret that I have but one life to give for my country," before being hanged by the British during the Revolutionary War for spying.

Country Clubs

The largest single type of private club is the country club, accounting for about 50% of private clubs. Country clubs are primarily recreational and social facilities for individuals and families who live in the area. These clubs often have separate children's facilities and do a large catering business, since it is common for members to hold bar mitzvahs, weddings, and other social events at them.

Country clubs are rapidly growing in popularity in the United States, due to what the *Wall Street Journal* terms a "nouveau revival" fueled by the baby boom generation.[6] According to the *Journal*, club memberships rose 9.5% during the 1980s after a two-decade slump. Since clubs are often limited by size—so that new members are not admitted unless someone leaves or dies—this surge lengthened the average wait for memberships at existing clubs to five years, double the waiting period in 1986, according to the National Club Association.[7] In fact, many clubs such as the Glen View Club in Golf, Illinois, and the Belle Haven Country Club in Alexandria, Virginia, are refusing to accept new applications until current rolls thin.[8]

With space so limited at established clubs, a national club construction boom is underway. The new clubs appeal to people with a sense of achievement who may have been excluded from older clubs. "We're establishing a new pecking order," says Frank Martinez, a medical equipment salesman who recently paid $19,500 to join the St. Ives Country Club near Atlanta. "I'm a minority from the inner city of New York, so this is a big deal for me."[9] Some who used to spurn country clubs because of what they represented have changed their minds:

> Tom McMillan, a lumbermill owner in Kansas City, has gone from social activist to social climber. Eighteen years ago he was taking over the ROTC building at the University of Vermont in protest, but now he takes his two children to the Homestead Country Club, a modern ranch style club with 20 tennis courts, a big pool, but no golf course. "In 1970, I thought country clubs symbolized the effete establishment and the Vietnam War machine," says the 36-year-old Mr. McMillan. "But today, the club is a safe harbor for my family."[10]

In some cases, members are asked to invest in the country club if they wish to become members. International Golf Management Inc. plans to build a dozen new prestigious clubs costing $50 million each. A member in one of these clubs will have to buy $150,000 worth of stock in the new company, and pay dues of at least $1,000 a month for "ultra-premier" surroundings, according to John Killip, senior vice president of marketing. The clubs will feature splits of champagne served at the tenth hole and a clubhouse designed for workaholics—complete with four boardrooms for corporate directors' meetings.[11]

Since country clubs need a great deal of land (one 18-hole golf course typically requires a minimum of 110 acres), they are usually located outside the city in suburban or rural locales. Exceptions sometimes occur when a nearby city develops to the extent that the urban sprawl comes up to or surrounds the club. The Hillcrest Country Club in Los Angeles is a case in point. When it opened in 1920, the locale was suburban Los Angeles. Now it is surrounded by Beverly Hills and Century City. Other once-suburban country clubs include the Chevy Chase Country Club in Washington, D.C., and the Everglades Country Club on fashionable Worth Avenue in Palm Beach, Florida.

In addition to a clubhouse with one or more dining rooms and function rooms, most country clubs have at least one golf course and one swimming pool. In the 1970s, the popularity of tennis grew to the point that tennis courts became almost a mandatory part of the recreational facilities for a country club.

There are a number of country clubs known for their beautiful facilities and exclusivity. One such is the Owentsia Country Club in Lake Forest, Illinois, its name derived from the Iroquois Indian word meaning "a meeting place in the country for sporting braves and squaws." Other clubs are famous for their outstanding golf courses and the tournaments held there. Examples include the Westchester Country Club and the Oak Hill Country Club in New York state, and the Pebble Beach Country Club in California.

Other Clubs

There are other types of private clubs that engage professional managers to operate their facilities and manage their social and recreational programs.

Yacht. Yacht clubs are located near large bodies of water. Their main purpose is to provide such facilities as marinas for boat owners. While many of these clubs have tennis courts, swimming pools, and elaborate clubhouses with dining rooms and lounges, others provide only the bare necessities of dock space, fuel, and boating supplies.

Fraternal. Organizations such as the Elks and the Veterans of Foreign Wars sometimes own or rent entire buildings or floors within a building. Some offer food and beverage service and overnight accommodations, as well as rooms for meetings and recreation. Fraternal clubs, too, require professional managers.

Military. The armed services operate officers clubs and non-commissioned officers clubs. Most have clubhouses with dining and function facilities. Some have lodging facilities, recreational facilities, and social programs similar to civilian private clubs and resorts. One such facility is the Hale Koa Hotel at the Armed Forces Recreation Center in Fort DeRussy, Hawaii, which is on one of the nicest parts of Waikiki Beach. In Europe, the armed forces operate hotels and recreation centers in Garmisch, Berchtesgaden, and Chiemsee—all in Bavaria. In recent years the Department of Defense has hired civilians to manage military clubs instead of using military personnel.

Club Ownership

Private clubs are usually owned in one of two ways. A club can be owned by some of its members; such clubs are called equity clubs. Those members who fund the purchase or development of an equity club are known as founder-members. Or a club can be owned by a company that sells memberships in the club. These for-profit clubs are also known as proprietary clubs.

Equity Clubs

Equity clubs are generally non-profit, since they are typically formed not for money-making purposes but simply for the enjoyment of their members. Members are either (1) founder-members, or (2) other members who pay a one-time initiation fee and annual dues. If an equity club has an excess of revenues over expenses, the profits are not given back to the founder-members, but are invested in improving the club's facilities and services.

Because equity clubs are not formed to make a profit, the non-profit statute of the tax law exempts the club from federal and state income taxes, although clubs may be required to pay taxes on unrelated income such as non-member catering as well as federal and state payroll taxes.

Non-transferring of profits to members is only one part of what gives an equity club its non-profit status. To receive a tax exemption, an equity club must be formed solely for pleasure and recreation, and must not discriminate on the basis of sex, race, or religion against anyone who wishes to become a member. Discrimination is often practiced on other grounds, however. Sometimes clubs charge very high initiation fees or require members to buy expensive bonds or membership shares. And it is perfectly within the rights of a club to turn down applicants because they are not qualified by reason of accomplishment; professional occupation; or, as in the case of the Bohemian Club, artistic talent.

Proprietary Clubs

As mentioned earlier, proprietary clubs operate for profit and are owned by individuals or corporations. Persons who wish to become members purchase a membership, not a share in the club. Members may or may not be involved in running the club.

Proprietary clubs proliferated with the real estate boom in office buildings, condominiums, and single housing developments. Just as having a dining club in office buildings helped developers rent office space, a country club at the center of a condominium or housing development was a good marketing tactic that not only helped to sell or lease properties but raised their prices by offering an added value to buyers.

The major proprietary company in the business of club management is the Club Corporation of America (CCA). The Dallas-based company operates 200 country and city clubs nationwide. Of the 200, 180 are company-owned and 20 are managed. Recently, CCA broadened its business by going into resort hotel management. This was not surprising in view of the similarity between country clubs and resorts.

Clubs managed by the same company, as well as individual city and country clubs, have various types of reciprocal agreements so that their members can use the facilities of similar clubs when traveling. The Downtown Athletic Club in New York City has reciprocal agreements with clubs all over the United States, including the Petroleum Club of Los Angeles, the Bankers Club in Miami, and the Boston Athletic Club, as well as with clubs in Hawaii, Australia, the Bahamas, Canada, England, Hong Kong, Japan, Germany, and even Hungary! Typically, members secure an introductory guest card or letter of introduction to the club they wish to visit before leaving on their trip, although simply presenting their current membership card in their own club will often get them into an affiliated club.

Club Organization

Clubs are organized in different ways depending to a large extent on whether the club is non-profit or proprietary. In a non-profit equity club, the members elect a board of directors (sometimes called a board of governors) to oversee the budget and set policy affecting membership and club use. Here the board is the governing body, and the club manager

Exhibit 7.1 Sample Organization Chart for an Equity Club

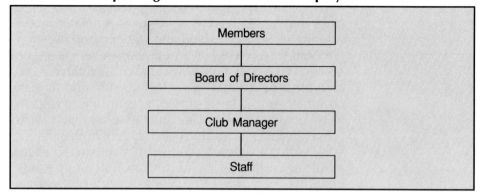

Exhibit 7.2 Sample Organization Chart for a Proprietary Club

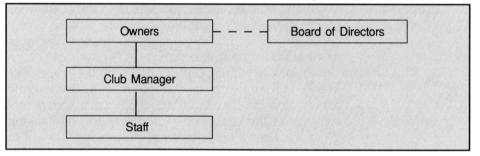

reports to the board and implements its policies and decisions (see Exhibit 7.1). In a proprietary club the club manager reports to and receives instructions as to club policies, procedures, and standards from the club's owners (see Exhibit 7.2). A proprietary club may have a board of directors made up of club members, if the owners wish to give the members some sense of authority, but generally this board does not make policy but merely advises the owners.

The number of members on an equity club's board usually ranges from 12 to 25, although sometimes it is even higher. Board officers typically include a chairman (usually last year's president), president, vice president, and treasurer.

Committees are extremely important to club morale and operation because they allow a larger number of members to participate in managing the club. In addition to special committees that are appointed for specific social or sporting events, clubs generally have five standing committees: a house committee, a membership committee, a finance and budget committee, an entertainment committee, and an athletic committee.[12] In some clubs with a house committee, the club manager reports to the chairperson of the house committee rather than to the board.

The club manager is the hired professional responsible for guiding all of the elements of the club's operation. A sample club manager's job description is shown in Exhibit 7.3.

A career in club management can be very rewarding, but a club manager's job is extraordinarily complex. The Thornblade Club, which opened in 1990 in Greenville, South Carolina, finally had to resort to an "executive headhunter" to find a qualified professional. "This guy has to know

Exhibit 7.3 Sample Club Manager's Job Description

As the chief operating officer of a club, the club or general manager is responsible for the proper management of all aspects of the club's activities and relationships. The club manager supervises, coordinates, and administers the policies of the club as defined by the club's board of directors. The club manager develops operational policies and procedures. All employees of the club are under the direction and supervision of the club manager.

Work Performed

1. Reports to the board of directors or its designated authority.

2. Employs, supervises, and terminates all management staff and has the authority to review the personnel policies and practices of the management staff.

3. Guides and assists the board of directors in the development and formulation of the club's long- and short-term objectives, goals, policies, and programs.

4. Coordinates inter- and intra-committee activities; guides and assists member committees in the development and preparation of recommended short- and long-term programs covering all phases of club member relations and activities.

5. Implements policies and operating procedures for the club.

6. Secures relevant data and, with the assistance of the club's treasurer, develops recommendations for the capital and operating budgets, presents recommendations to the board, and assures proper implementation. Reports the club's financial progress and its components to the board.

7. As head of all departments, has ultimate authority over inter-departmental disputes. Is consulted as to policy and changes in the operation of each department and suggests changes.

8. Develops, maintains, and disseminates throughout the club a basic management philosophy designed to effectively guide all club personnel toward optimum operating results, and keep employee morale and membership and guest satisfaction high.

9. Prepares reports regarding club history, surveys, trends, operations, etc., which serve as support material for committee and board decisions.

10. Maintains community relations with the police and fire departments and other county offices.

11. Finalizes approval of all contracts, all accounts payable, and all labor cost payouts.

Source: "Job Descriptions in the Private Club Industry," Club Managers Association of America, Bethesda, Maryland, 1982.

golf, tennis, pools, maintenance—not to mention 190 wines on the club's wine list," bemoaned Howard Covington, Jr., the club's president. "He's responsible for all the budget numbers, the pro formas, and responding to membership."[13] Wages for club managers who manage clubs that include one or more golf courses now range from $60,000 to $170,000, and perks often include housing, cars, and allowances for entertainment and travel.[14]

In one respect a club manager's job is more complex than that of a hotel or restaurant manager's. The jobs are similar to the extent that each manager must manage physical facilities, employees, and services in order to meet economic objectives. In addition, each must hire, train, fire, and set standards of service. Where the jobs differ—and what makes a club manager's job more complex—is that club managers must share planning and budgeting responsibilities with an on-site board of directors, and club members have a more direct say in whether a manager keeps his or her job than hotel or restaurant guests do. A club manager must find a way to keep two groups relatively happy: (1) a board whose members may have diverse points of view because they were elected by different factions within the membership who do not agree, and (2) a wide variety of members with differing wants and needs. To do this, a club manager must be a master politician.

Exhibit 7.4 Sources of Club Revenue

	Country Clubs	City Clubs
Dues	42.8%	38.5%
Food	28.9	34.5
Beverages	10.3	9.3
Rooms	—	7.8
Sports Activities	12.9	—
All Other	5.1	9.9
	100%	100%

Source: *Clubs in Town & Country 1989* (Houston, Texas: Pannell Kerr Forster, 1990), pp. 8, 18.

Advancement in the club management field may require more mobility than in the hotel field. According to the most recent surveys done by the Club Managers Association of America (CMAA), fewer than 20 percent of all CMAA-member club managers were employed as an assistant manager or department head at the same club they now manage.[15] An assistant manager or department head who wishes to advance usually finds it necessary to move to a different club. Club managers who wish to advance to a larger and more prestigious club obviously have to change jobs, which usually requires moving. But many club managers develop such a satisfying relationship with club members and officers that they never consider moving on.

Club Operations

Clubs are similar to other hospitality businesses in that they generate revenue and incur expenses. Differences between clubs and other hospitality businesses can be found in the clubs' sources of revenue.

Revenue Since a club is a private enterprise, limited for use primarily by members, the bulk of its revenue is derived from its members (see Exhibit 7.4). Typical sources of club revenue are:

- Membership dues
- Initiation fees
- Assessments
- Sports activities fees
- Food and beverage sales
- Other sources of revenue

Membership dues, initiation fees, assessments, and sports activities fees help set clubs apart from hotels and restaurants, since hotels and restaurants do not earn revenue from these sources.

Membership Dues. Membership dues are the cost to a member for the exclusivity of the club. Unlike an operation open to the public, a private club has a limited number of patrons and hence a limited source of revenue. Membership dues subsidize all of the club's operating costs and fixed charges. Dues vary based on the type of club (city or country), the number of members, and the extent of the club's facilities and services. Because country clubs are generally more expensive to operate than city clubs, they usually have higher dues. According to a 1990 study by Pannell Kerr Forster, in 1989 the income per member derived from dues alone averaged $1,793 for country clubs, compared to only $883 for city clubs.[16]

It is common for a club to have several different membership dues based on different types of membership. The reason for this is to make it possible for more persons to join and thus increase the membership base, which decreases costs for each member.

A good example of how a city club offers different types of memberships is the Cornell Club of New York. The Cornell Club occupies a 15-floor building with guestrooms, dining rooms, a lounge, and private meeting rooms. Here are the different memberships (each with a different dues structure) that are available:

- Resident—a member who resides within New York City

- Suburban—a member who resides within 50 miles of New York City but not within the city itself

- Non-resident—a member who resides more than 50 miles from New York City

Each of these memberships has six different levels of dues based on the number of years the member has been out of college. It is presumed, of course, that the ones who have been graduates for the greatest number of years can afford the highest dues.

In addition to these memberships, the Cornell Club offers special memberships for persons who are not Cornell graduates but are associated with the university (such as full-time faculty and staff). These special memberships are also categorized as resident, suburban, or non-resident. There is even a Cornell couple membership and a spouse membership.

Country clubs usually have a larger number of membership categories than city clubs. Some people are just interested in a social membership at a country club—they wish to eat there and socialize with friends at the swimming pool but are not interested in playing golf or tennis. Other members want to make full use of the club's recreational facilities and purchase a regular or active membership. Some clubs offer single or family memberships. A few country clubs have a non-resident category. Many have a lifetime membership option for those willing to make a large one-time payment for lifetime privileges.

An example of a club that offers its members a wide variety of memberships is the Grosse Pointe Yacht Club in Grosse Pointe Shores, Michigan. This club offers a choice of an active membership, an intermediate I membership for members aged 21–27, an intermediate II membership for members aged 28–34, two types of social memberships for those aged 21–34 and two for those 35-plus, two types of junior memberships, a non-resident membership, and even a special membership for clergy.

Exhibit 7.5 Golf Course Maintenance Costs

Average Cost per Hole, 1989	Overall Averages
Payroll	$14,300
Payroll Taxes and Employee Benefits	3,117
Course Supplies and Contracts	4,829
Repairs to Equipment, Course Buildings, Water and Drainage System, Etc.	2,437
All Other Expenses	3,045
Total Golf Course Maintenance	$27,728
Add: Golf Shop, Caddy, and Committee Expenses	6,898
Total Golf Expenses	$34,626
Less: Income from Golf Fees, Golf Carts, Etc.	18,387
Net Golf Expenses	$16,239

Source: *Clubs in Town & Country 1989* (Houston, Texas: Pannell Kerr Forster, 1990), p. 10.

Initiation Fees. Most clubs charge new members an initiation fee, which in most cases is non-refundable. Clubs vary as to their handling of initiation fees. Some consider them contributions to capital and show them as additions to founder-members' equity (for equity clubs) or owners' equity (for proprietary clubs). Others add them to reserve funds for specific capital improvement projects such as refurbishing the clubhouse. Initiation fees typically range from $500 to $10,000, although a few clubs charge $100,000 or more.[17] The median initiation fee for country clubs is $5,600; for city clubs, $1,100.[18]

Assessments. One-time or periodic assessments are sometimes imposed on members instead of increasing dues. Some assessments cover operational shortfalls. Others are used to raise capital for improvements to the club. Assessments are unpopular with members since they are unanticipated expenses. Therefore, instead of assessments, many clubs prefer to impose minimum spending requirements, usually on food and beverages. If a member does not spend a specified amount on food and beverages either on a monthly, quarterly, or annual basis, a bill is sent for the difference.

Sports Activities Fees. City clubs do not record revenue from sports activities because they typically do not charge members extra for using the club's recreational facilities. On the other hand, sports activities fees account for 12.9% of total country club revenues. In country clubs where golf and tennis are significant activities, a golf professional and a tennis professional are responsible for programs in these sports. Fees are charged for playing tennis or golf and, in the case of golf, rental fees are charged for golf carts.

A golf course is an expensive facility, each year costing almost $35,000 per hole to maintain (see Exhibit 7.5). As the exhibit shows, revenue derived directly from golf operations covers only a little more than half of golf costs. Membership dues or profits from other departments are necessary to make up the difference.

Sometimes other recreational facilities exist, such as a swimming pool, a health spa, and volleyball and/or squash courts. Members at most country clubs pay fees to use these facilities, with the exception of the swimming pools; swimming is free. If a club offers a lot of sports options, an athletic director might well be added to the staff to supervise all of the club's recreational facilities and programs.

Clubs with athletic facilities have committees for specific sports. A country club with a golf course would have a golf committee that would report to the club's board and advise on golf course policies such as appropriate course use and the course's hours of operation. The committee would work with the club's management in planning tournaments and preparing the golf course budget.

Food and Beverage Sales. Other than dues income, sales of food and beverages are the major source of revenue in both city clubs and country clubs. Like hotels and resorts, clubs often have more than one dining facility. City clubs with a single dining room tend to keep it formal and add a more informal tap room or grill. Country clubs usually operate snack bars at the pool or golf course, an informal dining room for lunch, and a formal dining room.

In recent years clubs have recognized that they must compete with their area's independent restaurants in terms of quality and value. The Lake Mead Golf and Country Club near San Francisco conducts wine tastings and frequently puts on special dinners prepared by renowned European chefs to draw members away from "too much" restaurant patronage, according to club manager Adair Chew.[19] Club chefs are often promoted heavily and in some instances have become celebrities. Executive chef Thomas Catherill of the Cherokee Town and Country Club in Atlanta is a gold medalist from the Culinary Olympics in Frankfurt, Germany. In Dallas the Club at San Simeon has lured a sizable share of banquet business away from prominent hotels by offering the locally renowned cuisine of club chef Richard Chamberlain to its tightly restricted membership.[20] In general, club members hold their club to higher standards of food quality and service than public restaurants. For this reason, in many cases food service becomes the main focus of the club, requiring the greatest part of the club manager's efforts. According to *Nation's Restaurant News*, clubs that are earning high marks for progressive food service are the Metropolitan Club in Chicago, the Hillcrest Country Club in Los Angeles, the Commerce Club in Atlanta, the New York Athletic Club, and the Dallas Country Club.[21]

Other Sources of Revenue. In addition to membership dues, initiation fees, assessments, sports activities fees, and food and beverage sales, there are other sources of revenue at some clubs. Most clubs charge visitors' fees for non-members who are guests of members and use rooms, buy food and beverages, or use recreational facilities. Often there are service charges on food and beverage sales, which may be distributed to employees or, as in most cases, are used to offset the club's labor costs. City clubs with

Exhibit 7.6   Sources of Club Expense

	Country Clubs	City Clubs
Operating Supplies and Expenses	30.4%	22.5%
Payroll and Related Costs	47.4	49.9
Cost of Food and Beverages Sold	14.6	14.9
Real Estate Taxes and Insurance	7.0	6.9
Balance Available for Debt Service, Capital Improvements, Etc.	0.6	5.8
	100%	100%

Source: *Clubs in Town & Country 1989* (Houston, Texas: Pannell Kerr Forster, 1990), pp. 8, 18.

overnight accommodations have revenues from guestroom sales and may offer laundry and valet services for a fee. Some city clubs have barbershops and newsstands. Country clubs have pro shops, operated by the club or by a concessionaire, that sell sports equipment, apparel, and, in some cases, a broad range of gift items.

Expenses   Payroll is the single largest expense in operating a club (see Exhibit 7.6). The largest segment of payroll expenditure is in the food and beverage operation, although this segment represents less than 50% of total payroll expense in both city and country clubs. Administrative payroll, which includes management and accounting staff, makes up about 10% of a club's payroll.

"Balance Available for Debt Service, Capital Improvements, Etc." shows how much income remains after all of the club's operating expenses have been paid. This income is used to pay fixed charges such as real-estate taxes, insurance on the club's buildings and their contents, and interest on borrowed money.

Control   Like hotels and restaurants, clubs have a uniform accounting system. The *Uniform System of Accounts for Clubs* is a manual published by the Club Managers Association of America.[22] In addition to a classification of accounts, the system provides for a reporting method that separates revenues and expenses into departments. This allows a club's managers, board of directors, members, and—if it is a proprietary club—owners to easily review operating results by department.

Chapter Summary

Private clubs date back to ancient Greece and Rome, but the true forerunners of American private clubs (which now number more than 14,000) are the social and golf clubs of England and Scotland. While there are many similarities between managing clubs and hotels, there are some differences as well.

There are two basic types of clubs—city clubs and country clubs. City clubs can be divided into the following types: athletic, dining, professional, social, and university.

Athletic clubs are often quite large, sometimes occupying entire downtown buildings, and may include lodging and dining facilities as well as gymnasiums, swimming pools, and courts for squash, handball, and racquetball.

Dining clubs are generally found in office buildings. Many of these clubs are open only for lunch.

A professional club is a dining or social club for people in a particular profession. These clubs exist for lawyers, actors, artists, journalists, and other professionals.

Social clubs were originally modeled after men's social clubs in England. Although most social clubs do not discriminate on the basis of sex, race, or religion, some try to limit their membership to persons of the same social and economic background.

University clubs are private clubs for university graduates. Some university clubs have dining and meeting rooms, guestrooms, and extensive libraries and recreational facilities.

Other kinds of clubs include yacht clubs, fraternal clubs, and military clubs.

Most private clubs are either equity clubs or proprietary clubs. Equity clubs are owned by a group of founder-members and are generally nonprofit, since they are formed not for money-making purposes but only for the enjoyment of their members. Proprietary clubs are for-profit clubs owned by companies that sell memberships in the clubs.

A club's organization depends on whether it is an equity or a proprietary club. The club manager is the hired professional responsible for guiding all of the elements of a club's operation. Unlike hotel managers, club managers share the responsibility for preparing budgets and planning activities with a board of directors elected by club members.

The bulk of club revenues is derived from club members. These revenues fall into the following classifications: membership dues, initiation fees, assessments, sports activities fees, food and beverage sales, and other sources of revenue.

Membership dues are the cost to a member for the exclusivity of the club. It is common for city and country clubs to have several different types of memberships. A city club might have different membership dues for resident, suburban, and non-resident members, reflecting the location of the member's residence in relation to the location of the club. Country clubs tend to use a different type of dues structure, based on use of recreational facilities, a member's age, and other factors. In addition to dues, clubs generally charge initiation fees and, in some cases, special assessments.

Next to dues, food and beverage sales are the major source of club revenue. In recent years clubs have realized that they must compete with public dining facilities to keep their members' patronage. Thus many have been upgrading their food service and hiring award-winning chefs.

In 1989 sports activities fees accounted for approximately 13% of the average country club's revenues. The most expensive recreational facilities country clubs offer are golf courses. The cost per hole of maintaining a golf course averaged approximately $35,000 in 1990.

Other sources of revenue include guestroom sales (for city clubs), visitors' fees, and service charges on food and beverage sales.

Payroll is the largest expense connected with running a club. It represents approximately half the costs for operating city clubs and slightly less for country clubs.

Like hotels and restaurants, clubs have their own uniform system of accounts that helps club managers control and manage operations.

Endnotes

1. Richard Martin, "Tradition Gives Way to Reform," *Nation's Restaurant News*, January 23, 1989, p. F-7.

2. Carole Klein, *Gramercy Park, An American Bloomsbury* (Boston: Houghton Mifflin, 1987), p. 159.

3. Stephen Birmingham, *America's Secret Aristocracy* (New York: Berkley Books, 1990), p. 209.

4. Birmingham, p. 210.

5. Birmingham, p. 213.

6. Robert Johnson, "Country Clubs May Be Old Line, but They're in a Nouveau Revival," *Wall Street Journal*, April 12, 1990, p. A-1.

7. Johnson, p. A-1.

8. Johnson, p. A-1.

9. Johnson, p. A-9.

10. Johnson, p. A-9.

11. Johnson, p. A-9.

12. Ted E. White and Larry C. Gerstner, *Club Operations and Management*, 2d ed. (New York: VNR, 1991).

13. Amanda Bennett, "Grass Looks Greener for Golf-Club Managers," *Wall Street Journal*, January 25, 1990, p. B-1.

14. Bennett, p. B-1.

15. Club Managers Association of America, *Club Management Operations*, 4th ed. (Dubuque, Iowa: Kendall/Hunt Publishing Company, 1989), p. 32.

16. *Clubs in Town & Country 1989* (Houston, Texas: Pannell Kerr Foster, 1990), p. 13.

17. Bennett, p. B-1.

18. 1987 Operational Profile Survey, Club Managers Association of America, Bethesda, MD 20817.

19. Jack Hayes, "Food Is 'In' at Clubs Nationwide," *Nation's Restaurant News*, February 12, 1990.

20. Martin, p. F-7.

21. Martin, p. F-7.

22. Club Managers Association of America, 7615 Winterberry Place, Bethesda, MD 20817.

Key Terms

assessment
club manager
equity club
golf committee

initiation fee
membership dues
proprietary club
visitors' fees

Discussion Questions

1. What is a basic difference between clubs and hotels?

2. What are the similarities and differences among the various types of city clubs?

3. What are the similarities and differences between city clubs and country clubs?

4. What are two basic ways private clubs can be owned?

5. What are some criteria an equity club must meet to maintain its non-profit status?

6. How is an equity club organized? a proprietary club?

7. What are some problems and opportunities associated with a career in club management?

8. What are typical sources of club revenue?

9. What are some common types of club memberships?

10. What are typical sources of club expenses?

Part III

Hospitality Management

Chapter Outline

The Job of a Manager
    Management Tasks
        Setting Objectives
        Organizing
        Motivating and Communicating
        Measuring Performance
        Developing People
The Evolution of Management Theories
    The Classical School
    The Behavioral School
    The Quantitative School
        Systems Theory
        Contingency Theory
    Other Management Theories
        Theory Z
        Customers First
Current Hospitality Management Practices
    Strategic Planning
        Tactical Planning
    Planning Problems in Capacity-Constrained Businesses
        Managing Supply
        Managing Demand
        Moments of Truth
    The Strategic Service Vision
        Targeting a Market Segment
        Focusing on a Service Strategy
Service Organizations and People Power
Chapter Summary

8 Management Basics

Chapter 8 begins by defining the task of managers. It traces the evolution of management theory and discusses three schools of thought on management—the classical school, the behavioral school, and the quantitative school. The chapter then turns to modern service management techniques and identifies the competencies needed by today's hospitality managers in the roles that they must play.

The Job of a Manager

Very often it is easy to single out the managers in any hotel, restaurant, or club. First of all, managers have titles. They have nice offices. Often their jobs come with all kinds of perks such as company cars, country club memberships, and expense accounts. But what exactly does a manager do? This question cannot be answered precisely or easily. Managers in different businesses do different things, and the entire field of management is changing rapidly as America moves from a manufacturing-based economy to a service-based economy.

Peter Drucker, probably America's greatest management theorist, says a manager has two broad goals. The first is "creation of a true whole that is larger than the sum of its parts, a productive entity that turns out more than the sum of the resources put into it."[1] Drucker compares a manager to a conductor of an orchestra who is able to pull together the individual musical parts played by each musician into a beautifully played symphony. The Four Seasons hotel company, in its statement of operating philosophy, compares its general managers to orchestra conductors. Managers are told that their role is to "keep all of the various pieces playing in proper tempo and harmony so the performance is pleasing to the customer."[2]

But unlike conductors, who have a composer's score in front of them and only have to interpret it, managers must do more, says Drucker. They must write their own score, and in that sense managers are composers as well as conductors. The second broad goal of a manager is to "harmonize in every decision and action the requirements of [the] immediate and long-range future."[3] In other words, a manager must consider not only the needs of today but also the needs of next year and beyond. "He not only has to prepare for crossing distant bridges—he has to build them long before he gets there."[4]

These two goals serve to separate managers from supervisors. Supervisors are generally concerned with implementing policies that have already been established. Although supervisors may act like orchestra conductors at times—that is, lead and direct their employees—it is not their job to compose the music as well; that has already been done by higher-level managers. Nor do supervisors worry about the long-range future. Their job is to take care of what is going on today.

This is not to imply that a manager does not do supervisory work. Managers do other things besides manage (see Exhibit 8.1), but they always focus their activities on creating and harmonizing—or should, if they want to be effective managers.

Management Tasks

Drucker says that a manager has five basic tasks:

- Setting objectives

- Organizing

- Motivating and communicating

- Measuring performance

- Developing people [5]

Setting Objectives. A manager sets objectives. Unlike a worker or supervisor, a manager must decide what goals and objectives his or her department or organization must strive to achieve. The manager then must decide what work needs to be done to reach those objectives and, lastly, direct and communicate with his or her employees to get the work done.

Tim Firnstahl is the founder and CEO of Satisfaction Guaranteed Eateries Inc., a company in Seattle that operates Jake O'Shaughnessey's and other popular restaurants. Firnstahl set the objective of making sure that guest satisfaction in all of his restaurants would be guaranteed. Then he developed a plan to reach that objective. He came up with a company slogan: "Your Enjoyment Guaranteed. Always." He reduced this to an acronym—YEGA—that all employees could easily remember. After a series of meetings in which he explained what he had in mind, all of Firnstahl's 600 employees signed a contract pledging that they would follow through on the YEGA promise. Then, says Firnstahl, "We created a YEGA logo and put it everywhere, on report forms, on training manuals, on wall signs. We started the *YEGA News*, and distributed YEGA pins, shirts, name tags, even underwear. We announced that failure to enforce YEGA would be cause for dismissal."[6] The final step was empowering the employees to make good on the YEGA promise. With this in mind, Firnstahl says, "I instituted the idea that employees can and should do anything to keep the customer happy. In the event of an error or delay, any employee right down to the busboy could provide complimentary wine or desserts, or pick up an entire tab if necessary."[7]

Organizing. A manager organizes. A manager must analyze the work that his or her department is responsible for, divide that work into various jobs, and assign the jobs to employees, some of whom might have to be trained. All of the classic texts on management emphasize that managers

Exhibit 8.1 Hospitality Management Skills

Here are some of the skills top hospitality managers should possess:

Management Skills

Managers must be able to:

- Plan and organize work in a timely and efficient manner
- Select and train subordinates
- Make decisions correctly and effectively
- Adapt leadership to the needs of workers
- Recognize the organizational structure and chain of command
- Understand, interpret, and apply company policies and rules
- Understand, interpret, and apply local, state, and federal laws and ordinances
- Apply current technology to problem-solving situations
- Supervise subordinates

Human Resources Skills

Managers must be able to:

- Function in stressful situations
- Establish functional relationships with superiors, peers, and subordinates
- Show sensitivity to employees' differences in age, sex, race, creed, national origin, and physical abilities
- Balance the needs and wants of employees and guests
- Establish a positive work environment
- Maintain objectivity in resolving differences within their work group
- Accept criticism and use the feedback constructively
- Convey to employees that following personal grooming, health, and safety rules is essential for effective performance
- Take personality differences into account when making decisions
- Think creatively

Marketing Skills

Managers must be able to:

- Understand the concept and purpose of marketing
- Know how to generate or locate marketing data
- Know proper research methods
- Create a marketing strategy
- Write a marketing plan
- Develop and implement media advertising
- Develop a media mix and schedule
- Create and implement public relations programs
- Understand sales techniques
- Plan and implement promotional activities

Accounting and Finance Skills

Managers must be able to:

- Understand the nature and limitations of the accounting system used at the firm
- Understand tools and techniques used to interpret financial statements
- Understand the importance of cash planning for business purposes
- Understand economic conditions affecting the hospitality environment
- Understand financing alternatives available to the hospitality industry
- Use ratio analysis for comparative purposes and assess the firm's weaknesses and strengths
- Implement internal control measures
- Understand budgeting as a management tool
- Understand the firm's goals and objectives, including the significance of profit and loss analysis
- Use accounting information in making business decisions
- View accounting as a management information system

From an industry survey conducted by Professor Joseph Gregg, Florida International University.

must know how to delegate. According to contemporary author Weiss Roberts, even Attila the Hun, a brilliant fifth-century leader who forged a conglomeration of 70,000 barbarians into a well-disciplined army, understood this concept. Attila is credited with expressing these thoughts:

- Chieftains should never delegate responsibilities necessitating their direct attention.

- Those actions that don't require a chieftain's direct handling are appropriately delegated to the one most able to fulfill the assignment.

- A chieftain cannot accomplish every responsibility of his office by himself. Should he prove otherwise, a leader should understand that he is, in fact, chieftain over little or nothing at all.[8]

Motivating and Communicating. A manager motivates and communicates. The manager must turn a group of individuals into a team that works together. To do this, managers need to have excellent "people skills." They must be good at listening to employees with problems and helping them work out solutions. They must make wise and fair decisions regarding compensation and promotions. They must instinctively understand how to encourage and reward superior performance. Mississippi Management, a hotel management company, "pays regular bonuses for such mundane tasks as carving prime rib properly or making more beds (the correct way, to be sure) than the norm."[9]

Above all, managers need to know how to communicate—both orally and in writing—with their superiors and peers as well as with the people who report to them. The need for communication skills is often not recognized by those who desire to become managers. Because of the very nature of their jobs, managers have to "sell" their ideas and solutions to problems to others. This requires abilities ranging from writing a convincing memo or report to standing in front of a group and making a well-organized presentation. Communication skills can be developed through training and practice.

Measuring Performance. A manager must measure performance. Managers decide what factors are important to the success of the organization and then establish standards against which to measure individual or group performance. Domino's Pizza measures performance weekly by calling back a number of consumers who ordered pizzas from them. The management at Marriott, besides regularly taking a scientific sampling of guests and non-guests, pay a great deal of attention to what is known as the "GSI" or Guest Satisfaction Index. This index is compiled from in-room survey forms that guests voluntarily fill out. As J. W. "Bill" Marriott, Jr., chairman of Marriott Corporation, puts it: "Measurement of customer perception causes a lot of focus just where we want it, on the customer."[10] To measure performance, managers must collect statistical, financial, and qualitative data on how an organization or a department is doing, and then analyze and interpret the data for subordinates, superiors, and colleagues. For this reason hospitality and business schools often stress statistical and writing skills in their curricula.

Developing People. A manager develops people, including him- or herself. This calls for continual learning so that people can move ahead. On-going employee training is one of the main tools used to accomplish this, along with outside seminars and educational programs. Good managers recognize that their most important resource is the people who work for

Managers must know how to communicate effectively, both orally and in writing.

them. They also know that setting an example is the surest and best way to develop people. It is by following a good leader that people learn how to become leaders themselves. "What a manager does can be analyzed systematically," said Peter Drucker. "What a manager has to be able to do has to be learned (though perhaps not always taught). But [there is] one quality [that] cannot be learned, one qualification that the manager cannot acquire but must bring with him. It is not genius; it is character."[11] J. Willard Marriott, founder of the hotel chain bearing his name, believed the same. In a letter to his son when Bill Jr. took over the reins of the company, Marriott senior wrote, "A leader should have character, be an example in all things. This is his greatest influence."[12]

The Evolution of Management Theories

Although discovering the best way to manage has been a concern dating back thousands of years, it was not until the nineteenth century, after the Industrial Revolution in England and the industrialization of other countries had begun, that the subject of management was systematically studied and written about.

Probably the first modern management theorist was a Scottish cotton mill manager, Robert Owen (1771–1858). Owen thought that a manager's job was to institute reform. He believed that the way to motivate his workers and increase their productivity was to treat them better. He reduced the length of the standard working day to 10½ hours, refused to hire children under the age of 10, and created an incentive pay system based on daily evaluations of an employee's work.

After Owen, other industrialists and theorists contributed their views about management. Over the years, three schools of thought on management have emerged:

- The classical school

- The behavioral school

- The quantitative school

The Classical School

The founder of the classical school was Fredrick W. Taylor (1856–1915), an American industrial engineer who managed the Midvale Steel Company in Philadelphia. Taylor revolutionized the manufacturing process by coming up with scientific principles of production. According to Taylor's theories of scientific management, there was one "best way" to do every job; if managers analyzed what needed to be done to perform a job, they could come up with that best or most efficient way of performing it. Taylor believed that workers should be trained to do their jobs using only the "best way" that had been devised by management, and paid according to how fast and how well they performed. He suggested using a "differential rate system of piece work," under which one of two rates would be paid for a job: "a high price per piece, in case the work is finished in the shortest possible time and in perfect condition, and a low price, if it takes a longer time to do a job, or if there are any imperfections in the work."[13] Taylor also advocated "discharging workers and lowering the wages of the more stubborn men who refused to make any improvement." In 1912, in testimony taken by a committee of the House of Representatives investigating the practicality of using the "Taylor System" in government, Taylor compared workers to horses and said that just as a trotting horse was a "first class" horse not suited for hauling coal, so there were "first class" men who were better suited for some jobs than other men and so should be given those jobs.[14]

While Taylor's methods were widely hailed, many thought his approach was too hard-nosed and rational and criticized him for comparing people to horses and failing to take into account the needs of workers. Because they felt that pushing workers to produce more was in some cases irrational and might ultimately result in fewer jobs, both unions and workers became very critical of Taylor's ideas. In a strike at the Watertown Arsenal, government workers refused to adhere to what they called Taylor's "Stop-Watch System" on the grounds that "it is not a question of what a job is worth, but is based upon the quickest time that one can make."[15] Taylor defended his point of view by saying that if labor and management cooperated, his system would work.

A one-time associate of Taylor's, Henry Gantt (1861–1919), added to Taylor's thinking by devising a control system for production scheduling so that management could forecast how much work should be expected from each employee. His Gantt Chart, which identifies work progress and deadlines in a visual form, is still used today.

Frank Gilbreth (1868–1924) and his wife, Lillian Gilbreth (1878–1972), contributed much to the classical school of management. Frank was an efficiency expert; Lillian was an industrial psychologist. By doing a series of motion studies, Frank was able to reduce the number of motions needed to lay a brick from 18 to 5. If bricklayers were trained to lay bricks using Gilbreth's five-step system, their productivity would triple. Gilbreth's research was a logical continuation of Taylor's idea that a "best way" could be found for every job. Lillian concentrated her efforts on studying worker fatigue. She advocated standard work days, lunch periods, and regular breaks for all employees. The Gilbreths also developed what they called a "three position plan of promotion," in which workers would do their own job while at the same time preparing themselves for promotion by learning the next higher job, and also training workers below them to take over their job when the promotion actually came. That way every worker would always be looking forward to, and preparing for, a better job.

While one group of classical management theorists was developing systems to increase worker efficiency and productivity, another group was concerned with organizational theory—that is, defining the duties and functions of managers. The leader in this area was Henri Fayol (1841–1925), a French engineer and the manager of a large coal mining enterprise. Fayol was interested in what managers contributed to a business and how businesses were organized. From his studies, Fayol came up with a number of management principles. Fayol believed that these principles were universal and that they could be taught and applied to any situation. Much of what we consider to be general management theory today was first articulated by Fayol in his 14 principles of management (see Exhibit 8.2). In Fayol's view, the manager's primary role is to be a regulator and integrator, taking all of an organization's rules, structures, and traditions and making them work together.

In summary, theorists of the classical school were mostly concerned with productivity. According to these theorists, workers are rational people who are interested primarily in making money. The classical school of management emphasizes satisfying employees' economic needs (pay them better for doing more work) and physical needs (don't tire them out) but ignores their social needs for respect and recognition. While many of the ideas developed by Taylor and his followers are still used today, we recognize now that scientific management ignores the human desire for job satisfaction. In service businesses such as hotels and restaurants, this human factor can make all the difference between providing a good product and a bad one.

The Behavioral School

In recent years, many managers have recognized that the classical approach to management has serious limitations, especially when applied to service industries. To begin with, the relatively stable and predictable business environment enjoyed by the classical theorists is a thing of the past. In today's business world, turbulence and ambiguity are the norm. This means that rigid systems and rules no longer work as well as they used to. Managers need to be more flexible and adaptable. In service industries especially, regulations and formal procedures may interfere with an employee's ability to satisfy consumer expectations. In addition, employees today are better educated and need and want to make their own decisions as much as possible.

For these reasons as well as others there has been a movement towards a behavioral or human relations school of management. Behaviorists attempt to find other ways of motivating workers besides the rules, systems, and wages proposed by classical management thinkers. One of the first behaviorists was Chester I. Barnard (1886–1961), president of the New Jersey Telephone Company. Barnard believed that only when the goals of employees as well as employers were being satisfied could an organization grow and prosper. People want to work within an organization, said Barnard, because they want to accomplish more than they can do alone. Therefore, if management can mesh the personal goals of its employees with the organization's overall goals, a company should be successful.

A landmark in the development of behavioral management theory occurred when George Elton Mayo (1880–1949), a Harvard Business School professor, evaluated some studies on human behavior in work settings

Exhibit 8.2 Fayol's 14 Principles of Management

1. *Division of work.* In Fayol's words, specialization leads to "more and better work with the same effort." This concept eventually led to the modern assembly line. Fayol believed specialization applied not only to workers but to management as well.

2. *Authority and responsibility.* Fayol defined this as "the right to give orders and the power to exact obedience." Managers need both authority and responsibility to accomplish things.

3. *Discipline.* This is a function of leadership. Poor leadership produces poor discipline. Management needs to enter into fair agreements with employees and then both sides must respect and adhere to all the rules. When the rules are violated, management must, for the well-being of the business, apply certain sanctions.

4. *Unity of command.* "For any action whatsoever an employee should receive orders from one superior only," said Fayol.

5. *Unity of direction.* Those activities in an organization having the same objective should be under the direction of one person with a single plan. In other words, one person should be in charge of sales, another finance, and so forth.

6. *Subordination of individual interest to general interest.* The interests of a single employee or group of employees are less important than the interests of the whole organization.

7. *Payment of personnel.* Workers should be paid at a rate that is fair and affords satisfaction to both employers and employees. Fayol advocated (1) paying workers by either time or piece or by the job, (2) giving bonuses, and (3) providing for employee welfare through better working conditions. He did not favor profit sharing except for senior managers on the grounds that is was impractical.

8. *Centralization.* "The issue of centralization or decentralization is a simple question of proportion; it is the matter of finding the optimum degree of centralization for the particular concern." Managers need to centralize things enough so that they can maintain control, but also need to give workers some authority so that they can perform their jobs. This balance will vary in different organizations so managers need to be flexible and seek the best degree of centralization.

9. *Scalar chain.* This is "the chain of superiors in a firm ranging from the ultimate authority to the lowest ranks." Generally, Fayol felt it was a mistake to deviate from this without reason, but he also believed that there were times when this might be necessary.

10. *Order.* "There must be a place appointed for each thing and each thing must be in its appointed place." Similarly, "there must be an appointed place for every employee. . . . As in the case of orderly material arrangement, charts or plans facilitate the establishment and control of human arrangements."

11. *Equity.* Managers need to be impartial and at the same time understanding in dealing with their employees. Fayol advocated both kindliness and justice.

12. *Stability of tenure of personnel.* A high employee turnover rate is not good for any organization. Organizations need to have policies and plans that help them retain workers.

13. *Initiative.* Employees must be encouraged to show initiative on the job. "Thinking out a plan and ensuring its success are two of the keenest satisfactions that an intelligent person can experience," said Fayol. While some mistakes might occur, allowing employee initiative injects zeal and energy into an enterprise.

14. *Esprit de corps.* "Union is strength." Promoting team spirit is a key factor in good management. "Dividing enemy forces to weaken them is clever, but dividing one's own team is a grave sin against the business." Fayol also advocated oral communications rather than written ones because written ones might cause misunderstandings.

Source: Adapted from Henri Fayol, *General and Industrial Management*, revised by Irwin Gray (New York: Institute of Electrical and Electronic Engineers Press, 1984), pp. 61–82.

performed at the Western Electric Company's plant in Hawthorne, Illinois. Conducted between 1924 and 1933, these "Hawthorne studies" revolutionized the way management looked at human relations problems. The experiments were originally designed and conducted by the company to assess the effects of lighting conditions on workers. In the first experiment, which spanned three years, two groups of workers were segregated from the rest and each group was placed into its own "test room." Each test room started out with the same amount of light, with both groups performing the same task. For one group the light level was gradually increased over a period of time and, as expected, the group's productivity increased. Next, the light level was then gradually lowered and, to the surprise of the researchers, productivity increased again. Moreover, in the other test room, where the light remained constant, productivity also increased! The company's researchers were puzzled by this ambiguity and decided that there must be other factors at work besides the amount of light.

At that point a second series of experiments was started, this time looking at other variables that might be affecting productivity. Five workers were placed in a separate test room and this time rest periods were varied, the work day and work week were shortened, and wages were raised. The researchers acted as supervisors in this set of experiments and allowed the workers a say in deciding when and how long their rest periods would be. On the whole, performance improved, but there were unexpected variations.

In the midst of these experiments, Mayo and his associates became involved, and they began to suspect that the real agent of change was the human factor:

The Hawthorne studies revealed that one of the most important ways for managers and supervisors to help motivate employees is to establish a good relationship with them.

The records of the test room showed a continual improvement in performance of the operators regardless of the [experimental] changes made during the study. It was also noticed that there was a marked improvement in their attitude toward their work and working environment. This simultaneous improvement in attitude and effectiveness indicated that there might be a definite relationship between them. In other words we could more logically attribute the increase in efficiency to a betterment of morale than to any of the . . . alterations made in the course of the experiment. . . . Comment after comment from the girls indicates that they have been relieved of the nervous tension under which they previously worked. They have ceased to regard the man in charge as a boss . . . [and] they have a feeling that their increased production is in some way related to the distinctly freer, happier, and more pleasant working environment.[16]

Subsequently, 21,126 workers of the plant were interviewed over a period of three years to check the findings of the test group. Mayo and his associates eventually determined that their findings were valid. The employees worked harder and more efficiently when they knew that management was interested in them and that they had the ear of a sympathetic supervisor. This was far more important in motivating them than the level of lighting or even the amount of money they were paid. This finding—that there was a clear link between supervision, morale, and productivity—was subsequently labeled the Hawthorne effect, and Mayo's book, *The Human Problems of an Industrial Civilization*, became a bestseller in business circles.

The idea of concentrating on motivation was developed even further by the work of Abraham Maslow (1890–1970). Maslow came up with the idea that we all have a system of priorities in our needs. Maslow defined a hierarchy of needs and theorized that we try to satisfy our needs progressively—that is, we satisfy one group of needs first because they are the most basic (or strongest), then go on to the second group, and so forth.

Group I needs are physiological. These are our most powerful needs, and until they are satisfied we are not interested in anything else. They are our needs for water, food, and shelter.

Group II needs are the safety needs—our needs for protection and security. As soon as we are satisfied that we have a roof over our heads and something to eat, these needs emerge as primary.

Social or belonging and love needs are in Group III. Once we have food and security, the next thing we hunger for is love, affection, and a feeling that we belong to a community or group. These needs are all part of a need to relate to others around us.

Group IV needs are esteem needs. All of us need or want to think well of ourselves and to have others think well of us. We want to be appreciated and recognized, and to achieve some degree of independence.

Self-actualization needs make up Group V. These are needs for fulfillment—to express ourselves and reach our full potential. These needs are the highest of all and they emerge only after all other needs are met.

Another theory of how human beings are motivated was suggested by Douglas McGregor (1906–1964), a professor of psychology at Massachusetts Institute of Technology. McGregor said managers tend to believe one or the other of two basic sets of assumptions about human nature and behavior, and these assumptions governed a manager's behavior and management style. McGregor labeled the first set of assumptions Theory X, and said they represented the "traditional view of direction and control." Theory X assumptions are:

- The average human being has an inherent dislike of work and will avoid it if possible.

- Because people dislike work, most people must be coerced, controlled, directed, and threatened with punishment to get them to put forth adequate effort toward the achievement of organizational objectives.

- The average employee prefers to be directed, wishes to avoid responsibility, has relatively little ambition, and wants security above all.[17]

McGregor thought that while most managers believed these assumptions, they were really nothing more than self-fulfilling prophecies. In fact, McGregor said, if more managers would change their assumptions to Theory Y, which is based on a whole different set of ideas, workers would behave entirely differently. The assumptions of Theory Y are:

- Working is as natural as playing or resting. The average human being does not inherently dislike work.

- External control and the threat of punishment are not the only means of encouraging employees to work towards organizational objectives. Employees will exercise self-direction and self-control in the service of objectives to which they are committed.

- Commitment to objectives is a function of the rewards associated with achieving those objectives. The most significant of such rewards, e.g., the satisfaction of ego and self-actualization needs, can be direct products of effort directed toward organizational objectives.

In the final analysis, McGregor believed that managers who did not try to control their employees through formal structures but instead tried to motivate them by encouragement and challenge would be the most successful.

The Quantitative School

While the behavioral school of thought founded by Barnard and Mayo influenced a great number of managers, there were still some unanswered questions. For one thing, not all companies that improved working conditions achieved the expected results. It turned out that in many instances the corporate culture, salary levels, or the way the company was organized played a more important part in determining motivation and productivity. In other words the problem of how to motivate workers turned out to be much more complex than was realized by any of the early behavioral researchers.

A new approach that would integrate the management ideas of the classical and behavioral schools was needed. The quantitative school, which is still evolving, tried to accomplish this. Theorists in the quantitative school take a much broader view of management and believe that there are other factors that need to be considered besides simple organizational and motivational problems. These factors include the collective "personality" of the company and its employees, the personal relationships within the company, the personal values represented by the various informal groups within the company, and the general conditions of society.

There are two main theories in the quantitative school: the systems theory and the contingency theory.

Systems Theory. According to the systems theory, a company is a system composed of many interrelated departments, which in turn is part of a larger external environment (made up of such things as competing companies, the economy in general, societal values) that influences its behavior. Therefore managers cannot act independently—what they can and cannot accomplish depends on other managers inside of their company and on outside environmental factors. For example, in a hotel the decisions made by the food and beverage director as to what kind of food will be served and at what price will affect the kinds of groups that the sales department can attract to the hotel. Similarly, the number of rooms the sales department sells to groups affects the number of rooms that the rooms department has to sell to individual travelers. All of these decisions are affected to a great degree by the external environment—how many other hotels are nearby, what their rates are, how strongly they are competing for each other's business, and consumer needs and wants.

Recognition of this interdependence has led to the growth of management information systems (MIS) and property management systems (PMS). These computer systems make it possible for managers to examine and interpret data from many different "systems" at the same time—the many systems in the outside environment and those within the business itself. For example, managers at the corporate headquarters of hotel or restaurant chains can use computers to instantly see how reservations and sales are doing for units scattered around the world, and compare this information with environmental information, such as the state of the economy, in order to make wise marketing decisions.

Contingency Theory. The second approach to quantitative management utilizes the contingency theory. Contingency management, sometimes referred to as situational management, recognizes that every situation is different and every manager is different. Contingency theorists suggest that there are few management principles that are as universal as Taylor, Fayol, and Mayo believed. Managers must be pragmatic and decide what is likely to achieve the needed results in any given situation. The solution may use classical, behavioral, or quantitative management ideas, depending on what the problem is and what resources are available to the manager to solve it. Managers must constantly adapt to changing circumstances, and the way to do this is to be very flexible, to keep an open mind, and to be able to change one's own behavior to fit the situation at hand.

Other Management Theories

Theory Z. William Ouchi introduced Theory Z in 1981.[18] Ouchi compared Japanese and American management practices in matters such as employment, promotion, and decision-making. He found that Japanese companies tend to employ people for a lifetime, while American companies do not. In Japan, promotion can be quite slow, while in America a manager can be promoted very rapidly. Japanese companies make decisions on a collective or consensus basis, while in American companies a single manager can often call the shots. Ouchi then studied the management techniques of successful companies in America and noted that they had much in common with successful Japanese companies. For instance, consensus decision-making, employee participation, and long-term employment are all hallmarks of the best American companies. Ouchi suggests that more American companies should develop a style of management similar to the Japanese style, which he calls Theory Z. A Z-type organization must be committed to its employees, trust them, involve them in decision-making, but nevertheless encourage specialization and responsibility.

Customers First. Another attempt to make sense out of all of the different management approaches came in 1982 from two McKinsey & Company management consultants, Thomas H. Peters and Robert A. Waterman, Jr., who wrote *In Search of Excellence,* a study of 43 excellent, very large companies. In summarizing their findings, Peters said, "In the private or public sector, in big business or small, we observe that there are only two ways to create and sustain superior performance over the long haul. First, take exceptional care of your customers . . . via superior service and superior quality. Secondly, constantly innovate. That's it. There are no alternatives in achieving long term superior performance, or sustaining strategic competitive advantage, as business strategists call it."[19]

Peters and Waterman were the first to turn the management spotlight onto customers and suggest that while all of the various management theories and systems had their place, managers must never forget that they are in business to satisfy customers, and all the systems in the world to motivate employees and organize them using scientific principles will not succeed unless the final outcome is a satisfied customer. Although quantitative management theorists generally recognized the importance of the external environment—including customers—Peters and Waterman said that customers should be the *most* important consideration when managers decide how to run their business. Peters, in fact, suggested that companies start drawing their organization charts upside down with customers at the top and presidents on the bottom![20]

An example of how customers should help run a business is provided by Domino's Pizza, which, as mentioned earlier, conducts regular and extensive phone surveys of their customers to ask about Domino's service and products. "The survey not only covers quantitative/technical issues e.g. response time—but also qualitative ones: 'Did anything we do bug you?' Monthly evaluation and compensation for all hands (up through the president!) are predicated on the results, which are instantly summarized and made available to everyone."[21] Under the Peters and Waterman model of excellent management, the principles of scientific management apply only so long as they help the company please the customer, and even wages should be tied to customer satisfaction. We have come a long way from Fredrick Taylor, who believed in paying workers according to how well they met their manager's expectations, not their customers'.

WE VALUE YOUR OPINION

Thank you for ordering a Domino's Pizza®. We would appreciate any comments or suggestions which will help us improve our service and product.

Date _____

Name _____

Address _____

City _____

Please check which pizza you ordered. ☐ **PAN PIZZA** ☐ **ORIGINAL**

PIZZA (Please circle your response.)

1. Did you receive your pizza as ordered? Yes No
   If not, what was wrong?
2. Was your pizza damaged upon arrival? Yes No
   (eg., items stuck to top)
   If yes, how was it damaged?
3. Was your pizza: Too Hot   Just Right   Too Cold
4. Amount of toppings? Too Much   Just Right   Too Little
5. Thickness of crust? Too Thick   Just Right   Too Thin
6. Amount of sauce? Too Much   Just Right   Too Little
7. Overall, was your pizza: Excellent   Good   Fair   Bad
8. Have you ordered a
   Domino's Pizza® before? Yes No
9. Have you tried a pan pizza other than
   Domino's Pan Pizza®? Yes No
   Name of other brand?
   How would you rate our product
   next to theirs? Better Than   As Good As   Not As Good As

DELIVERY (Please circle your response.)

1. When you ordered your pizza were you placed
   on hold? Yes No
   If yes, how long?
2. Was the phone person courteous? Yes No
3. Did you receive your pizza in 30 minutes or less? Yes No
   If not, did you receive our service guarantee? Yes No
4. Was the delivery person courteous? Yes No
5. Was the delivery person neat and clean? Yes No
6. Overall, was the service: Excellent   Good   Fair   Bad

Please write any comments or suggestions on the back of this form.

Present this flyer with your next pizza purchase.

Thanks for taking the time to respond.

$1.00 OFF!
Order any original or Domino's Pan Pizza® with **ONE** or more toppings and **get $1.00 OFF!**

Offer valid through ® February 28, 1990

Valid at participating stores only. Not valid with any other offer. Customer pays applicable sales tax. Delivery area limited to ensure safe driving. Our drivers carry less than $20.00. ® 1990 Domino's Pizza, Inc.   COUPON NECESSARY

OPINION

Overall, were you satisfied with this order?
☐ **YES** ☐ **NO**
CALL US!
Location Serving You:

D O M I N O ' S   P I Z Z A®

In addition to telephone surveys, Domino's attaches customer survey cards to its pizza boxes. Courtesy of Domino's Pizza.

Current Hospitality Management Practices

As can be seen from the previous section, most management theories have been the work of people involved in large bureaucracies such as armies, or industrial engineers concerned with the best way to manage manufacturing companies such as coal mines and steel mills. One reason for this is that, until recently, service businesses have been very small and were not able to support extensive research. This has changed, however, now that hotels, restaurants, hospitals, banks, airlines, and other service businesses represent approximately two-thirds of U.S. economic activity.

One assumption made by managers up to now has been that the principles of management developed by industrial managers are universal and can be applied equally well in any type of enterprise. This, among other reasons, is why most management courses taught at universities use many more examples and cases drawn from manufacturing industries than from service industries. But this assumption is slowly changing. According to Professor Chistopher H. Lovelock of the Harvard Business School, "A growing body of research suggests that managers in the service sector face many problems that are not commonly encountered by their colleagues in manufacturing."[22]

In this text we have taken a view similar to Lovelock's, and thus the management principles presented in the rest of this chapter are drawn mostly from the work of Lovelock; Peters and Waterman; James L. Heskett, author of *Managing in the Service Economy;* and Karl Albrecht and Ron Zemke, authors of *Service America.* We do not rule out the necessity of understanding traditional management principles, which is why we described them earlier in some detail; we simply suggest that there are unique problems in service businesses that require a shift in traditional thinking.

The remainder of this chapter explores a number of management concepts that are receiving widespread acceptance in the hospitality and other service industries. These include the need for strategic planning, strategies for managing supply and demand, the strategic service vision, and the key managerial/leadership roles that today's service managers should be comfortable with.

Strategic Planning

As pointed out earlier, the most important operational competency of top-level service managers is the ability to plan for the future. While day-to-day operations can be performed by others, someone must be thinking about tomorrow, next week, next year, and beyond. This is the job of top managers—to develop the strategy for survival and growth that any business needs if it is to succeed.

Broad, long-range planning is called strategic planning. Strategic planning is an important ingredient in business success. Companies must formulate general business objectives for themselves, otherwise there is confusion about where they are going and how they intend to get there. Here are some strategic planning objectives of one top company, Hewlett-Packard:

> *Profit.* To achieve sufficient profit to finance our company growth and provide the resources we need to achieve our other corporate objectives.

> *Customers.* To provide products and services of the greatest possible value to our customers, thereby gaining their respect and loyalty.

> *Our People.* To help HP people share in the company's success, which they make possible; to provide job security based on their performance; to recognize their individual achievements; and to insure the personal satisfaction that comes from a sense of accomplishment in their work.[23]

Tactical Planning. Once strategic objectives have been formulated, the next step is to make plans to achieve them. This is done by formulating more specific tactical objectives. For instance, a restaurant chain might have a strategic objective of becoming the largest operator of seafood restaurants in California. Tactical objectives might include opening three new restaurants in Los Angeles, two in San Francisco, and one in San Diego. To make sure that these tactical objectives are not forgotten, there is a management technique called management by objectives (MBO). Peter Drucker believes in this concept and thinks that for a company to succeed, very specific objectives need to be articulated in all areas. Douglas McGregor, the originator of the Theory X and Theory Y concepts of behavior, also believed in MBO.

Under the MBO system, management objectives and deadlines for achieving them are first formulated by a company's top managers. For instance, "increase food and beverage sales by 10% within the next six months" might be one of the strategic objectives of a hotel's general manager. Based on this, the food and beverage manager has to come up with some objectives for his or her department in order to meet that goal. "Design a new menu cover within the next 30 days" and "introduce five new menu items within the next three months" might be two of the food and beverage manager's objectives.

Whenever an objective is set under the MBO system, an appropriate measurement of success is agreed on. For the food and beverage manager just mentioned, there might be several separate measurements of success: whether the new menu design and the five new items were actually introduced, whether they were introduced on time, and whether sales increased by 10% as anticipated.

While MBO is widely practiced, many companies feel this system has several weaknesses, including its emphasis on short-term goals and its lack of flexibility (since the system discourages changing goals in the middle of a time period).

Planning Problems in Capacity-Constrained Businesses

One important difference between service organizations and manufacturing firms is the inability of service firms to inventory finished products. In manufacturing, the peaks and valleys of supply and demand are managed by finishing and storing goods in advance of when they will be needed. Thus it is seldom, if ever, necessary to produce anything instantly to satisfy demand. Because service firms cannot finish and store services, their financial success depends on how efficiently they are able to match their productive capacity—their staff, equipment, and resources—to consumer demand at any given moment. This is very difficult. When demand is low, production capacity will be wasted because there will be more workers than customers; when demand is higher than production capacity, business will be lost—there will be more guests than the workers can handle. In other words, hotels and restaurants are, by their very nature, capacity-constrained organizations and therefore must constantly manage both supply (production capacity) and demand.

Managing Supply. Let's first look at strategies for managing supply. In the case of hotels and restaurants, the ability to supply the products manufactured in the service "factory" is fixed. A hotel has a fixed number of beds, just as a restaurant has a fixed number of seats. These cannot be altered to increase capacity whenever demand is greater than capacity—that is, when there are more guests than there are hotel beds or restaurant seats. That means that a good part of the time hotels and restaurants must follow a level-capacity strategy in which the same amount of capacity is offered no matter how high the demand.

However, some hospitality firms can follow a chased-demand strategy—in which capacity can be varied to suit the demand level—in a limited way. For example, there is a certain flexibility in some parts of a hotel, such as the space set aside for meetings and conventions. Another tactic that is common in hospitality firms is to have a certain number of part-time employees such as food servers who work only when the demand is high. Sometimes firms such as caterers can rent extra equipment and thus increase their capacity as needed. Finally, companies such as Embassy Suites cross-train employees so that employees can be shifted temporarily or promoted to other jobs as needed. In the long run, of course, a hotel or restaurant organization can increase its capacity by enlarging its property or building a new one.

Managing Demand. Because hotel and restaurant capacity is limited, it is important to put most of the emphasis for strategic planning on managing demand. One of the goals of managers in a service business is to shift demand away from periods when it cannot be accommodated (because the operation is already filled to capacity) to periods when it can be accommodated. One way to do this is to encourage business during slow periods. Restaurants offer early-bird specials to increase demand earlier in the day, and lounges have happy hours for the same reason.

While supply cannot be inventoried, sometimes demand can. This happens when managers or employees encourage customers to stand in line or sit in the restaurant's lounge until the next table becomes available. Reservations systems also are an example of demand inventorying.

The most common method used to influence demand in the hotel industry is price. Pricing strategies as a means of controlling demand are risky unless they are carefully understood. Hotels are faced with pricing decisions every day, such as whether to accept meeting and convention reservations at low group rates, or hold on to those rooms for later sale at higher rates to individual business travelers. One approach used in making such decisions is yield management.

Sometimes the product itself can be varied to help balance supply and demand. Restaurants routinely change menus and level of service between lunch and dinner, for example. Cruise ships reposition themselves to call on ports in the Caribbean in the winter and Alaska in the summer. Sometimes different services can be offered at the same time to accommodate the demand levels of different groups. Concierge floors in hotels and first-class or business-class airline seats are examples of this.

Finally, communication strategies can play a large part in balancing levels of demand. A carefully thought out advertising schedule can enable resorts to influence demand by appealing to new market segments with special rates during the off season, and keeping demand levels high during the season by attracting those guest groups willing to pay full rates.

One of the hard realities that prompts all of these tactics to manage demand is that hotels and restaurants have a high level of fixed expenses because of their physical plant. These fixed expenses by definition cannot be altered (lowered), so strategies and tactics must be found to utilize a hotel or restaurant to its fullest possible extent. Even a marginal increase in business can produce a significant increase in profit once the break-even point is reached.

Moments of Truth. In order to achieve maximum profits, many successful hospitality firms have turned to computers and other modern technology. But this sometimes produces a depersonalized atmosphere and guests may feel that they are being treated as mere numbers. To combat this guest perception, some companies have identified what they call "moments of truth." Moments of truth are instances when important personal contact is made between guests and employees. Good businesses concentrate their efforts on making sure that moments of truth are handled correctly. For hotels, moments of truth occur when guests check in or out and come face-to-face with a hotel employee. Although there are certain check-in/check-out routines that must be followed, guests should be given individual attention so they feel their needs are being addressed in a personal way. Thus, front desk employees should look up from their computer screens to give guests a warm welcome (by name if possible), and continue to smile and make eye contact as they perform their duties for the guests.

The Strategic Service Vision

James Heskett, professor of business administration at the Harvard Business School, says that all successful service companies share what he calls a "strategic service vision"—a blueprint for service managers. The components of this blueprint are:

- Targeting a market segment

- Focusing on a service strategy[24]

Let's discuss these elements in more detail, drawing from examples and ideas from the work of Heskett and others.

Targeting a Market Segment. There is no such thing as a product or service that will appeal to everyone. Some people want hotels that have a very good restaurant because they like to eat well while they are traveling. Others don't care that much about food but value a hotel with a fitness club and spa where they can relax and exercise. Some travelers want a comfortable guestroom with a desk where they can work; others plan to spend little time in their room. Similarly, a restaurant can't appeal to everyone. People have different tastes in food, different ideas of what constitutes a pleasant experience when dining out, and differ in how much they are willing to pay for a meal. Since hotels and restaurants cannot hope to appeal to everyone, they single out groups or market segments and attempt to provide products and services that, in the eyes of their consumers, are superior to those of their competitors. For example, McDonald's primary market has always been families with young children. Wendy's targets adults who want a hamburger cooked to order; it makes little effort to attract children because it suspects they might scare

The best hospitality businesses train their employees to handle "moments of truth" correctly.

away the adult customers. At the high end of the scale is Fuddruckers, which serves larger and more expensive hamburgers and beer in an atmosphere designed to appeal to adults. The Omni Parker House hotel in Boston focuses on individual business travelers and does not accept business from bus tour groups except on weekends during July and August, which are traditionally slow periods. Mini-vacation weekend packages are offered only when large numbers of business travelers are not in the hotel.

Focusing on a Service Strategy. The various service concepts that hospitality businesses adopt are not simply amorphous marketing ideas. A hotel or restaurant, including its services, is carefully designed to appeal to a limited segment of the market, and the way service is delivered is tailored to match the expectations of that segment. Research has shown that most people believe buying an intangible service like a vacation or even a meal in a restaurant is more risky than buying a manufactured product. With a manufactured product, buyers have a better idea of what they're getting for their money, while with intangible products there may be some surprises. It is that element of surprise that poses the biggest challenge to service businesses. That is why it is so important to provide consistent services that meet an operation's standards.

  Service standards. Another service strategy concern is establishing service standards. Successful hospitality companies focus a good deal of management attention on establishing service quality standards, communicating them through training programs, and measuring performance.

  For example, one service standard that is frequently established and easy to measure is waiting time. McDonald's and Burger King have strict standards for how long customers are expected to wait for their food once it has been ordered. Many airlines and hotels with busy telephone reservation systems have set time limits for how long customers can be kept on hold before their call is handled. In some cases an effort is made to manage expectations so that customers feel that they are being taken care of promptly. Restaurants often do this by telling guests they will have to wait longer for a table than is in truth necessary. When they are given their table earlier than expected they conclude that they have been given special attention—thus their feeling of receiving good service is reinforced.

Another quality control technique restaurants use is to set service standards as to the amount of time between when a customer sits down and when contact is first established by a server. At some properties the standard is for a server to go to the table immediately and say, "I'll be with you in a minute." Another restaurant may require bread and butter to be served at the same time to further acknowledge the presence of the diners.

The truth is that providing consistent services is extremely complex where customer contact is involved, especially when some of the lowest-paid employees make the contacts. A former Marriott executive, G. Michael Hostage, described one strategy he used to deal with the problem:

> 'The Marriott Bellman' booklet is designed to convince our uniformed doormen that they represent an all-important first and last impression for many of our guests, that they must stand with dignity and good posture, and that they must not lean against the wall or put up their feet when sitting. . . . Bellmen are often looked at subconsciously by guests as being "Mr. Marriott himself" because many times a guest will speak to and deal with a bellman more often during a visit than with any other employees of the hotel. . . . They are coached to smile often and to do all they can to make the guest feel welcome and special.[25]

Marriott is known for setting exact standards—including service standards—for all of its jobs, and communicating them clearly in writing as well as in training sessions. Marriott continually measures how well standards are being met with frequent inspections, and encourages its employees to provide good service through profit sharing, stock options, and other bonus programs. Recently Pizza Hut announced that it was going to reward its employees with company stock so that everyone would feel a personal interest in doing a good job. Avis Car Rental has a similar program in place.

Job restructuring. An effective service strategy must also provide a means of achieving levels of productivity that will satisfy economic needs as well as customer expectations. One way managers do this in service companies is by job restructuring—changing the nature of the work or the way it is done. For example, at Benihana of Tokyo, the chef prepares the food at a hibachi in front of the guests, combining the jobs of food server and chef. Observes Heskett, "Given the nature of a service concept that combines quality food and entertainment at reasonable prices as well as the exotic format of a Japanese restaurant, customers of Benihana readily accept a highly economic combination of jobs that is carried out in their full view."[26]

Payroll control. Along with controlling the quality of services goes controlling payroll and other costs involved in providing that service. It has been observed by several researchers that the companies that do the best job of controlling service quality also do the best job of controlling labor and other costs, since they are closely connected. Payroll control can be achieved by careful scheduling techniques and enhanced employee training, a combination that almost always produces higher productivity and better service.

Earlier we told the story of Tim Firnstahl and YEGA (Your Enjoyment Guaranteed. Always). One of the reasons Firnstahl designed the YEGA service system was to identify systems that were not working and control costs that were out of line. Every time an employee gave a guest a free meal, this was reported and considered by Firnstahl to be a "system failure cost." Whenever a meal was given away, Firnstahl asked, "Why is the system failing?" not "Why is the employee failing?" Asking the question proved to be highly productive. "Our search for the culprit in a string of complaints about slow food service in one restaurant led first to the kitchen and then to one cook. But pushing the search one step further revealed several unrealistically complex dishes that no one could have prepared swiftly."[27] Thus a service strategy helped identify a production problem.

Service Organizations and People Power

A prime function of managers is to organize their companies. Company organization tends to be different in successful service firms than in manufacturing firms. One difference we have already discussed is that in successful service firms the employees who deal with customers are encouraged and empowered to take responsibility for customer satisfaction. At Delta, for example, gate agents are empowered to upgrade passengers and even give them free airline seats if they have been bumped or needlessly delayed. But there are many other elements in the organizational structures of service companies that can make a difference.

As Peters and Waterman observed and as Heskett confirms, successful service companies have relatively small executive groups at the top that meet frequently and informally. Managers spend a good deal of their time out of their offices, managing by walking around (MBWA). The idea is to have as few levels of management as possible between the top of the organization and the bottom, so that people will be encouraged to work together, not prevented from doing so by layers of management and numerous closed doors. Given the importance of people and their relationships in service organizations, selecting, training, and promoting the right people is of paramount importance.

In conclusion, we have tried to illustrate that in the management of hospitality organizations there is no single model or style of managing that is appropriate in all circumstances or for all organizations. Managers have different personalities, and thus any two managers are likely to adopt different solutions to the same problem. There are no absolutely right or wrong ways of doing things. There are, however, certain management principles involving market segmentation, operations strategy, and human resources that are used in excellent companies and that seem to produce the best results. In order to apply those principles, managers need to be able to do certain things, many of which cannot be taught in a classroom but must be learned by experience. Four management professors—Robert E. Quinn, Sue R. Faerman, Michael P. Thompson, and Michael R. McGrath—have put together eight managerial/leadership roles and their key competencies (see Exhibit 8.3). Managers and aspiring managers would do

Exhibit 8.3 Eight Managerial/Leadership Roles

Director Role

As a director, a manager must be a decisive initiator who defines problems, establishes objectives, generates rules and policies, and gives instructions. A manager directs by taking charge of a situation, focusing on results, and making things happen. As directors, managers must also set goals and define the action plans that will be needed to reach them. Finally, managers must know how to delegate effectively by recognizing that they cannot accomplish very much by themselves. It is only through the work of others that things get done.

Producer Role

In the role of producer, managers are expected to be task-oriented, work-focused, and highly interested in the task at hand. Managers must be able to motivate themselves to a high level of productivity, respond to challenges in a positive manner, and have the drive and ambition to continuously desire to improve their performance. Just as managers must motivate themselves, they must also motivate others by understanding that what they expect of their employees and how they treat them largely determine their employees' performances and career progress. In the role of producer, a manager must also learn how to cope with and minimize the effects of negative stress that occurs regularly in many hospitality jobs, because often there are slow periods followed by peaks of frenzied activity.

Coordinator Role

In the coordinator role, a manager's task is to make sure that work flows smoothly and that activities are carried out according to their relative importance with a minimum amount of conflict among individuals, departments, or groups of workers. This is accomplished by planning the use of financial and human resources to ensure the most effective delivery of services. Managers must establish standards and priorities and schedule work by task and by employee. Managers must also establish lines of authority by clarifying who reports to whom and who is supposed to perform which jobs. Finally, as coordinators, managers must learn to use controls as effective mechanisms that provide feedback on whether actual performance is consistent with planned performance and whether customers are actually receiving the level of service intended.

Monitor Role

As monitors, managers are expected to know what is going on and make sure people are complying with rules and producing as expected. Managers must be able to keep track of facts such as food costs or occupancy rates, analyze them, and decide what is important. To do this, managers must be good at handling paperwork, reading memos, and taking notes at meetings. Managers must also know how to make effective use of information by keeping an open mind and using good judgment. To solve problems, managers must be able to discover and weigh all possible factors and then decide which solution is likely to produce the desired result(s). This requires clear analytical judgment. Managers must also be able to present information to others by writing effective memos, proposals, and letters.

Mentor Role

In this role a manager is expected to be helpful, considerate, sensitive, approachable, open, and fair. Managers do this by understanding themselves and others, by interpersonal communication—including developing active listening skills, and by developing employees through performance evaluation and training.

Facilitator Role

In this role a manager fosters collective effort, builds cohesion and morale, and manages interpersonal conflict. This can be accomplished through team building. Effective managers are first of all team players. They believe that working together is better than working in isolation. They are able to get others to share that belief. Managers who are facilitators practice participative decision-making. When an important decision comes up, they involve the individuals whose work lives are affected by the decision. Furthermore, they are skillful in conflict management, which research shows may take between 20 and 50 percent of a manager's time. These managers know how to use collaborative approaches to resolve disputes.

Innovator Role

In today's rapidly changing environment, the ability of managers to initiate and implement change so that they can keep up with the times is an essential survival skill. Nowhere is change more evident than in the hospitality field, where new lifestyles and demographic profiles are constantly affecting how and where people travel as well as their diets and tastes. Innovative managers must learn how to live with changes that are unplanned and sometimes unwelcome. Doing this requires the creativity to generate new ideas and solutions. Innovative managers know how to plan for and manage change. They welcome new technology, new ideas, and are willing to take risks to find new and better ways of doing things.

Exhibit 8.3 *(continued)*

Broker Role

In organizations, good ideas work only if people see a benefit in adopting them. Managers must be brokers who know how to build and maintain a power base, negotiate agreement and commitment, and present ideas effectively. These managers understand that power and authority are not the same thing. Real power comes not from a title or a position, but from the shape and impact a person's presentation of self has on others—the personal characteristics that people find attractive or influential or persuasive. Power can also be gained through the expertise a manager may possess in special areas like food or computers. Managers who are effective brokers are good negotiators and know how to get agreement among groups or individuals with opposite ideas. They are also competent public speakers and know how to communicate not only on a one-to-one basis but to an audience.

Source: Adapted from Robert E. Quinn, Sue R. Faerman, Michael P. Thompson, and Michael R. McGrath, *Becoming a Master Manager* (New York: Wiley, 1990).

well to keep these various management roles in mind and try to develop their skills in them as they pursue their careers.

Chapter Summary

A manager's job is similar to that of a conductor of an orchestra, in that he or she must take all of the individual parts of a company and harmonize them into a whole. The manager must also compose the music that the orchestra is going to play. Managers have five basic tasks to perform. They are: setting objectives, organizing, motivating and communicating, measuring performance, and developing people.

The classical school of management was founded by Fredrick Taylor, who advocated scientific management. Taylor believed there was a best way to perform every job. Frank and Lillian Gilbreth looked for new ways to make people more efficient and studied worker fatigue. Henri Fayol developed 14 principles of management that included division of labor, unity of command, and centralization, among others. His work is the basis of the current systems approach used in industrial management today.

The behavioral school was founded by Chester Barnard, who believed in satisfying the needs of both employers and employees, and George Elton Mayo, who was a researcher involved in the Hawthorne studies. Mayo found that when managers paid positive attention to employees, employees worked harder and had better morale. Abraham Maslow identified a hierarchy of needs, starting with basic physiological needs and ranging up to needs to know and understand. Douglas McGregor developed Theory X and Theory Y, which represent opposing views about how people are motivated to work.

There are two theories in the quantitative school of management. The systems theory holds that all organizations are a system and therefore events or decisions that occur in one part affect every other part. The contingency theory proposes that every situation is different and every manager is different and thus there are no universal principles of management.

Theory Z tries to combine scientific management techniques with human relations concepts. Peters and Waterman, the management theorists who wrote *In Search of Excellence*, found that excellent companies took exceptional care of their customers, and concluded that this was the only path to real success.

Current hospitality management practices focus on the idea that managing service businesses can be very different from managing manufacturing businesses. Because services cannot be stored, strategies must be developed to balance supply and demand. Service businesses can be seen as service factories where the workers are part of the product.

Strategic planning is another important element of managing. Strategic planning starts with formulating broad objectives and continues with creating specific tactical objectives. Some companies practice management by objectives (MBO) in order to track their success at meeting objectives.

Because service businesses such as hotels and restaurants have finite capacities, they require unique strategies in order to maximize revenues. Supply can be managed either by pursuing a level-capacity strategy or a chased-demand strategy. Demand can be managed by offering weekend specials, early-bird dinners, and other price incentives.

Service businesses must work especially hard to manage "moments of truth," those times when important personal contact is made between employees and guests. Heskett developed the idea of a strategic service vision—a blueprint for service managers consisting of targeting a market segment and focusing on a service strategy.

Effective service organizations believe in people power and managing by walking around (MBWA). They focus a lot of attention on selecting, training, and promoting the right people.

There are eight managerial/leadership roles that a manager must play. These are director, producer, coordinator, monitor, mentor, facilitator, innovator, and broker.

Endnotes

1. Peter F. Drucker, *Management: Tasks, Responsibilities, Practices* (New York: Harper & Row, 1974), p. 398.

2. Ron Zemke and Dick Schaff, *The Service Edge* (New York: NAL Books, 1989), p. 43.

3. Drucker, p. 399.

4. Drucker, p. 399.

5. Drucker, pp. 400–401.

6. Timothy W. Firnstahl, "My Employees are my Service Guarantee," *Harvard Business Review,* July-August 1989, p. 29

7. Firnstahl, p. 29.

8. Weiss Roberts, *Leadership Secrets of Attila the Hun* (New York: Warner Books, 1990), pp. 74–75.

9. Zemke and Schaff, p. 71.

10. Zemke and Schaff, p. 48.

11. Drucker, p. 402.

12. Robert O'Brien, *Marriott: The J. Willard Marriott Story* (Salt Lake City: Desert Book Company, 1987) p. 265.

13. Fredrick W. Taylor, "A Piece Rate System," *Scientific Management: A Collection of the More Significant Articles Describing the Taylor System of Management*, edited by Clarence Bertrand Thompson (Cambridge: Harvard University Press, 1914), p. 637.

14. "The Taylor System of Shop Management at the Watertown Arsenal," *Scientific Management: A Collection of the More Significant Articles Describing the Taylor System of Management,* edited by Clarence Bertrand Thompson (Cambridge: Harvard University Press, 1914), p. 755.

15. "The Taylor System of Shop Management," p. 743.

16. George Elton Mayo, *The Human Problems of an Industrial Civilization* (Boston: Macmillan, 1933), pp. 75–76.

17. Daniel A. Wren, *The Evolution of Management Thought* (New York: Wiley, 1979), p. 484.

18. William Ouchi, *Theory Z* (New York: Avon Books, 1982).

19. Tom Peters and Nancy Austin, *A Passion For Excellence* (New York: Random House, 1985), p. 4.

20. Peters and Austin, p. 34.

21. Peters and Austin, p. 88.

22. Christopher H. Lovelock, *Managing Services: Marketing, Operations, and Human Resources* (Englewood Cliffs, N.J.: Prentice-Hall, 1988), p. 23.

23. Ouchi, pp. 194–197.

24. James L. Heskett, *Managing in the Service Economy* (Boston: Harvard Business School Press, 1986), pp. 5–25.

25. Heskett, pp. 96–97.

26. Heskett, p. 93.

27. Firnstahl, p. 30.

Key Terms

Barnard, Chester I.
behavioral management school
capacity-constrained businesses
chased-demand strategy
classical management school
contingency theory
Fayol, Henri
Gantt, Henry
Gilbreth, Frank
Gilbreth, Lillian
Hawthorne effect
Hawthorne studies
job restructuring
level-capacity strategy
management by objectives (MBO)

Maslow, Abraham
Mayo, George Elton
McGregor, Douglas
moments of truth
Owen, Robert
Peters, Thomas H.
quantitative management school
scalar chain
systems theory
Taylor, Fredrick W.
Theory X
Theory Y
Theory Z
three position plan of promotion
Waterman, Jr., Robert A.

Discussion Questions

1. Managers must perform which five basic tasks?

2. Who are the founders of the classical school of management?

3. What are Taylor's and Fayol's contributions to management theory?

4. What are the Hawthorne studies?

5. What are Maslow's and McGregor's contributions to management theory?

6. How is the systems theory different from the contingency theory?

7. Can the principles of management developed by industrial managers apply as well to service managers? Why or why not?

8. How can a service organization manage supply and demand?

9. What is a moment of truth?

10. What are some of the roles that a manager must play?

Chapter Outline

9 Managing Human Resources

In the previous chapter, a manager was compared to a conductor, whose job it is to instruct and direct all of the various musicians so that they perform well together. But before a conductor can direct a beautiful performance, all of the individual musicians must be able to play their instruments well. What kind of performance could you expect if the violinists did not know how to play their instruments or the flutists could not read music?

So it is in the hospitality industry. Before a manager can direct and shape employees' individual contributions into an efficient whole, he or she must first turn employees into competent workers who understand how to do their jobs. Employees are the musicians of the orchestra that the members of the audience—the guests—have come to watch perform. If employees are not skilled at their jobs, then the performance they give will get bad reviews. Just as an orchestra can have a fine musical score from a great composer and still perform poorly because of incompetent musicians, so a hotel or restaurant can have the finest standard recipes, service procedures, and quality standards and still have dissatisfied guests because of poor employee performance.

That is why managing human resources is of tremendous importance. No other industry provides so much contact between employees and customers and so many opportunities to either reinforce a positive experience or create a negative one. In this chapter we will talk about the shortage of workers, high turnover rates, and labor-related legislation—elements contributing to what can only be called a labor crisis. We will then turn our attention to the chief strategy used by hotel and restaurant managers to combat this crisis: good human resources programs designed to help managers hire, train, motivate, and retain employees.

Labor Trends

By any measure, one of the most serious problems the hospitality industry faces today is a shortage of labor. In a survey of *Lodging Hospitality* readers, 58% of those responding recognized that a shortage of workers and the poor quality of workers are the biggest problems facing the industry, ahead of even overbuilding and foreign competition concerns.[1] A

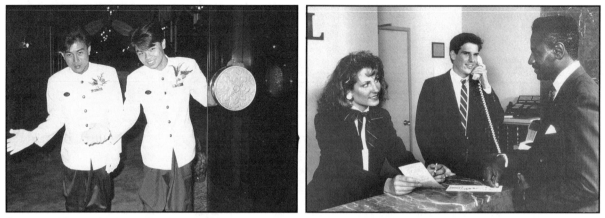

Opportunities to make a positive impression on guests abound in the hospitality industry. Left photo courtesy of The Dusit Thani, Bangkok.

survey of National Restaurant Association members showed that there is a shortfall of about 200,000 persons in the restaurant industry, and that the problems managers face included: (1) fewer applicants for jobs, (2) jobs staying vacant longer, (3) turnover edging upward, and (4) lack of qualified applicants.[2] The study went on to note that:

- The shortage is most severe in the East, followed by the Midwest.

- Chain and franchise operators are more likely than independent operators to feel the impact of the shortage.

- Fast-food operations are no more likely than their table-service counterparts to be affected.

- Large operations (in terms of customer counts and food purchases) report more labor-shortage problems than small ones.

- It is most difficult to fill such back-of-the-house positions as cook and dishwasher.[3]

There are a number of factors that contribute to the labor crisis:

- Changing demographics

- High turnover

- Legislation

Changing Demographics

Most observers and analysts agree that there are at least five demographic trends that will have a significant impact on the American work force and consequently on all U.S. businesses in the next decade.

The Decline in the Birth Rate. In the 1950s the U.S. population was growing at a rate of as high as 2% annually. Today's population growth rate is only slightly more than .5%, and the rate is projected to gradually decrease for many years to come. This slow population growth means that there will be fewer workers in the decades ahead, which means slower economic growth. Many people in the hospitality industry are asking: If the population of America is only growing at .5% annually, how are we going to find enough workers for an industry that depends on people and is growing at the rate of 1% to 3% annually?

The Middle-Aging of America. In 1985, 50% of American workers were between the ages of 16 and 34, 38% were between 35 and 54, and the remaining 12% were over 55, according to the U.S. Bureau of Labor Statistics. But by the year 2000 the situation will have changed dramatically. It is estimated that by 2000 the number of workers within the 16–34 age bracket will have declined by 12%, so that the total for this group will be only 38%; while the number of workers between the ages of 35 and 54 will have increased 13%, from 38% to 51%. The number of workers over 55 will decline to 11% in the same period. There is good news and bad news in these statistics. The good news is that middle-aged workers are usually more experienced and dependable than their younger counterparts. The bad news is that there will be fewer young workers available to start at the bottom and work their way up.

The Increase in Women Workers. Because of the rising cost of living and the increase in the number of single family households, the number of women joining the work force has been growing steadily since the middle of the century. In 1955 only 35% of women worked outside the home, but the Hudson Institute estimates that this figure will reach 60% by 2000. Already, two-thirds of all U.S. mothers are in the work force, and more than half of all women work. Again, there is both good and bad news in these figures for the hospitality industry. The growing number of working women is a boon for the restaurant business, since these women have less time for homemaking and they (and their families) eat out more. The bad news is that employers who wish to attract women may have to provide care for dependents, which was not necessary when they were dealing with a predominantly male work force.

The Shifting Population. For years, the population in the United States has been moving away from the Northeast and Midwest and settling in the Sunbelt and western states. In addition, there has been a large influx of immigrants from the Caribbean and Central and South America who have settled in those same areas. This means that the labor shortage will hit some areas of the country harder than others.

The Decline in Education. Some claim that education in America has been under-funded for many years. Others think the education system needs to be overhauled. In any event, the current pool of workers available for all jobs is of exceptionally poor quality. And there is no indication that the situation is going to improve. The *Wall Street Journal* tells a typical story of the problems faced by a service company employing minimum-wage workers—Southwestern Bell. According to the *Journal*, of 3,700 people who took Southwestern Bell's 85-question entry-level test to determine if they could understand simple mathematics and could read, only 800 managed to get a passing score of 55. Here are samples of the questions most applicants could not answer:

- If Ralph makes $7.23 per hour, how much will he make if he works 12 hours? Do you (A) add (B) subtract (C) multiply (D) divide to get the answer?

The number of women employed in the hospitality industry continues to grow.

- John knew from the dismal look on the face of the police officer that the situation was serious. Dismal means (A) bright (B) cheerful (C) cheerless (D) distant.[4]

So we can add to the problem of having fewer workers the fact that many of the ones who will be looking for jobs are hardly able to read, add, or subtract.

High Turnover   High turnover rates are another labor problem that hospitality managers have to cope with. According to the National Restaurant Association, median crew turnover for the restaurant industry is about 250% per year. One hotel operator reports that most departing employees are room attendants, food servers, and bus help, and nearly half of them leave during the first two weeks of employment.

It is difficult to pin down all of the reasons for the industry's high turnover rates, but there are a few that may be universal:

- *Inefficient hiring systems.* Because it is so difficult to find employees, managers hire many individuals without screening them or fully explaining what their jobs involve. For example, a hotel is open and needs to be staffed 24 hours a day, seven days a week. New employees often don't understand what it is like to work all night, or on holidays or weekends, and that they are likely to be called on to fill some of those shifts. When they discover what a hospitality job can involve, they often get discouraged and look for other work.

- *Limited opportunities for advancement.* Most people want to better themselves. Few people are satisfied with only the minimum wage at a hotel or restaurant if they can find a better job. Often they can. Moreover, many hotels and restaurants have no training programs where entry-level workers can learn skills that will make them promotable within the company. A worker who wants to get ahead may have to quit and go somewhere else.

- *Lack of training and supervision.* People hired for entry-level positions need to be trained to do their jobs. Many receive inadequate training, make mistakes, get discouraged, and leave. While on-the-job training may be the cheapest form of training, it is also the most traumatic for employees.

Legislation

It is important for hospitality managers to understand legislation that will have an impact on the labor crisis in the years ahead. A 1990 law raised the minimum wage to $4.25 an hour, along with instituting a tip credit of 50% under certain conditions and specifying a training wage.[5] Consequently, many employers are re-examining ways to increase productivity and decrease staff. This makes sense at a time when there aren't enough workers to go around, but laying off employees is potentially disruptive, especially in hospitality operations that are unionized. Unions as a whole seem to be catching their second wind in the United States. Indeed, 1989 was a turn-around year in which union membership, which had been declining steadily for years, actually increased. Hospitality managers at properties with unionized workers must gain union cooperation to deal with the labor shortage successfully.

There are many employee issues being discussed today that could be addressed by future legislation. Because the number of women in the work force is increasing, benefits such as family leave (for men as well as women) are receiving more attention from legislators. There are issues concerning young employees and senior citizens that need resolving. Child labor laws restrict people under 18 from operating hazardous pieces of equipment, and some believe that the slicers and deep fryers used in many restaurants fall into that category. Senior citizens, who lose social security benefits if they earn more than a certain amount after they are 65, have been lobbying for a relaxation of these restrictions, and if they succeed a tremendous pool of new labor will become available.

What does all of this mean for hospitality managers? In a market where there is a shortage of labor and tough competition for good workers, employers are going to be forced to do more than is required by the law and union contracts if they wish to attract and retain good employees.

Human Resources Programs

In order to deal with the labor problems just outlined, many successful hospitality operators have developed human resources programs.

A good human resources program typically contains the following elements:

- Job analyses

- Productivity standards

- Recruitment

- Selection

- Training

- Motivation

- Evaluation

Job Analyses

Before the right person can be hired to perform a particular job, managers must understand exactly what the job involves so that an applicant's skills and the requirements of the job can be matched accurately.

The task of analyzing a job is somewhat more complicated in the hospitality industry than elsewhere. The job of a spot welder, for example, is exactly the same whether the welding takes place on top of a skyscraper or in a machine shop. But a food server's job can vary tremendously, depending on whether he or she is working at a local diner or a fine-dining restaurant. Not only will the type of establishment dictate the nature of the job, but also the time of day, the operation's physical layout and design, the operation's equipment, and the guests' expectations. Even merchandising techniques can affect a food server's job: in most restaurants, guests order off a printed menu; in others, servers are expected to show a blackboard to diners or memorize the daily specials.

Since the same job can differ from property to property, independent hotels and restaurants must perform their own job analyses in order to understand how jobs are done at their particular properties. Hotels and restaurants that belong to chains do not typically perform their own job analyses; this task has been done at corporate headquarters. Several years ago, Days Inn's franchise division commissioned the School of Industrial and Systems Engineering at the Georgia Institute of Technology to prepare an analysis of Days Inn's room-cleaning procedures. The Georgia Tech analysts concluded that all major tasks in room cleaning fall into "natural groupings" or job blocks, and recommended that Days Inn adopt the room cleaning sequence shown in Exhibit 9.1.

Once a job has been analyzed, then a number of documents can be prepared to help employees understand and learn the job, among them job lists, job breakdowns, and job descriptions.

Exhibit 9.1 Sample Guestroom Cleaning Sequence

Preliminary

The room attendant enters the room, turns on the light, and opens the curtains. He/she places the in-room cart at the side of the vanity. He/she then makes a forward sweep through the room, dumping ashtrays in the trash can bags, picking up these bags, and picking up room trash. He/she deposits the trash in the main cart outside the door and returns to the room, picking up ashtrays and washing them in the sink or leaving them there to soak if necessary.

Block 1

From the vanity, the room attendant makes a second sweep through the room, gathering all dirty terry, placing terry on the used bed, and wrapping the dirty linen around it. If two beds are used then he/she places the ball on the second bed, wrapping the dirty linen from that bed around it. Note that the procedure eliminates stuffing linen and terry into a pillow case. This is a time-consuming procedure. The room attendant takes the ball and places it in the main cart outside the door.

Block 2

From the main cart, he/she takes all necessary clean linen, re-enters the room, and makes the bed.

Block 3

From the beds he/she goes directly to the vanity and performs all necessary work, including terry re-stocking. He/she does not need to move away from the vanity due to the convenience of the in-room cart.

Block 4

He/she moves the in-room cart next to the bathroom. Here he/she performs all bathroom cleaning tasks.

Block 5

He/she makes a circuit of the room to dust. Returning to the in-room cart, he/she moves it next to the desk, cleans the desk mirror, replaces the trash can bag, re-stocks necessary stationery supplies, and replaces the desk ashtray. Then, moving the in-room cart toward the door, he/she replaces the air conditioner ashtray, and takes the in-room cart outside the room.

Block 6

Removing the vacuum (or other carpet cleaning tool) from the main cart, he/she vacuums the room.

This is only part of the job analysis of a Days Inn room attendant. The complete description would also cover the room attendant's responsibility for stocking his/her carts with sheets, pillow cases, towels, glasses, soap, toilet paper, stationery, and other items, as well as more detail on how beds are to be made, toilets cleaned, and so on. Source: "Industrial and Systems Engineers Study Room Cleaning Procedures," *Lodging,* January 1977, p. 33.

As the name implies, a job list is simply a list of the tasks that must be performed by the individual holding that particular job (see Exhibit 9.2). Job lists are useful as training tools and can serve as reminders for new employees.

Job lists are the foundations for job breakdowns—specific, step-by-step procedures for accomplishing a task (see Exhibit 9.3). The first column in Exhibit 9.3 shows a task (7) from the job list shown in Exhibit 9.2. The second column breaks down the task by identifying the steps that an employee must take to accomplish the task. These steps are written as performance standards. The third column, "Additional Information," explains why each step of the task is performed and may also include such information as desired attitudes when performing the step, safety tips, or pointers on how to reach the performance standard. In column four, managers can record information for quarterly performance evaluations. As you can see, a job breakdown can be useful in evaluating employees as well as training them.

Exhibit 9.2 Sample Job List

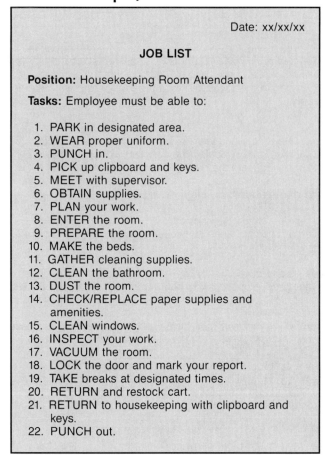

Date: xx/xx/xx

JOB LIST

Position: Housekeeping Room Attendant

Tasks: Employee must be able to:

1. PARK in designated area.
2. WEAR proper uniform.
3. PUNCH in.
4. PICK up clipboard and keys.
5. MEET with supervisor.
6. OBTAIN supplies.
7. PLAN your work.
8. ENTER the room.
9. PREPARE the room.
10. MAKE the beds.
11. GATHER cleaning supplies.
12. CLEAN the bathroom.
13. DUST the room.
14. CHECK/REPLACE paper supplies and amenities.
15. CLEAN windows.
16. INSPECT your work.
17. VACUUM the room.
18. LOCK the door and mark your report.
19. TAKE breaks at designated times.
20. RETURN and restock cart.
21. RETURN to housekeeping with clipboard and keys.
22. PUNCH out.

Once a job list and a job breakdown have been developed for a particular job, a job description can be written that outlines (1) the title that goes with the job, (2) the person to whom the employee reports, (3) the work to be performed (in general terms), and (4) the education or skills the employee must have (see Exhibit 9.4). A job description can be useful in a number of ways: it can be used as a recruiting tool to show prospective employees the nature of the work to be performed; it is an excellent training tool; supervisors can use it to monitor work in progress; and it can be used as the basis for employee evaluation. Job descriptions can also ease employee anxiety because they specify in writing the person to whom the employee reports and the responsibilities of the employee.

Productivity Standards

A good human resources program has productivity standards. Productivity standards tell managers how long it should take employees to complete tasks using the best methods management has devised, and how much work can be performed in a given time period. Productivity standards are often based on a manager's personal experience, the business's historical records, and industry standards.

In order to know if productivity standards are being met, employee productivity must be measured. Productivity can be measured in dollars or units produced or served.

Exhibit 9.3 Sample Job Breakdown

			1st Qtr. 2nd Qtr. 3rd Qtr. 4th Qtr.
POSITION: Housekeeping Room Attendant, morning shift **NAME:** **SUPERVISOR:**			
JOB LIST	**PERFORMANCE STANDARDS**	**ADDITIONAL INFORMATION**	1st Qtr. 2nd Qtr. 3rd Qtr. 4th Qtr. Yes/No Yes/No Yes/No Yes/No
7. PLAN YOUR WORK.	A. STUDY your assignment sheet.	Early service requests, rush rooms, check-outs, VIP's and no-service requests will be noted on your chart.	
	B. CLEAN check-outs first, whenever possible.	Cleaning check-outs first gives the front desk rooms to sell.	
	C. CLEAN early service requests as noted on your report.		
	D. CLEAN VIP rooms before lunch, whenever possible.	A VIP is our most important guest.	
	E. LOCK your cart room door and proceed to your section.		
	F. HONOR "do not disturb" signs.	We must honor the privacy of guests. Many guests like to sleep in. Never knock on a door that has a "do not disturb" sign.	
	G. CHECK rooms marked c/o and then check the rooms which are circled on your report. These are rooms due to check out.	Rooms marked c/o have already checked out at the front desk. Check-out time is noon.	
	H. PLAN your work around early service requests.	If you have early service requests, be sure to clean these rooms at the proper time.	

When productivity is expressed in dollars, it can be calculated by two different methods. The first consists of dividing sales by payroll costs:

$$\frac{\$10,000,000 \text{ (sales)}}{\$2,500,000 \text{ (payroll)}} = \$4$$

In this example, every $1 of payroll expended produced $4 of sales.

The second method of calculating productivity using dollars consists of dividing sales by the number of full-time-equivalent (FTE*) employees:

$$\frac{\$10,000,000 \text{ (sales)}}{280 \text{ (FTE employees)}} = \$35,714 \text{ (rounded)}$$

In this example, $35,714 was generated for every FTE employee.

Units produced or served divided by the number of employees can also yield a measure of productivity. For instance, suppose a restaurant with ten FTE employees serves 500 covers on a particular evening:

$$\frac{500 \text{ covers (units produced or served)}}{10 \text{ (FTE employees)}} = 50$$

In this example 50 covers were served per FTE employee.

---

*A "full-time-equivalent employee" is a measure used for statistical purposes in which two or more part-time employees whose hours add up to 40 hours a week (the number of hours one full-time employee would work) equal one full-time-equivalent employee.

Exhibit 9.4 Sample Job Description

JOB DESCRIPTION	
JOB TITLE: Executive Housekeeper	
IMMEDIATE SUPERVISOR: Resident Manager/Assistant Resident Manager	
JOB SUMMARY	Supervises all housekeeping employees, has the authority to hire or discharge, plans and assigns work assignments, informs new employees of property regulations, inspects housekeeping personnel work assignments, and requisitions supplies.
DUTIES	Supervises all housekeeping employees, hires new employees as needed, discharges employees when necessary, and writes warning notices when policy has been violated. Evaluates employees in order to upgrade when openings arise.
	Plans the work for the Housekeeping Department and distributes assignments accordingly. Assigns Housemen, Inspectresses, and Linen Room Attendants to their regular duties, or any special assignments that need to be accomplished. Schedules employees and assigns extra days off according to the occupancy forecast. Maintains a time log record book of all employees within the department.
	Informs new employees of regulations. Trains and assigns new employees to work with experienced help. Checks on the work of these employees occasionally and observes the reports made by the Inspectress or Section Housekeeper.
	Inspects the housekeeping staff periodically to determine if they are on duty and checks the quantity and quality of their work, checking places likely to be overlooked.
	Approves all supply requisitions, such as spreads and bathroom rugs. Maintains a lost and found department and is responsible for all lost and found items. Determines the rightful owner and mails to appropriate address.
PREREQUISITES	Education — High school required.
	Experience — Minimum three (3) years as an Assistant Housekeeper or Inspectress.
	Skills — Ability to plan and implement housekeeping programs and policies and to work and communicate with management, associates, and subordinates.
	Approved_____ Date_____

Fifty is the number of covers that were actually served that evening, but fifty covers might or might not meet the work productivity standard for the restaurant. The restaurant's standard might be that 65 covers should be served for every FTE employee, in which case the 10 FTE employees should have served 650 covers. Managers then have several options. They can investigate why employees served fewer covers that evening. It could be that guests at many tables stayed longer than average, so that the restaurant didn't seat enough guests to meet the productivity standard. Or it could be that several new food servers were scheduled that evening and they did not serve guests as quickly as the more experienced servers. Depending on the circumstances, managers might then decide to re-train the new servers or conclude that they just need a little more experience. Or managers might wait to see if an investigation is really necessary. Managers may decide not to investigate what happened that evening at all, but to keep a close eye on the covers per FTE employee for the next week or two. Only if covers per FTE employee stay below standard for a significant period would they take the time to investigate the causes.

Productivity standards are not only essential for payroll control, they are also important in job analysis and as measures of expectation for the employee in recruiting, training, and evaluating. Exhibit 9.5 shows some sample productivity standards at hotels.

Under no circumstances should managers assume that high productivity equals guest satisfaction and business success. While managers of service businesses must watch their productivity measures carefully in order to achieve their economic goals, they must also remember that success in business has both qualitative and quantitative dimensions. In other

Exhibit 9.5   Sample Productivity Standards

	Motor Hotel Chain*	1,000-Room Hotel[#]	350-Room Hotel
Food server covers per 8 hours	80–100	40–50	70–80
Preparation covers per 8-hour employee	200	80	150
Warewasher covers per 8 hours	250–300	125	250
Occupied rooms per day room attendant	16	14	15
Occupied rooms per houseperson	150	7	44

*The motor hotels are franchise Holiday Inns.

[#]Luxury class.

Source: C. Everett Johnson, "How to Staff and Schedule to Conserve Dollars," *Lodging*, October 1975, p. 11.

words, successful businesses base their productivity standards in part on guest expectations, not on profitability or efficiency objectives alone. For example, the Bob Evans restaurant chain bases many of its productivity standards on its guests' expectations and carefully measures how well it meets those expectations. Guests should not have to wait for a table for more than 15 minutes; after guests are seated, an employee should come by with water and a greeting within 60 seconds; food should arrive at the table no longer than 10 minutes after the guests order it; and a vacated table must be readied for new guests within 5 minutes.

Recruitment

Once the various jobs have been defined and productivity standards established, recruiting workers becomes the top priority. A major goal of recruiting is to find the best workers available who are willing to work for the wages offered by the business. This task is complicated by the fact that in the hospitality industry work skills alone are not a sufficient measure of a person's suitability for a job. Personality must also be taken into consideration if the position involves guest contact.

To a large extent, whether an operation can recruit people who have the personality and skills to fit into a service-oriented business depends on the labor market in which it is functioning. Market areas differ as to levels of unemployment, diversity of the work force, and competitive industries. Hotels and restaurants might have trouble recruiting good employees in locales with a low level of unemployment and a number of large businesses with high wage scales. Even in some areas with high levels of unemployment, there may not be a wide selection of people with the basic skills and temperament to work in a hospitality organization. In some unfavorable market areas, employees need to be transported daily from nearby towns to their place of work—a very costly procedure. When McDonald's opened a new restaurant in Boca Raton,

Florida—a town where the leading employer is IBM—it found it necessary to transport workers by bus from Miami, 50 miles away! The Hyatt Regency Hotel in Greenwich, Connecticut, assists workers who commute to the area by train from places like Mt. Vernon, New York, or Stamford, Connecticut. The hotel leases a van and has hired two full-time drivers to pick up employees at the train station, ensuring the workers get to work on time and saving them taxi fare.

Internal and External Sources of Employees. All sources of new employees fall into one of two categories: internal or external. Of these, internal sources are the least costly and often the most reliable. One internal source consists of recruits recommended by current employees. Since employees have a good understanding of the nature of the work involved, and since they tend to be careful about whom they recommend, employees often bring in recruits who do very well. Bulletin boards and company newsletters are ways of getting the news of job openings to employees.

Very often employees will suggest friends and relatives for positions. Some operators have rules prohibiting family members from working together. These rules are typically a result of previous negative experiences, or of fears that if one member of a family leaves the company other members may leave as well. While these concerns are sometimes justified, there are many examples of family members working for an employer quite successfully.

Another internal source of applicants for a vacant job is the current staff. Promoting from within establishes the operation as a good place to work—one in which opportunities are available for those who want them and work hard for them. In fact, a strong internal-promotion policy is in itself a valuable recruiting tool, and many companies spell out career ladder progressions as part of their recruitment program. For example, just about all of the Domino's Pizza franchisees were once store managers—owning your own store is part of the career track that is offered as a recruitment incentive. A full 30% of Marriott's managers started out as hourly employees. At Embassy Suites at any given time, between 25% and 80% of the firm's hourly workers are in training programs that help them upgrade or expand their skills and qualify for better paying jobs.[6]

There are also some potential problems associated with internal promotion. An employee-applicant who loses a position to another employee (or to an outside applicant) might turn his or her disappointment into negative actions such as not performing up to standards or complaining on the job (which could affect the morale of others). In general, employers who use internal promotion effectively also have strong employee counseling programs.

External sources for employees can be informally tapped. Managers and supervisory staff often are able to locate new personnel through their social and professional contacts. In many cases this procedure involves recruiting from competitive operations. Companies find that being heavily involved in local community affairs makes them more approachable, and that a larger number of people apply for job openings than would otherwise.

Classified advertising and direct mail are examples of formal external recruiting methods. Classified advertising can be placed in local daily newspapers, in industry journals, and even on radio stations. Direct mail to schools, colleges, and seniors' groups is also a good way to reach job candidates. An advantage of advertising and direct mail is that they generally produce a large number of applicants—everyone looking for a job is likely to apply for what sounds like an attractive position. A disadvantage is that many applicants are not qualified and must be screened out by the human resources department. This can be time-consuming and expensive.

Other formal external sources that are often used to recruit employees are state government employment offices and private employment agencies. People who are out of work and wish to receive unemployment compensation are usually required to register with state employment offices, so these offices usually have sizeable lists of candidates. Many of these individuals may not be qualified for hospitality jobs, however, and so they must be screened carefully. There are some private employment agencies that charge a fee for placing an individual with a company; the fee is paid by either the employee or the employer. These agencies are mostly used to find supervisory and management personnel.

In some communities, there are atypical external sources that can provide recruits. The city school systems in New York City and Miami, Florida, have their own "Academies for Tourism." The purpose of these academies is to help high school students gain an awareness and understanding of the hospitality industry. All of the students work in an internship in their senior year; some continue into hospitality programs in college, others go directly into the work force. In many communities, students in hospitality programs offered by junior colleges and four-year institutions are eager to gain work experience while in school.

The National Restaurant Association (NRA) has identified some population groups that can answer the needs of the restaurant industry and other hospitality organizations. These groups include minorities, handicapped workers, senior citizens, and workers with limited skills. The NRA points out that some individuals within these groups might need help in improving their English-speaking skills. Special job trainers or equipment might be needed for handicapped workers, and new career ladders might be needed for older workers. Some of the best job programs singled out by the NRA are summarized in Exhibit 9.6.

Recruitment of Supervisors and Managers. Since most of you reading this text are supervisors or managers or aspire to be in the future, in this chapter we concentrate on how supervisors and managers recruit, select, hire, and train workers for hourly staff positions. However, in this section we'd like to say a brief word about how you might be recruited for a supervisory or management position.

A good deal of recruiting is done by companies at colleges that teach hospitality management. A hotel or restaurant chain may offer graduates an opportunity to enter a management training program that, upon completion, qualifies them for a supervisory position in one of its properties. Or graduates may receive direct placement offers. With these, graduates are put directly into supervisory or management positions and are given on-the-job training. Very often, direct placement recruiting is done by independent companies and clubs that do not offer full-scale management training programs.

Exhibit 9.6 Sample Job Programs

> **English as a Second Language** (Marriott and other hotels, along with the Wilson School, Arlington, Virginia)
>
> The Wilson School, working with the Arlington, Virginia, chamber of commerce, has received a grant from a federal pilot program—the Workplace Literacy Partnership Program—and funding from the State of Virginia to provide basic English and communication skills to 400 employees in nine hotels in the area. Because of the low unemployment rate (1.6 percent) in the area, hotels are hiring workers who barely speak English. Under the guidelines of the program, the business partner must match the school's contribution one-to-one. Companies can do this by donating space for classes, paying the teacher and employees for attending the class, and offering bonuses for employees who complete the class.
>
> **Training and Employment Programs for the Disabled** (Marriott Corporation)
>
> In Chicago, working with the Department of Rehabilitation Services (DORS) and Goodwill Industries, Marriott contracts to provide skill-specific training in the food service industry to DORS clients at Marriott business sites. At the end of the training period, clients are placed with Marriott or another industry employer. This project serves 25 to 30 clients annually with a placement rate approaching 90 percent. Clients include the hearing impaired, developmentally disabled, and emotionally impaired.
>
> **McMasters Job Coach Program** (McDonald's Corporation)
>
> This nationwide program recruits and trains persons over 55 years old. Groups of six to ten seniors are started as a cohesive unit to provide peer support. The trainees work one-on-one with a job coach who is a McDonald's manager on leave for one year. They receive 15 to 20 hours of training each week for a period of four weeks. Jobs have been designed to suit older people: salad maker, biscuit maker, host/hostess, maintenance, and some swing management positions for those who have had store management experience. At the end of training, graduates receive a diploma from Hamburger University, along with a commemorative pin and spatula. They are "mainstreamed" into a crew and become employees at one of the company's restaurants. Currently, approximately 71 percent of participants are retained in active employment. A prime-time television commercial, "The New Kid," which features an older man preparing for his first day on the job, has been a successful recruiting tool.

Source: NRA Current Issues Report, *Foodservice Employment 2000: Exemplary Industry Programs,* January 1989.

Some hotels and food service companies employ the services of executive recruiters or "headhunters." Companies usually engage these recruitment firms to find people for senior management positions. Executive recruiters receive substantial fees for their services.

Another recruitment technique is popularly called "networking." With networking, individuals either contact or are contacted by friends, classmates, and former associates about a job opening. Most observers agree that most management positions are filled via networking rather than through advertising.

Of course, many graduates from hospitality programs—and supervisors and managers already employed in the industry—find their own positions by directly contacting the companies they would like to work for.

Selection

Selecting the right employees has long been considered one of the keys to operating a successful hospitality business. As mentioned earlier, personality must be considered as well as skills. Almost 100 years ago, Ellsworth

Statler was telling his hotel managers to "hire only good-natured people." That is still a good idea today.

Selecting an employee to fill a position involves five steps:

- Receiving and processing applications

- Interviewing applicants

- Evaluating applicants

- Checking references

- Hiring the selected person

These steps should not be taken lightly. Top-notch companies go about hiring people for even the lowest-paid positions in a very careful way. Selectivity is the watchword. At the Walt Disney Corporation no one is hired on the basis of one interview or on the recommendation of one interviewer; at least two are required.[7]

Receiving and Processing Applications. Most hotels and restaurants use exactly the same application form whether they are hiring unskilled or skilled personnel. It is considered a good practice to have applicants fill out these forms on-site. This is to make sure that the applicant fills out the form him- or herself, because the completed application serves as an indication of the applicant's neatness and literacy.

Applications generally cover an applicant's name, address, telephone number, work experience, references, and education, as well as some other miscellaneous items. Some applications also contain a clause in which the applicant agrees, upon accepting the job, to submit to a drug-screening test at any future time should the employer request it. After someone is employed, whether he or she can be tested is a matter for negotiation. Most employers believe it is better to secure permission up front so they can administer the tests on an as-needed basis.

Human resources managers are often more interested in a person's intellect and attitude than in his or her specific skills. With today's sophisticated training techniques, almost any entry-level job can be learned in a matter of weeks, so the key factors that managers look for are a person's adaptability to a job, enthusiasm, and willingness to learn. That means a job application, at least in the hiring of entry-level employees, is a pre-screening tool more than anything else—it helps weed out people not suitable for a position, rather than identify the best candidates. Paul Breslin, director of human resources for the Fontainebleau Hilton in Miami, puts it this way: "We are no longer looking for people with five years' experience to be a front office clerk. They can learn that job in two weeks. What we want are people who can adapt to a new environment and retain what they are taught."[8]

Interviewing Applicants. Once an application is filled out and submitted, the applicant is often given a short screening interview by someone in the human resources office. In this interview, the interviewer reviews the facts on the application and notes the applicant's personal grooming and language skills. In small operations this interview can be extended to cover all aspects of the candidate's history, because the person doing the interviewing will also do the hiring. In large operations the human resources department only does the screening and first interviews; there is usually a second interview by the manager for whom the new employee will work.

Breslin has some advice about interviewing prospective employees:

> Don't ask them anything you wouldn't want to tell someone yourself. Don't ask them any questions you don't need to know the answer to, such as "Are you married?" or "How many children do you have?" Also, don't ask any questions that are deemed related or will indicate any discriminatory discussion relating to race, religion, national origin, or sexual orientation.[9]

As far as physically disabled individuals are concerned, Breslin feels that they should be asked, "Are you physically able to do this job?" but that's all. "If they feel they can do it, if they want to do it, and if they are qualified to do it, then they ought to be given the opportunity," he says.[10]

Some areas should be avoided altogether, since questions relating to them may be interpreted as violations of the applicant's rights. Topics to avoid during an interview include an applicant's birthplace, age, race or color, religion or creed, height, weight, marital status, national origin, citizenship, membership in lodges and religious or ethnic clubs, and arrest record. The general rule of thumb to apply is: Don't ask a question unless it has a direct bearing on whether the candidate can successfully perform the job in question. Since the standards for what constitutes discriminatory or otherwise unlawful questions vary from state to state and year to year, interviewers must keep abreast of current federal and state laws.[11]

Evaluating Applicants. The goal when evaluating applicants is to fit the person to the job. Don't put someone in a position where there's a lot of guest contact if he or she is more suited to a back-of-the-house position. Room attendants in hotels must bend over to make a bed or scrub the bathroom floor or tub; obviously, someone with a bad back would not be suitable for this kind of work.

Pick the most interested candidate who enjoys the kind of work that needs to be done. Make sure that he or she has the necessary language, writing, and physical skills, and (of course) look carefully at cleanliness and personal grooming. Beyond these traits, having an enthusiastic and optimistic attitude and the ability to function as part of a team are paramount.

One interesting technique that is being used in some quarters to help managers evaluate applicants is video-assisted testing. Hospitality authors Casey Jones and Thomas A. Decotiis advocate "work sampling" as a method of predicting the performance of employees in guest-contact positions before they are hired. Work sampling tests employees by presenting them with situations simulating the actual job. Working with a major hotel company, Jones and Decotiis developed a video-based work-sample test that could be administered easily to large numbers of applicants and scored quickly.[12] Forty guest-service simulations based on actual guest/employee incidents were filmed. After each simulation is presented, a prospective employee is asked to choose among four possible responses to the guest's behavior. Here is a typical simulation:

The scene is the front desk, where a single front desk agent is on duty, checking out a guest. Several other guests are in line to check out. Suddenly, another guest rushes to the desk and says, "Hey, I'm going to miss my plane. I need to check out right now or I'm going to miss it." The frame freezes. The agent should: (A) ask the people in line if it's okay to check out the guest ahead of them; (B) say, "I'm sorry, sir, but I'll get to you as soon as I finish with Mr. Steinberg here," (C) say, "Yes sir, right away," or (D) look for a supervisor.

Action B is the best. It acknowledges the guest's special need by serving him next, but allows the agent to continue serving the guest who is at the head of the line (and may also have a time problem). Action A would shift the problem to the other guests, and if one of them objected, an embarrassing situation would arise. Action C would be viewed as extremely inconsiderate to guests in line and the guest being served. Action D is a last resort; supervisors should be called for help only in very difficult situations.[13]

According to the researchers, a work-sample test such as this one has proved valid as a predictor of job performance. It also has proven to be especially useful to applicants for whom English is a second language, because they can both see and hear the test problem.

Checking References. Before offering a person a position, always check the person's references. Checking references is one of the most important steps in the hiring process, according to Breslin and other experts. "Calling references can really give you more firsthand knowledge of the applicant," says Breslin. "In addition, applicants usually know when you have called and that sends the message to them that they are important to you and that you are hiring them for the long term."[14] Of course, a former employer of the applicant may only confirm that the applicant worked for the organization from date X to date Y and decline to say anything more. Even that much information is useful, since it will help you check the accuracy of the candidate's application or résumé.

Some companies have a third party such as a detective agency do a further check on candidates for certain positions. If the candidate is interviewing for a position that involves being responsible for large amounts of money, you may want to run a credit check. If the applicant is seeking a hotel position as a parking attendant or as a driver of a courtesy van, you may run a check on the applicant's driver's license. You must be careful, however. Such checks are unlawful unless they clearly relate to the job the candidate is applying for.

Hiring the Selected Person. The key points to keep in mind when hiring applicants is to make sure they clearly understand the position they are being offered; what they will be required to do; what their hours will be; whom they will report to; their vacation and other benefits; the dress code or uniform requirements (if applicable); how much pay they will be getting to start; and when and under what circumstances they can expect a pay increase. If managers do not make these matters absolutely clear to applicants, misunderstandings can occur that could permanently spoil manager/employee relationships before they even get off the ground.

Training

Training is one of the most crucial parts of a human resources program, but it is talked about more than it is practiced. When an operation gets busy, training is often overlooked or temporarily suspended because of either a lack of time or a lack of trainers. The fact is that training is enormously demanding. It needs to be an ongoing process for all current employees; for new employees the training process or program has to be

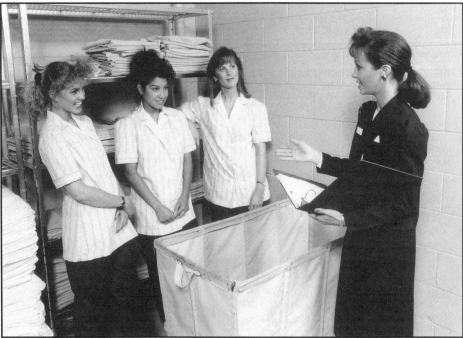

Training helps give employees confidence.

started all over again at square one. Training is also expensive, for employees who are learning are not fully productive. For these reasons, there is a great temptation to take shortcuts in training procedures. Managers often rationalize their negligence by telling themselves that current employees don't need to be trained, and on-the-job training is good enough for new hires. Yet without training at all levels within the organization, there can be no consistency of product and service. Training is the process that teaches trainees the knowledge and skills to operate within the standards set by management. Training also attempts to develop within employees a positive attitude toward guest service.

Poor training contributes to high turnover and substandard job performance. Employees should feel comfortable in their jobs and be able to do them well so that they do not become discouraged and quit. To train their employees well, many companies use modern technology such as the video-assisted testing described earlier for new job applicants. At Domino's, McDonald's, and Wendy's, frontline training is accomplished through videotapes sent to individual stores and played on an on-site VCR. These videos introduce new items and emphasize product consistency and control standards. Domino's has gone so far as to invent an animated cartoon character—Vincent Van Dough—to carry the gospel of consistency, safety, and cleanliness to employees via videotapes.[15] Sonesta International Hotels uses a board game that all of its employees play to sensitize themselves to guest needs. You advance on the board by giving the right answers to guests and lose spaces by giving the wrong answers.

According to Lewis C. Forrest, Jr., author of *Training for the Hospitality Industry*, the basic steps in the training process are:

1. Establish a training policy

2. Define training needs

3. Plan the training

4. Prepare the employees

5. Conduct the training

6. Evaluate the training

7. Follow through with ongoing coaching[16]

Training should be continuous and ongoing. A company with an active training program expresses a commitment to its employees. A training program should define who will be trained (ideally, all categories and levels of employees), who will be responsible for training (corporate staff, on-site managers, supervisory personnel), and the training aids and techniques that should be used (see Exhibits 9.7 and 9.8).

Regular ongoing training on basic job tasks is necessary at all levels of an organization. Unless continuing positive reinforcement is provided, employees tend to forget some of what they learned. In addition to ongoing training in employees' regular duties, it is often necessary to hold extra training sessions on topics such as wine, sanitation, fire safety, CPR, and terrorist threats.

Exhibit 9.7 Sample Training Aid

TRANSLATION ACTIVITY OUTLINE

(S logo)

TASK: ADMINISTER GUEST MAIL

OBJECTIVE: Upon completion of this training activity the learner will be able to record, send up or store guest's mail according to the procedure in effect at the Front Office.

STANDARD: Proper handling of guest's mail requires receiving all mail which arrives prior to their stay at the time of registration, notifies in-house guests of mail on the day it arrives, delivering telexes within thirty minutes of arrival, and stamping all messages with the time received.

RESOURCES: Computer system (if available), mail log, handouts, mail slots.

METHOD OF TRAINING	TRAINING STEPS	TIME
LECTURE	Trainer notes when mail arrives, when mail is collected, and the process to follow when mail, telexes or other messages for a guest are received by the hotel.	10 min.
DEMONSTRATION	Trainer takes learner through a step-by-step series of instructions to show how to time-stamp messages, record mail received and notify a guest mail is being held.	15 min.
REVIEW	One-on-one discussion of the job skill learned to determine the degree of comprehension.	5 min.
TEST	Trainer administers the test provided on the following page.	10 min.
		40 min.

TRAINING ACTIVITY TEST

(S logo)

EMPLOYEE _____ DATE _____

TASK: ADMINISTER GUEST MAIL

INSTRUCTIONS: Respond to the following questions in writing:

1. Why is it important to time-stamp all guest messages?

2. Telexes received are forwarded to a guest: (Circle the best answer.)
   A. within 30 minutes
   B. on the same day received
   C. within one hour
   D. other

3. Fill in the blanks:
   A. Mail arrives at the hotel at _____ a.m. and at _____ p.m.
   B. Mail departs the hotel at _____ a.m. and at _____ p.m.
   C. Stamps can be purchased at _____.

4. Under what circumstances would guest mail be delivered to a guest room?

5. What should you do with guest mail addressed to a guest who will not arrive at the hotel for five days?

6. How does a guest know mail is being held at the Front Office?

7. What should you do if a letter arrives at the hotel for a guest who has already checked out?

These pages are from a training manual developed by the Sheraton hotel chain. A series of training activity outlines within the manual show the manager/trainer what should be covered when training an employee to perform a particular task, and the approximate time training should take. Once the training is completed, the trainee takes a test to see how well he or she has learned. Courtesy of the Sheraton Hotel Corporation.

Exhibit 9.8   Sample Training Aid

	NEW EMPLOYEE TRAINING PROFILE					EMPLOYEE GUEST SERVICE AGENT -2- POSITION	

PRIMARY TASK	PERFORMANCE STANDARD	TRAINING METHOD	HOURS PROFILE	HOURS ACTUAL	EMPLOYEE'S SIGNOFF TRAINER'S SIGNOFF	DATE DATE
3. Register Guest (cont.)	e) Hands pen to guest with point facing employee, f) Verifies payment, obtains signature and confirms registration,					
	(Travel Vouchers are verified in the Sheraton Travel Voucher Manual), g) Uses upselling techniques to obtain higher revenue, h) Accepts cash for payment after					
	obtaining identification from guest. "No Posts" the account to ensure no outstanding balance, i) Ensures registration card is time stamped and dated.					
	j) Listens attentively to guest, k) Becomes familiar with names of V.I.P., complimentary, and pre-registered guests at the start of each shift by reviewing report					
	provided by Front Office Management, l) Assists in pre-keying and pre-registering guest rooms, m) Treats each guest as an individual.					
4. Room the Guest	a) Guest Service Agent selects a room within the specified room category,	Introduce task, provide handout	60 min.			

Here is an example of how job breakdowns can be used in training. As you can see, the job task is listed in the extreme left column; the second column lists the performance standards of the hotel. Column three shows the manager/trainer what training method should be used. Column four shows (1) the suggested or target time for training ("Profile"), and (2) the actual training time. Then there is space for the manager/trainer and the employee to sign off, indicating that the employee's performance meets the property's standards.
Courtesy of Sheraton Hotel Corporation.

One hotel that takes training seriously is Washington D.C.'s 128-year-old Sheraton Carlton, located two blocks from the White House. This historic landmark reopened in 1988 after a $16 million renovation. And, according to *Lodging* magazine, the hotel spent $500,000 on training before the first guest arrived.[17]

In developing its training program, Sheraton Carlton's management focused on a single theme that could guide managers and line employees: "Bring the guest back." Once the theme was established, management concluded it could rely on Sheraton's Guest Satisfaction System (SGSS) for implementation. Whatever job employees were assigned to do, they would be trained to do it with four points in mind:

- Every time they saw a guest they would smile and offer an appropriate hospitality comment.
- They would speak to guests in a friendly, enthusiastic, and courteous tone and manner.
- They would answer guest questions and requests quickly and efficiently, or take personal responsibility for getting the answers.
- They would anticipate guests' needs and solve their problems.[18]

After establishing the theme, management drew up job lists for 58 positions with accompanying procedures for meeting SGSS standards. The front desk agent had 137 tasks, for example, while the busperson's list contained 25 tasks. First, all employees had to be trained to accomplish each of their job tasks. The hotel's managers were given a three-day seminar in effective training techniques. Two weeks before the hotel opened, all 200 employees attended a special orientation where SGSS standards were taught through speakers, skits, role-plays, and videos. Skill-training sessions for individual employees and groups of employees were established. Employees learned how to perform a task, and then they would be observed performing the task by the manager/ trainer and other employees. In guest-contact situations, employees not being trained played the role of guests. Some sessions were videotaped; the videotapes were then critiqued by the employees involved as well as their trainers. After the training sessions were completed, each employee received a certificate of completion signed by the manager/trainer and the employee certifying that the employee had the knowledge to perform effectively in his or her position.

Motivation   Finding a way to motivate workers is perhaps a manager's most difficult challenge. The importance of having employees who are motivated is clear. The present shortage of workers demands that the productivity of individual workers increase. How can managers increase productivity? According to a National Science Foundation report that reviewed three hundred studies of productivity, pay, and job satisfaction,

> increased productivity depends on two propositions. First comes motivation: arousing and maintaining the will to work effectively— having workers who are productive not because they are coerced, but because they are committed. Second is reward. Of all the factors that help to create highly motivated and highly satisfied workers, the principal one . . . appears to be that effective performance be recognized and rewarded in whatever terms are meaningful to the individual—financial, psychological, or both.[19]

The message is clear. Motivation is a matter of commitment. A manager can only motivate employees to do their best at what he or she wants them to do if it is something the employees want to do as well. Bill McClean, former CEO of a major bank, puts it this way: "You need not read further concerning motivation unless you genuinely understand that to get employees to perform minimum duties, one only needs to drive them. To gain their top performance, one must inspire them to drive themselves."[20]

Techniques. There are four techniques managers can use to create an environment that helps employees motivate themselves.

Here a room attendant/butler is learning through role-playing to understand the responsibilities of a floor supervisor. Courtesy of New World Hotels International Limited.

Remove the fear of failure. Hospitality enterprises are busy places where at times there is a good deal of stress. For workers to function well, they must be well-trained and secure in the fact that they are valued and that they can count on keeping their jobs. Delta Airlines and IBM are known for doing all they can to avoid laying anyone off for economic reasons. Employees who are respected and know that they are important are not afraid of taking risks to do their best. Many hospitality companies don't even refer to their workers as "employees." At McDonald's they are crew members; at the Walt Disney Corporation they are cast members. These terms are intended to help give workers a sense of importance.

Pay a fair wage. Employees who are worrying about how they're going to pay next month's rent or a big car-repair bill aren't usually in the mood to take care of other people's problems—they're too worried about their own. In a best-selling book on management called *Leadership Secrets of Attila the Hun,* the author attributed this management advice to Attila: "Grant your Huns the benefit of your interest in the welfare of their families and the condition of their stores; share your riches with those who are loyal and stand in need. They will be certain to willingly follow you into the mouth of Hell, should the occasion arise."[21] Many excellent companies view themselves as an extended family. Thomas Peters and Robert Waterman, Jr., the authors of *In Search of Excellence*, reported that "we found prevalent use of the specific terms 'family,'

Mom, working when she wants to.

JOIN THE FAMILY.

APPLICATION ON INSIDE.

Always, An Equal Opportunity/Affirmative Action Employer.

This ad asks job seekers to join the McDonald's "family." The ad has special appeal for non-traditional workers who may need to work something other than a 9 to 5 shift. Courtesy of McDonald's Corporation.

'extended family,' or 'family feeling' at [such successful companies as] Disney, McDonald's, [and] Delta."[22]

Offer incentives and rewards for performance. People like to get rewarded. It makes them feel good. The more rewards and awards a company gives, the more motivated its employees are likely to be. Incentives do not have to be monetary to be important. Peters and Waterman put it this way:

> We were struck by the wealth of non-monetary incentives used by excellent companies. Nothing is more powerful than positive reinforcement. Everybody uses it. But top performers, almost alone, use it extensively. The volume of contrived opportunities for showering pins, buttons, badges, and medals on people is staggering at

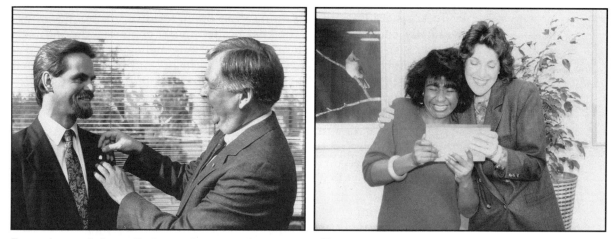

Rewards can help motivate employees and managers alike.

McDonald's, Tupperware, IBM, and many other top performers. They actively seek out and pursue endless excuses to give out rewards.[23]

At Delta Airlines the employee newsletter always includes a section reporting awards given to employees for exceptional service to passengers. Recognition and celebration are another way of letting employees know they are important to the company. That helps make the company important to them.

Operate with an open-door policy; keep everyone informed about everything. It's no secret that companies with highly motivated employees have no secrets. Communication is a two-way street in these companies. Everyone at the bottom knows what everyone at the top is thinking about important issues, and vice versa. When Ed Carlson was president of United Airlines, he said: "Nothing is worse for morale than a lack of information down in the ranks. I call it NETMA—Nobody Ever Tells Me Anything—and I have tried to minimize that problem."[24] United has always been known as a company that communicates with all of its employees all of the time. It publishes a daily *Employee Newsline* and a monthly employee newspaper. It also issues *Supervisors Hotline* every other week. At Walt Disney World, employees receive weekly newsletters called *Eyes and Ears* and *Resort Report,* which focus on cast (employee) recognition and resort information. Walt Disney World managers also get *Five Star Team,* a monthly newsletter that discusses current management issues and management development. Finally, Disney has designed a series of property-specific employee handbooks.

Besides using newsletters and newspapers, effective managers communicate with their employees via regular meetings, bulletins, and even paycheck stuffers. Operating results are posted where everyone can see them. A variety of techniques are used to make sure management at the top knows what workers on the front line think. Bill Marriott, Jr., still spends nearly half of his time in the field, first listening and then talking to employees (the sequence is important). In addition to other forms of communication, the Marriott company conducts annual attitude surveys of all employees. One Marriott executive calls it "our early warning system."[25]

To keep the lines of communication open, top executives at Shoney's (frequently cited as one of the best limited-menu chains in the industry) regularly visit Shoney's restaurants. Operations managers are expected to spend as much as four days a week in the field. And they do more than listen and talk: Chairman Ray Danner has been known to clean out a dirty washroom himself—then clean the collective clocks of the restaurant crew that let it get that way.[26]

Many companies practice the open-door policy—literally. At Delta Airlines the doors of the executive offices have always been open to any Delta employee. Pilots, mechanics, flight attendants—anyone can walk into the president's office and say what's on his or her mind or ask for help.

To ensure communication continues right to the end, excellent companies almost invariably hold exit interviews with departing employees. Hospitality companies generally regard such interviews as a necessary evil to help prevent possible lawsuits from disgruntled former employees. According to professors Robert H. Woods and James F. Macaulay, writing in the *Cornell Quarterly*, "This is neither the intended use of exit interviews nor their most common use outside of the hospitality industry. Most companies use exit interviews to collect information on why employees leave. Correctly used, these interviews point to problems that cause turnover."[27]

Evaluation

Although we are discussing evaluation last, it should be clear by this time that evaluation occurs in almost every part of a human resources program, from selection and hiring to training and motivating. Companies that do a good job in retaining, developing, and motivating employees are constantly evaluating employees informally and letting them know how they are doing. When they do well, employees are rewarded promptly; when they do poorly, they receive more training. In addition to this continual evaluation process, most companies have formal employee evaluations or performance reviews.

Performance reviews are typically held every three, six, or twelve months. New employees are usually reviewed more frequently than experienced employees. The purpose of performance reviews is not to confront employees with their shortcomings. The performance review is a natural step that follows selection, training, and motivating. It lets employees know how well they have learned to do what the company expects of them, and it lets managers know how well they are doing in hiring the right people and training them. Performance reviews are also coaching tools that managers can use to improve employee performance.

Good performance reviews are specific and objective. Some managers fill out a review form before meeting with an employee, on which they can rate the employee's knowledge, skills, and personal attributes—often on some kind of numerical basis. During the review the manager shares these ratings with the employee and gives him or her a chance to comment on them. Some companies have the employee fill out the same form before the review meeting so that the manager and the employee can compare ratings. The manager can recommend follow-up training, coaching, and counseling if this seems called for. Some companies have the manager and the employee draw up a joint goal-setting agreement in which the two agree as to (1) what will be done on both sides to improve the employee's performance in his or her current job, and (2) what the manager and employee will do to prepare the employee for a more rewarding position.

Chapter Summary

The hospitality industry is facing a labor crisis. There are fewer applicants for jobs, jobs are staying vacant longer, turnover is increasing, and there is a lack of qualified applicants. This crisis is largely a result of changing demographics, although some businesses make the situation worse by using inadequate hiring procedures, offering employees few opportunities to advance, and improperly training and supervising employees.

Other issues that have an impact on the hospitality industry include unions, family benefits, child labor laws, and social security legislation affecting senior citizens.

As part of their strategy to deal with the shortage of employees, many hospitality companies have developed human resources programs. A human resources program typically involves job analyses, productivity standards, recruitment, selection, training, motivation, and evaluation.

Jobs need to be analyzed so the best way to do them can be established. Once jobs are understood, job lists, job breakdowns, and job descriptions can be prepared. These are helpful in training and recruiting employees.

Productivity can be expressed in dollars or in units produced or served. But productivity standards cannot be based on numbers alone—they must take into account quality goals and guest expectations as well.

Effective recruiting demands an understanding of the local labor market. The major recruiting goal is to find the best workers available for the wages the business can pay. Recruiters can use internal sources (current employees, and people recommended by employees) and external sources (those recruited through advertising, community involvement, and employment agencies). Groups that can help answer the hospitality industry's labor needs include minorities, handicapped workers, senior citizens, and workers with limited skills. There are several job programs already in place to help hospitality businesses find and train potential employees in these groups.

Selecting an employee to fill a vacancy involves five steps: receiving and processing applications, interviewing applicants, evaluating applicants, checking references, and hiring the selected person.

Training is one of the most crucial parts of a human resources program. Unfortunately, training is often neglected. Basic steps in the training process are: establishing a training policy, defining training needs, planning the training, conducting the training, and evaluating the training. Today many companies supplement traditional training methods with interactive videotapes and games.

To have motivated workers, managers must gain their commitment to the company and its goals. There are four techniques managers can use to accomplish this: (1) remove the fear of failure, (2) pay a fair wage, (3) offer incentives and awards for performance, and (4) operate with an open-door policy—keep everyone informed.

Evaluation is the final step in a human resources program. Employees need to know how they are doing. Regularly scheduled performance reviews help accomplish this.

Endnotes

1. Doreen Bell, "Employees Hold Key to the 90s," *Lodging Hospitality*, January 1990, p. 78.

2. National Restaurant Association, *A 1988 Update: Foodservice and the Labor Shortage*.

3. *Foodservice and the Labor Shortage*.

4. Bill Richards, "Wanting Workers," *The Wall Street Journal*, February 9, 1990, p. R-10.

5. The 1990 law will become fully effective in 1992.

6. Ron Zempke and Dick Schaff, *The Service Edge* (New York: New American Library, 1989), p. 123.

7. Zempke and Schaff, p. 59.

8. Paul Breslin, Director of Human Resources, Fontainebleau Hilton, Miami, Florida. Personal interview with authors, May 16, 1990.

9. Breslin, personal interview.

10. Breslin, personal interview.

11. Adapted from David Wheelhouse, *Managing Human Resources in the Hospitality Industry* (East Lansing, Mich.: Educational Institute of the American Hotel & Motel Association, 1989), pp. 89, 93.

12. Casey Jones and Thomas A. Decotiis, "A Better Way to Select Service Employees: Video Assisted Testing," *Cornell Hotel and Restaurant Administration Quarterly*, August 1986.

13. Jones and Decotiis.

14. Breslin, personal interview.

15. Zempke and Schaff, p. 62.

16. Lewis C. Forrest, Jr., *Training for the Hospitality Industry*, 2d ed. (East Lansing, Mich.: Educational Institute of the American Hotel & Motel Association, 1990), p. 5.

17. Kathleen Keenan, "A Cool Half Million for Training Creates Warm Luxury," *Lodging*, December 1989, p. 25.

18. Keenan, p. 25.

19. Zempke and Schaff, p. 72.

20. J. W. McClean, *So You Want to Be the Boss* (Englewood Cliffs, N.J.: Prentice Hall, 1990), p. 44.

21. Weiss Roberts, *Leadership Secrets of Attila the Hun* (New York: Warner Books, 1990), p. 79.

22. Thomas H. Peters and Robert J. Waterman, Jr., *In Search of Excellence* (New York: Harper & Row, 1982), p. 261.

23. Peters and Waterman, p. 269.

24. Peters and Waterman, p. 267.

25. James L. Heskett, *Managing in the Service Economy* (Boston: Harvard Business School Press, 1986), p. 127.

26. Zempke and Schaff, pp. 286–287.

27. Robert H. Woods and James F. Macaulay, "R$_x$ for Turnover: Retention Programs That Work," *Cornell Hotel and Restaurant Administration Quarterly*, May 1989, p. 84.

Key Terms

back of the house	job description
front of the house	job list
full-time-equivalent employee	performance review
job breakdown	productivity standards

Discussion Questions

1. What factors contribute to the labor crisis?

2. What five demographic trends will have a significant impact on U.S. businesses within the next decade?

3. What are some common reasons for the hospitality industry's high turnover rates?

4. What are the differences between job lists, job breakdowns, and job descriptions?

5. What are some internal and external sources of employees?

6. What steps are involved in filling a vacant position?

7. What should an interviewer keep in mind when interviewing job candidates?

8. Why is training important?

9. What are some techniques for motivating employees?

10. Performance reviews serve what purpose?

Chapter Outline

The Marketing Concept
    The Four Ps of Marketing
Developing a Marketing Plan
    Situation Analysis
    Objectives
    Strategies
    Action Plans
    Controls
Sales Management and Personal Selling
    How to Be a Successful Salesperson
    Basic Qualities of a Salesperson
Making the Sales Call
    Prospecting and Qualifying
    Preparation
    Presentation
    Overcoming Objections
    Asking for the Sale
    Follow-Up
Selling Through Travel Agencies
    Types of Travel Agencies
    What Travel Agencies Do
    How Travel Agents Are Trained
    How Travel Agents Get Paid
Chapter Summary

10 Hospitality Marketing and Sales

Chapter 10 discusses the marketing concept, marketing plans, and personal selling. It concludes with a section on selling through travel agencies.

The Marketing Concept

As we have stated before in this text, the purpose of a business is to get and keep customers, for without customers there is no business. Professor Theodore Levitt points out that:

> customers are constantly presented with lots of options to help them solve their problems. They don't buy things, they buy solutions to problems. . . . No business can function effectively without a clear view of how to get customers, what its prospective customers want and need, what options its competitors give them, and without explicit strategies and programs focused on what goes on in the market place.[1]

That is what marketing is: the effort to determine and meet the needs and wants of current and potential customers.

There is an important distinction between selling and marketing that many students fail to recognize. This is due to a confusing terminology that is often used in business. Very often, people whose jobs are in sales are called "marketing representatives." The title suggests that the words "sales" and "marketing" are interchangeable; they are not. Marketing is a much broader term that includes sales and a great deal more. The difference between the two has often been stated this way: selling is getting rid of what you have; marketing is having what people want.

Some marketers look at it this way: marketing is the art of *buying from* customers, which is exactly the opposite of *selling to* customers. In other words, customers have money in their pockets that you, the salesperson, want to "buy." How can you buy the customer's money? By paying for it with a product or service. This marketing approach to selling can help you sell in two ways. First, your focus is on the customers rather than on your products. Instead of focusing on the attributes of your products, you focus on persuading customers to "sell" you their money—which usually leads you to study your customers and their needs and wants. Second, you have a different attitude toward customers—you value them more and approach them more carefully because you realize you are trying to convince them to give up something of value.

The Four Ps of Marketing

The list of activities that can be included in the efforts to get and keep customers is quite extensive. For a restaurant, for instance, the things that influence whether customers eat there include the location, decor, menu, type of service, and prices. All of these are marketing decisions first and foremost. To make these decisions, a restaurant's managers need to determine (1) what their current and potential customers need or want, (2) how to provide it, and (3) how to persuade current and potential customers to patronize the restaurant. These activities break down into four basic responsibilities that are popularly called the "Four Ps of Marketing": product, place, price, and promotion.

How businesses allocate their resources among product, place, price, and promotional efforts varies widely, depending on the objectives of each business. In a sense, the four Ps are like the ingredients in a recipe for success, and the relative proportion of resources allocated to each effort and the way these four marketing efforts are combined is often referred to as the marketing mix.

Product: What Do You Sell? As we have seen throughout this text, the term "product" as used in the hospitality field can have several meanings. Obviously, a product can be a meal or some other tangible item that a hotel or restaurant provides to guests. A hospitality product can also be an intangible service, such as a food server serving a meal. Product can also refer to a hotel or restaurant's concept—as in, "A La Quinta motel is an economy product." In this case, product refers to all the things that make the experience of staying at a La Quinta what it is—its philosophy, facilities, amenities, level of service, and the tangible products it sells to guests.

For many small business owners, determining the concept for a hotel or restaurant was not considered a marketing decision. For example, many

Not all hospitality products are tangible. A hospitality product can be a service or a property's business concept. Photo on right courtesy of La Quinta Motor Inns, Inc.

ethnic restaurants in the United States got their start because immigrant families from such countries as Italy, Greece, and France decided to open eating establishments offering the kind of food they knew how to prepare. Since these families generally opened their restaurants in neighborhoods where other people of the same origin lived, their restaurants enjoyed a built-in market. It was not necessary for the owners to be marketing-oriented—they simply sold what they knew how to make, and as long as they did it well there were plenty of customers.

This approach no longer works, because those built-in markets have for the most part disappeared. While it is still true that people who have the same tastes and lifestyles are likely to live in the same neighborhood, consumers today have so many different choices that simply opening a business in a location, no matter how good that location, cannot ensure success. This is especially true in the hospitality field, where there are no revolutionary new developments that are likely to convince customers to give up their old buying habits and form new loyalties. People have been eating and sleeping the same way for thousands of years. While the surroundings have gotten nicer, the basic services offered by dining and lodging establishments have not changed. And yet, surprisingly enough, many hotels and restaurants still market themselves as if they were offering something truly unique in a marketplace without competitors. They first decide what they are going to sell and then wrestle with the problem of how to sell it.

The point to keep in mind is that the concept of a hotel or restaurant should be first and foremost a marketing decision that is based on providing a better solution to a customer's problem—which might be anything from finding a place for a quick bite to eat, to searching for a site to hold a wedding reception for 300 people. To come up with a successful concept requires a very clear understanding of what people are looking for and what competitors already offer them. Only a business that understands what problems consumers are hoping to solve—and can offer better solutions—has a hope of succeeding.

This reinforces what Professor Levitt of the Harvard Business School says about people never buying a product but rather the utility they expect to receive from it. In a speech for the American Association of Advertising Agencies at the Greenbriar in White Sulphur Springs, Virginia, a few years ago, Levitt put it this way: "When you go into a hardware store you do not buy a quarter-inch drill, you buy the expectation of a quarter-inch hole." Similarly, when people walk into a hotel they are not buying a room or a bed, but rather the expectation of a comfortable night's rest. This clearly has far-reaching implications in terms of what features are important in a hotel to different groups of people and what people are willing to pay for them.

Place: Where Do You Sell It? "Place" also has several meanings in hospitality marketing. To begin with, it clearly refers to the physical location of a facility or property, which, as we have seen previously, can be crucial to the success of a hotel or restaurant.

Place can also have a profound effect on marketing methods. For instance, the fact that a large number of Holiday Inns are located all over America means that people are reminded of the Holiday Inn name wherever they go, so when they are in a strange town the Holiday Inn there is a familiar place. Moreover, because Holiday Inn is everywhere, its corporate management can advertise on national television or in national magazines, which would be too costly and inefficient for many of its competitors.

Place has another meaning as well, which is the physical location not of the hotel but of the site where the reservation for the hotel or the sale is made. This can be via telephone at a central reservation system office, at a travel agency, or even on a home computer. Obviously, the more places from which it is possible to buy a hotel room, the easier it will be to fill up that hotel.

Price: What Do You Sell It For? Too often, hotels and restaurants set their prices on a cost-plus basis. It is assumed that food costs, for example, should be 30% of the menu item's total cost to a guest. But this orientation ignores how guests feel about what they are getting and what they are willing to pay for it. The basic flaw with cost-plus pricing is that guests don't care what your costs are. Moreover, it doesn't take into account a notion that all retailers understand: that some items are loss-leaders—items that are not profitable in themselves but attract customers to their stores so they will buy other items that are profitable. Typically, bars and lounges that offer a free or nominally priced buffet during happy hour are purposely sacrificing the low profit margin on their food in order to gain higher profits from beverage sales.

Cost-plus or product-driven pricing is used by many businesses to set prices, but ultimately consumers decide whether they will pay for what is being offered, and if they won't pay the price set by management, the price must be adjusted or the product or service must be dropped. Therefore, consumer-based pricing is a much more realistic method of setting prices. With consumer-based pricing, companies first determine what customers want, what they are willing to pay for it, and then figure out a way to deliver that product and service at the desirable price.

There are many other methods of pricing besides cost-plus and consumer-based pricing. One is competitive pricing. With competitive pricing, hotels base room rates on what competitors charge. This strategy can work only as long as consumers see all of the hotels in the area as being equal. If there is a perceivable difference (such as one hotel being brand-new while the others are much older), then competitive pricing will favor the hotel that appears to offer the most, the newest, or the nicest facilities. Another problem with competitive pricing is that your competitors may be willing to lose money, or have lower costs and can therefore make money charging prices that would mean losses for you.

Most businesses practice customer-based pricing. This is a pricing method based on what the customer perceives to be a good value. Hotels and restaurants which use this system try to give customers what they expect or more for the price being charged. Businesses that set prices with the customer in mind also recognize that consumers may perceive a larger difference between $9.95 and $10 than there actually is, and so try to keep their prices at the lower figure. There is another psychological factor at work in pricing—the assumption that quality costs money, and that you must pay more to get better quality. Many people are willing to pay more and refuse to stay in the cheapest motel because they believe that there are no free lunches and you always get what you pay for. Restaurants that have a real quality advantage over competitors in terms of product and/or service also have a definite pricing advantage. Even if it costs them less than it costs their competitors to produce a meal, they can charge more and their sales will actually increase, since many people believe that extra quality is worth more money.

Elasticity of demand. Hospitality authors Robert Lewis and Richard Chambers observe that:

> foodservice in convenience stores owes a good part of its growth to the raising of food prices in fast-food restaurants. Even supermarket business increased because of the raising of restaurant prices. Consumers traded down and down until many, and not just at the lowest level, decided to stay home and eat. Many who preferred higher-quality restaurants maintained that quality level by eating better at home.[2]

In economics, this phenomenon is known as elasticity of demand—the response by customers to changes in price. In the Lewis and Chambers example, restaurants have been steadily increasing their prices. Some consumers have responded by refusing to pay the higher prices, instead turning to other alternatives such as convenience store food or preparing food at home.

Elasticity of demand is important to understand, because if demand for a product or service is elastic, then managers can raise or lower consumer demand through various strategies, including raising or lowering prices. If demand for a product or service is low at one price, then lowering that price may increase the demand. For example, in New York City, rates

Elasticity of demand is something most resorts must cope with. Courtesy of Hotel Egoth Oberoi, El Arish, Egypt.

for hotel rooms are high during the week because business travelers will pay high prices for the rooms. Those same guestrooms may go unoccupied, however, on weekends when demand from business travelers drops off significantly. However, the rooms may be sold if the prices for them are lowered enough so that they appeal to a different guest group—families or singles wanting a weekend getaway package, for example.

If demand is inelastic, then demand will vary little if at all, no matter what type of adjustments are made. This is the experience of resorts in areas such as Bermuda (in the winter when it is too cold) and Palm Springs, California (in the summer when it is too hot), where lowered room rates and special promotional advertising have not been entirely successful in raising room occupancies to an acceptable level during the off-season. Many people do not want to go to Bermuda or Palm Springs during the off-season, no matter how attractive the price.

Many critics charge that the hotel industry has been unwilling to accept the reality of elasticity of demand, and that the low occupancy rates, which are still endemic in many parts of the country, are not a result of over-building, but rather of a failure of hotel managers to recognize that when prices are above what consumers perceive is a good value, they will find something else to do or somewhere else to go.

Promotion: How Do You Spread the Word? The fourth P in marketing stands for promotion. It is placed last because promotional decisions ideally should be made after product, place, and price decisions have been made. Promotion consists of all the ways an enterprise uses to persuade people to buy its products and services. All promotional activities fall into one of four categories:

- Personal selling
- Advertising
- Public relations
- Sales promotion

Personal selling is discussed in this chapter; advertising, public relations, and sales promotion are discussed in the next.

Promotional categories should be looked at separately, not as a group. Each of them has its own unique strengths and objectives. Personal selling, for instance, is used as the primary way to attract corporate and group business. Advertising is often targeted at leisure travelers (who cannot be reached by direct sales), or designed to build an image for a brand name such as Hilton or Sheraton. Public relations often has a much wider audience and attempts to influence individuals and groups not reached by traditional personal selling or advertising—employees, community opinion leaders, financial institutions, unions, and others. Sales promotion is used to level out peaks and valleys of business by providing a mechanism designed to generate immediate response.

To succeed, a hotel or restaurant must know how to use promotional activities and how to organize and combine them so they work together to produce a synergistic effect—one where the whole is greater than the sum of its parts. The principal tool used to accomplish this is the marketing plan.

Developing a Marketing Plan

All business activities should be planned. Although this rule seems obvious, it is often ignored. Managers sometimes feel that planning takes too much time and is not very useful. They argue that it is better to go out and get something done than sit around and figure out how to do it. Nevertheless, in the case of marketing, where the expense involved can be astronomical, planning may be regarded as a survival tool. Companies like McDonald's spend more than $1 billion a year on marketing and advertising activities. If those funds were not spent effectively and did not produce the desired results, McDonald's would go out of business very quickly. Even a small restaurant owner with a marketing budget of $25,000 must make those dollars return themselves very rapidly in the form of increased revenue, or the dollars available for marketing will disappear in no time at all.

A marketing plan is a blueprint for organizing, in the most efficient way possible, a business's marketing strategies and activities. New marketing plans are usually created on a regular basis; many businesses create one every year, others may create one every two years, three years, or five years. Good plans are always reviewed and often revised on a quarterly basis to take current conditions into account.

A good marketing plan consists of several parts:

- Situation analysis
- Objectives
- Strategies
- Action plans
- Controls

Situation Analysis
Developing a marketing plan may sound like an intimidating procedure, but it is relatively uncomplicated and follows a series of logical steps. The first of these is the situation analysis. A marketing department's situation analysis is in some ways very similar to feasibility studies prepared for proposed hotels or restaurants (discussed in Chapter 3), except that the marketing department's situation analysis is prepared for an already existing property and is even more marketing oriented.

A situation analysis prepared by a marketing department typically consists of a marketplace analysis, a competition analysis, a review of internal data, a consumer profile, and a problems and opportunities section.

Marketplace Analysis. Before we can do anything about a situation, we must understand it. Therefore, the situation analysis contains first a description of the marketplace. If we were doing a situation analysis for a hotel, our first step would be to write down the important data that is likely to affect hotel occupancy in our area in the year ahead. Are businesses opening or closing? Is the economy growing? What is the outlook for tourism? Is the state or city planning any major new campaigns to attract tourists? Is the airport projecting more traffic or less?

Competition Analysis. Marketplace information is very general, in that it concentrates on overall or macro trends that are likely to affect your business in the years ahead. In addition to this kind of information, the situation analysis should include a competition analysis. The competition analysis seeks to pinpoint who your competitors are. These are not always easily spotted. For example, the Greenbriar Hotel in White Sulphur Springs, West Virginia, competes with the Boca Raton Hotel & Country Club in Florida for conventions. As we pointed out earlier, fast-food establishments compete with convenience stores and supermarkets for market share.

Besides simply listing competitors, it is important to get down on paper a description of the competitive establishments and how they compare with your facility, both in terms of the physical plant and the quality of service. Prices of all competitors should be noted, and a comparison of value made. A competition analysis for a hotel also includes the number of hotel rooms or beds in the market, average occupancy rates, and the kinds of properties found in the area—resorts, city hotels, motels, and so on. If the market is overbuilt, it should be noted. Finally, a careful look needs to be taken as to who the competitors' guests are, where they come from, and whether you can reasonably expect to lure them from your competitors. New business almost always comes from the competitor's customer-base—customers who either are unsatisfied or believe that you can offer them something superior.

Internal Data. There should be a section in the situation analysis that deals with internally generated sales data. Occupancy rates by month is an example of sales data for hotels. Among other sales data, restaurants should note their busiest times and track their food sales by individual menu item.

Consumer Profile. The most important part of the situation analysis is the consumer profile. You should begin with the demographics—that is, what you know about the ages, income, and geographic location of your guests. What is their family size? You need to know as much as you can about your guests' lifestyles. How often do they travel or eat out? Where do they eat? Who makes the decision? This information will help you organize your sales efforts and select advertising media. It will help you decide how to appeal to your guests as well as match up age and household characteristics with specific radio stations, TV programs, magazines, and newspapers.

Ideally, a consumer profile should help you identify your current or potential heavy users. Are they businesspeople grabbing a quick breakfast on the way to work, or mothers with young children meeting friends for lunch? A restaurant's heavy users sometimes represent only 25% of the guest base, but as much as 75% of sales because they come in regularly several times a week. The same is true in hotels, where a small base of corporate guests can easily represent more than half of a hotel's total sales.

Problems and Opportunities. Once you have completed the fact-finding phase of the situation analysis, the work really begins. Now you have to interpret what those facts mean. Does the fact that there are no Italian restaurants in your neighborhood mean that there is an opportunity to convert yours to one, or does it simply mean that people in the area do not like ethnic restaurants? Does the fact that all of the hotels in your city are mid-priced mean that there is a market for a luxury one? There may indeed be a market, but it may be so small that upgrading your property to go after it would not be a profitable venture. Many restaurateurs who are convinced that they can operate a catering service start one, believing that competence is sufficient to attract customers and earn profits. This is an illusion. There may already be several competent caterers in the area with established reputations and a loyal customer base. In such a situation it can be a long and costly process to start a new catering operation, and it might never succeed unless there is a real point of difference between the established caterers and the new operation. Even then success is not guaranteed. As the old proverb goes, "The man who built a better mousetrap and then waited for the world to beat a path to his door starved to death."

The problems and opportunities section is the place to list as objectively as you can the problems that stand in the way of significantly increasing your sales or your market share. For example, if you operate a downtown dinner restaurant in a city where fewer and fewer people are coming downtown for dinner in the evening, put that down on paper. You have a genuine problem. You also may have an equally genuine opportunity to open a second restaurant in the suburbs, or open for lunch in your city location.

Similarly, with airline deregulation many carriers found themselves faced with new competition on routes that previously had been exclusively theirs. That was a problem. But in turn they were free to seek out new and profitable markets previously denied them and thus could develop their own new opportunities. Remember, however, as we pointed out earlier, all new opportunities are not profitable. It was mainly Eastern Airline's expansion under deregulation that caused its bankruptcy, because it invested in expensive new aircraft in anticipation of business that never materialized.

Objectives

Once facts have been gathered and analyzed, managers can create marketing objectives. Marketing objectives are nothing more than clear and concise descriptions of exactly what managers want the marketing program to accomplish. These objectives are usually very specific and measurable.

A business usually has several different kinds of objectives. At the top is most often a financial objective. Most companies base their company-wide expense budget on expected income; expected income is stated in the marketing plan as monthly profit goals. Then there are usually growth objectives. Objectives to significantly increase your sales or expand into new markets are growth objectives. Sometimes financial objectives and growth objectives conflict with each other—building a new wing onto the hotel may diminish profits temporarily, for instance. Quality objectives are clearly very important in the marketing plans of service organizations. Quality objectives may encompass introducing new amenities or improving existing products or services. Finally, there are philosophical objectives that may address problems such as better working conditions for employees, more environmentally conscious waste management, or support of local charities and cultural programs.

Strategies

After marketing objectives are established, marketing strategies can be devised. Strategies are simply descriptions of how the marketing objectives are going to be achieved. For example, suppose one of your objectives is to raise the amount of leisure business at your hotel from 20% to 30%. Your strategies to do this might include:

- Generating support from more travel agents

- Increasing consumer advertising expenditures

- Developing special honeymoon and other travel packages

To be sure that these strategies are realistic, projected cost figures should be attached to each of them. How much money is going to be spent on generating support from more travel agents, on advertising, and on promoting the new travel packages? If a strategy costs too much, it can be eliminated, modified, or replaced with a less expensive one.

Action Plans

Strategies are general in nature. How are you going to go about "generating support from more travel agents"? Are you going to invite travel agents to visit your property on familiarization (FAM) tours? Are you going to offer them special rates? Are you going to visit them in their offices and leave brochures? How many visits will you make? Who will make them? Which travel agencies will you visit? When will this be done?

The answers to all of these questions help managers develop tactics or action plans for achieving marketing objectives. Without action plans, a marketing plan is a useless document. It is not a plan at all. A real marketing plan contains action plans for every strategy so that anyone with a copy can pick up the ball and run with it.

Controls

Control is as important in marketing as it is in operations. If marketing's action plans are specific, you should be able to tell what is supposed to happen every month and how much it is expected to cost. Results too can be anticipated. Advertising a special honeymoon package ought to produce a number of reservations by honeymooners. If it doesn't, something is wrong. Marketing plans should not be inflexible—they should be reviewed on a regular basis and revised when necessary. That is the function of controls—to monitor and correct deviations from the plan.

Sales Management and Personal Selling

Some hotel and restaurant chains have millions of dollars to spend on advertising, public relations, and sales promotion, but most hotels and restaurants have very limited marketing budgets. Therefore, personal selling by the owners, managers, or sales force is the business-building tool hotels and restaurants most frequently employ.

Most hotels have a marketing and sales or a sales department. Some of these departments are quite sophisticated. Salespeople generally report to a director of sales, who may in turn report to the director of marketing and sales (remember, sales is only one of the functions of marketing). In mid-size to small hotels, the director of marketing and sales and the director of sales are often the same person, although the functions of each job are very different. Clubs, restaurants that have private meeting rooms, and caterers all utilize at least one full-time salesperson (unless the owner or manager takes on this function, which is not a good idea).

The director of sales is in charge of the sales office and is responsible for overseeing the sales staff. Some sales directors assign salespeople according to source of business. There may be a salesperson in charge of selling corporate programs targeted at individual business travelers, for example; another in charge of booking meetings and conventions business; and a third in charge of tour business. Other salespeople may be in charge of travel agency sales, military and government sales, and catering sales. Or, sales directors may use a regional approach—there may be an eastern sales manager, a western sales manager, and even an international sales manager, depending on the size and nature of the business. According to James Abbey, author of *Hospitality Sales and Advertising*, the general goals of a director of sales include:

- Increasing property revenue through personal sales calls, telephone calls, and correspondence

- Establishing guidelines for the number of personal sales calls, telephone calls, and sales letters required from each salesperson

- Assisting the general manager with obtaining the maximum sales effort from all employees

- Holding weekly and monthly sales meetings

- Maintaining sales reports and establishing a sales filing system to insure that all files are processed and kept up to date[3]

In order to accomplish these tasks, a director of sales must first recruit and train salespersons. The ability to be an effective salesperson can be learned; it is not a skill that is inherited or based purely on natural talent. Nevertheless, some people are better at it than others.

There are individuals who do not like the idea of selling to someone else. They consider it to be manipulative behavior and not very ethical. To be sure, unethical salespersons are a part of American folklore. Early salespeople in America were peddlers whose wares included snake oil, charms, and fake antiquities, all of which required a certain amount of deception to sell. Even today, surveys show that used-car salespersons are some of the least-trusted of all individuals, and salespeople as a group are considered less trustworthy than most other professionals. Nevertheless, sales can be an honorable and rewarding career, and, as often as not, today's salesperson is regarded as an important partner, counselor, and helper. At IBM, for example, the mission of the sales team is to help companies solve problems, which is very different from selling them computers. However, because IBM salespersons are very good problem solvers, they also sell a great many computers.

How to Be a Successful Salesperson

There are certain characteristics that successful salespersons share, according to Professor Charles Garfield, a clinical professor of psychology at the University of California. Garfield, who has studied super-achievers in all areas, says that exceptional salespersons are similar in these ways:

- They are always taking risks and making innovations to try and surpass previous levels of performance.

- They have a powerful sense of mission and set short-, intermediate-, and long-term goals to fulfill that mission. Their personal sales goals are higher than those set by their managers.

- Super-salespeople are more interested in solving problems than in placing blame or bluffing their way out of situations. Because they view themselves as professionals, they are always upgrading their skills.

- Super-salespeople see themselves as partners with their customers and as team players rather than adversaries. They believe their task is to communicate with people.

- Super-salespeople do not take rejection personally; rather, they treat it as information they can learn from.

- Like other peak performers Garfield has studied, such as athletes and performers, super-salespeople use mental rehearsal. Before every sale, they review it in their mind's eye, from shaking the customer's hand when they walk in to discussing his or her problems and asking for the sale.[4]

How does one become a good salesperson? One characteristic is essential in sales: intelligence. Derek Taylor, a successful hotel sales director in England for more than 30 years, puts it this way:

> Sales . . . is a cerebral occupation. It takes a great deal of thought, for in trying to convince a client to buy the product, you are trying to influence his mind. I have often been asked what book a prospective hotel salesperson should read to understand his job; my answer remains Freud's *Two Short Accounts of Psychoanalysis*. It is a nice simple book that tells you the rules of the game. The capacity to outthink the client who is not all that keen on buying your hotel is the vital difference between success and failure.[5]

Four Types of Personalities. Most professional salespeople would agree with Taylor that an understanding of how people think and how to relate to them is the most important characteristic of any salesperson. The idea, for instance, that extroverted, sociable people make better salespersons than those who are quiet and introverted has little basis in fact. They make different kinds of salespeople, but studies have shown that there is no difference in sales effectiveness between people who are outgoing and sociable and those who are quiet and reserved. The key is the ability to relate to other people, to be able to listen to them, and then to communicate with them in terms that they understand and in a manner that they can empathize with. In other words, the first step in successful sales is to recognize the kind of person you are dealing with and then use that information to decide how to sell to him or her.

Exhibit 10.1   Four Personality Types

High Responsiveness

Amiable Style

Slow at taking action and making decisions

Likes close, personal relationships

Dislikes interpersonal conflict

Supports and "actively" listens to others

Weak at goal-setting and self-direction

Has excellent ability to gain support from others

Works slowly and cohesively with others

Seeks security and belongingness

Good counseling skills

Expressive Style

Spontaneous actions and decisions

Likes involvement

Dislikes being alone

Exaggerates and generalizes

Tends to dream and get others caught up in his dreams

Jumps from one activity to another

Works quickly and excitingly with others

Seeks esteem and belongingness

Good persuasive skills

Low Assertiveness   *High Assertiveness*

Analytical Style

Cautious actions and decisions

Likes organization and structure

Dislikes involvement

Asks many questions about specific details

Prefers objective, task-oriented, intellectual work environment

Wants to be right and, therefore, overrelies on data collection

Works slowly and precisely alone

Seeks security and self-actualization

Good problem-solving skills

Driving Style

Decisive actions and decisions

Likes control

Dislikes inaction

Prefers maximum freedom to manage himself and others

Cool, independent, and competitive with others

Low tolerance for feelings, attitudes, and advice of others

Works quickly and impressively alone

Seeks esteem and self-actualization

Good administrative skills

Low Responsiveness

Source: Anthony J. Alessandra, Ph.D., and Phillip S. Wexler, *NON-MANIPULATIVE SELLING,* ©1979, p. 22. Reprinted by permission of Prentice-Hall, Englewood Cliffs, NJ.

One useful way of doing this that was originally developed by sales consultant Tony Alessandra is to think of all personalities as falling somewhere on a grid consisting of two dimensions (see Exhibit 10.1). One dimension defines personalities as ranging from high responsiveness to low responsiveness, the other from high assertiveness to low assertiveness. High-responsive people are very open; they are relaxed and warm and are willing to share personal feelings. Low-responsive people tend to hide personal feelings and be formal and guarded. Highly assertive people are willing to take risks, are impatient, extroverted, and express opinions readily. People with a low degree of assertiveness are supportive, easygoing, and reserve opinions.

As can be seen from Exhibit 10.1, depending on where on the grid a person falls, he or she can be characterized as an Amiable, an Expressive, a Driver, or an Analytical.

Amiables. People who are Amiables consider personal relationships to be of utmost importance. They are interested in buying from people with whom they have established a personal relationship. Amiables are easy to recognize because their conversation often deals with relationships they have with others. They also tend to be indirect and slow-paced.

Most Amiables are hesitant to talk business until they feel comfortable with a person, and thus a salesperson who tries to come to the point quickly will not make a favorable impression on them. Amiables are particularly susceptible to buying from individuals who went to the same school as they did, belong to the same club, or live in the same neighborhood. Often you can tell when you are sitting in an Amiable's office by the way it is decorated. An Amiable's desk may have family pictures or personal items on it. The seating arrangement is open and informal.

Expressives. An Expressive is also open and interested in relationships, but, unlike an Amiable, an Expressive moves faster and is much more direct. Expressives do not hesitate to open up and tell you about themselves and their ideas and opinions. To successfully sell to Expressives, you must respond to what they say in a lively and interesting manner, and draw them out so that they will feel they are dealing with someone who is really interested in them.

Again, one way to recognize an Expressive quickly is to look around his or her office. While an Expressive's office may contain family pictures (just like an Amiable's), it may also have a golf or fishing trophy, a souvenir of a trip to Europe, or a picture of him or her running in the Boston marathon. Sometimes Expressives have a sign or plaque with a favorite saying on it. All of these mementos suggest a person who likes to remember and talk about personal experiences and ideas.

Drivers. The Driver is also a fast-paced person, but, unlike an Amiable or an Expressive, a Driver is not interested in small talk. Drivers want to get down to business. They are not interested in knowing more about you or telling you anything about them; they only want facts, figures, and results. Drivers are take-charge individuals. They only buy from a salesperson who they feel is taking directions from them. Drivers are leaders, not followers, and if they feel they are being manipulated or pressured they will not respond no matter how good the deal is. Success in selling to Drivers often involves giving them several options and letting them pick one—that way they can feel that they are in charge of the transaction.

Because they are action-oriented, Drivers generally have desks with lots of paperwork and projects on them. Sometimes there is a large planning sheet or calendar on the wall. There are few or no personal mementos to be seen. If a Driver has received any certificates or awards for achievements, these may be displayed to give visitors the idea that they are dealing with a highly competent, knowledgeable person. Seating arrangements are usually formal and the Driver sometimes has a large desk to suggest power.

Analyticals. The fourth kind of person is the Analytical. Analyticals are very logical people. They too have little time for socializing—they know they are there to get a job done and they want to get on with it. But unlike Drivers, Analyticals are more slow-paced and careful when making decisions. They need to be convinced that they are doing the right thing before they will buy, and the only way to convince them is with facts and figures. Analyticals want to see documentation that everything you say is true. They are less likely to take anything on faith, no matter how much they may like you. Testimonial letters from people who have held meetings in your hotel, or newspaper reviews from food critics of your restaurant, are the most convincing things you can show Analyticals.

An Analytical's office usually contains nothing distracting in it; it is all business. It often contains business and reference books, charts, and graphs that can be consulted if necessary.

Clearly, we cannot neatly categorize everyone and say that he or she is an Amiable, an Expressive, a Driver, or an Analytical. All of us have some of each of these personality styles within us. But, generally speaking, we tend to fit into one of these personality types more than the others. Successful salespeople take time before they start selling to establish which kind of personality they are dealing with. From that point on it is a question of modifying their own behavior so that it matches that of the person on the other side of the desk.

If you are selling to an Amiable, for example, the conversation might start with a question about how long he or she has been in that job or in the city. This may be followed by sharing some similar information about yourself to see if common ground can be established. If you are dealing with an Expressive, you might briefly comment on his or her tennis trophy. A Driver wants you to come to the point quickly—tell him or her why you are there and what you hope to accomplish. Analyticals want to see pictures, plans, and facts supporting your sales presentation, and will take the time to go over these support materials carefully.[6]

Basic Qualities of a Salesperson

Besides inherent intelligence, an interest in people, and an ability to relate to them, a prospective salesperson needs some other qualities. The late DeWitt Coffman, international hotel consultant and author of *Hospitality for Sale* and other sales and marketing books, pointed out that nearly all textbooks prepared on personal selling emphasize the following basic qualities:

- Courtesy
- Deportment
- Appearance
- Knowledge of product or service
- Willingness to work
- Personality[7]

Courtesy. According to Coffman, courtesy is best defined as "a combination of friendliness and politeness, tempered by conservatism and reserve. It is the use of 'please' and 'thank you' and all the other terms for showing appreciation. It is consideration and respect and interest in the other person's comfort, pleasure, and deportment." Without courtesy, a salesperson is doomed from the start. While you may accept service from a discourteous food server in a restaurant where you are already seated, you are not likely to entrust the planning of your next meeting to a person who strikes you as being rude or uncaring.

Deportment. Deportment is related to physical posture. Individuals who deport themselves well don't slouch, and they look alert, pleasant, and enthusiastic.

Appearance. Appearance can make a huge difference in a person's ability to be a successful salesperson. Appearance in this context refers to personal grooming and dress, not physical attractiveness. Incidentally, there is no evidence that beauty or handsomeness offers the slightest advantage in making a sale. Indeed, some salespeople have reported that being physically attractive has actually hindered their sales efforts, because their prospects are distracted!

Sales training programs constantly refer to presenting a "professional" image. What is a professional image? For one thing, it is very conservative. There is nothing wrong with choosing clothes for your personal wardrobe that make a statement about what kind of a person you are, but when you are selling, the objective is to get the prospect to concentrate on your product or service, not on you. That is why almost all salespeople avoid dressing too colorfully; displaying the latest fashions; or wearing large rings, bracelets, or earrings.

There is also research to indicate that people are more likely to respond favorably to persons who dress in a manner that suggests that they have already achieved success. John T. Molloy, who calls himself a wardrobe engineer and has written several books on how to dress properly for business, noticed that upper-class people tended to wear beige raincoats, while lower-class people usually wore black ones. To see how this affected behavior, he bought 25 copies of the *Wall Street Journal* and, wearing a black raincoat, tried to deliver them to the head person in 25 randomly selected offices. It took him a day and a half; the receptionists assumed he was a glorified messenger boy. Then he did the same thing wearing a beige raincoat. He was able to deliver all of the papers successfully in one morning; the receptionists assumed he was a friend of the boss![8]

A professional image is also enhanced by neat grooming: pressed clothes, shined shoes, clean fingernails, and combed hair. If a salesperson looks shoddy and unkempt, prospects generally assume that the company he or she represents is the same.

Knowledge of Product or Service. A knowledge of your product or service is essential. Says Coffman:

> the salesman promoting banquet business should know exactly the seating capacity of the various rooms in his establishment under all possible set-ups. He should know the complete price range of menus

Salespeople dress conservatively so that their clothes do not distract potential customers from the sales message.

available and all the additional services available such as music, loud speakers, and flowers. The waiter or waitress should know every item on each day's menu and the general type of preparation of each of these items. The room clerk should have a mental image of every room, or every type of room, he is selling. All of the personal charm in the world cannot overcome ignorance or lack of knowledge.[9]

In the same vein, knowledge of the prospect's needs is equally important. There is no point in going to a meeting ready to discuss how well your property handles banquets when the prospect is interested in talking about his or her company's annual training meeting.

Willingness to Work. Willingness to work sounds like an obvious qualification, but it is not. Salespersons often get discouraged because most of the calls they make do not produce immediate business. The truth is that sales is a game of numbers. The more calls you make, the more sales you will make. But on the way to making those sales, you will receive a large number of rejections because it is hard to locate good prospects. In the insurance industry it takes nine prospect calls to create one customer. Selling computers to businesses is even harder: 125 phone calls to prospects may produce 25 interviews that lead to 5 sales presentations and 1 sale.[10] Hanging tough requires a lot of determination, or what Derek Taylor calls tough-mindedness. Taylor says he likes to hire salespeople who are considered "stubborn, difficult, awkward, or bloody-minded. These are the ingredients professional salespeople need to bolster their persistence and fuel their determination to get the account."[11]

Personality. The final quality a successful salesperson needs is personality. This often frightens some people who would otherwise be interested in a sales career. "I don't have the right personality," they tell themselves, "I'm not interesting enough as a person," or "I'm too shy." The secret of personality is to come across as being interested in others, not yourself. Think of your friends whom you consider to have the best personality. The ones who come to mind are usually the ones who are interested in what you have to tell them. Sometimes we confuse liveliness and playfulness with personality. They are not the same. Anyone who is courteous, friendly, and a good listener is judged by most others to have a good personality.

Making the Sales Call

An effective sales call consists of six steps. These are:

- Prospecting and qualifying

- Preparation

- Presentation

- Overcoming objections

- Asking for the sale

- Follow-up

Let's discuss each of these steps in sequence.

**Prospecting
and Qualifying**

Even experienced salespeople often waste a lot of effort calling on people who are not legitimate prospects. One reason is that many companies establish quotas for the number of calls a salesperson is expected to make in a day or a week. There isn't any doubt that the only way to sell is to make a large number of calls, but the more carefully the prospects are selected, the greater the return will be.

There are several good sources of leads for hospitality enterprises besides the inquiries that come in through the mail and on the telephone daily. To begin with, current guests are often the best source of new leads. Another excellent source are the companies you do business with—your vendors, suppliers, bankers, insurance people, and accountants. All of these people have other clients that might be interested in using your

Salespeople spend a lot of time prospecting for potential customers.

facilities. Trade publications and newspapers are another excellent source of leads. Many hotels, restaurants, and caterers look in their local newspapers for people who are getting married and contact them promptly. Many cities have a convention and visitors' bureau, whose job it is to develop leads for meetings and conventions and distribute them to all local hoteliers. Airlines have group sales departments that are constantly negotiating rates with groups such as the AFL-CIO who plan conventions and will have a large number of people flying to the convention location. Airlines will very often contact hotels to seek their cooperation in creating flight/hotel packages.

Preparation

There are two parts to the preparation process. The first is to decide exactly what you hope to accomplish with the sales call. "Make the sale" is not a good objective because actually making a sale is not the objective of most sales calls. It usually takes several calls to close a sale. A hotel salesperson's objective for a first sales call might only be to "introduce our property," or "gather information about the prospect's 1994 annual meeting so we can make a proposal." Only after another meeting or two might the objective become "make the sale."

Equally important to the preparation process is to research the prospect and his or her company so that everything that might be needed is at hand during the meeting. On a first call, it is important to know as much about the company as possible beforehand. What are its products and/or services? How well is it doing? Who are its competitors? A well-informed salesperson can ask specific and intelligent questions that will convey the impression to the prospect that the salesperson is really interested in his or her company. In fact, as we have pointed out, this cannot be an illusion. Effective salespersons are truly interested in their prospects' companies— that is what makes them effective!

Presentation

By the time a salesperson is in a face-to-face meeting with a prospect, he or she should already know what the prospect is interested in buying. In the real world, however, that is not always the case. Without this information, a sale is not possible, so you should not try to sell anything until you get it. If the prospect hasn't told you what he or she might be interested in buying, ask. Let them tell you about their problems and then maybe you can suggest some ways in which you can help solve them.

In a good presentation, the salesperson always focuses on benefits, not features. The prospect is interested in benefits—"What's in it for me?"—not in what you are selling. For example, one of your convention hotel's features may be its ten lighted tennis courts. But if you merely mention this fact, the prospect might think, "So what?" The benefit should be spelled out clearly. Rather than saying "We have ten lighted tennis courts," you should say something like: "There are always enough tennis courts available for your delegates to use after their meetings, no matter what time they finish."

Successful presentations almost always employ the use of visual aids. However, don't make them the focus of the presentation. They are simply there to reinforce what you are saying.

Overcoming Objections

Even with the best of presentations, you can expect a prospect to raise some objections. It is normal for people to ask tough questions or try to put off decisions, especially if they have a fear of deciding incorrectly. You should not be discouraged by objections. An objection usually signals that the prospect is interested, but that you haven't correctly identified the prospect's needs or clearly pointed out how your hotel or restaurant can fill them. You should respond to an objection with further questioning to determine what the prospect is really looking for.

It should be recognized that there will be many instances when objections can't be overcome. A prospect may simply not be interested in what you have to sell. For example, your property may not have a golf course and a golf tournament may be the highlight of your prospect's annual meeting. In that case, the best strategy is to end the presentation, thank the prospect for his or her time, and withdraw gracefully. By doing so, you can retain your relationship with the prospect and you may do business with him or her in the future.

Asking for the Sale

This is the part of selling that most inexperienced salespersons fear most. No one wants to be rejected, and asking for the sale and not getting it can be discouraging.

Timing is everything in closing. Experienced salespeople seldom get rejected, simply because they don't ask for the sale until they sense that the prospect is ready to buy. Signs that a prospect is ready to buy are usually obvious to a careful observer. The prospect nodded in agreement throughout the presentation. He or she looked relaxed. At the end of the presentation he or she asked you to confirm some details of your proposal. That is the time to ask for the sale. Salespeople should not be tentative at this point; the prospect expects you to ask. Very often experienced salespersons simply assume that the sale has been made and ask questions such as, "How many rooms shall I reserve for you?" or "When can we expect your deposit?"

Follow-Up

It is an established principle of salesmanship that the sale really begins once the order is signed. This is especially true in the hospitality industry, where good service and word-of-mouth recommendations are keys to increasing business. Careful follow-up can keep the customer sold permanently and produce repeat business.

The follow-up process typically starts with a letter sent to the client within a day or two after your last meeting, thanking him or her for the sale and confirming the details. But that is only the beginning. Professional salespeople stay with the client every step of the way. They check to make sure that everything that happens is exactly what the client wants and, if possible, sees that he or she gets more than was expected. Sales depend on a continuing relationship, where the client comes to view the salesperson as a partner and friend.

Repeat sales depend on a trusting relationship.

Selling Through Travel Agencies

One of the most prominent trends in the travel industry in recent years has been the growing importance of travel agencies in the distribution of travel products. This is quite a change from the early days of travel, when there were no travel agents, and travelers had to arrange for transportation and accommodations on their own.

The first travel agent was Thomas Cook. In the mid-1850s, Cook recognized that with the emergence of railroads and steamships there was a need for someone willing to make arrangements for people who wished to explore England and the Continent, but were somewhat nervous about traveling on their own to foreign places. Soon Cook had established himself as a sales agent for these new and convenient forms of transportation, and in 1856 he offered his first "Grand Tour" of Europe.

About the same time (1850), the American Express Company was formed in the United States. Originally started with the purpose of shipping merchandise and money across America and then to Europe, the company soon grew to the point where it also offered travelers checks and dispensed information on foreign destinations. Not until 1915, however, did the company decide to go into the business of handling tourist travel and offering tours.

Modern travel agencies represent airlines, hotels, car rental firms, and wholesale tour operators. As representatives, their job is first and foremost to dispense information about these various services to the public at large. In this sense they are information brokers. However, because travel agents buy airline tickets, make hotel reservations, and make other travel arrangements for clients, they are also distributors and salespersons and, as such, they receive commissions from the organizations whose products they distribute and sell.

Today there are more than 35,000 travel agencies in the United States. This figure is more than double the number of agencies before airline deregulation took effect. Most travel agencies are small businesses with average annual sales in the neighborhood of $2.6 million. Sixty-six percent of agency locations have yearly revenues of under $2 million, while 34% have revenues of more than $2 million. Only 9% of locations exceed $5 million in sales.[12] The average travel agency has six employees.

Types of Travel Agencies

There are various types of travel agencies, and new variations seem to spring up all the time because of new technology and the ease of entry into the business. The most common travel agencies are full-service, commercial, in-plant, and group and incentive.

Full-Service. Although full-service agencies handle all types of travel, in most cases a little more than half of their business comes from vacation and personal travelers booking airline tickets and hotel rooms. Before airline deregulation, air fares did not vary much from airline to airline, and many travelers—especially business travelers—called the airlines directly to make their travel arrangements. Agencies were used more for convenience than for any other reason. However, with today's complicated and competitive airline fare structures, it is a formidable task for anyone to figure out which airline offers the best fares and the most convenient schedules without the aid of a computer. This has led many more travelers to buy their airline tickets through travel agencies. Today, American Express and Thomas Cook are two of the largest full-service agencies in the world, with branch offices in all major countries.

Commercial. Commercial agencies specialize in commercial business and frequently have little or no walk-in clientele at all. Travel agents at these agencies deal with corporate customers on the telephone and book primarily airline tickets, hotel rooms, and car rentals. Very often they handle meeting arrangements for their clients as well. Rosenbluth Travel in Philadelphia is an example of a highly sophisticated commercial agency with a separate meeting planning facility.

In-Plant. In-plant agencies are located in the offices of large corporate clients so that ticketing and other arrangements can be booked instantly and in person. In-plant agencies are branch offices of commercial agencies. In 1989, in-plant agencies accounted for 11% of total travel agencies.

In some cases, commercial agencies do not need to open an in-plant office staffed with an agent, but instead install satellite ticket printers (STPs) in clients' offices. Under this arrangement, the client calls the agency to arrange travel, but instead of the agency printing the ticket in its office and then delivering it or mailing it to the client, the ticket is instantly printed on the satellite ticket printer in the client's office.

Group and Incentive. Group and incentive travel agencies specialize in creating customized travel programs for groups and corporations. Many companies reward their top salespersons with trips to exotic places. Others hold annual conventions in Hawaii and the Caribbean for all managers and their spouses. Then there are church groups that wish to visit religious sites such as the Vatican, for example, or veterans groups who wish to return to the beaches of Normandy. Group and incentive agencies specialize in this kind of business. Two of the largest are Maritz and the E. F. McDonald Company.

Other Agencies. In addition to the travel agencies just mentioned, there are several less common types of agencies that should be noted.

Direct-response agencies. Direct-response agencies do not have any walk-in offices, but market their products through the mail, usually to senior citizens or other special groups such as disabled persons or alumni associations. Many direct-response agencies offer extended-stay options for clients who, for example, may wish to spend a month in Spain in their own apartments. One of the largest programs of this kind is offered by the American Association of Retired Persons (AARP). In addition, there are direct-response agencies that operate with 800 numbers and offer no travel advice, but instead provide rebates to clients who make their own airline reservations and simply call the agency to issue the ticket(s) that they have already reserved. Travel Avenue in Chicago operates in this manner.

Tour operators. Although travel agencies represent many tour operators, in many cases tour operators sell directly to the public, thereby acting as their own travel agents. Tours are frequently sold by mail and are often advertised in magazines such as *Travel & Leisure* and *The New Yorker*. Many "adventure" vacations, such as African safaris, treks to Nepal, and trips to the Galapagos Islands, are marketed in this fashion. Companies like Society Expeditions and Tauk Tours are good examples of tour operators.

Cruise-only agencies. For travel agents, an essential part of selling cruises is knowing the layout of as many cruise ships as possible, so that the agents can recommend the most favorable cabins (the ones with the least noise and motion) to their clients. Understanding which ports of call offer the most interesting attractions is also important. Because of these complications, almost all cruise tickets are sold through travel agents. As a practical matter, most travel agents simply do not have enough experience or have inspected enough ships to be able to give authoritative advice on cruises. For this reason, many travel agencies have been formed in recent years to handle cruise business only. These agencies go to extra lengths to train their agents to become familiar with cruise ships, their menus, on-board services, and ports of call. Since the cruise business is growing rapidly (today there are 100 cruise ships operating out of American ports alone), these agencies tend to do very well in markets where cruises are popular.

Consolidators. Consolidators are travel agencies that have negotiated special arrangements with certain airlines that allow them larger commissions on certain routes and flights, or simply have been able to obtain more favorable fares or larger commissions based on unsold seats or other marketing considerations. For example, an airline may have 50 unsold seats on a particular flight a few days or weeks before departure. It may then call a consolidator and say, "We'll pay you a 25% commission on every unsold seat you can move for us. Although we sell the seats for $200, you can sell them for $125, because we'd rather get a lower profit than nothing at all." Sometimes there is a catch: the airline will try to sell the 50 unsold seats at the airline's $200 price right up until a day or two before the flight leaves, and only at the last moment let the consolidator know how many seats are still available at the $125 price.

Some consolidators sell to individual clients and advertise regularly in Sunday travel sections of major metropolitan newspapers. However, most consolidators do not deal directly with the public—they purchase seats at bulk rates and then re-sell them to travel agencies. Many travel agencies refuse to deal with a consolidator, despite the fact that they can obtain cheaper fares through it, on the grounds that they can't offer an adequate level of protection for their clients. This is because many flights booked through consolidators may not be confirmed until a few days or even a few hours before departure.

Travel clubs. Travel clubs charge an annual fee (usually $35 to $50) and in return offer their members packaged vacations at special prices. These vacations are usually developed on short notice by the clubs, working with tour operators that have unsold airline seats and hotel rooms and are willing to sell them to clubs at substantial discounts. Discount Travel International (DTI), R&R Travel, and Stand-Buys are three well-known agencies in this category.

What Travel
Agencies Do

We have mentioned the principal products sold by travel agencies in the previous sections. Some of these products need further elaboration and clarification. The three products travel agents sell that we will discuss in this section are airline tickets, hotel rooms, and tours.

Sell Airline Tickets. Airline tickets make up more than two-thirds of sales for most travel agencies. In order to be able to sell tickets for all major airlines throughout the world, agencies need to be accredited by the Airlines Reporting Corporation (ARC) and the International Airlines Travel Agent Network (INTAN). Monies that travel agencies collect from clients are forwarded weekly to these organizations through area settlement banks, which then distribute the money to the airlines.

Ninety-five percent of all travel agencies subscribe to one or more of the four computer reservation systems that, for the most part, are owned or controlled by the major airlines. The major systems are APOLLO (United); SABRE (American); System One (Texas Air and General Motors); and a system created by Worldspan Travel Agency Information Services (a partnership of Delta, Northwest, and TWA airlines) that replaced the DATAS II and PARS systems (formerly operated by Delta and TWA). Of these computer reservation systems, the largest is SABRE. In addition, there are two major multinational European systems—AMADEUS and GALILEO—owned by a group of European carriers; and a Far Eastern system called Abacus, owned by Singapore Airlines. All of these airline systems are linked together. This makes it possible for a travel agent to compare schedules, fares, and seat availabilities from different airlines, make an instant reservation, issue a ticket, and in some cases issue a boarding pass as well. Agencies with computers use them to book 95% of the domestic airline tickets they sell and 82% of the international airline tickets they sell. Seventy percent of the car rentals and 52% of the hotel reservations they sell are booked electronically as well.

Computer systems are a major expense for travel agencies. An agency with $2 million in annual sales typically has five computer reservation terminals per location and spends more than 6% of its gross income on computer rentals and supplies. However, rental fees charged by airlines are negotiable, depending on the volume of business or the market share that an agency is able to generate for the airline supplying the system.

Sell Hotel Rooms. Some hotels can have their guestrooms booked through the airline computer systems that travel agents use. However, these are only hotels in the major hotel chains. On the whole, the lodging industry has not kept up with the airlines or travel agents in computer technology. Many hotels still do not have computerized property management systems, and even those that do in most cases do not have hardware and software that is compatible with the airline reservation systems. As a result, computer reservation systems are used to book hotel rooms only 51% of the time.[13]

Industry analysts expect this to change, however. As travel agencies become more involved in making hotel reservations for their clients, the lodging industry is expected to accelerate programs to interface with travel agency computer systems.

In the meantime, just about every travel agency subscribes to the Official *Hotel & Resort Guide, Hotel & Travel Index,* or a similar publication from which they draw their information about guestroom rates. Guestrooms are booked by telephone, or—especially in the case of foreign countries—by mail, telex, or facsimile. Some hotels are represented by hotel representatives (or "reps") who are able to instantly confirm reservations on behalf of the hotels they represent.

Travel agencies and hotels have not yet established an entirely satisfactory business alliance. Despite the fact that travel agencies book the majority of airline seats and virtually all cruises, the AH&MA reports that travel agencies account for only 20% of guestroom reservations at hotels owned by AH&MA members. There are two principal reasons for this. In the past, many hotel chains have bypassed agents in their marketing efforts, urging consumers via TV, radio, and magazine advertising to call the hotels directly for reservations using a toll-free 800 number. Travel agencies have opposed this practice because it deprives them of commissions. The second reason is that some hotels have developed a reputation among travel agencies for not paying the commissions they owe to travel agents. According to Eric Friedheim, chairman and editor-in-chief of *Travel Agent Magazine:*

> Tardy remittances or refusal to pay still plague the agency/hotel relationship, already strained by persistent bypass. . . . Only chains, hotel reps, and top flight establishments aggressively solicit agency support with FAM trips, advertising seminars, overrides, and other incentives. . . . Careless or cumbersome accounting procedures by hoteliers more often than not deprive the agent of rightful compensation.[14]

Hoteliers have responded recently to these challenges. The Marriott Corporation has instituted a commission guarantee program, under which Marriott has pledged to pay twice the commission owed if a commission check is not issued within two business days of the guest's departure. According to Bruce Wold, Marriott's vice president of distribution marketing, "We want agents to feel comfortable in booking Marriott in terms of receiving the commission owed. Otherwise they won't aggressively sell our hotels."[15] Other chains, such as Days Inn, Holiday, and Radisson have instituted similar programs.

Since consumers are expected to place as much as 50% of all their hotel reservations through agencies in the next decade, both agencies and hoteliers continue to explore ways in which the two can work together on a fair and equitable basis. According to *Travel Weekly's 1990 U.S. Travel Agency Survey,* in the eyes of travel agents there are several ways in which hotels can better their relationships with agents:

- Pay commissions
- Pay commissions promptly and on time
- Honor reservations
- Provide updated information on rates and specials
- Improve the efficiency and reliability of reservation systems
- Avoid overbooking

- Improve overall service

- Provide trained, knowledgeable, and courteous staff

- Provide better information on hotel facilities and amenities[16]

Sell Tours. Tours are another popular product with travel agents. Like cruises, tours are often all inclusive. Basically, tours fall into three classifications: escorted, independent, and package.

An escorted tour is a group of travelers traveling with a guide who has travel experience and has set up an itinerary for the group. Escorted tours appeal to people who are inexperienced travelers or who do not enjoy traveling alone. However, some experienced travelers—who recognize that escorted tour operators are able (through volume discounts) to secure airline seats and hotel rooms at a far lower cost than they can—book these tours simply to take advantage of the low prices that are available. Some escorted tours are very expensive, however. For example, Lorraine Travel in Miami has put together escorted tours around the world on a Concorde jet that cost $40,000 and up per person.

Independent tours, known in the trade as FITs (Foreign Independent Tours), are tours created for individuals or families that walk into the travel agency and tell an agent what country or area they would like to visit and what they would like to see and do there. Independent tours are usually tailored exactly to the needs of the client and require agents to do a good deal of detail work. The travel agent must arrange for transportation, work out daily itineraries, make hotel reservations, and set up sightseeing excursions or buy theater tickets. Many agencies charge a special fee for this kind of careful planning in addition to the regular commissions they earn.

Package tours are similar to independent tours in that travelers who buy a package tour travel by themselves rather than with a large group. The difference is that travelers do not put their own tours together—they buy a tour that has been planned by a packager or tour operator. Certified Tours in Ft. Lauderdale, Florida, is such a packager. It assembles its own tours as well as the Dream Vacation tours for Delta Airlines. When agents or customers call the Delta Dream Vacation desk, they actually get a Certified Tour travel agent, who books a Dream Vacation tour for them for one package price that is considerably lower than if the elements of the tour (airline tickets, hotel rooms, and so on) were purchased separately.

How Travel Agents Are Trained

Many travel agents start their careers by attending one of the many vocational training schools that teach the basic skills required. While these schools (which offer courses lasting anywhere from a few weeks to several months) will not guarantee placement, many travel agencies recruit from the graduates of these schools. Community colleges also offer travel agent training programs. Courses in these colleges generally focus on the technical skills needed to make airline reservations and issue tickets, as well as on basic geography, since many students have not had the opportunity to travel.

Travel suppliers have learned that the best way to train agents is to give them an opportunity to see the places they are asked to sell. The two trade associations of travel agencies, The American Society of Travel Agents (ASTA) and the Association of Retail Travel Agents (ARTA), sponsor numerous meetings and events where agents can learn to improve their skills. So

Familiarization tours allow travel agents to get acquainted with all of a destination area's hotels, restaurants, and sights. This is an open market in Jerusalem. Courtesy of Moriah Hotels Ltd., Tel Aviv, Israel.

does the Cruise Line Industry Association (CLIA), which runs "schools at sea" where agents learn to sell cruises while taking one. Airlines offer agents a 75% discount on fares and hotels; tour operators and cruise lines all have special rates so agents can become familiar with their products. Many times, destinations and tour operators or airlines will get together to offer, for a small price, familiarization trips to agents in which a group of agents is taken to a particular place and given a chance to inspect all of the hotels and other sights. These are working trips—it is not unusual for agents to visit more than a dozen hotels, plus a couple of restaurants and a sightseeing attraction, in a single day. Most agents take careful notes and are often expected to write reports for other agents in their office when they return. In addition to all of these methods, there are numerous trade shows in the industry such as those run by ASTA at their world congresses, and the traveling Henry Davis shows, where many suppliers put up booths and pass out literature about their hotels and destinations. Also, airlines, tour operators, and destinations frequently hold in-depth training seminars for agents.

There is a formal certification program for travel agents as well, run by the Institute of Certified Travel Agents. Agents that complete this five-year study program earn the designation of CTC (Certified Travel Counselor), considered the most prestigious in the industry.

How Travel Agents Get Paid

Many travel agents advertise that "our services are free." This is not exactly correct. While services are generally free to consumers, agents are paid a commission, as noted earlier, from all major travel suppliers. The standard commission from domestic airlines and hotels is 10%, although commissions can be higher or lower. In some cases, consumer activists have noted this may cause a conflict of interest in that the amount of commission may influence the agent's advice, which is supposed to be impartial. To compound this problem, in recent years many agencies have banded together into "consortiums"—groups of agencies that use their combined strength to negotiate lower rates for their clients and higher commissions for their agencies. Two such associations are Travel Trust International and Hickory. One result of this is that sometimes agencies may be tempted to suggest airlines, hotel chains, or cruise lines which may not be in the best interest of their clients, but with whom they have negotiated special deals for themselves. Good agents adamantly refute any charge that they might be tempted to do this. They say their first interest must be their client, or else they will not get any repeat business. Nevertheless, many consortiums have "preferred suppliers" and instruct their agents to offer the products of these suppliers before any others simply because they are more profitable to sell.

Chapter Summary

There is a real difference between selling and marketing. Selling is getting rid of what you have, marketing is having what customers want. The marketing concept can be defined as "the effort to determine and meet the needs and wants of current and potential customers."

The Four Ps of marketing are:

- *Product.* The concept of a restaurant or hotel is first and foremost a marketing decision. To make it correctly requires a clear understanding of what consumers are looking for and what competitors already offer them to satisfy their needs. People almost never buy a product—they buy the utility they expect to receive from a product.

- *Place.* Place refers to the physical location of a property. It also refers to the place where a sale of a guestroom is made, which can be over the telephone or at the offices of a travel agency.

- *Price.* There are four methods of pricing commonly used in the hospitality industry. These are cost-plus pricing, competitive pricing, market-demand pricing, and customer pricing.

- *Promotion.* Promotion decisions are made after the other marketing Ps are established. Promotion consists of all of the ways an enterprise uses to persuade consumers to buy its products and services. All promotional activities fall into one of four areas: personal selling, advertising, public relations, and sales promotion.

To properly allocate marketing resources, a company needs to begin with a marketing plan. A good marketing plan consists of several parts: situation analysis, objectives, strategies, action plans, and controls.

Hotel sales department personnel are often assigned to specific types of travelers or given specific regions. The director of sales is in charge of sales efforts. He or she is expected to: increase property revenues through sales calls, establish guidelines for selling, assist the general manager with obtaining maximum sales efforts from all employees, hold weekly and monthly sales meetings, maintain sales reports, and establish a sales filing system.

Successful salespersons have certain characteristics in common. The main ones are an ability to understand how people think and an ability to relate to them. To do this, it helps to understand and be able to recognize four basic personality types: Amiables, Expressives, Drivers, and Analyticals. Effective salespersons learn to recognize each style and interact with prospects in the way that makes them most comfortable.

Salespersons need certain basic qualities in order to succeed. These are courtesy, deportment, a good appearance, knowledge of product or service, willingness to work, and personality.

A sales call consists of six steps: (1) prospecting and qualifying, (2) preparation, (3) presentation, (4) overcoming objections, (5) asking for the sale, and (6) follow-up.

Travel agencies help hospitality businesses such as hotels and cruise companies in their sales efforts. Modern travel agencies act as representatives of airlines, hotels, car rental firms, and wholesale tour operators. There are several types of agencies: full-service agencies, commercial agencies, in-plant agencies, group and incentive agencies, direct-response agencies, tour operators, cruise-only agencies, consolidators, and travel clubs.

Travel agencies use airline reservation computer systems to book airline tickets, hotel rooms, and car rentals. Agencies also obtain information on hotels through hotel directories and representatives.

Travel agents obtain training in several ways: by attending special schools, through trade association programs, and by taking familiarization (FAM) tours. They also attend trade shows and may participate in a certification program.

Agents are paid on a commission basis by the travel businesses they represent. The standard commission is 10%.

Endnotes

1. Theodore Levitt, *The Marketing Imagination* (New York: Macmillan, 1983), pp. xii–xiii.

2. Robert C. Lewis and Richard E. Chambers, *Marketing Leadership in Hospitality* (New York: VNR, 1989), p. 354.

3. James R. Abbey, *Hospitality Sales and Advertising* (East Lansing, Mich.: Educational Institute of the American Hotel & Motel Association, 1989), p. 66.

4. Philip Kotler and Gary Armstrong, *Marketing: An Introduction,* 2d ed. (Englewood Cliffs, NJ: Prentice-Hall, 1990), p. 444.

5. Derek Taylor, *Sales Management for Hotels* (New York: VNR, 1987), p. 23.

6. These sections on personality styles were adapted from Anthony J. Alessandra and Phillip S. Wexler, *Non-Manipulative Selling* (Englewood Cliffs, NJ: Prentice-Hall 1979), pp. 13–41.

7. C. Dewitt Coffman, *Marketing for a Full House* (Ithaca, New York: School of Hotel Administration, Cornell University, 1984), p. 183.

8. John T. Molloy, *Dress For Success* (New York: Wyden, 1975).

9. Coffman, p. 183.

10. Vincent L. Zirpoli, "You Can't Control the Prospect, So Manage the Presale Activities to Increase Performance," *Marketing News,* March 16, 1984, p. 1.

11. Taylor, p. 25.

12. *Travel Weekly's Louis Harris Survey,* June 28, 1990, p. 14.

13. Melinda Bush, "Exploding Common Myths about Travel Agents," *Lodging Hospitality,* August 1988, p. 28.

14. Eric Friedheim, "Agents Continue Hunt to Capture Elusive Hotel Commissions," *Travel Agent Magazine,* April 30, 1990, p. 96.

15. "Marriott Makes Good on Pay Promise," *Travel Weekly,* May 10, 1990, p. 1.

16. *Louis Harris Survey,* p. 84.

Key Terms

commercial agency
competitive pricing
consumer-based pricing
cost-plus pricing
cruise-only agency
direct-response agency
elasticity of demand
the Four Ps
full-service agency
group and incentive agency

in-plant agency
loss leaders
marketing
marketing mix
promotion
sales
satellite ticket printer (STP)
tour operator
travel club

Discussion Questions

1. What is the difference between marketing and selling?

2. What are the Four Ps of marketing?

3. Which four methods of pricing are commonly used in the hospitality industry? How do they differ from one another?

4. Promotional activities fall into which four areas?

5. What are the differences between marketing objectives, strategies, and action plans?

6. How do the four personality types proposed by sales consultant Tony Alessandra differ from one other?

7. What basic qualities should a good salesperson possess?

8. A sales call consists of what six steps?

9. What are the four most common types of travel agencies?

10. Why do many hotels and travel agencies have strained business relationships?

Chapter Outline

Advertising
    Definition of Advertising
    What an Advertiser Needs
        Competitive Advantage
        Unique Positioning
        Market Segmentation
    Advertising Agencies
    Creating Effective Advertising
        The Anatomy of a Print Ad
        Using Broadcast Media Effectively
        What Works and What Doesn't
Choosing Advertising Media
    Newspapers
    Magazines
    Radio
    Television
    Direct Mail
Public Relations
Publicity
Sales Promotion
Chapter Summary

11 Advertising, Public Relations, Publicity, and Sales Promotion

The codfish lays a thousand eggs
The homely hen lays one
But the codfish never cackles
To show what she has done.
And so we praise the homely hen
The codfish we despise
Which clearly shows to you and me
It pays to advertise!

Anonymous

Advertising

In the previous chapter we pointed out that there are four basic components to the marketing mix: product, price, place, and promotion. Promotion can be further broken down into personal selling, advertising, public relations, publicity, and sales promotion. Personal selling was covered in Chapter 10; in this chapter we will take a look at advertising, public relations, publicity, and sales promotion.

All these forms of communication have one important difference from personal selling: they communicate with many people at the same time. Personal selling talks to one person at a time. For this reason, personal selling is the most effective form of sales. You can tailor your message to fit each prospect's needs, watch the prospect react to the message, and make any changes to the sales presentation that might be necessary. Unfortunately, every business has far more prospects than it has salespersons, and in most cases many of the prospects are unknown. Therefore it is necessary to find a way to broadcast your sales message to a wider audience—to talk to not one person at a time but to hundreds and thousands of them.

Advertising is a substitute for personal salesmanship. Through advertising, we attempt to talk to those prospects who, for one reason or another, will never get a personal sales call, as well as to prospects who never directly communicate with an advertiser. Advertising also has some unique advantages over personal selling. For instance, advertising can get into offices and homes where a salesperson can't. Many companies use advertising for exactly that reason—to get a "salesperson" past a closed door.

Another advantage of advertising is that it can be repetitive. Once we've seen a salesperson and heard his or her pitch, we are not likely to listen to the pitch again, but print and broadcast ads can reach us many times. This is an important feature, for many people need repeated exposures to sales proposals or messages before they understand and remember them.

Advertising can, and often does, increase the value of products and services in the customer's eyes. It does this in several ways; one way is by inspiring consumer confidence. Consumer confidence in a product or service can take a number of forms. A customer wants the security of knowing that he or she is not wasting money; a brand name can provide that through the assurance of consistent quality. Hotel names like Four Seasons, Hyatt, Sheraton, Hilton, Marriott, and Holiday Inn all assure travelers that they are going to get whatever quality or value they have been promised. "We Didn't Invent the Word Satisfaction—We Defined It," says Sheraton. "A Good Night's Rest Guaranteed," promises Suisse Chalet. These companies understand that they risk everything if too many guests are disappointed, so they are careful to provide consistent products and services that guests can count on.

Another form of confidence is developed when a product is advertised in a way that boosts the consumer's self-esteem, telling a person that using it will make them feel more successful, more important, or more self-confident. Travelers who stay at hotels like the Pierre or The Ritz-Carlton in Manhattan, The Four Seasons in Washington, D.C., and the Stanford Court in San Francisco know that they are paying for the best money can buy. When businesspeople stay in a hotel that has achieved the reputation of being for top executives, it makes them feel successful and it signals to their associates in that city that they have achieved that status. Many people seek experiences that make them feel important. Advertising can let large groups of people know what status a hotel or restaurant has earned.

This concept is known as "added-value." Added-value means that advertising adds to the value of a product. The American Association of Advertising Agencies cites Dr. Thomas S. Wuster, vice president of the Boston Consulting Group:

> Chickens, water, and payment systems are all considered commodities. But Perdue has used advertising and quality controls to change chicken from a commodity into a product with distinct features; Perrier has used attractive packaging and advertising to make water into a drink of choice; American Express has continued to upgrade its brand value added through its gold- and platinum-card introductions. In each case a company has added something of value to consumers.[1]

Many hotel and restaurant managers say that, while stressing the value of what they offer is an interesting concept, they get better results by featuring in their advertising the low prices of their accommodations and meals. Wuster thinks otherwise:

> Many believe that advantage based on lower costs is more real and lasting than advantage based on higher price realization and "elusive" concepts of superior consumer value. In fact, however, our experience and research suggest that the opposite is true: Value-based advantage is even more enduring than cost-based advertising.[2]

THIS WINTER, REKINDLE YOUR RELATIONSHIP.
SPEND A WEEKEND SOMEPLACE WARM.

If one of the greatest luxuries in life is time together, imagine how meaningful
that time can be in the very special warmth and elegance of The Ritz-Carlton.
Join us for A Weekend to Remember. The Newbury Street Spree. Who but Boston's
Five Diamond Hotel could offer A Weekend of Social Savvy for Children?
And of course, one of the nicest things about giving someone you love a weekend at
The Ritz-Carlton—you get to come, too. Call or write for our Weekend Catalog today.

THE RITZ-CARLTON
BOSTON

The Ritz-Carlton in Boston does not use price to compete in this newspaper ad. The ad's layout and design elements reinforce the hotel's image of elegance and quality.
Courtesy of The Ritz-Carlton, Boston, Massachusetts.

The bottom line, according to the Boston Consulting Group, is that "loyalty is a longer-lasting competitive barrier than low cost" and that companies that use advertising to make their name stand for quality will be able to hold on to their customers longer than those who compete by lowering their prices. Someone can always offer a lower price or a newer hotel, but a name that stands for superior value or service will outlast them.

To illustrate this, the Boston Consulting Group pointed out that in 19 of 22 consumer categories, the leading brand in 1925 was still the leader 60 years later. For instance, in 1925 Kellogg was the leading cereal brand, and it still is. Gillette razors, Hershey chocolate, Wrigley chewing gum, Nabisco crackers, Ivory soap, Campbell's soup, Coca-Cola soft drinks, and Colgate toothpaste are other examples of leading brands that have held on to their position by competing on the basis of quality and value rather than price.

Although the Boston Group did not study hotels and restaurants, the same inferences can easily be drawn. The Plaza Hotel in New York, the Willard in Washington, D.C., and the St. Francis in San Francisco are hotels that have never competed on the basis of price. Nor have such famous restaurants as Anthony's Pier Four and Locke-Ober in Boston; or Galatoire's, Antoine's, or Brennan's in New Orleans. These establishments have transformed themselves into institutions that cannot be displaced by newer or more trendy offerings.

Advertising, of course, is not the only way to do this. A brand's image is reinforced through use, experience, pricing, distribution, and packaging. For example, take a plain two-story building. It doesn't stand for much until we put two words on it—Holiday Inn. Now, even though you don't know exactly what the inside looks like, you do know that you'll get a good night's sleep in a clean room, the service is reliable, the amenities have been well thought out, and—best of all—you'll get all this at a reasonable price.

Research shows that advertising is crucial for consumer products of all kinds. A study by the Strategic Planning Institute indicates that brands that advertise much more than their competitors average a return on investment (ROI) of 32%, while brands that advertise much less than their competitors average only 17% ROI. According to the Institute, "Relative advertising influences relative perceived quality, market share, and relative price. These in turn influence profitability and growth."[3]

The need for those in the hospitality industry to understand the role of advertising is underscored by the fact that the largest advertiser in the United States today—the company that spends more money on advertising than anyone else—is a restaurant chain. According to *Advertising Age,* in 1989 McDonald's was the nation's largest advertised brand name, with expenditures of $424.8 million dollars in paid media.[4] Clearly McDonald's uses advertising as its principal tool to stay ahead of its competitors and to generate customers and profits. Exhibit 11.1 shows other hospitality companies among the top 200 advertisers.

No discussion of the role of advertising would be complete without mentioning the social concerns that are sometimes raised when advertising is discussed. Critics frequently charge that advertising makes people buy things they do not need and cannot afford. This is not true. Consumers' wants and needs are determined by society, not by advertising. Most advertisers have learned through experience that it is very difficult to change consumers' buying behavior. Usually, therefore, advertising is used to get them to choose a different brand in a category where they have already decided to buy something.

Critics also say that advertising is sometimes tasteless, it reinforces undesirable stereotypes, it exerts an unhealthy effect on social values, and it influences the character of the media. It would be foolish to deny that some advertising does some of these things some of the time. But these claims are similar to saying tourist development destroys the environment and causes social unrest. Sometimes it does, but most of the time it does not. On the whole, most economists believe that advertising supports a highly diverse media structure at a low cost to consumers. For example, usually only one-third of the cost of publishing a newspaper is paid for by its subscribers. The rest is covered by advertising. In the United States, commercial television programs are free to the public and paid for entirely by advertisers. In countries where advertising is restricted, television programs are subsidized by the government, which collects taxes from the public to pay for them.

Definition of Advertising

According to Professors Charles H. Patti of the University of Denver and Charles F. Frazer of the University of Colorado at Boulder, advertising has a number of characteristics that distinguish it from other forms of communication. Some of these are:

- *It is paid for by the sponsor rather than run at the discretion of the medium.* This distinguishes advertising from publicity—publicity is not paid for and is run at the discretion of the medium.

Exhibit 11.1 Hospitality Companies Among the Top 200 Advertisers

RANK	ADVERTISER	MEASURED AD SPENDING
1	McDonald's	$424,789,900
9	Burger King	170,358,500
18	Kentucky Fried Chicken	118,400,700
30	Pizza Hut	94,466,900
33	Wendy's	92,523,000
61	Domino's Pizza	60,120,600
63	Taco Bell	59,211,900
68	Red Lobster	57,965,700
114	Hardee's	40,628,200
158	Hyatt hotels	29,824,500
168	Royal Caribbean Cruise Line	28,790,000
173	Holiday Inns	28,526,600
186	Long John Silvers	27,036,800
193	Jack in the Box	25,763,900
200	Walt Disney World	25,270,200

Source: "The Top 200 Brands," *Advertising Age*, May 21, 1990, p. 25.

- *It is impersonal.* That is, advertising is disseminated to a mass audience. This distinguishes it from personal selling.

- *It identifies the sponsor of the message.* Advertising is distinguished from propaganda in that the source of the message is identified within the message itself.

- *It is persuasive.* Advertising is rarely designed to tell all sides of the story about a product or service; it is not designed to be objective information. Advertising is a tool organizations use to persuade people to accept products, services, or ideas.[5]

In short, Patti and Frazer define advertising as "planned communication activity in which messages in mass media are used to persuade audiences to adopt goods, services, or ideas."[6]

Many people say, "I depend on word-of-mouth advertising to promote my business." These people do not understand what advertising is. Word-of-mouth is not a message a sponsor pays to place in mass media, it is not planned, nor does it necessarily persuade. It does help promote a business, but it is not advertising.

What an Advertiser Needs

Advertising does not work equally well for all products and services under all conditions. To produce an effective advertising campaign, an advertiser needs:

- A competitive advantage
- Unique positioning
- A segmented market

Competitive Advantage. One of the key factors for advertising success is product differentiation—in other words, there needs to be a clear difference between what you sell and what your competitors offer. Produce wholesalers, for instance, do not need to advertise their lettuce or tomatoes to restaurants because most wholesalers sell similar grades and quality of produce. But if one wholesaler has a demonstrable difference, such as guaranteed fast delivery or lower prices, that is another matter. Advertising works best when a business has a demonstrable competitive advantage that it wants to communicate to consumers. This advantage might be superior service, lower prices, or higher quality.

The advantage must not only be demonstrable—that is, one that can be seen or experienced—it must be one that satisfies an important consumer need. For example, Hyatt Hotels, in promoting its weekend getaway packages in major cities, offered an 8 p.m. check-out on Sundays instead of the industry's usual 12 noon check-out time. This was an important difference to guests because the 8 p.m. check-out allowed them to spend Sunday afternoon at the beach or pool and even have dinner at the hotel before checking out.

Too often advertisers ignore the principle of featuring an important difference and advertise features that consumers don't care about. A survey of the nation's most frequent travelers found that

> large numbers [of travelers] don't care much about in-room bars, computerized travel directions or other new gimmicks. What they really want are simple pleasures—quiet hotel rooms, clean rental cars, comfortable airline seats. . . . Having newspapers delivered to rooms—which many hotels don't bother with—appeals far more to travelers than a health club.[7]

Sometimes a business may have an important feature that competitors have as well, but if no one has advertised it, the first business that does can gain an advantage. In an airfare war, all airlines may cut their prices to the same level, but the one that advertises the fare reduction first usually gets the lion's share of the business. Almost 80% of hotels offer a "kids-stay-free" plan, but many don't advertise it. The ones that do are more likely to get family business.

Unique Positioning. Another factor that contributes to effective advertising is positioning. This theory, first articulated by advertisers Jack Trout and Al Ries in the 1960s, asserts that because of the overcrowding of information in our minds, we only have so much room for storing information about products. So we categorize information and retain just enough to be useful in any one area. In order to be remembered, a product needs to occupy a very clear and sharply focused position in our minds relative to filling our needs and also relative to the competition. Companies that aspire to stand for everything in their advertising messages don't stand for anything at all, because consumers can't categorize and remember the messages.

Companies that have created successful positioning strategies include Avis, which positioned itself as number two against Hertz (the market leader) and promised that "We Try Harder." While Hertz held the position in consumers' minds as the biggest car rental company, Avis was able to create a position for itself as the company that would go the extra mile to get business. Avis still continues to occupy that position by advertising that all its employees are stockholders, and as owners of the company they will go out of their way to provide good service.

Here are some other positions of hospitality and travel businesses that may be familiar:

- Delta Airlines—We Love To Fly And It Shows

- British Airways—The World's Favourite Airline

- Bermuda—A Short Trip to the Perfect Holiday

- Carnival Cruise Lines—The Fun Ships

- Princess Cruise Lines—The Love Boats

- Holiday Inns—Stay with Someone You Know

Advertising slogans sometimes reflect positioning, but not always. Slogans may only be catchy phrases that have nothing to do with a company's positioning strategy.

Market Segmentation. This brings us to the third factor that boosts advertising's effectiveness: a segmented market. Market segmentation refers to a company's ability to identify different segments of its market and separately promote its products and services to these segments. This is also called niche marketing. Companies that practice niche marketing make different products for each market segment and then create different advertising campaigns.

As mentioned in Chapter 3, the Marriott Corporation practices market segmentation very thoroughly. Marriott has Fairfield Inns for the economy segment of the market—those people who buy based on price and look for a room for under $30 a night. Courtyard by Marriott is aimed at business travelers willing to pay for mid-price rooms. Residence Inns, which offer mini-suites with cooking facilities, are targeted at business travelers who must spend an extended period of time in one location. Marriott Suites are full-service properties for travelers who want a larger-than-average guestroom. Then there are traditional Marriott Hotels and Resorts, targeted at the upscale segment of the market.

Marriott has different names and different advertising campaigns for each of these products. Instead of viewing their market as just "people who go to hotels," they have segmented their market into smaller groups that they can identify, designed products with features that appeal to those groups, and then communicated those different features.

Almost all hotels practice some form of market segmentation. City hotels seek to appeal to traveling businesspersons on weekdays and tourists on weekends. Hotels in Bermuda advertise water sports to families in the summer months, but offer golf and tennis packages in the winter when it is too chilly to go swimming. Resorts may go after affluent consumers at the height of their season, then try to attract other groups by advertising lower prices in the off-season.

Price is only one way to segment customers. American Express segments its travel agency customers into different groups according to how

Marriott designed Residence Inn properties to appeal to business travelers on extended stays. Courtesy of Marriott Hotels and Resorts.

they react to different travel products. With help from the Gallup organization, American Express has identified five basic customer types:

- *Indulgers* are wealthy and confident people willing to pay for their comfort. They like to be pampered. These people look for cruises and resorts with health spa programs. Twenty-seven percent of American travelers are Indulgers.

- *Dreamers* read and talk a great deal about travel but lack confidence in their travel skills. They like to go to places recommended in guide books and tend to buy tried-and-true travel packages. Dreamers represent 24% of the market.

- *Economizers* see travel as an outlet for stress and a chance to relax. They scrimp on services and amenities even when they can afford them. These people are interested in price and value.

- *Adventurers* are young, confident, and independent. They prefer new experiences, cultures, and people. Many are interested in trips to the South Pacific and the Orient. Forty-four percent of adventurers are between 18 and 34 years old.

- *Worriers* are afraid to fly and have little confidence in their decision-making while on the road. Half of them are over 50. They need well-traveled, experienced agents to help them choose a destination and tell them how to get there.[8]

By dividing their markets into small market groups, advertisers can tailor an advertising campaign to fit the wants and needs of each group and place ads in the media that appeal to each group. (More about this later in the section on media selection.)

Advertising Agencies

The first decision hotel or restaurant owners/managers encounter when putting together an advertising campaign is: Should they attempt to take care of their advertising themselves, or hire an advertising agency? Advertising agencies help clients create and place advertising. Agencies employ marketing strategists, artists, writers, production managers, and media selection experts. Agencies generally work on a commission basis of 15%, so that an advertiser who spends $100,000 on an ad campaign pays $15,000 for advertising agency services and $85,000 for space in the media where the advertising runs. Sometimes agencies work for a fee when a 15% commission is not enough for the work involved, or, conversely, when the work the agency is expected to perform does not justify a 15% commission. Agencies bill their clients for the cost of media space or airtime and then—after receiving full payment from the client—are allowed by the media involved to deduct 15% from the client's payment before distributing the balance to the media.

Many advertisers opt to handle their advertising themselves by hiring freelance writers and artists to design their advertising, and then negotiating with the media directly for space and time. For a small advertiser this can mean considerable savings, since agency retainers plus fees for writing and designing ads can sometimes be substantial. On the other hand, many advertisers have found that there can be a very large difference between customer response to a good ad and a bad one, and argue that even small advertisers will get better results by using an agency instead of doing it themselves. While this may be true, there are some freelancers who can and do create outstanding ads (many freelancers are hired by ad agencies for certain projects), and therefore much depends on the nature of the advertising to be created, the freelancers available in an area, and the media to be used. Sometimes media prices are negotiable, and advertising agencies are in a better position to obtain the most favorable rates.

There is a wide variety of books and articles on how to chose an advertising agency, but one of the best ways is to simply take note of the advertising you like and then find out who did it by calling the advertiser or the media. Good agencies do not accept competing accounts, unless they are located in different market areas.

Creating Effective Advertising

Movies and television shows have produced an oversimplified and glamorous impression of how advertising is created. Typically, writers and artists are shown as becoming suddenly inspired with an idea for an ad campaign—almost as if a bolt of lightning has come down from above. The truth is far more mundane. Good campaigns are based on marketing plans, which in turn are based on thorough market research. Therefore, effective advertising is almost always the product of a rational, methodical process. Most ads reflect a position that has been carefully worked out in advance, and are written to appeal to a specific target market. The people who create the ads are not geniuses who pull great ideas out of thin air. There is no doubt that talent is involved, but it is a special kind of talent, a talent that includes sorting out and synthesizing facts. Indeed, it is not uncommon to find advertising copywriters with strong backgrounds in research. Most professional advertising writers thrive on research reports, profiles of target audiences, demographics, and psychographics.

Think of the inventor Thomas Edison. He did not sit in his laboratory with his feet on his desk until the idea for a light bulb popped into his head. The idea grew out of years of collecting information about the properties of electricity and conductors. So it is with good advertising.

The Anatomy of a Print Ad. Print advertisements consist of three basic elements:

- Headline
- Body copy
- Signature

The headline is the heading or the title of the ad. It is similar to the headline of a newspaper story. The purpose of the headline is to draw readers' attention and get them to read the rest of the ad. Effective headlines often contain the main promise of the ad. Some advertisements contain a sub-headline that spells out the promise made in the headline.

The body copy is the main portion of an ad. This is text that usually contains an amplification of the promise or benefit offered in the headline.

Finally, ads usually contain signatures or logotypes. A "signature" is the name of the advertiser; a logotype or "logo" is "a unique trademark, name, symbol, signature, or device to identify a company or other organization."[9] McDonald's golden arches are an example of a logo; so is the unique type that Coca-Cola uses to spell its name.

There are few rules as to what works and what doesn't in advertising. Since advertising is an art and a craft as much as a science, new techniques of getting and holding consumers' attention and persuading them are always being tried. Over the years many advertising studies have been done by independent research companies, advertisers, and agencies, and there are some general guidelines that most advertisers follow.

Print ad guidelines. Every good ad contains a promise. The promise can be stated or merely implied, but it is there, usually in the headline—the first thing most people read. Five times as many people read the ad's headline as read the body copy. That means that unless a headline sells, the advertiser has wasted most of its money.

Why does an ad need a promise? To attract readers. People won't remember an ad just because an advertiser wants them to, no matter how eloquently or clearly it is written. To be remembered, messages must include something that has personal meaning for readers. Consumers don't care about your resort's features per se—they care about how those features can benefit them.

If you are advertising something that is only available to certain groups, it is a good idea to put something in the headline to flag them down. When Marriott advertises discounts available only to members of the American Association of Retired Persons (AARP), it usually puts a banner across the top of the ad that says "AARP Members Only."

There is conflicting evidence on how long a headline should be. While some studies show that headlines with less than ten words do better than longer ones, other studies show that people will read very long headlines as well as long advertisements if they are interested in what the advertiser is saying. David Ogilvy, who founded Ogilvy & Mather Advertising and went on to be elected to the Advertising Hall of Fame, wrote one of the most famous automobile ads of all time for Rolls-Royce. The 17-word headline—"At 60 miles an hour the loudest noise in this new Rolls-Royce comes from the electric clock"—was followed by 607 words of factual copy. Colonial Williamsburg used a 10-word headline and five columns of copy interspersed with photos, illustrations, and a coupon to tell its story in a successful full-page newspaper ad.

Jim Johnston, chairman and co-founder of Jim Johnston Advertising, in an advertisement run by the *Wall Street Journal,* says this about headlines and advertising copy: "Headlines *can* be visuals; words can stop readers. They can attract, intrigue, provoke—and pull the reader into the copy. But that's only the beginning. Copy is no task for tyros. It must work word for word, line for line. Effective copy is *simple* but not *simplistic;* intelligent but not obtuse; interesting but not frivolous. People *will* read long copy. They won't read dull, confusing copy, no matter how short."

In the body copy of the ad, advertisers should try to "make the sale"—that is, present the reasons why you should buy their product, stay at their hotel, or eat at their restaurant. The Regency Hotel in New York uses a headline to focus on its location: "As Preferred as Park Avenue." The body copy amplifies this promise: "Located in one of the world's most exclusive neighborhoods, it promises an enclave of quiet elegance. Here are superb accommodations, a restaurant, lounge, fitness center and select meeting facilities . . . and of course, uncompromising service."

The final part of an ad should contain a call to action. In most cases ads don't make sales—salespersons make sales. The purpose of most ads is to interest the reader and put him or her in touch with a salesperson. "Call this number for reservations," "See Your Travel Agent," or "Send For Our Free Brochure" are typical calls to action. Salespeople who don't ask for the sale aren't successful—neither are ads that don't include a call to action.

An ad should always contain the signature or name of the advertiser and the advertiser's logo (if it has one). Sometimes advertisers are reticent about making their name too large—it is as if they are ashamed of who they are. But if the signature is not large and clear, people could miss it entirely. Very often the only thing people see in an ad is the headline, picture (if any), and signature. This is why some advertisers always try to put their name in the headline. Readership studies show that many ads succeed in attracting attention and getting readership, but fail entirely in getting prospects to remember what company placed it. The Hong Kong Tourist Association puts its name in the headline as well as in the bottom of its ads where it invites readers to take action.

Using Broadcast Media Effectively. Unlike print media, in which a consumer chooses to read advertisements that are of interest, ads in broadcast media are intrusive. Listeners and viewers have tuned in to a program and in the middle of that program they are interrupted by a commercial that they may not be interested in. Newspapers and magazines are primarily informational media, but radio and television are entertainment media. Commercials interrupt that entertainment. Broadcast advertisers therefore often seek to entertain in order to make their messages more palatable.

One way to entertain consumers is through humor (see Exhibit 11.2). However, using humor requires great skill because commercials are surrounded by professional entertainment and amateurish commercials stick out like a sore thumb. Moreover, a commercial needs to have "staying power" so listeners will enjoy hearing it or viewing it more than once, and unless it is well done they will tune out fast.

Some advertisers use a local broadcast personality in markets where he or she has a strong presence. Local TV talk-show hosts or radio deejays often have a great deal of credibility with their listeners.

Music, too, can be effective in broadcast ads when it is correctly used. Music is not suitable for telling the whole message—commercials that are sung in their entirely are seldom remembered (with a few exceptions, such as the award-winning "I'd Like to Buy the World a Coke" TV commercial)—but music can enhance the ad's theme. McDonald's still uses the memorable music to its "You Deserve a Break Today" jingle although it has since changed its slogan.

What Works and What Doesn't. At an *Advertising Age* conference in Frankfurt, Germany, David Ogilvy summed up what he believed worked best in advertising. As a founder and pioneer of much of modern advertising, his advice is worth noting:

> Put your brand name as well as your promise in your headline. Don't be cute. Readers will not take time to decipher your double meanings and word plays.
>
> All things being equal, twice as many people are captured by the picture in both a print ad and a television spot, than by the headline or copy. TV stations know this. On a national basis, if during the broadcast of your spot the picture is lost, you'll get a rebate 75 percent of the time. But if only the sound is lost rebates are given 25 percent of the time. Photographs increase recall over illustrations an average of 26 percent. Cartoons and animation (on TV) don't work as well on adults as live actors. Don't use them unless you're selling to children.
>
> One big picture in an ad works better than several small pictures. Use photos that suggest a story—something that is happening. The more story appeal you inject in an ad, the more people will read it. [Authors' note: Ogilvy & Mather created the highly successful American Express Travelers Check commercials which tell stories about people losing their travel checks while on a trip.]
>
> For your radio commercials to work you need to be intrusive. The average radio station plays 15 commercials an hour and unless you stand out, you haven't a prayer of being remembered. Research shows that people who hear your commercials on car radios remember them better than those who hear them at home. As in radio, television spots need to attract attention immediately. The first five seconds are the most crucial. The average viewer sees 38,000 TV commercials a year and has learned to ignore most of them. For quick reach and high impact consider outdoor (billboard) advertising. A Nielsen study shows you can reach up to 45 percent of all households the first day with this medium.

Exhibit 11.2 Humorous Radio Ads

SAWGRASS Radio :60		PIER 66 Radio :60	
(office sounds in background)		TOM:	Boy, it's good to be home again. I wonder who called? *SFX: (Click, rewind phone message machine)*
WOMAN #1:	Stella, you notice anything weird about Mr. Hastings?	RAY:	*(telephone voice, beep)* Tom. It's Ray. I'm going to spend the weekend at Pier 66. Meet me there. They've got this great Get Aquainted Summer Deal. Just 25 bucks a day if we share the room.
STELLA:	Ahhh, you mean like wearing sunglasses in the office?		
WOMAN #1:	Well, ya.	JONI:	*(second message; SFX/Beep)* Tom, this is Joni, Sally's friend. Meet me at the Pier Top Lounge at Pier 66 Friday night. Bye.
STELLA:	Mmmm, mmm.		
WOMAN #1:	And look at his feet.	RAY:	*(third message; SFX/Beep)* Tom, Ray again. Sunday night. Where have you been?! You missed a great weekend at Pier 66. I met this terrific gal named Joni.
STELLA:	He's wearing golf shoes.		
WOMAN #1:	Right.		
STELLA:	Uh!	DON PARDO:	*(SFX soap opera music)* Will Ray find out about Tom and Joni? Will Joni find out about Tom and Ray? Find out at Fort Lauderdale's Pier 66 Hotel and Marina, the 22-acre island resort on the Intracoastal. They'll be talking about it around the pool, on the courts, in the jacuzzis, at the restaurants and high above it all in the revolving Pier Top Lounge. Make your reservations now. Call 525-6666. So long for now from Pier 66.
WOMAN #1:	You know at the coffee area, he asked me if he could play through.		
STELLA:	Oh, well, listen, I caught him at his desk, hanging ten, yelling		
BOTH WOMEN:	Surf's up!		
WOMAN #1:	I know, I heard that.		
STELLA:	Mmmm, mmm.		
WOMAN #1:	Well, at least he's still wearing a tie.		
STELLA:	Ya, but with a tennis outfit?		
ANNOUNCER:	People all over Jacksonville are driving themselves to distraction. A beautiful distraction. Sawgrass. With our Commuter Vacation Package, you can go from desk to dunes in 30 minutes or less. Stay in the Sawgrass Resort Village, play golf, tennis or just relax on the beach after work and be back in the office the next day. Give your family a week or weekend at Sawgrass, complete with supervised programs for the children. Call 285-2261 and say you want to drive yourself to distraction. No one at work will know you're on vacation, unless you get carried away.		
(office sounds in background)			
WOMAN #1:	Stella, what's he doing in the secretarial pool?		
STELLA:	I don't know. Look's like a half gainer.		
(springboard)			
STELLA:	Stand back.		
(splash)			

Source: *The Art of Hotel & Travel Advertising, A Look at the Past—A Guide to the Future* (Washington, D.C.: Hotel Sales & Marketing Association International, 1987), pp. 53–54.

And if you use direct mail, remember response rates are seasonal. Using January as 100 percent, June mailings get only a 67 percent response, but August will get you 87 percent, and October almost 90 percent.[10]

Choosing Advertising Media

In planning an advertising campaign, once the message is decided on the next important decision an advertiser needs to make is where to run it. Should the advertising be placed entirely in local newspapers? What about magazines? Radio? Television? Direct Mail? There are many considerations in answering this basic question. One way to approach the problem is to consider whether what you are advertising is a planned purchase. If so, newspapers are probably the best media. Because their very nature is informational, newspapers are good places for any advertising message whose real thrust is information. The consumer can study it, re-read it, and even tear it out and carry it around in a purse or wallet. Airlines advertise new fares in newspapers; restaurants can print their menus and specials in a newspaper.

But what about an item that is not a planned purchase—one the consumer has to be motivated to buy? Or an image-building campaign to attract younger customers to a new restaurant? In these cases, the excitement and immediacy of broadcast media can make a real difference. An iceberg in Alaska's Glacier Bay, the pink sand beaches of Bermuda, and storybook castles in Europe all look much more enticing on television than they would in a black-and-white newspaper ad.

Ideally, an advertiser should use more than one medium to sell anything. There's a synergistic effect in advertising that has been proven time and time again: the use of any two media together is more powerful than the sum of the same media used independently.[11]

Budget is also a powerful consideration when choosing media. The more people an advertiser attempts to reach, the less frequently it will be able to reach them. The campaign might end up selling no one. The purpose of an advertising campaign is to persuade people to buy, and even 5 fully persuaded people who become customers are better than 500 half-persuaded people who buy nothing. Most advertisers cannot afford to advertise everywhere. They invest their money in key markets in which they are already drawing customers, rather than advertising in new markets where they are unknown. And they run their campaigns long enough to have an impact. Here's what Thomas Smith, a British advertiser writing in the nineteenth century, had to say on the subject:

> The first time a man looks at an advertisement he does not see it.
> The second time he does not notice it.
> The third time he is conscious of its existence.
> The fourth time he faintly remembers having seen it before.
> The fifth time he reads it.
> The sixth time he turns up his nose at it.
> The seventh time he reads it through and says, "Oh, bother."
> The eighth time he says, "Here's that confounded thing again."
> The ninth time he wonders if it amounts to anything.
> The tenth time he thinks he will ask his neighbor if he has tried it.
> The eleventh time he wonders how the advertiser makes it pay.
> The twelfth time he thinks it may be worth something.
> The thirteenth time he thinks it must be a good thing.
> The fourteenth time he remembers he has wanted such a thing for a long time.
> The fifteenth time he thinks he will buy it some day.[12]

Mr. Smith may have overstated the case a bit, but the principle is as sound today as it was then: it takes more than one exposure to reach anyone via advertising. The available evidence indicates the average is probably around three exposures, and that by six exposures we have probably made 80 to 90 percent of the target market aware of our message. By the time we have reached ten exposures we are probably at 99+ percent in most cases.[13]

Newspapers   Despite the growth of electronic media, newspapers remain America's largest advertising medium, with 26.3% of total 1988 U.S. advertising expenditures.[14] Sixty-four percent of American adults read a daily newspaper weekdays. Six out of ten adults also read a Sunday newspaper. The average newspaper reader spends 62 minutes reading the Sunday newspaper and 45 minutes reading one or more newspapers on a weekday.

Newspapers have many different rates for different kind of advertisers and for different editions. Local advertisers generally pay lower rates for ad space than national advertisers. In addition, most metropolitan newspapers offer "zoned" editions that carry news and advertising of interest to a single suburb. This makes it possible for a suburban restaurant to buy advertising space targeted directly at people who live in the immediate area. Finally, newspapers offer different rates for different kinds of advertising. Classified advertising is the least expensive. Usually there are rates for travel agencies, movie theaters, hotels, and restaurants that are lower than the rates paid for the regular display advertising that department stores and other advertisers run.

Most newspaper space is sold on a run-of-paper (ROP) basis. This rate, which is the lowest, allows the paper to place the advertising anywhere it wants in the paper. For a higher price advertisers can specify the section in which they want their ads to appear. Hotels and restaurants often use several different sections of a newspaper for maximum effectiveness. The entertainment section is used for restaurant advertisements. In some papers there is a special weekend section, which can be useful for restaurant ads, since readers who consult this section are looking for places to go and things to do. Meeting facilities are sometimes advertised in the business section. Around Christmas many hotels and restaurants advertise private rooms for office holiday parties.

Businesses that do a lot of newspaper advertising can buy ad space on a contract basis in which the advertiser agrees to buy a certain amount of space in a year and in return gets a volume discount depending on how much space has been ordered.

Advantages. Newspapers appeal to a large spectrum of people and thus have a very broad audience. On the whole newspaper readers tend to be somewhat more affluent, better educated, and older than the general population. There is no difference in newspaper readership between the sexes, however—an equal number of men and women read newspapers. It is interesting to note that most Americans who read newspapers also watch TV, listen to the radio, and read magazines. People who want to be informed use many sources.

One of the great advantages of newspapers is their sense of immediacy. Newspapers contain information about what happened yesterday and what is happening today and tomorrow. While television reporting is mostly concerned with what has already happened, newspapers print the exact time and place where movies are playing tonight, what is going on sale in the next few days, and calendars of events for the upcoming weekend. This quality of immediacy makes newspapers especially good for the kind of advertising that calls for an immediate response—a Thanksgiving or Easter "getaway weekend" package at a hotel for instance, or a Mother's Day champagne brunch at a restaurant.

Newspapers also invite involvement. Consumers react to newspapers differently than they do to radio and television, where they are passive and information is thrown at them. Newspaper readers decide what they are going to read and how much time they are going to spend reading it. It is involvement that helps make newspapers powerful persuaders.

UP AND RUNNING.

The Ocala Hilton is now up and running. Like a real thoroughbred, we are eager to prove ourselves. And ready to take the lead as Ocala's most elegant hotel ever.

Months of planning, construction, decorating and training have gone into this exciting new beginning. And we invite you to share in celebrating our big start. Join us for a fine gourmet meal at Arthur's, an evening of entertainment at the Gentry Bar or a nightcap at The Lobby Court. Some are even considering a weekend stay for a chance to get away without leaving

town. All of our guests will enjoy a heated pool with Jacuzzi, two lighted tennis courts and personal service from the warm welcome of our bellman to the attentive housekeeper. And for our most discriminating guests, our most luxurious accommodations are on the Tower Level.

For reservations and information regarding meetings, banquets, guest rooms and suites, call now, 854-1400. Find out what makes the Ocala Hilton an outstanding hotel. And a real winner.

Announcing The Birth Of A Thoroughbred.

OCALA HILTON
1-75 and S.R. 200, 3600 SW 36th Ave., Ocala, Florida 32674

This newspaper ad announces that the Ocala Hilton is open for business.

Newspapers offer other advantages that cannot be matched by other media. First of all they are flexible. An ad can usually be placed just a day before publication—and in some cases, less than a day before. That means the information in them is usually "hot."

Newspapers are local. They carry local news and they're written for local audiences. That makes them ideal for local businesses to display their addresses and telephone numbers and include maps showing their locations. Newspapers also carry coupons, many of which are unavailable elsewhere. Many shoppers value these coupons and plan their purchases to take advantage of them.

Newspaper advertising is also relatively inexpensive on a per-insertion basis, especially for local advertisers, who get a lower rate than national advertisers.

Disadvantages. Newspapers also have some major disadvantages. They are the least selective of all media. Because they are a mosaic of information of interest to everyone, their circulation is composed of a cross-section of the population. Because newspaper rates are based on their total audience, advertisers pay to reach a lot of readers who are not prospects for their products.

Newspapers are printed on newsprint, which has poor reproduction qualities—especially when it comes to photographs. In addition, newspapers have a short readership "life," ranging from a day to less than an hour. It is a cliché that there is nothing as useless as yesterday's paper.

Finally, advertisers have limited control over where their advertising will appear in a newspaper and what it will appear next to. A restaurant ad can appear next to a critic's review panning that same restaurant. Contrary to the belief held by those who think advertisers influence what appears in a newspaper, at large daily papers the editorial department and the advertising department have little or no contact, and editorial policy is rarely influenced by advertising considerations.

Magazines
In the years before radio and television, magazines were the only national advertising medium. Unlike newspapers, which were local in scope, magazines allowed an advertiser to reach broad groups of people not only in the United States but internationally. Today magazines are still a major international advertising medium—*Readers Digest, Time,* and even *Ladies Home Journal* have international editions that go to every corner of the globe.

However, on the domestic front magazines can serve a different purpose for advertisers. Whereas newspapers carry information that is of interest to a broad spectrum of people, magazines target their audiences very narrowly. In other words, within one newspaper we might find news items and features about travel, food, entertainment, and sports, but each of those subjects by themselves are the focus of a host of magazines. Would-be travelers can read *Travel & Leisure, Condé Nast Traveler,* and *European Travel & Life.* Those interested in food can choose from *Gourmet, Food and Wine,* and others. There are magazines for stereo enthusiasts, sailors, apartment dwellers, single people, golfers, homemakers, beekeepers, soap opera fans, entrepreneurs, and dog breeders. Of course, some of these groups are larger than others. Not surprisingly, *TV Guide* has the largest group of readers, with a circulation of 17 million people.

Advantages. The main advantage of magazines is their ability to advertise to only those people who are likely to be interested in and perhaps buy your product or service. Not everyone who reads *Travel & Leisure* travels; some are armchair travelers. But all readers are interested in travel, all are interested in the travel advertising that appears in that magazine, and a large percentage of the readers do take frequent trips. Some types of specialized magazines fare very well with lodging advertisers because their readers are prone to choose resorts that appeal to their special interests. Bob Stein—of Gardner, Stein, and Frank advertising in Chicago—puts it this way:

> The tennis player, reading a tennis magazine, is influenced in his choice of vacation resorts (he may, for example, choose to vacation at a certain hotel solely because an advertisement in the magazine

This ad was placed in a magazine for brides.

focuses on the hotel's first-rate tennis courts). . . . The newly engaged young woman, in planing her wedding, consults bridal magazines that advertise honeymoon retreats (idyllic scenery, heart-shaped tubs, mirrored ceilings, 24-hour room service) that may also interest her. In short, hospitality marketers can expect a better response from readers who regularly turn to magazines for information on subjects in which they have a particular interest than they can from a mass-media audience.[15]

Another advantage of magazine advertising is that it is long-lasting. Television and radio messages are fleeting. If you don't catch them at the moment they are broadcast, you lose them until they come on again. Newspaper ads may last a day or so, then they are destroyed or recycled. But magazines stay around for weeks, even months, and continue to build an audience. Daniel Starch's 30-year study covering 12 million inquiries generated by magazine ads found that, for monthly magazines, 54% of all inquiries that an ad generates are likely to come in the first month after publication, 22% more come in the second month, and by the sixth month

94% of the expected return is in. In other words, a hotel that places a coupon ad in a January magazine issue offering a free brochure can still expect to receive some coupons as late as June. Because magazines have a long life they also have a lot of readers—about 3.6 adults read a single copy of the average magazine. For this reason, the measure of a magazine's readership or audience is as important as its circulation numbers.

Finally, magazines offer superb reproduction to advertisers. Because they are printed on high-quality paper with sophisticated four-color presses, magazines can reproduce pictures with a clarity and brilliance unavailable in any other media. Magazines like *Travel & Leisure* and *National Geographic Traveler* are as valued for their photographs as for their articles.

Disadvantages. In spite of their many advantages, magazines also have some serious disadvantages. For one thing, magazines have very long "closing" dates. In other words, the date on which a magazine "closes"—when all advertising for the issue in question must be submitted—is usually two months or more in advance of the publication date. In addition, color advertisements often take many weeks to prepare, so that it is not unusual for an advertiser who wishes to run an ad in September to put it together in May. It is not possible to cancel an ad or change it after the closing date.

Another disadvantage of magazines is that their circulation, which is generally national in scope, often does not match the regions advertisers are most interested in. Some magazines have regional editions, but most don't. Because hotels have fixed locations, most of their business is not equally divided around the country but comes from a few areas. Resorts in Las Vegas get most of their business from California, and it makes little sense to advertise in a publication like *Gourmet*, which carries a substantial amount of travel advertising but has many readers in New England and the South, areas that contribute relatively few tourists to Las Vegas.

Finally, magazines are a very expensive advertising medium on an absolute dollar basis. The cost per thousand readers (CPM) is sometimes as much as ten times higher than for other media. This cost is often justified in that most magazines reach a specific audience.

Trade Magazines. Besides consumer magazines, there is a classification of magazines called trade or business publications in which companies advertise to each other. *Lodging* magazine, published by the American Hotel & Motel Association (AH&MA), and *Restaurants USA*, published by the National Restaurant Association (NRA) are two such publications. Magazines like these have controlled circulations in that they go to members of these associations only. They are good advertising media for businesses that wish to sell products such as furniture and kitchen equipment to hotels and restaurants. *Hotel & Travel Index*, *Travel Weekly*, and *Travel Agent* are the principal magazines used by airlines, hotels, cruise lines, and destinations to reach travel agents. The trade advertising that appears in these magazines often differs from consumer advertising in that the advertising is more detailed and informational in nature. This is because a trade magazine's audience is interested in the products advertised—indeed, they often read a trade magazine to keep up with the latest products in their field.

Radio   More than 99 percent of all homes in America have radios. In fact, the average home has 5.5 radios located all over the house—living room, bedrooms, kitchen. Moreover, 95% of all cars are equipped with radios and those radios are on 90% of the time the car is in use. The average adult has his or her car radio on 42 minutes a day.

Some groups of people listen to radio more than others. For example, 99.4% of young people ages 12–17 listen to the radio weekly. College students have an unusually high allegiance to radio. One study showed that radio for this group accounts for 49% of total time spent with radio, TV, newspapers, and magazines combined.

Hospitality enterprises use a large amount of radio because barter is very common in both businesses. Unsold hotel rooms and unsold radio spots are perishable commodities. A spot on the six o'clock news that is not sold is worth nothing after 6:01 p.m. Since there are always some unsold spots—just as there are always some unsold hotel rooms—radio stations and hotels often enter into a barter arrangement in which the radio stations exchange airtime for rooms and meals at the hotels. The stations use these credits to entertain guests, to hold station parties, or to give to listeners as prizes in on-the-air contests. For the most part these arrangements are advantageous to both parties, and by using them hotels and restaurants can increase the size of their advertising budgets substantially.

The standard unit of radio-ad airtime is the 60-second commercial. Most stations offer 30-second commercials as well, but since 30-second spots are often priced at 80% of the cost of a 60-second spot, they are seldom used.

It is often advisable to use a professional advertising agency in buying radio time because the cost of ad spots is highly negotiable. Stations have many package plans, bonus spots, and other complicated deals that make it very difficult for an amateur to obtain the best prices.

Advantages. One of radio's unique characteristics is that it is a very personal medium. It speaks to one listener at a time and is a very private form of communication that evokes different responses in each of us. Unlike media that supply a picture to go along with the words, radio gives us no visual clues at all. This can be a real advantage, because radio induces us to use our imaginations, to add our own mental pictures to the words. Thus it is a more involving medium.

To demonstrate the power of radio to stir the imagination, comedian Stan Freberg created a radio commercial for the Radio Advertising Bureau. Here is part of it:

> Okay, people, now when I give the cue, I want the 700-foot mountain of whipped cream to roll into Lake Michigan, which has been drained and filled with hot chocolate. Then the Royal Canadian Air Force will fly overhead, towing a ten-ton maraschino cherry which will be dropped into the whipped cream, to the cheering of 25,000 extras.[16]

Effective radio commercials induce people to create a picture in their mind's eye of what the announcer is saying.

Another advantage of radio is that it is highly selective. Because radio stations have different formats, they attract very different types of audiences. According to Arbitron, a service that measures radio and television audiences, here are the formats currently in use at AM and FM radio stations:

- Contemporary Hit
- News/Talk
- Adult-Oriented Rock
- Easy Listening/Beautiful Music
- AM Adult Contemporary
- FM Adult Contemporary

- Country
- Urban Contemporary/Black
- Classical
- Nostalgia/Big Band
- Religion
- Spanish

Each of these formats attracts listeners with different demographics. For example, adult-oriented rock stations attract the largest number of adults in the 18–25 and the 25–34 age brackets. Only a small percentage of the listeners of news/talk stations fall in this age group; the largest groups of listeners to these stations are in the 35–49 and 50–64 age brackets. More teenagers listen to contemporary hit radio than any other format, and seniors constitute the bulk of listeners to nostalgia/big band stations.[17] A restaurant featuring fine dining with moderate to expensive prices would do best advertising on a classical or an AM adult contemporary station because these stations attract large numbers of 35- to 49-year-old adults, which are the heavy users of restaurants of this kind. On the other hand, restaurants such as TGI Friday's and Bennigan's would get the most responses from adult-oriented rock and FM adult contemporary stations, which draw listeners in the 25–34 age group.

For restaurants, radio has the advantage of reaching a large part of their potential customers when they are literally in the market ready to buy. The highest radio listenership takes place when people are driving to and from work. It is the ideal time to suggest a good place to have breakfast this morning, lunch today, or dinner this evening.

Disadvantages. Despite these strong advantages, radio does have some disadvantages that make it less than an ideal medium. First of all, there are a huge number of AM and FM stations in almost every market. Because there are so many stations, listeners are fragmented into many groups, and if an advertiser wishes to reach a large segment of the population it must buy ad spots on many different stations.

Also, radio listenership at any given moment is small—an advertiser who wishes to reach all of a radio station's listeners has to buy many spots at different times on different days. Because people's habits vary, some of a radio station's listeners only hear it when they are driving; others hear it after school or after work. Some listen to a station while they are working, but never hear it at home. The bottom line is that while the cost of an individual radio spot might be low, it requires a lot of spots on a lot of radio stations for an advertiser to "cume"—that is, accumulate a large audience—and that can turn an inexpensive medium into an expensive one.

Moreover, radio signals cover a large area and when a local restaurant uses radio it must recognize that many of the people who listen are not legitimate prospects because they live too far away. Of course, for those restaurants that draw patrons from a large region this can be an advantage. Finally, if it is necessary to include telephone numbers or directions in an ad, radio is not a good medium because most people will not remember them and it is often not convenient to write them down.

Television   About 98 percent of U.S. households have at least one television set. Television is by far the most powerful and persuasive of all advertising media. There is no other way to reach so many people so fast. The average household has a television set turned on for more than seven hours every day. Programs like "The Cosby Show" and "L.A. Law" routinely reach more than a third of all of these homes every week, and special programs like the Super Bowl have been known to reach close to 50 percent of all American households.

Advantages. It is television's large reach and powerfully persuasive nature that makes it so attractive to advertisers of all kinds. As mentioned earlier in the chapter, McDonald's is the largest single advertiser in America. It also buys more television time than any other advertiser. Travel advertisers such as destinations (Jamaica or Hawaii, for example), hotels, and resorts accounted for $230 million dollars of TV advertising in 1986, making them the sixth largest user of national and regional television in the country.[18]

Television is the only medium that appeals to our eyes and ears at the same time. It is this characteristic that makes it such a powerful persuader. It allows an advertiser to show and demonstrate the product or service right in the prospect's living room. Moreover, most Americans believe television is more exciting, interesting, and entertaining than other media.

There is no doubt that well-done television sells. One reason is that television mirrors all of our hopes, fears, and values in its commercials and programming and thus captures our attention. In 1985, for instance, when relations between the United States and the Soviet Union were at a low point, Wendy's ran a commercial that reflected the American view of Soviet society at the time. The commercial featured a Soviet fashion show where there was only one kind of garment to choose from, and contrasted this with the large number of choices on a Wendy's menu. The commercial won many awards and boosted the awareness of Wendy's tremendously.

The Wendy's commercial is also an example of the effective use of humor in TV advertising. Research shows that humor can sell on television, but only if it's well done. David Ogilvy cautions advertising copywriters: "I must warn you that very very few writers can write funny commercials which *are* funny. Unless you are one of the few, don't try."[19]

When Florida wanted to demonstrate that there was more to see in Florida than Walt Disney World, it created a commercial that showed other attractions and urged viewers to "See Florida Coast to Coast." Another technique that works well in television is what is called "slice of life." Slice-of-life commercials show actors simulating a real-life situation. American Express uses this to sell their travelers' checks by showing someone being robbed of a purse or wallet in a foreign country.

Disadvantages. Despite the advantages of television, up to now television advertising has been confined to advertisers who have substantial budgets. By its very nature television is an expensive medium. On prime time—8 p.m. to 10 p.m., when most sets are in use—a typical network spot can cost $150,000 for 30 seconds of airtime, and even on daytime television a $25,000 price tag for 30 seconds is not unusual. A single 30-second spot in the 1991 Super Bowl cost $800,000! Local spots that run in a single market are of course much less expensive. A few hundred dollars will buy a 30-second commercial next to the evening news in most places, but still—like advertising placed in other media—a good TV ad campaign requires several spots per week for a number of weeks, so even a modest campaign is likely to cost $10,000 or more to run in one market on a single station.

In addition, television commercials are costly to produce. The simplest commercial made in the studio of a local TV station costs $5,000; the average production price for a local spot today is $15,000. Many network commercials cost $100,000 or more. Some advertisers have been known to spend three or four times that much to produce a single 30-second spot.

As with radio stations, television stations generally base their prices for airtime on the expected number of people who will be exposed to the ad during its time slot. This is determined by rating services such as A. C. Nielsen and Arbitron, which measure listenership by means of diaries and electronic meters placed in people's homes. Just as with prices for radio airtime, prices for TV airtime are highly negotiable.

Even for advertisers that have the funds to advertise on television, there exists a serious question as to TV advertising's effectiveness in the face of ever-increasing "clutter." Clutter refers to the proliferation of commercials, which reduces the impact of individual commercials. It is not unusual for a viewer to be subjected to 20 or more commercials in an hour's time, and with this number many advertisers question how much viewers remember of any of them.

Direct Mail   Direct mail has grown rapidly in the past decade as advertisers have sought to direct their messages to increasingly well-defined target audiences.

Advertisers can get mailing lists from various sources. First of all, many hotels maintain lists of previous guests. Travel agencies that issue airplane tickets, book cruises, and book hotel rooms also have the names and addresses of customers who have used their services. Many corporate directories list companies in an area, the names of their owners and principal officers, and the number of their employees. Then there are companies that compile lists from various sources and sell them. These companies buy lists of car owners from car dealers, or lists of credit card holders, magazine subscribers, people who send for various catalogs in the mail, and so forth. Mailing list companies "rent" these lists to customers by supplying them with a complete set of mailing labels.

Aside from the mailing list, the most important part of a direct mail campaign is to have a good offer that is properly packaged in an attractive and interesting direct mail piece so that it will be read and not thrown away.

Advantages. Direct mail advertising offers some unique advantages:

Postcards can be inexpensive yet effective direct mail pieces. Courtesy of Inter-Continental Hilton Head at Port Royal, Hilton Head, South Carolina.

- *Direct mail is highly selective.* Advertisers can direct their messages to people who live in specific neighborhoods or even on selected city blocks, or select recipients by other characteristics—profession, income, lifestyle, or possessions (such as cars or boats).

- *Direct mail enhances response.* A direct mail piece can include a postage-paid card or envelope to encourage responses.

- *Direct mail is a personal medium.* Computerized letters have made it possible to personalize a direct mail piece to each individual reader. Recipients handle direct mail pieces one at a time, which means they get the advertiser's message without any competition at the moment it is read.

- *Direct mail offers flexibility of timing and format.* Material can be timed to go out exactly when it will produce the greatest impact and can be easily varied by region.

- *Direct mail can be measured.* Advertisers can measure exactly how many responses a particular direct mail piece produces and relate that to the cost of creating and mailing the piece. This is one medium where you can tell exactly what you get for your money.

Direct mail is used extensively in the hospitality business. Restaurants often mail coupons to homes. Airlines and hotel chains use direct mail to build loyalty among frequent flyers and repeat guests. Writing in Lodging magazine, Michael D. Sena, president of Alvin B. Zeller Inc. in New York, says:

> Guest segmentation is a must for today's hotel marketer. Managing your property's [guest] mix has never been more important. Direct mail enables you to do both.
> For example, if your objective is to increase mid-week meetings business, you might target corporations within your surrounding zip codes, and select those with more than 100 employees and individuals that carry the title of VP sales or marketing. Similarly, you could select clubs, associations, or fraternal groups with prescribed limits.[20]

Disadvantages. Many mailing lists are expensive, and may become ineffective quickly. Not all of the people on a mailing list will be interested in what an advertiser has to offer, and a certain percentage of names and addresses will be inaccurate. Also, a direct mail piece takes a lot of time to plan and produce, especially if it has color. It also takes time to process the mailing (folding, stuffing, addressing, sorting). Finally, some recipients of a direct mail piece will view it as junk mail and throw it away without reading it.[21]

Public Relations

A company does not function in a vacuum, but rather as part of a society that consists of the people who work for it, the people and companies who do business with it, the public at large, and the government that regulates and taxes it. These groups are known as a company's "publics." In order for a company to effectively deal with these publics, a relationship of trust must exist. Employees will not cooperate with or put forth their best efforts for a company that they do not trust or that they feel is taking advantage of them. The public will not buy services or products from a company that, in their estimation, is not responsible or trustworthy: if they can't trust the company or its owners, how can they trust the products or services it sells? And the government, as the protector of the society it governs, is especially vigilant in dealing with a company that it regards as not operating in the public interest. Given these circumstances, every hotel, restaurant, travel agency, tour company, and other hospitality business needs to give some thought to the relationships it has with all of the various publics it interacts with. The techniques that a company uses to improve these relationships are known as "public relations," also called "PR" (see Exhibit 11.3).

The goal of public relations is usually to improve the climate or atmosphere in which a company operates. Here are some results a company might expect from a successful public relations campaign:

- Its products and services are better known

- Its relationship with employees has improved

- Its public reputation has improved

A successful public relations campaign can get people to do something that will help a company, stop them from doing something that might hurt it, or at least allow the company to proceed with a course of action without criticism. "An organization with good public relations has a favorable image or reputation, perhaps as a result of public relations activities," says Richard Weiner, an award-winning public relations counselor and the author of *Webster's New World Dictionary of Media and Communications.*[22]

In developing and implementing public relations plans, companies often use a simple five-step process:

1. *Research or fact-finding.* The purpose of research or fact-finding is to identify the attitudes of the publics, who the key opinion leaders are, and what needs to happen to change bad perceptions or reinforce good ones.

2. *Planning.* A public relations strategy is devised that will produce the desired outcome(s).

3. *Action.* Action steps are taken to implement the strategy.

4. *Communication.* The company's actions are communicated to the interested publics.

5. *Measurement or evaluation.* The results of the public relations campaign are studied to see if the desired outcomes have been achieved or if more action is needed.

A classic example of public relations at work in the hospitality industry is McDonald's. It has always been important to McDonald's to be known as a company that values cleanliness. Indeed, founder Ray Kroc emphasized cleanliness along with quality, service, and value as being the four most important things in any McDonald's operation. For that reason Kroc instructed the first McDonald's franchisees to pick up all litter within a two block radius of their stores, whether it was McDonald's litter or not.[23] However, by the mid-1970s McDonald's had grown so large that its discarded packages were found everywhere, from nearby city streets to campgrounds and beaches miles from the nearest restaurant. As public consciousness grew about the importance of not polluting, more and more critics pointed to McDonald's as a leading culprit, and the company realized it needed to take further action.

In 1976, McDonald's commissioned the Stanford Research Institute to do an environmental impact study comparing the paperboard packaging McDonald's was using at the time with polystyrene packages, an economical alternative that also offered some other product benefits. The study concluded that polystyrene was better from an environmental perspective when all aspects of the problem were taken into consideration. "Paper and paperboard used with food have to be coated, making them 'mixed materials' that are nearly unrecyclable. Polystyrene uses less energy than

Exhibit 11.3 Examples of Public Relations Efforts

Here are some examples of public relations efforts that were given awards by the American Hotel & Motel Association at its "AH&MA Stars of the Industry 1991" national awards program.

Ramada Renaissance Hotel, Atlanta, Georgia

In 1990 the Ramada Renaissance Hotel set out to establish several programs to help the local environment. Their successes have been many. To name a few, they began to find ways to improve the quality of the area surrounding the hotel, and they started recycling programs.

The first program implemented was the "Adopt-A-Street" program, in which hotel employees gathered weekly to pick up trash along a one-mile stretch of the highway near the hotel. In addition, to reduce landscape waste the hotel replaced its flowerbeds of annuals with perennials, which grow back each year.

Recycling is also an integral part of the hotel's ongoing operations. Even though recycling is not revenue producing due to the time it requires in additional labor, the Ramada Renaissance Hotel recycles cooking grease and oil, white paper, glass bottles, and aluminum cans.

Four Seasons Hotel, Houston Center, Houston, Texas

The Four Seasons Hotel in Houston Center has been a pillar in the Houston community, playing an integral role in supporting dozens of civic and charity organizations. Along with donating over $50,000 in gift certificates to needy organizations in 1990, the Four Seasons Hotel participated in several major charitable events, including sponsoring "Evening with the Masters." This benefit raised $110,000 for the Texas Gulf Coast Chapter of the Cystic Fibrosis Foundation.

The Four Seasons Hotel also sponsored the "Terry Fox 5K Run, Walk and Kids Race," which raises funds for cancer research. The hotel was responsible for obtaining corporate sponsors, creating publicity, recruiting volunteers, and coordinating the race. In addition, the Four Seasons helped underwrite the annual Channel 8 Tennis Tournament, promoting awareness of Houston Public Television, for the eighth consecutive year.

Hyatt Hotels Corporation, Chicago, Illinois

In 1990 Hyatt Hotels & Resorts launched FORCE—a *F*amily *o*f *R*esponsible and *C*aring *E*mployees. Recognizing the need for more community involvement and the long hours worked by Hyatt managers, FORCE was developed to allow managers to meet the unique needs of each of their communities. Hyatt Hotels provided managers at least one paid day off during the months of July through October, 1990, to volunteer with local organizations.

The program has been so successful that FORCE is enabling every interested manager to take one paid day each quarter to volunteer in 1991. The reaction from volunteers and organization recipients has been overwhelming.

Source: Adapted from *AH&MA Stars of the Industry 1991*, a national awards program created by the American Hotel & Motel Association.

paper in its production, conserves natural resources, represents less weight and volume in landfills, and is recyclable."[24] McDonald's accepted the study's recommendations and switched to polystyrene wherever it could.

But in the 1980s new questions were raised. Environmentalists pointed out that the manufacturing process for polystyrene released halogenated chlorofluorocarbons into the earth's atmosphere, which harmed the ozone layer. By 1987 McDonald's had directed all of its packaging suppliers to eliminate these dangerous chemicals from the manufacturing process. At the same time it reduced by 29% the thickness of its containers, and by 20% the weight of plastic straws. It used a lighter paper for wrapping sandwiches and began using recycled paper for napkins and tray liners. At the same time the company launched a new investigation into recycling programs.

To make sure that everyone knew what it was doing, McDonald's made its concern for the environment the theme of its 1989 annual report and printed the report entirely on recycled paper generated from paper waste from its offices and restaurants worldwide.[25] This was followed in 1990 by the announcement of McRecycle USA, a program in which McDonald's committed itself to buy $100 million in recycled materials for use in building and remodeling its restaurants.

Despite all of these positive actions, many critics continued to question whether McDonald's was really an environmentally friendly company. So in November 1990 the company made a decision to turn back the clock by phasing out polystyrene packaging and returning to paper while investigating other alternatives.

It is important to understand the role public relations has played in all of these decisions. McDonald's has always been socially responsible and extremely concerned about its image. These two facts are part and parcel of its public relationships. To McDonald's, public relations activities go much deeper than simply sending out press releases and having corporate officers serve on various charitable boards. The company understands that real public relations means taking significant actions first, then announcing them to the public. Without the first step, the second would be meaningless. Many companies do not understand this basic principle: if you want to make news, you must first do something newsworthy.

Publicity

Public relations and publicity are often confused with each other, but they are not the same thing. Richard Weiner defines publicity as "a public relations technique in which information from an outside source—usually a public relations practitioner—is used by the media. A message is developed and distributed, without specific payment to the media, through selected outlets (magazines, TV, and so on) to further particular interests of the clients."[26]

Publicity is sometimes called free advertising, but this is a misnomer. Advertising is paid for and advertisers control the message in their ads. Publicity is not paid for by the advertiser, and the media—not the advertiser—control the message, because they are writing or broadcasting stories that they consider newsworthy, which just also happen to mention a company or be about a company. Because publicity is not paid for by an advertiser, it has more credibility with consumers than an ad. Unfortunately, publicity can be unfavorable as well as favorable. A newspaper article about a restaurant's discrimination in hiring or a TV story about a hotel fire are examples of bad publicity.

New hotels and restaurants usually work hard to publicize their grand openings and often receive a good deal of attention and publicity. Press kits are the most common publicity materials prepared by a property. These kits generally consist of a series of fact sheets about the property; some news releases about the building, the architects, the general manager and other key personnel; and several 8" × 10" glossy black and white photos that can be reproduced in newspapers.

However, grand openings occur only once and businesses need publicity throughout their lives. Newspapers receive thousands of press releases every week and generally discard most of them. Therefore it is often necessary to stage special events or create new products or services to focus the media's attention and give them something newsworthy to write

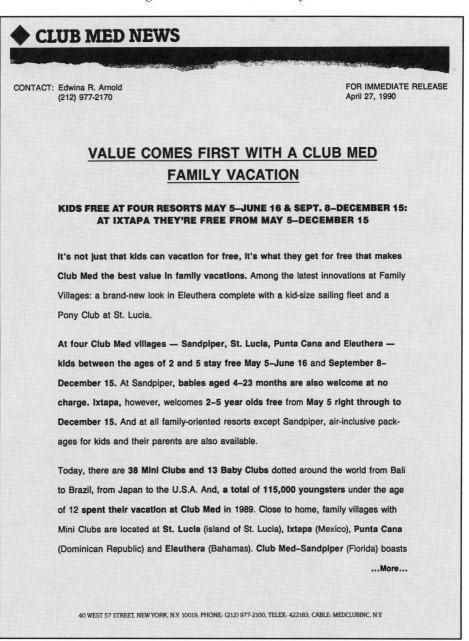

This press release announces special family vacation packages. Courtesy of Club Med.

about (see Exhibit 11.4). One of Richard Weiner's most celebrated publicity stunts was the Texas Armadillo Race he created for Lone Star Beer. Weiner recruited "professional" armadillo racers and had them compete against one another. The cost was minuscule but the armadillo race (and Lone Star) appeared on several network TV shows.

Hotels and restaurants often try to stimulate publicity by inviting travel editors and writers to visit. Sometimes these invitations are arranged by publicists who organize all-expenses-paid press tours. However, while freelancers often accept invitations to go on these tours, many of the top newspapers and travel magazines will not publish anything that a

Exhibit 11.4 Examples of Publicity Efforts

Here are some examples of publicity efforts that were given awards by the American Hotel & Motel Association at its "AH&MA Stars of the Industry 1991" national awards program.

Days Inns of America, Atlanta, Georgia

In honor of its 20th birthday, Days Inns created a truly unique celebration campaign that culminated in a huge birthday blow-out attended by almost 1,000 current and former employees. Days Inns set out to raise public awareness, improve employee morale, and show that they care about the community. All their efforts were a phenomenal success.

First they went on a nationwide hunt for Days Inns memorabilia from employees and hotel guests. They gathered hundreds of items that they could proudly display, from a 16-year-old bar of soap to one of the original Days Inns hotel directories. Next, Days Inns highlighted dedicated workers by showing taped interviews of employees who had been with the company longer than ten years. This program created a bond for long-time employees and generated interest in the company by newer workers. Finally, Days Inns introduced a program to recycle their old hotel furniture in the Atlanta area to homeless families.

Fontainebleau Hilton Resort and Spa, Miami Beach, Florida

The Fontainebleau Hilton's Chocolate Festival and Fair has become the largest and most acclaimed chocolate festival in terms of attendance and worldwide recognition. The festival began seven years ago to capitalize on the national chocolate craze and to increase room revenue. It has grown into the "Best Chocolate Show in America" according to *Chocolatier* magazine.

The Chocolate Festival and Fair is a marketplace filled with chocolate vendors, music, children's activities, chocolate carvings, and special chocolate events and contests. Attendance for the 1990 festival was over 12,000, an increase of 8,000 over the year before, and food and beverage revenues were up 47%. The Fontainebleau Hilton received tremendous publicity, increased revenues, and created excitement for attendees and exhibitors alike.

Super 8 Motels, Aberdeen, South Dakota

Christmas Eve 1990 at Super 8 Motels started a new tradition of Christmas spirit and goodwill. The chain offered free lodging for people visiting friends and relatives in a nursing home, veteran's home, or hospital or treatment center. A total of 525 rooms were given away as a result of this "Room at the Inn" promotion.

Press coverage of the event was astounding. TV stations filmed some of the participating properties and "Room at the Inn" was mentioned on Paul Harvey's radio show and in *USA Today.* The results were so remarkably positive that major franchisees plan to expand the offer to include Thanksgiving in 1991.

Source: Adapted from *AH&MA Stars of the Industry 1991*, a national awards program created by the American Hotel & Motel Association.

freelancer writes while enjoying a free trip because they believe he or she is likely to be biased. Their editors and writers usually pay for everything when they visit a hotel or restaurant, and report on both the positives and the negatives they encounter.

Sales Promotion

Unlike advertising and public relations, which aim to achieve results over time, sales promotion consists of sales tools and techniques to encourage immediate action—not only by consumers, but by others in the trade. Extra commissions paid to travel agents, cooperative advertising, contests, and familiarization trips for agents are all examples of hospitality industry sales promotions directed at the trade. For many years Carnival Cruises had a mystery-shopper program in which travel agents were handed $1,000 in cash on the spot for recommending a Carnival Cruise to someone who asked about a Caribbean vacation.

Probably the most widely used form of sales promotion directed toward consumers is loyalty marketing programs such as Marriott's Honored Guest, Hyatt's Gold Passport, and American Airlines AAdvantage frequent-flyer program. All of these programs reward people who travel frequently and do business with these companies. Such programs stimulate additional travel by offering incentives to fly and stay at hotels. For example, in 1990 American and other airlines offered one free round-trip flight to customers who bought three round-trips within a specified period of time.

Tie-ins are another form of sales promotion in which marketers of diverse products or services team up to create consumer awareness and generate sales. Delta Airlines and Poloroid ran one successful sales promotion in which, in exchange for proof of purchase of a Poloroid 600 camera, customers received a certificate good for a free round-trip ticket to anywhere Delta flew (when they bought a ticket of equal or greater value).

Sweepstakes are a popular form of sales promotion. In the spring of 1986, faced with a decrease in trans-Atlantic traffic due to fear of terrorism, British Airways created an ambitious and very successful "Go For It America" sweepstakes. Launched in June with entry blanks printed in newspapers, British Airways offered readers 5,200 free round-trip tickets for two to London with free first-night lodging. The July prize was 100,000 British pounds; in August the winner received a five-year London townhouse lease; and in September the prize was a new Rolls Royce. The airline also included travel agents in this promotion—agents got an opportunity to win prizes every time they booked a passenger on British Airways.

Sales promotions are very effective in stimulating business in the short term. However, they are no substitute for long-term advertising and public relations efforts. While sales promotions do work, they are in effect a way of "buying business" and can be very costly.

Chapter Summary

Advertising acts as a substitute for a personal salesperson. Advertising is valuable because it is repetitive and thus helps consumers understand and remember sales messages. It increases the value of products and services by adding value to the name and reputation of a company.

Some critics charge that advertising induces people to buy things they don't want or need, but in fact most advertising is used to influence the choice of brand of something that consumers have already decided to purchase.

Advertising is paid for by the sponsor, is impersonal, identifies the sponsor, and is persuasive. It is a planned communication activity in which messages in mass media are used to persuade audiences to adopt goods, services, or ideas.

There are certain factors that favor the use of advertising. These include a demonstrable competitive advantage, unique positioning, and market segmentation.

Some hospitality advertisers employ an advertising agency. Advertising agencies consist of marketing strategists, artists, writers, production managers, and media selection experts. Agencies generally work on a 15% commission. Whether to use an agency depends on the nature of the advertising, the advertising agencies or freelancers available in an area, and the media to be used. Sometimes media prices are negotiable, and advertising agencies are in a better position to obtain the most favorable rates.

Effective advertising is not only inspired; it is almost always the product of a rational and methodical process.

Print advertisements consist of several elements. Usually there is a headline; some advertisements also contain a sub-headline. The main portion of an ad is called the body copy. Finally, ads usually end with a signature and a logotype ("logo").

There are some general guidelines that most print advertisers follow: (1) put a promise in the headline, (2) "make the sale" in the body copy, and (3) close with a call to action.

Broadcast advertisers seek to entertain because commercials interrupt the entertainment provided by the medium.

Once the ad message is decided on, an advertiser must determine where to run it. Any advertising message whose real thrust is information works well in newspapers. For (1) purchases that are not planned, and (2) image-building campaigns, the excitement and immediacy of broadcast media can make a real difference. Ideally, an advertiser should use more than one medium to sell something.

Budget is also a consideration when choosing media. The more people an advertiser attempts to reach, the less frequently the advertiser will be able to reach them. It takes more than one exposure to persuade anyone via advertising.

Despite the growth of electronic media, newspapers remain America's largest advertising medium. Newspapers appeal to a large spectrum of people. One of the great advantages of newspapers is their sense of immediacy. Newspapers are also flexible, local, and relatively inexpensive for local advertisers. Newspapers have disadvantages too. They are the least selective of all media. They have poor ad reproduction capabilities and a short life. Advertisers have limited control over where their advertising will appear in a newspaper.

Whereas newspapers carry information of interest to a broad spectrum of people, magazines target their audiences very narrowly. The main advantage of magazines is their ability to reach a particular market segment. Another advantage is that magazines have a long life—magazine ads continue to build an audience for weeks and even months. Finally, magazines offer superb ad reproduction.

Disadvantages of magazines include long closing dates, limited circulation flexibility, and high advertising costs.

More than 99 percent of American homes have radios. Radio is a very personal medium that induces listeners to use their imaginations. Because radio stations have different formats, they attract very different types of audiences. Radio's disadvantages include the large number of radio stations in most markets, the small listenership of a station at a given moment, and the difficulty of using phone numbers and directions effectively in a radio ad.

Television is by far the most powerful and persuasive of all advertising media. It is the only medium that appeals to our eyes and ears at the same time. But high costs and declining ad effectiveness due to "clutter"—the sheer number of commercials on TV—have kept some advertisers away from the medium.

Direct mail advertising has some unique advantages. Direct mail is highly selective, encourages a response, is a personal medium, offers flexibility of timing and format, and can be measured. The two most important parts of an effective direct mail program are the mailing list and the offer. Direct mail's disadvantages: mailing lists can be expensive and inaccurate, direct mail pieces take a lot of time to plan and produce, and direct mail may be viewed by recipients as junk mail.

Every hotel, restaurant, travel agency, tour company, and other hospitality enterprise needs to give some thought to its public relationships—that is, the relations it has with all of the various "publics" it interacts with. The techniques that a company uses to improve these relationships are known as "PR" or public relations.

In developing and implementing public relations plans, companies often use a simple five-step process: research or fact-finding, planning, action, communication, and measurement.

Publicity is a public relations technique in which information from an outside source—usually a public relations practitioner—is used by the media. Hotels and restaurants often receive a lot of publicity at their grand openings. But the need for publicity continues throughout the life of the business.

Sale promotion consists of sales tools and techniques to encourage immediate action by consumers or the trade. Probably the most widely used form of sales promotion directed towards consumers are loyalty marketing programs such as Marriott's Honored Guest, Hyatt's Gold Passport, and American Airlines AAdvantage frequent-flyer program.

Tie-ins are a form of sales promotion in which marketers of diverse products or services team up together to create consumer awareness and generate sales. Sweepstakes are widely used as a form of sales promotion among travel and hospitality companies.

Endnotes

1. *The Value Side of Productivity* (New York: American Association of Advertising Agencies, 1989), pp. 17–18.

2. *Value Side of Productivity,* p. 18.

3. Bradley T. Gale, "How Advertising Affects Profitability and Growth for Consumer Businesses," in *Value Side of Productivity,* p. 35.

4. "The Top 200 Brands," *Advertising Age,* May 21, 1990, p. 25.

5. Charles H. Patti and Charles F. Frazer, *Advertising: A Decision-Making Approach* (New York: Dryden Press, 1988), p. 4.

6. Patti and Frazer, p. 5.

7. "Giving People What They Don't Want . . . Travel Industry Is Out of Touch Customers Say," *Wall Street Journal,* November 30, 1989, p. B-1.

8. "Profiles in Travel," *Travel Agent Magazine,* October 16, 1989, p. 40.

9. Richard Weiner, *Webster's New World Dictionary of Media and Communications* (New York: Simon & Schuster, 1990), p. 272.

10. Andrew Vladimir and Donna Vladimir, *Fundamentals of Advertising* (Chicago: Crain Books, 1984), p. 147.

11. Vladimir and Vladimir, p. 174.

12. Vladimir and Vladimir, p. 146.

13. Vladimir and Vladimir, p. 175.

14. Facts about newspapers supplied by the American Newspaper Publishers Association, Box 17407, Dulles Airport, Washington, DC 20041.

15. Bob Stein, "Reaching Your Audience through Special-Interest Magazines," *Cornell Quarterly,* November 1982, p. 37.

16. Vladimir and Vladimir, p. 206.

17. J. Thomas Russell and Thomas Lane, *Kleppner's Advertising Procedure,* 11th ed. (Englewood Cliffs, New Jersey: Prentice-Hall, 1990), p. 217.

18. Television Bureau of Advertising, New York.

19. David Ogilvy, *Ogilvy On Advertising* (New York: Crown Publishers, 1983), p. 105.

20. Michael D. Sena, "Leaping Direct-Mail Hurdles: A Hassle-Free Approach," *Lodging,* May 1990, p. 62.

21. The information in this paragraph was adapted from James R. Abbey, *Hospitality Sales and Advertising* (East Lansing, Mich.: Educational Institute of the American Hotel & Motel Association, 1989), p. 323.

22. Weiner, p. 381.

23. Scott Hume, "The Green Revolution," *Advertising Age,* January 29, 1991, p. 32.

24. Hume, p. 32.

25. Hume, p. 32

26. Weiner, p. 380.

Key Terms

added-value

advertising

body copy

closing date

clutter

cost per thousand (CPM)

"cume"

headline

logotype ("logo")

positioning

publicity

public relations (PR)

run-of-paper (ROP)

sales promotion

signature

Discussion Questions

1. What are the advantages of advertising?

2. What factors favor advertising?

3. What are some guidelines for creating print ads?

4. How can advertisers use broadcast media effectively?

5. What advice does David Ogilvy give advertisers?

6. What are the advantages and disadvantages of newspaper advertising? magazine advertising?

7. What are the advantages and disadvantages of radio advertising? television advertising?

8. What are direct mail's advantages and disadvantages?

9. What are the differences between public relations and publicity?

10. What is sales promotion?

Chapter Outline

What Is a Franchise?
    Types of Franchises
The History of Franchising
    Product or Trade-Name Franchising
    Business-Format Franchising
Owning a Franchise
    Advantages
        Site Selection Assistance
        Easier Credit
        Construction Expertise
        Fixtures and Equipment Assistance
        Good Training
        Opening Support
        Promotional Assistance
        Economies of Scale
        Ongoing Support
    Disadvantages
        Restrictions
        Unwanted Products or Procedures
        Unwanted Advertising
        Unprotected Territories
        Cancellation
        Inadequate Training
    Advantages and Disadvantages for Franchisors
How Franchising Works
    Initial Investment
    Franchise Regulations
The Future of Franchising
Chapter Summary

12 Franchising

This chapter deals with franchising in the hospitality industry. It covers the history of franchising, the reasons for its popularity, the advantages and disadvantages of owning a franchise, and how franchising works. Finally, there is a brief look at the future of franchising.

What Is a Franchise?

In its simplest form, the word "franchise" refers to the authorization given by a company to another company or an individual to sell its unique products and services. Franchising is a marketing or distribution system: the franchisor grants an individual or company the right to conduct business according to the franchisor's guidelines for a specified time and in a specified place.

Franchising is big business. According to a U.S. Department of Commerce report, the estimated sales of goods and services in the country's 509,000 franchised outlets in 1988 totaled $640 billion—a 91% increase over sales just eight years earlier. Franchised units employed 7.3 million people in 1988.[1]

Let's review the following terms, which will be used throughout the chapter:

- *Franchise*—in addition to the meaning mentioned earlier, franchise can also refer to the name of the business format or product that is being franchised. The Marriott Corporation grants Residence Inns franchises as well as Courtyards by Marriott franchises.

- *Franchising*—The major trade association in franchising, the International Franchise Association, defines franchising as "a continuing relationship in which the franchisor provides a licensed privilege to do business, plus assistance in organizing, training, merchandising, and management in return for a consideration from the franchisee."[2]

- *Franchisor*—the franchise company that owns the trademark, products, and/or business format that is being franchised. Red Lobster is a franchisor.

Courtyards are Marriott franchises. Courtesy of Marriott Corporation.

- *Franchisee*—the individual or company granted the right to do business under the franchisor's name. A person who buys a Dairy Queen franchise is a franchisee.

Franchise rights vary. Most franchisors grant franchisees the right to use the franchise name and its distinctive trademark, logo, architecture, and interior design. Some franchisors also sell their method of operation or designate territories in which the franchisee may operate. In some cases, the franchisor may grant the franchisee the right to sell the franchisor's product(s); for example, A&W Restaurants have the right to sell A&W Root Beer.

Types of Franchises

There are two types of franchises: the product or trade-name franchise and the business-format franchise.

The product or trade-name franchise is a supplier-dealer arrangement whereby the dealer (franchisee) sells a product line provided by the supplier (franchisor) and, to some degree, takes on the identity of the supplier. This is the type of franchise that exists in the automobile, gasoline service station, and soft drink industry. The majority of total franchise sales in the United States are from product or trade-name franchising—70% in 1988.

Business-format franchises, which include fast-food restaurants and lodging chains, are "characterized by an ongoing business relationship between franchisor and franchisee that includes not only the product, service and trademark but the entire business concept itself."[3]

Since 1950, the majority of the growth in franchising has been in the business-format franchise category. Besides food service operations and hotels, this category includes non-food retailers, personal and business services, real estate services, and other service businesses. By 1988 there were 50 hotel companies and 488 restaurant companies offering business-format franchises.

Business-Format Franchise Growth[4]

	Estimated Sales (billions)	Number of Establishments
1972	28.7	189,640
1988	190.1	368,458

Restaurants make up the majority of business-format franchises, with 63,762 units and sales of over $41 billion.[5] The top five states in number of franchise restaurants are as follows:

State	Number of Franchise Restaurants[6]
California	6,039
Texas	4,394
Ohio	2,779
Florida	2,651
Illinois	2,184

As of 1988, PepsiCo was the largest franchisor of food service establishments, with a total of 14,000 Kentucky Fried Chicken, Taco Bell, and Pizza Hut restaurants. McDonald's was second domestically but first internationally in number of units.7

In 1988, the number of franchise hotels, motels, and campgrounds was 9,007 units, with total sales of just under $14 billion. The states with the largest number of franchise hotels are as follows:

State	Number of Franchise Hotels
Florida	620
California	593
Texas	485
Virginia	296
Georgia	274

The History of Franchising

Franchising is not a new concept. A precursor of modern franchising occurred in Roman times, when private citizens bid for the right to operate tax collecting "franchises" for the government. These "franchisees," called "publicans," kept a percentage of the taxes they collected for themselves. It was a lucrative business—especially for the unscrupulous—and publicans were generally detested, as the Biblical phrase "publicans and sinners" reminds us.[8] This form of franchising existed in the Middle Ages as well when royalty and church officials rewarded important citizens with the right to collect revenues in return for "various services or considerations."[9]

Product or Trade-Name Franchising

All of the early franchises were product or trade-name franchises that allowed individuals or companies willing to put up their own capital to sell and, in some cases, make the product of the franchisor. The only restrictions on franchisees was on what they sold and the territory where they sold it.

In 1851, I. M. Singer & Company used franchising to develop a network of sewing-machine dealers all over the United States. Under the Singer concept, a dealer was allowed to open a Singer Sewing Machine store in return for an agreement to sell only Singer machines and supplies. Since women did not know how to use these new sewing machines, the dealers also provided service in the form of sewing lessons and classes. This was the beginning of modern franchising systems.

Because the Singer company had a unique product that was very much in demand and one that dealers could not obtain unless they agreed to open a Singer Sewing Machine store, the company did very well. However, franchising did not catch on in a big way until the early 1900s, with the production of soft drinks and automobiles.

Just as in the case of Singer sewing machines, automobiles were new and complicated mechanical devices requiring service and repair. No one was willing to buy a horseless carriage unless there was someone nearby who would fix it if it didn't work. Automobile manufacturers, most notably General Motors at first, came up with a solution similar to the Singer company's: they established dealerships to sell and service their cars. Because dealers were located right in the communities where the cars were sold, they were trusted neighbors who could be relied on to back up the promises made by the automobile manufacturers. Not surprisingly, the petroleum companies that grew along with the automobile dealers adopted the same form of distribution, and even today gas stations are for the most part individually owned small businesses that have the right to use the trade name of a single company and sell products purchased from one of the major oil refiners.

The first Coca-Cola franchise was granted in 1899. Franchising was necessary because Coca-Cola was packaged in a unique glass bottle that consumers paid a deposit for and returned to the company. Handling those bottles required local bottling companies that could pick them up, wash them, and re-use them. Moreover, it was very expensive to ship bottled drinks all over the country from the company's headquarters in Atlanta, Georgia. In order to expand, Coca-Cola gave franchisees the right to build Coca-Cola bottling plants in return for purchasing Coca-Cola's bottles and syrup. Coca-Cola also agreed to train its bottlers in the areas of production techniques and marketing. Soon Coca-Cola bottling plants were established all over America.

Each Singer or General Motors franchise involved a relationship between the manufacturer (franchisor) and the retailer (franchisee) who sold the manufactured product(s) directly to the public. Note that in both cases the retailer performed a service (product servicing and repair) for the franchisor in addition to just selling the product, which was one reason why franchising was the most efficient form of distribution for these products. In the case of Coca-Cola, the relationship was between the manufacturer/franchisor and a wholesaler (franchisee). Coca-Cola's wholesalers did not sell directly to the public—they delivered Coca-Cola to retail soda fountains and grocery stores. Again, however, the franchisee (wholesaler) performed a service for the franchisor—in this case, bottling the product. It was because these new products—sewing machines, cars, and soft drinks—required the seller to provide services as well as the product itself that franchising became so necessary and practical.

Business-Format Franchising

The first person to pioneer the idea of the business-format franchise was Howard Johnson, founder of the Howard Johnson Company. As we said in Chapter 2, Johnson started his chain in 1925 with a drug store which he successfully converted into an ice cream parlor. By 1928 he had two thriving ice cream parlors and decided to open a third that would serve food as well. This was his first restaurant. When a friend offered Johnson some land so Johnson could build a second restaurant, Johnson, who had no more capital to invest, convinced his friend to build the restaurant. Johnson would provide him with a franchise to sell Howard Johnson ice cream as well as assist in the design and supervision of the restaurant.

The friend's restaurant was an instant success, and Johnson realized that without investing any money of his own he had found a way to expand his business. He decided to continue with the strategy of encouraging others to build Howard Johnson restaurants, which would sell Howard Johnson ice cream and other products that he would supply. He decided to assist in the design and management of these new restaurants so that he could help make them a success. Johnson did not ask for a royalty on sales for these extra services; his sole profit came from the sale of Howard Johnson products. By the end of 1936 there were 61 Howard Johnson restaurants, most of which were franchises. By 1939 there were a total of 107 restaurants operating in a half dozen states.[10] In 1958 Johnson started the Howard Johnson hotel chain with 23 lodges comprising 3,500 rooms. By 1969 there were 391 lodges, 90% of which were franchises. After almost two more decades of continued growth, Howard Johnson, Jr., son of the founder, sold the lodging chain to Prime Motor Inns.

In spite of the Howard Johnson success, franchising did not catch on with the rest of the hospitality industry until the early 1950s. Lodging's most notable early franchising success was Holiday Inn. Kemmons Wilson and a partner owned three successful Holiday Inn motor hotels in the early 1950s and wanted to expand nationwide. They decided to finance their expansion by selling Holiday Inn franchises to franchisees who would build their Holiday Inns according to a set format and contribute some money from each guestroom for advertising. The rest is history.

The beginning of the franchise giant McDonald's was a drive-in self-service restaurant in San Bernardino, California, built in 1948 by two brothers, Maurice and Richard McDonald. In 1954, Ray Kroc, a milkshake-machine salesman, called on the McDonald brothers to deliver eight of his Multimixer machines. What he found was an efficient octagonal assembly-line operation turning out beverages, french fries, and 15-cent hamburgers. As Kroc tells it, "When I saw it working that day in 1954, I felt like some latter-day Newton, who'd just had an Idaho potato caromed off his skull."[11] Kroc understood what made the restaurant a success. In his book, *Grinding it Out: The Making of McDonald's,* he explained what went through his mind:

> I've often been asked why I didn't simply copy the McDonald brothers' plan. They showed me the whole thing and it would have been an easy matter, seemingly, to pattern a restaurant after theirs. Truthfully the idea never crossed my mind. I saw it through the eyes of a salesman. Here was a complete package. I could get out and talk up a storm about it. . . . Besides, the brothers did have some equipment that couldn't be readily copied. They had a specially fabricated aluminum griddle for one thing, and the set up of all the rest of the equipment was in a very precise step-saving pattern. Then there was the name. I had a strong intuitive sense that the name McDonald's was exactly right. I couldn't have taken the name. But for the rest of it, I guess the real answer is that I was so naive or honest that it never occurred to me that I could take their idea and copy it and not pay them a red cent.[12]

The McDonald brothers, who drove Cadillacs and lived together in a luxurious home, were not interested in expanding. They were happy with what they had achieved and did not want to work any harder. They granted Kroc an exclusive ten-year franchise. He agreed to put up buildings exactly like the one their architect had drawn up, complete with the golden arches. The McDonald brothers inserted contractual clauses that obligated Kroc to follow their plans down to the last detail—even to signs and menus. And there was a clause that prohibited Kroc from doing anything differently without a registered letter of permission from the two brothers. It was agreed that Kroc could charge franchisees 1.9% of their gross sales and that he would give .5% of that to the McDonalds. Kroc was also allowed to charge a franchise fee of $950 to cover the expenses he incurred in finding a suitable location for each franchise and a landlord who would build to the McDonalds' specifications.

Kroc brought in Harry Sonneborn to assist him, and the two planned the future of their new enterprise. They realized that for their franchise to succeed they had to do more than simply sell prospective franchisees a name and a menu. Besides, a hamburger—ready-made according to the franchisor's specifications—could not be sold to a franchisee like Howard Johnson's ice cream; franchisees would have to cook their own hamburgers. Kroc writes:

> We agreed that we wanted McDonald's to be more than just a name used by many different people. We wanted to build a restaurant system that would be known for food of consistently high quality and uniform methods of preparation. Our aim, of course, was to insure repeat business based on the system's reputation rather than on the quality of a single store or operator. This would require a continuing program of educating and assisting operators and a constant review of their performance. It would also require a full-time program of research and development. I knew in my bones that the key to uniformity would be in our ability to provide techniques of preparation that operators would accept because they were superior to methods they could dream up for themselves.[13]

Here Kroc expresses the heart of the concept of modern franchising: a franchise company's reputation depends on the quality and consistency

A McDonald's franchise. Courtesy of McDonald's Corporation, Oak Brook, Illinois.

of all of its franchises, and quality and consistency is maintained by on-going training and development. In 1961 Kroc bought out the McDonald brothers for $2.7 million. Today there are over 10,000 McDonald's units in 51 countries, 75% of which are franchised.

Owning a Franchise

Franchising has not only been a boon to companies seeking to expand quickly; it is one of the safest ways for individuals to have their own business. Ray Kroc considered it the quickest way to capture the American

Dream and was proud of the fact that people credited him with making many of his associates millionaires.

Starting a business from scratch is very risky. According to studies done by the U.S. Department of Commerce, 80% of all private enterprises eventually fail, most of them in the first year. Franchises, on the other hand, do very well in comparison. Fewer than 3% of the nation's franchises fail each year.[14]

Franchising gives an individual entrepreneur a chance to compete in the market place against giant companies. It provides some insurance for success, for when franchisees buy a franchise, they buy (1) a format and formula that has already been tested, and (2) the experience of the franchisor, who is expected to teach them what they need to know to succeed.

The Development Group, a consulting firm that sells franchises for its clients, asked prospective franchisees why they wanted a franchise. Their answers were revealing:

- Self-management was the most important reason given; 73% of applicants saw owning a franchise as a way to be their own boss.

- Financial independence was a close second: 69% of applicants thought owning a franchise was a better way to ensure financial security than depending on a paycheck from someone else.

- Career advancement ranked third (53% of applicants). If you own your own franchise you don't have to wait for someone else to promote you. You can move as fast as you are able.

- New skills/training was cited by 49% as their main reason for buying a franchise. Many people, for example, would like to own their own hotel or restaurant but simply don't know how. Good franchise companies provide training and assistance.

- A franchise was seen by 32% as a long-term investment that would appreciate in value.[15]

Advantages   There are many advantages to owning a franchise in addition to those just cited in the Development Group Survey, including:

- Site selection assistance

- Easier credit

- Construction expertise

- Fixtures and equipment assistance

- Good training

- Opening support

- Promotional assistance

- Economies of scale

- Ongoing support

Site Selection Assistance. The first advantage for franchisees is that their franchisor will help them select a good site for their business. Almost all successful franchisors know exactly what kinds of sites work best for their franchises. In many cases the franchisor selects the site, buys or leases the land, puts up the building, and then leases it to the franchisee. In other instances, the franchisees do all of this for themselves, but even then franchisors almost always approve sites based on their experience of the amount and kind of population needed in an area, traffic patterns, and other considerations.

Quality International, which franchises Clarion, Comfort, Quality, and Sleep Inns, offers prospective franchisees help with not only site selection but also site acquisition and site and market assessment. The Subway sandwich chain, which was named the best franchise in America by *Franchising* magazine for three years in a row (1988–1990), is a good example of how this works. In its franchise-offering circular, filed with the Federal Trade Commission in Washington, D.C., Subway states:

> The location of the store must be approved by the franchisor and the franchisee. The franchisor, or a corporation it designates, will then endeavor to lease the approved site and sublet the premises to the franchisee at cost. The responsibility for finding a site rests solely with the franchisee, and the franchisor will not unreasonably withhold approval of a location found by a franchisee. In rendering its assistance, the franchisor considers the population in the area of the site.

While Subway requires franchisees to find their own locations, McDonald's prefers to pick locations for its franchisees, based on sophisticated airplane and helicopter surveys and demographic studies.

Easier Credit. Obtaining credit is often easier for a franchisee than for individuals starting their own business. Banks and other lenders are reluctant to loan money for starting small businesses because of their high failure rate. Franchises are a much better risk. Very few national franchises fail, because franchisors work very hard to keep their franchises going, and so lenders are usually more willing to make capital available.

Some lodging franchisors provide some financing to qualified applicants. Hampton Inns sometimes helps franchisees raise capital through various methods. Red Carpet Inns and Scottish Inns assist in locating potential lenders and preparing a loan package. Quality International offers "lender introductions" to franchisees. In its franchise-offer package, Sheraton says its assistance can take the form of "helping the franchisee prepare a mortgage package, possibly identifying a lender who may be interested in his type of project, and, in some cases, accompanying the franchisee in his presentation visit to the lender."

Construction Expertise. Virtually all franchisors supply franchisees with architectural and floor plans for the franchise building. Quality International has plans available for three different styles of two-story 100-unit Sleep Inns, and furnishes all interior and exterior designs and site plans, including landscaping. McDonald's and Burger King have a large variety of building interior designs to choose from, depending on the market and the amount the franchisee is able to invest.

Some franchisors also help with employing the builder and supervising the construction. Since most franchisees do not have experience in this area, the assistance of a construction professional can mean considerable savings. Quality International provides preliminary and code-modified working drawings, elevations, and floor plans, as well as all structural, mechanical, plumbing, and electrical drawings necessary to complete the project. When the hotel is finished, a Quality International representative conducts a final site inspection to make certain that everything was done properly.

Fixtures and Equipment Assistance. Franchisors help franchisees select, purchase, and install fixtures and equipment. The Subway chain has an equipment-leasing program for those franchisees who do not have sufficient capital to purchase necessary fixtures. Sheraton has a division called the Sheraton Supply Company, which is a one-stop shopping center for all of the items needed to open a new Sheraton or refurbish an existing one. The company issues a product catalog as well as a guestroom design catalog with different interior design schemes that fit in with the Sheraton image.

Good Training. Classroom and on-the-job training is a major part of most franchise programs. As noted earlier, 49% of all franchisees list training as their main reason for buying a franchise. Most franchisors have extensive training programs because it is in their best interest to see that franchisees meet franchise standards.

Kentucky Fried Chicken or KFC offers an intensive three-week training program at the company's headquarters in Louisville, Kentucky. Tuition is included in the initial franchise fee, but attendees are responsible for most of their own travel expenses. An allowance for meals and lodging is provided. The curriculum covers every aspect of operating a KFC restaurant, from bookkeeping to sanitary systems. In addition, a KFC representative visits every restaurant on a regular basis to troubleshoot and offer guidance. McDonald's has a four- to eight-week program at Hamburger University in Oak Brook, Illinois. A unique aspect of the McDonald's franchise training program is that prospective franchisees must successfully complete the training program *before* being considered for a franchise. Holiday Inn provides its franchisees with an intensive two-week training program at Holiday Inn University in Memphis, Tennessee. The curriculum includes hotel organization, daily operations, food and beverage control, back office systems, marketing, promotion, and personnel administration. The program is supplemented by a staff of field advisors who work with franchisees at their properties.

A set of operations manuals and training videos is a part of most franchise packages. Some operations manuals are very detailed. The Dunkin' Donuts manual instructs franchisees in everything from how to make donuts to how to interview prospective job applicants. It also has sections on marketing, bookkeeping, and equipment operation. Sheraton gives each of its Sheraton franchisees a set of manuals outlining Sheraton's basic policies and procedures. Topics include pre-opening, operations, food and beverage, advertising, sales, budget and forecasting, housekeeping, front office, and security.

Opening Support. Just about all franchisors help their franchisees prepare and open their franchise units for business. International Tours, a travel

McDonald's trains managers at Hamburger University. Courtesy of McDonald's Corporation, Oak Brook, Illinois.

agency franchise headquartered in Tulsa, Oklahoma, sends a company representative to each new franchise. This representative oversees the first few days of operation to make sure that everything runs smoothly. He or she also attends the grand opening party. The grand opening package usually consists of a party and a series of other events to introduce the franchise to the local community, as well as suggested press releases and advertising materials. McDonald's opens its restaurants with a series of champagne receptions for local politicians and families of the crew. In 1990, when the company opened its first Russian franchise on Pushkin Square in Moscow, 700 people attended a champagne and caviar reception!

Promotional Assistance. Advertising, sales, and public relations help is one of the main strengths a franchisor can offer a franchisee. Most franchisors charge franchisees a marketing or advertising fee that is used to purchase television time, radio spots, newspaper ads, and produce other promotions including coupons, sweepstakes, or contests. Jack In The Box, a 600-unit fast-food restaurant chain headquartered in San Diego, California, charges each franchisee an advertising fee equivalent to 4% of monthly sales. This money is used for newspaper and magazine advertisements, mailers, promotional displays, and television and radio commercials. The company also helps franchisees with cooperative advertising plans, offers ongoing sales incentives, and sponsors periodic awards for superior sales

Franchisors help franchisees by producing merchandising materials such as this tray liner. Courtesy of Wendy's.

and quality. Dunkin' Donuts' advertising fee is 5% of retail sales. Wendy's charges 2% of gross sales for national advertising and another 2% for local advertising efforts.

Advertising and sales efforts in the lodging industry can be quite complicated. For Sleep Inn franchisees, Quality International has a fee of $25,000 for the large entrance signs that are important in attracting visitors; a monthly reservation fee of 1% of gross revenues, plus $1 per room night confirmed through the reservation system; as well as a monthly marketing assessment of 11% of gross revenues plus 24 cents per room per night. In return, franchisees receive advance reservation services; listings in travel directories; participation in trade shows; the services of Quality's meeting sales department; direct mail, telemarketing, and other sales programs; as well as sales seminars, workshops, and blitzes. Sheraton has established a Group Rates Availability Bank (GRAB) and staffed it with professional salespeople who sell for hotels throughout the Sheraton system. They handle group reservations of ten or more rooms and confirm arrangements to clients on a same-day basis. In addition, Sheraton has a special toll-free number for frequent travelers, travel agents, tour operators, and corporate and industry accounts.

A franchisor's regional representatives give franchisees ongoing support. Courtesy of McDonald's Corporation, Oak Brook, Illinois.

Economies of Scale. Because they are part of a franchise chain, franchisees receive the advantages of economies of scale in purchasing supplies, equipment, and advertising.

Ongoing Support. The franchisor remains available to the franchisee on an ongoing basis after the franchise unit becomes operational. All franchisors have regional representatives and district managers who constantly meet with franchisees. Franchisors help franchisees with merchandising and day-to-day problems. Franchisees have access to many types of specialists that they would have to hire if they were not members of a franchise organization.

Disadvantages   Despite all of the advantages of franchises, there are problems with franchising that have caused some franchisees to regret their decision to purchase a franchise. Disadvantages include:

- Restrictions
- Unwanted products or procedures
- Unwanted advertising
- Unprotected territories
- Cancellation
- Inadequate training

Restrictions. A major disadvantage of franchising is that most franchise contracts restrict franchisees a great deal. A franchisor's success depends on having a consistent quality throughout the system. When people check into a Holiday Inn anywhere in America they expect to find the same kind of room, similarly priced and furnished, with the same kind of amenities; a Big Mac or a Whopper is expected to taste exactly the same whether it is purchased in Bangor, Maine, or Los Angeles, California. This means that franchisors must strictly enforce their standards. For operators of Holiday Inns, guestrooms *must* be furnished and maintained in a certain way, kitchens *must* adhere to certain standards, staffing *must* be at required levels. A McDonald's franchisee *must* throw away unsold hamburgers after ten minutes no matter how much it costs, and a Dunkin' Donuts franchisee *must* make new donuts every four hours. A Travelodge Motel *must* achieve a minimum Two Diamond AAA rating to keep its franchise. All of these franchisors run regular and unannounced inspections, and franchisees who fail to adhere to standards run the risk of having their franchise cancelled. This is not an idle threat. Every year some franchisees have their contracts cancelled for failure to follow company guidelines.

These restrictions mean that some franchisees cannot be as creative as they'd like to be. They can't come up with their own advertising campaigns or introduce new menu items on their own. Restaurant chains are especially strict about their menus; franchisees cannot add or subtract anything from menus or change recipes in any way without permission, which is seldom granted. There are rare occasions when a franchisee will get an idea approved, however. McDonald's likes to point out that many of its menu items evolved from the ideas of its operators. Ray Kroc credited franchisee Lou Groen with inventing Filet-O-Fish to help him in his battle against the Big Boy chain in the Catholic parishes of Cincinnati. Jim Delligatti in Pittsburgh came up with the idea for the Big Mac. Herb Peterson in Santa Barbara created the Egg McMuffin; and Harold Rosen in Enfield, Connecticut, came up with the Shamrock Shake, a special green shake to serve on St. Patrick's Day.[16]

Unwanted Products or Procedures. When new products or procedures are introduced, franchisees must embrace them whether they want to or not. Originally, many McDonald's operators did not want to open for breakfast—it meant dramatically increased labor costs and a whole new shift. They doubted that they would sell enough breakfasts to make it pay. But when the company decided to introduce breakfast on television, every franchisee was forced to open at 6 a.m., even in areas where there was no business. Breakfast is still a losing proposition for some McDonald's franchisees.

Unwanted Advertising. A franchisor's advertising program can be another cause of franchisee dissatisfaction. When Burger King decided a few years ago to launch a television campaign featuring "Herb the Nerd," many franchisees did not like it. They felt it actually drove away customers. Nevertheless they were forced to accept it and pay for it until the company itself decided the campaign was not effective and cancelled it. In some cases franchisees feel the franchisor's national campaign does not help them, although it may benefit franchisees elsewhere.

Unprotected Territories. Another area of dispute between franchisors and franchisees involves territories. Many franchisors do not grant specific territories. This means they allow a franchisee to establish a new unit as close as a mile or two away from an existing unit if business in the area warrants it.

Cancellation. Franchisees are not always guaranteed that they will be able to renew their franchise after the initial 20-year period (the usual length of a franchise contract). If a franchisee has not been adhering to the standards set by the company, for example, the franchisor may decide not to renew his or her franchise. The franchisor may decide not to renew for reasons outside the franchisee's control. Theoretically, a franchisee might spend a lifetime building a business and then not be able to pass it on to his or her children because the franchise contract expired and was not renewed.

Inadequate Training. Not all franchisors provide high-quality training programs to their franchisees. Sometimes a franchisor's salespersons misrepresent what franchisees are going to receive.

Advantages and Disadvantages for Franchisors

Franchising has advantages and disadvantages for the franchisor as well. Little to no capital is required to expand because the franchisees provide the funding. This allows franchisors to expand quickly while transferring the investment risk to the franchisees. A company can develop quickly through franchising without the need of a large system of corporate staff and administration. Because a franchise unit is owned by a local individual or company, the franchisor gains an involved and motivated on-site manager who is a member of the community. This means the franchisee is likely to be accepted by the local community, and the franchise is in the hands of someone who knows local authority and ordinances.

The downside is that the franchisor gives up the profits generated by its franchise units, settling for royalties instead. Also, the franchisor surrenders a certain amount of control to the franchisees. In a company-owned unit it is easier to make changes in operating procedures and marketing approaches and get feedback from unit managers.

How Franchising Works

In order to obtain a license from a franchisor, a franchisee must pay a fee for the privilege of using the franchisor's name, identity, business systems, operating procedures, marketing techniques, and (in the case of hotels) reservation system. The typical franchise fee arrangement has two parts: (1) an initial franchise fee upon signing the franchise agreement, and (2) ongoing fees.

Initial franchise fees vary. They are calculated by assigning a monetary value to the following:

- The franchisor's goodwill
- The value of the new franchise unit's trading area or territory
- The average cost of recruiting a franchisee

- The cost of training a franchisee
- The cost of signs, ads, plans, and other aids[17]

The goodwill of a business—the reputation or prestige it enjoys among customers—is an intangible asset that is easier to estimate for an established franchisor such as McDonald's than for a new franchisor. Although intangible, goodwill can be calculated by relating it to the profits, profits being one measure of the amount of goodwill a franchisor enjoys. For example, if a franchisor's franchises average $150,000 in profits per year, the value of the goodwill for a new franchise might be 2½ times that, or $375,000. A percentage of the goodwill charge—anywhere from 4% to 12%—could be part of the initial franchise fee. Franchisors differ in how they calculate goodwill and how they charge it to their franchisees.

Some territories are more valuable than others due to their demographic makeup and the propensity of their residents to eat out. Therefore, a new franchise's location would be considered in setting the initial franchise fee.

The value of recruiting, training, and other aids is easier for the franchisor to calculate since it can refer to actual costs.

Restaurant franchisors generally charge a flat franchise fee for one unit; some franchisors charge a reduced rate for additional units. On the other hand, hotel franchisors base their initial franchise fees on the number of rooms the franchisee builds, with a minimum fee for those franchisees whose hotels fall below a certain number of rooms. Here are some examples of franchise fees charged in 1990:

Subway Sandwiches & Salads	$ 7,500
Little Caesar's Pizza	$15,000
Sheraton Inns	$15,000
McDonald's	$22,500
Hilton Inns	$25,000
Hampton Inns	$35,000

Ongoing franchise fees vary. All franchisors charge a royalty fee, usually calculated on a percentage of the franchisee's sales. As with initial franchise fees, royalties are related to the value of the franchise. Here are some typical royalty fees:

	Percent of Gross Sales
Holiday Inn	4%
Kentucky Fried Chicken	4
Hilton Inn	5
Subway Sandwiches & Salads	8
McDonald's	12

Other initial franchise and royalty fees are shown in Exhibit 12.1.

Some hotel franchisors operate a central reservation system and charge franchisees a reservation fee. The fee is to cover the cost of operating the system. The calculation of this fee varies. It is usually a percentage of rooms revenue, an amount per available room per month, or an amount per reservation.

Exhibit 12.1 Typical Franchises and their Costs

	Began Operations	Began Franchising	1990 Franchised Outlets	Initial Franchise Fee	Monthly Royalty	Adv. Fee	Training Program	Term
Arby's Sandwiches (Roast Beef)	1964	1965	2033	$25,000–$37,000	3%	4.2%	4 wks	20 yrs.
Carl's Jr. (Hamburgers)	1956	1984	71	35,000	3–4%	4%	1 wk.	20 yrs.
Domino's Pizza	1960	1967	3548	1,300–3,250	5.5%	3%	yes—not stipulated	10 yrs.
Kentucky Fried Chicken	1930	1956	5833	20,000	4%	5%	3 wks.	20 yrs.
McDonald's	1955	1955	7733	22,500	12%	4%	4 wks.	20 yrs.
Sonic	1953	1975	921	15,000	1% to $10,000 sales. Graduated ½% for each additional 10,000	1.5%	2 wks.	15 yrs.
Days Inn	1970	1971	321	Varies	6.5%	None	2 wks	20 yrs.
Hilton Inn	1947	1965	223	25,000–60,000	5%	None	Varies	20 yrs.
Holiday Inn	1952	1954	1490	Minimum 30,000 (300 per room)	4%	1.5%	2 wks	
Ramada	1954	1959	800	Varies	3%	3.5%	Varies	20 yrs.
Sheraton Inns	1937	1962	304	30,000	5%	None	5 days	10 yrs.

Initial Investment

Although most restaurant franchises are still considered small businesses, the initial investment required to buy a successful franchise is creeping up. The total investment, including the initial franchise fee, to open a McDonald's is $375,000 to $400,000. The land is owned by McDonald's and the rent is included in the continuing royalty fee of 12%. (McDonald's also has a leasing plan where a new franchisee who cannot afford to buy a franchise can lease one for around $65,000.) It costs $866,000 to open a Wendy's—including land, building, and signs.

Hotel franchises cost more. The typical price tag for a Days Inn franchise is $500,000 to $1.5 million; Hilton Inns, $10 million. Thriftlodge, a Trusthouse Forte economy concept, estimates construction costs for their motels at approximately $20,000 per room.

Franchisors want to be sure that franchisees will have enough capital to operate their franchises until they start making a profit. For this reason, some franchisors require their franchisees to have a minimum personal net worth. Wendy's requires a personal net worth of $250,000, Hardee's $300,000 to $1 million depending on the size of the market. Carl's Jr., a 430-unit hamburger chain based in California, requires "a net worth of

$250,000, excluding personal residence, and liquidity of $176,000 within 30 days."

Franchise Regulations

Franchising is regulated in the United States by the Federal Trade Commission and by fifteen states. In those states with special regulations, a franchisor must register with the proper state authority before offering a franchise for sale within the state. State and local restrictions take precedence if they are more demanding than federal requirements.

All franchisors must comply with Federal Trade Commission Rule 436.1, which requires that a prospective franchisee be given a prospectus—the Uniform Franchise Offering Circular (UFOC). This prospectus is a disclosure document, the purpose of which is to inform the franchisee about certain vital aspects of the franchisor and the franchise agreement before the agreement is signed. The law states that this disclosure statement must be in the hands of the prospective franchisee ten business days prior to signing the franchise agreement so that the franchisee will have ample time to study it and understand the risks involved. The UFOC covers everything from the franchisor's history and financial condition to the detailed terms of the sales agreement. Franchisees should study the UFOC carefully before buying a franchise. See the Chapter Appendix for more information on what a UFOC must contain.

The Future of Franchising

There is no doubt that franchising will continue to be a major force in the expansion of the hospitality industry. There are some problems, however, that will affect franchising in years to come.

The franchising of multiple units to a single franchisee has created a new breed of franchisee which is stronger and more sophisticated than ever before. In 1988, for example, unhappy Burger King franchisees played a major role in arranging the buy-out of the company by Grand Metropolitan. At Arby's, owner Victor Posner was faced with a rebellious group of franchisees who would not approve his choice of a new chief executive. And Kentucky Fried Chicken franchisees resisted an attempt by the company to require them to remodel their restaurants every seven years.

According to the *Wall Street Journal*, these events "illustrate the upheavals taking place at many older franchise systems. Franchisors' desire to overhaul their operations often puts them at odds with old allies: their long term franchisees."[18] Holiday Inn is another example of this situation. Holiday Corporation sold its Holiday Inns to Bass (a British company) because of slow growth, which was partly due to problems with franchisees. "As its older contracts with Holiday Inns have expired, Holiday Corp. has insisted on tougher terms and more investment in remodelling and expansion. It's part of a strategy calling for fancier hotels and higher room rates," according to the *Journal*. "Holiday says it forced out some balky franchisees, and others have quit. Some 185 franchisees have joined rival Days Inn of America according to a Days Inn spokeswoman."[19]

Franchising has now reached a mature stage of growth, where new concepts are much more difficult to come by and franchise chains and individual franchisees are competing for market share with each other. A good example of this problem is McDonald's, which according to *Advertising Age* "faces a list of problems longer than its menu":

> The company is finally running out of room to grow in the U.S. without cannibalizing its own stores. The chain also is watching the consumer base outgrow its menu and is confronting the unfamiliar possibility that massive marketing spending isn't enough to boost U.S. sales in the face of industry saturation, lower demand, and tougher competition.[20]

McDonald's is not taking this lying down. Its new McLean Deluxe burger with reduced fat (introduced in 1991) is a hit among nutrition-minded consumers. It is opening international franchises at an increasingly rapid rate, as well as testing new dinner items like pizza and pasta and new service concepts such as home delivery. Other hamburger franchises are facing similar problems in trying to sustain growth. According to the International Franchise Association, most growth in franchised restaurants will come from "licensed sandwich and snack places" such as Subway. The number of these units was expected to increase by 26.4% in 1990, compared to a 9.6% increase in hamburger restaurants.[21]

Entrepreneur magazine rated franchises as possible investments in their 11th Annual Franchise 500 Issue (January 1990). The top five franchises were all restaurants:

1. Subway
2. Domino's
3. McDonald's
4. Little Caesar's Pizza
5. Burger King[22]

In the lodging industry, too, franchising is in transition. The industry seems to have run out of new niches to occupy, so that the major thrust in the 1990s will be price and product segmentation. We can expect to see more chains extending their brand names to offer products in the suite, economy, and luxury markets. International growth too will play an important role. According to *Entrepreneur*, the top lodging franchises for potential investors will be:

1. Holiday Inn
2. Days Inn of America
3. Quality Inns International
4. Super 8 Motels Inc.[23]

Chapter Summary

Franchising is a marketing or distribution system. In its simplest form, the term "franchise" refers to the authorization given by one company to another to sell its unique products and services.

There are two types of franchises: the product or trade-name franchise and the business-format franchise. The product or trade-name franchise is a supplier-dealer arrangement whereby the dealer (franchisee) sells a product line provided by the supplier (franchisor) and to some degree takes on the identity of the supplier. Business-format franchises are ongoing business relationships between the franchisor and franchisees in which franchisors sell their product(s), service, trademark, and the business concept itself to franchisees in return for royalties and other franchise fees.

Franchising is not a new concept. In 1851, I. M. Singer & Company used franchising to develop networks of sewing-machine dealers all over the United States. The first person to pioneer the idea of the business-format franchise was Howard Johnson, founder of the Howard Johnson Company.

The evolution of franchising was driven by the desire of some companies to expand their business, coupled with the desire of entrepreneurs like McDonald's founder Ray Kroc to take a successful idea and build on it rather then risk starting from scratch. Franchising also provided an alternative method of financing growth other than through company-owned units.

Franchising is one of the safest ways for an individual to have his or her own business. Compared to the national failure rate for small businesses, very few franchises fail. When people buy a franchise, they are buying (1) a format and formula that has already been tested, and (2) the experience of the franchisor, who will teach them what they need to know to succeed. One study showed that prospective franchisees had the following reasons for being interested in owning their own franchise: self management, career advancement, new skills/training, and long-term investment.

There are many other advantages to owning a franchise. Franchisors help franchisees with site selection; credit; construction; fixtures and equipment; training; pre-opening and opening activities; and advertising, sales, and public relations.

Franchising is not for everyone, however. Many franchisees do not like the restrictions imposed on them by their franchise agreement. Franchisors have tough standards and usually do not hesitate to cancel the franchises of operators who will not adhere to those standards. Franchisees must also go along with the franchisor's advertising and marketing program whether they agree with it or not. Sometimes there are disputes over territories.

Franchising has disadvantages for the franchisor as well. While little or no capital is required to expand because funding is provided by the franchisee, the franchisor gives up the opportunity for the profits generated by the franchise units, settling for royalties instead. Also, the franchisor surrenders a certain amount of control to the franchisees.

The typical franchise fee arrangement has two parts: (1) an initial franchise fee upon signing the agreement, and (2) ongoing fees, which consist of royalties (based on monthly gross sales) and advertising and marketing fees. In addition to these fees, there is an initial investment required to purchase the physical facility, equipment, and supplies necessary to operate the franchise.

Before selling a franchise, franchisors are required by the Federal Trade Commission to submit a Uniform Franchise Offering Circular (UFOC) to the franchisee. The UFOC must contain the sections shown in the Chapter Appendix.

There is no doubt that franchising will continue to be a major force in the expansion of the hospitality industry. But there are many upheavals taking place, due to the increasing strength of franchisees, the reluctance of some franchisees to upgrade their units, and the predicted slow growth for some franchisors.

Endnotes

1. *Franchising in the Economy 1986–1988,* U.S. Department of Commerce International Trade Administration, Office of Service Industries, February 1988.

2. *Franchise Opportunities Handbook,* U.S. Department of Commerce International Trade Administration and Minority Business Development Agency, 1988, p. xxix.

3. *Franchise Opportunities Handbook,* "Franchising in the Economy" section.

4. *Franchise Opportunities Handbook,* "Franchising in the Economy" section.

5. *Franchise Opportunities Handbook,* p. 74.

6. *Franchise Opportunities Handbook,* p. 76.

7. Remus L. Foster, *The Rating Guide to Franchises* (New York: Facts on File Publications, 1988).

8. N. G. L. Hammond and H. H. Scullard, eds., *The Oxford Classical Dictionary* (Oxford: Clarendon Press, 1979), pp. 613, 898–899.

9. Charles L. Vaughn, *Franchising* (Lexington, Mass.: Lexington Books, D. C. Heath and Company, 1974), p. 11.

10. Vaughn, pp. 15–17.

11. Ray Kroc and Robert Anderson, *Grinding It Out: The Making of McDonald's* (New York: Berkeley Books, 1978), p. 71.

12. Kroc, pp. 72–73.

13. Kroc, p. 86.

14. Dennis L. Foster, *The Complete Franchise Book* (Rocklin, Calif.: Prima Publishing & Communications, 1989), p. 6.

15. *Franchising in the Economy 1986–1988,* pp. 18–19.

16. Kroc, pp. 173–174.

17. Foster, p. 42.

18. "Firms Try To Tighten Grip On Franchisees," *Wall Street Journal,* January 15, 1990, p. B-1.

19. "Firms Tighten Grip," p. B-1.

20. "McD's Faces U.S. Slowdown," *Advertising Age,* May 14, 1990, p. 1.

21. "Franchised Restaurants' Sales Forecasted to Outpace Industry's," *Restaurant News,* Franchising Insert, April 16, 1990.

22. *Entrepreneur,* January 1990, p. 190.

23. *Entrepreneur,* January 1990, pp. 156–157.

Key Terms

business-format franchise
franchise
franchisee
franchisor

product or trade-name franchise
Uniform Franchise Offer Circular (UFOC)

Discussion Questions

1. What's the difference between a franchisor and a franchisee?

2. What are two types of franchises?

3. How did I. M. Singer, General Motors, and Coca-Cola contribute to franchising?

4. According to a poll by the Development Group, why do franchisees purchase a franchise?

5. From a franchisee's point of view, what are the advantages and disadvantages of franchising?

6. Why do franchisors hold franchisees to such strict standards?

7. From a franchisor's point of view, what are the advantages and disadvantages of franchising?

8. How are initial franchise fees determined?

9. What is the Uniform Franchise Offering Circular?

10. What trends in the industry affect the future of franchising?

Chapter Appendix

All franchisors must comply with Federal Trade Commission Rule 436.1, which requires that a prospective franchisee be given a prospectus—the Uniform Franchise Offering Circular (UFOC). The purpose of a UFOC is to inform the franchisee about certain vital aspects of the franchisor and the franchise agreement *before* the franchisee signs the agreement. A UFOC must contain the following:

1. *Background.* The franchisor's background, including the franchisor's personal and business background and financial history, must be disclosed. Franchisors must state if they have any previous experience operating the kind of business they propose franchising. However, they are not required to disclose background that is not connected with their current enterprise.

2. *Key associates and managers.* The franchisor must identify and give the backgrounds of directors, trustees, partners, principals, and other managers of the franchising company.

3. *Litigation.* The franchisor must disclose any criminal or civil action involving unfair business practices, fraud, or violations of the franchise law. In those states where laws forbid revealing criminal records, only civil actions are revealed.

4. *Bankruptcy.* The statement must reveal whether the franchisor, partners, officers, or predecessors in the business have declared bankruptcy in the last 15 years.

5. *Initial Fee.* This section describes the initial franchise fee and how it must be paid. The refund policy must also be stated.

6. *Other fees and ongoing royalties.* Here the franchisor states the amount of monthly royalty plus advertising, marketing, reservation, and other fees the franchisee must pay. If the franchisor charges for training or for the time and expenses of its field representatives, such charges must be disclosed.

7. *Initial investment broken down into components.* In this section the amount of investment needed to open the franchise is stated. This includes the cost of the real estate, equipment, and supplies. If the amount is likely to vary due to local conditions, a range must be stated. In some cases, these figures do not include a figure for working capital, but anyone considering a franchise needs to add this to cover the period until the business starts making a profit.

8. *Designated suppliers.* The franchisor must state whether the franchisee is required to purchase or lease products, services, and equipment from a specified source. Generally this practice is frowned upon—and in some cases, is unlawful—except in certain instances. For example, the franchisee may be required to lease the building and land from the franchisor and buy certain signs from the franchisor.

9. *Obligation to purchase supplies according to franchisor specifications.* Franchisors cannot force a franchisee to buy from them or suppliers they designate (except as noted above), but in most cases it is reasonable to expect that the supplies a franchisee buys must meet franchise specifications. In the case of fast-food franchises, the specifications for all products to be used is often contained in the operating manuals. In lodging franchises, typical specifications include such items as size and quality of furnishings and construction materials.

10. *Financing.* In cases where financing assistance by the franchisor or others is offered, details of the parties involved and conditions should be set forth.

11. *Obligations of the franchisor.* Here the franchisor must describe all of the services promised to a franchisee after the agreement is signed. These include services provided before and after opening, such as site selection and training. If a franchisee is expected to pay for personal travel and living expenses while being trained at the

franchisor's headquarters, this must be disclosed.

12. *Exclusive territory.* In many cases, the territory of the franchise is limited to the actual location. In others, protection may extend to a certain geographical area or be described in terms of population density. In any case, the franchisor must disclose what protection, if any, is offered to the franchisee. Even when the franchisor forbids another franchise unit from being built within the franchisee's territory, the franchisor cannot protect the franchisee from other franchisees who may wish to solicit business within the franchisee's territory. For instance, several franchised travel agencies with different owners located in different parts of a city may compete with each other by advertising the same tours in the same newspaper.

13. *Trademarks, logotypes, and commercial symbols.* Since a franchisee often is buying the use of a recognized name, the franchisor is obligated to state whether that name is fully protected, and, if not, what steps are being taken to register and protect it. It should be noted that names of particular products served as well as that of the establishment can be protected. For example, McDonald's has registered not only its name and its golden arches but also names like "Big Mac."

14. *Patents and copyrights.* Some franchisors have unique, patented equipment or designs as part of their franchise. If this is part of the franchise, it must be disclosed.

15. *Obligation of the franchisee to participate in the conduct of the business.* If the franchisor requires the franchisee to personally operate the business, such a requirement must be stated. Some franchisors allow absentee ownership, others forbid it.

16. *Restrictions on goods and services.* Almost all restaurant franchisors restrict the variety of menu items that franchisees can sell. Lodging franchises usually limit the sales of goods and services on the premises to those that are normally incident to the operation of the facility.

17. *Renewal, termination, repurchase, and assignment.* This section covers the rights of both of the parties to renew, terminate, or assign the franchise. It is often the clause that is most litigated, because franchises can be terminated for non-performance and because franchisees sometimes wish to sell or otherwise terminate their franchise.

18. *Arrangements with public figures.* Some franchises are named after real people or use the names of celebrities in their promotions. If there is a formal arrangement with one or more public figures to use their name or reputation, the details and compensation must be disclosed.

19. *Projected earnings.* If franchisors project earnings, they must disclose the formula used in the calculation process. Names and addresses of units that have achieved these earnings are sometimes given. However, most franchisors do not project any sales or profits, since these figures can easily be misleading or misinterpreted and lawsuits can be filed for misrepresentation.

20. *Information regarding the franchises of the franchisor.* Franchisors are required to list the number of franchises they have sold as well as the franchises' addresses and the names of their owners. Prospective franchisees are well-advised to contact current owners for information before purchasing their own franchises.

21. *Financial statement.* An audited financial statement of the franchisor that is no more than six months old must be a part of the UFOC.

22. *Contracts.* The franchise agreement and any other agreements—such as a lease that the franchisee will be required to sign— must be attached to the UFOC.

Chapter Outline

Why Management Companies Exist
The Evolution of Management Companies
Management Contracts
    Contract Provisions
        Operating Term
        Fee Structure
        Reporting Requirements
        Approvals
        Termination
        Operator Investment
        Operating Expenses
        Employees
        Other Provisions
    Advantages and Disadvantages
Chapter Summary

13 Management Companies

This chapter covers hotel management companies and their methods of operation. First it explains the beginnings of management companies and continues by describing their history and evolution. It then focuses on management contracts between owners and management companies, identifying and explaining major contract provisions and the reasons for them. Finally, the chapter describes the opportunities and risks for both owners and management companies when entering into a management contract.

Why Management Companies Exist

The growth and prosperity of hotel management companies and the unique and changing nature of their relationships with hotel owners underscore the fact that hotels are special kinds of real estate. They are very different from office buildings and shopping malls, for example.

To begin with, unlike most other kinds of businesses, hotels operate 24 hours a day. Moreover, unlike 24-hour operations such as all-night gas stations or drugstores, hotels must provide a multitude of readily available specialized services. At most properties, guests expect that food and beverage service will be provided—in some cases on a 24-hour basis. Rooms need to be cleaned daily. Full-service hotels may also offer laundry and valet services, meeting and convention rooms and services, fitness clubs, tennis courts and golf courses, airport limousines, concierge services, business centers, and secretarial services. The number and range of facilities and services a property offers depends on the property's biggest guest group, which may be business travelers, tourists, or conventioneers.

In fact, a hotel is a miniature self-sustaining society. Managers of large hotels often compare what they do to running a small city. Many large hotels have their own energy-generating facilities, security forces, and shopkeepers. Guests sleep, eat, work, play, and sometimes die in hotels. The hotel is the guests' headquarters—their office and home, the center of their daily business and social life. Because a hotel can be so many things, managing it can be complex and extremely demanding. Managers and their staffs must be well trained and prepared to cope with a variety of activities and emergencies while maintaining and controlling the hotel's physical plant.

Managing a hotel requires special expertise. Buying a franchise hotel is one way frequently used by inexperienced hotel owners to acquire that expertise. When they buy a franchise, they buy an established image, a tested and successful operating system, management and employee training programs, and marketing and advertising programs.

However, while a franchise may provide systems, programs, and training, it does not provide the cadre of experienced people necessary to run a hotel. For this reason, when hotel chains such as Hilton and Sheraton first expanded, they managed every new property themselves rather than sell franchises. They understood that they could not write down everything they knew in training manuals, and that mastery of the science of running a hotel could not be easily acquired in a short training course.

For some inexperienced owners, franchising was not the answer. And they did not know enough about the hotel business to run their hotels themselves. Rather than buy a hotel franchise, some inexperienced owners decided the best way to make sure their hotel was profitable was to hire professional hotel management from established hotel chains such as Hilton, Sheraton, and others. The hotel management company was born.

The Evolution of Management Companies

For hundreds of years hotels were started and operated by hoteliers, just as restaurants were started by chefs. These hoteliers were professionals who knew how to manage a hotel.

But as the lodging industry grew in the last half of the twentieth century, a new breed of owners appeared. These new owners were entrepreneurs who regarded the buildings and land they occupied as attractive investments, or they were real estate developers who felt that a hotel would be the best use for a piece of property they owned. These new owners, who knew nothing about the hotel business and usually were not interested in it, had several options for running their hotels. Many hired professional hotel managers and operated their hotels as independent properties. In order to generate business and name recognition they sometimes tied in with a referral service such as Best Western, or a marketing group like Preferred Hotels.

Another option was to turn management of the property over to a hotel company. Hotel companies such as Hilton were receptive to the idea because it was a way to expand their earning base without the financial risk of developing a hotel from the ground up.

From the standpoint of these new owners—who were real estate investors, not hoteliers—the most logical way to employ a hotel company was a lease, an instrument that they were very familiar with. Under this arrangement, a hotel owner or developer—which might be an individual, a company, or even a government—would simply rent out a structure to a hotel company either as a fully developed and furnished turnkey operation or, more likely, as an unfurnished building that had to be outfitted by the hotel company. For instance, in Bermuda the government constructed the first hotel in the town of Saint George, expecting the hotel would bring tourists to that part of the island. The building was then leased to the Holiday Inn Corporation.

Under early lease arrangements, the hotel company was responsible for hiring and managing the entire staff of the hotel, collecting all the revenues from sales, and paying all operating costs. They also paid rent to the owners for the use of the facility. In return they received a share of the hotel's gross operating profit. Gross operating profit was determined by deducting actual operating costs from total revenue. Obviously, the hotel's fixed charges—such as depreciation, interest on borrowed capital, and real estate taxes—were paid by the owner of the building. For a few leased hotels, the rental agreement was based on a percentage of total sales. Sometimes the rent was based on a combination of a percentage of sales as well as a share of the gross operating profit.

Another typical arrangement was the two-thirds/one-third lease. Here, two-thirds of the gross operating profit went to the owner and one-third went to the hotel company. This kind of arrangement was the basis of the contract made in 1954 between Hilton Hotels and the Puerto Rican government, the lessee and lessor, respectively, of the Caribe Hilton Hotel in San Juan, Puerto Rico.

While Hilton was growing by leasing new properties and creating new types of leases, the Inter-Continental Hotel Corporation (IHC) was pioneering the management contract. In the early 1950s, IHC signed its first management contracts with the respective owners of the Techendama in Bogota, Colombia, and the Tamanaco in Caracas, Venezuela, while the hotels were still under construction. Instead of paying rent and keeping the hotels' profits, IHC did not pay rent and received from each owner a management fee (which originally was based on a fixed fee per room) and an "incentive fee." The incentive fee was a percentage of the hotel's gross operating profit plus reimbursement of IHC's overhead—specific expenses incurred by IHC in managing the property.

Incentive fees are now a regular part of management contracts, but in the 1950s this concept was a real innovation. The term "incentive fee" describes that portion of the management fee that is based on a percentage of income before fixed charges (also known as gross operating profit), or on a percentage of cash flow after debt service. It is called an incentive fee because it is designed to motivate the hotel company to produce maximum revenue and control costs so that the maximum profit is achieved and the hotel company can collect the maximum incentive fee. As it gained more experience with this concept, IHC switched from a fixed fee per room to a percentage of gross revenue plus a percentage of gross operating profit with no reimbursement of company overhead. At first, IHC made a small investment in each of the hotels it managed, to entitle it to a director on the boards of the companies that owned the hotels. Later, in Europe and the Far East, IHC invested as much as one-third of the project cost.

One of the pioneers of management companies in the United States was Robert M. James, CHA, now president of Regal-AIRCOA, the parent company of three management companies: MHM, AIRCOA Hospitality Services, and HMS Properties. With 150 properties, Regal-AIRCOA is the largest U.S. management company (see Exhibit 13.1).[1] When James started his company in 1971 there were not many hotels operating under management contracts in the United States.[2] In 1970 there were just 10 management companies operating 22 properties.[3]

Exhibit 13.1 *Lodging Hospitality's* **Top 25 Management Companies**

Rank	Hotel Group	Number of rooms	Number of properties	Own	Manage	Develop
1	Regal-AIRCOA	30,000	131	x	x	x
2	Prime Motor Inns	18,250	129	x	x	x
3	VMS Realty Partners	18,000	56	x	own properties	
4	The Continental Companies	16,000	58	x	x	x
5	Omni Hotel Corp.	14,410	39	x	x	x
6	Servico Inc.	13,000	52	x	x	x
7	Larken, Inc.	12,953	72	x	x	x
8	Commonwealth Hospitality Ltd.	10,500	40	x	x	x
9	United Inns Inc.	9,872	36	x		x
10	Weingardner & Hammons Inc.	8,556	42	x	x	x
11	Interstate Hotels Corp.	8,279	26	x	x	x
12	Outrigger Hotel Hawaii	8,910	23	x	x	x
13	John Q. Hammons Hotels Inc.	7,750	30	x	x	x
14	Hotel Investors	7,200	45	x	x	x
15	Mariner Corp.	7,150	22	x	x	x
16	Colony Hotels & Resorts	6,904	36		x	
17	Integra, A Hotel & Motel Co.	6,485	40	x	x	x
18	Loews Hotels	6,383	13	x	x	x
19	Integrated Resources Inc.	5,701	35		x	
20	Drury Inns, Inc.	5,599	52	x	x	x
21	Horizon Hotels Ltd.	5,500	22		x	
22	Victor Management Co.	5,497	32	x	x	x
23	Landmark Hotel Group	5,300	26	x	x	x
24	The Registry Hotel Corp.	5,000	14	x	x	x
25	Aston Hotels & Resorts	4,651	36	x	x	x

Source: *Lodging/Hospitality*, August 1988, p. 94.

Since contracting with a hotel owner to manage the hotel for him or her was virtually a new field, there was little information or experience to guide the first U.S. management companies. To help remedy this situation, James started the International Council of Hotel and Motel Management Companies—a committee of the American Hotel & Motel Association—which enabled management companies to network with one another and learn more about management contracts.

As a result of the economic recession in the early 1970s, management companies' services were in great demand because they could provide professional management for U.S. hotels that had been taken back by the investors—many of them insurance companies. By 1987, the management

The Kona Village Resort in Hawaii, a property managed for many years by Regal-AIRCOA. Courtesy of Regal-AIRCOA.

company field had grown to a point where there were approximately 1,650 hotels and motor hotels operated under management contract by 20 chains such as Hyatt, and 60 independent management companies such as those under James' management.[4]

Management Contracts

A management contract, as defined by Professor James Eyster of Cornell's School of Hotel Administration, is "a written agreement between an owner and an operator of a hotel or motor inn by which the owner employs the operator as an agent (employee) to assume full responsibility for operating and managing the property."[5] The operator (management company) can be a hotel chain with a familiar name and market image, such as Hyatt or Sheraton. It can also be an independent management company. Independent management companies operate franchise hotels as well as independent hotels. For example, The Continental Companies manages 55 properties under various franchises such as Sheraton, Omni, and Hampton Inns, as well as many independent resorts such as the five-star Grand Bay Hotel in Miami and the Pier House in Key West, Florida.

After an extensive study of management contracts, Dr. Eyster concluded that there are three provisions common to almost every contract:

1. The operator has the sole and exclusive right to manage the property without ownership interference

2. The owner pays all operating and financing expenses and assumes ownership risks

The Grand Bay Hotel in Miami. Top: Exterior. Bottom: Lobby. Courtesy of The Continental Companies.

3. The operator is indemnified from its actions except for gross negligence or fraud[6]

Management companies can run their properties in any manner they see fit, while at the same time they are relieved of the financial burden, which is carried by the hotel's owners. In short, the management company gets to make most of the decisions while the owner pays for them! This is the major difference between a lease and a management contract. In a typical lease, the hotel operator uses its own money to start the business and keep it operating. The operator has to pay rent to the owner of the building, and pay all of the employees of the property as well. The operator, in other words, takes all of the financial risk and receives all of the profit. On the other hand, under a typical management contract the owner must bear the costs of operating the physical plant and paying the employees. The operator pays no rent and is merely an agent who acts on behalf of the owner. If the hotel makes a profit, the owner and the operator share in it, with the owner getting the greater amount since he or she bears most of the financial risk.

Under the earliest management contracts, the operator was simply regarded as a company hired to perform a service, much as an architectural firm might be hired to draw the plans for a hotel. The management company got paid for performing those services, but took no financial risk and therefore was not entitled to any profits. However, as noted previously, that basic concept has evolved over time. There are a variety of reasons for this:

- According to Robert James, 20 years ago most owners of lodging facilities were insurance companies. They invested for the long term, hoping to realize both profits and appreciation on the value of the property. Today, most new investors are banks and governments. Their objectives are very different. They are not interested in staying in the hotel business. These owners want to develop, open, stabilize, and then sell off all or part of the hotel.[7]

- The U.S. building boom of the 1970s and 1980s is over. The pace of hotel development has slowed because hotels no longer offer the tax incentives they once did. International companies that invest in the United States usually take over existing properties rather than build new ones.

- Environmental concerns have also slowed development in the United States and abroad. Today it is recognized that hotels and resorts might damage ecologically sensitive areas, so it is harder to get approval to build. Often the cost of meeting environmental requirements can substantially increase the capital required to develop a new property.

- The business climate has dramatically shifted. Writing in the *Cornell Quarterly*, James Eyster says that since 1980 there has been a significant change in the relationship between owners and operators due to: (1) increased competition among operators due to the emergence of new domestic and international chains and market segmentation, (2) increased sophistication of owners' knowledge about the hotel industry, and (3) the more active role of lenders in management contract negotiations.[8]

Because of these reasons, owners have become even less willing than they were before to take all of the financial risk by themselves. The stakes have gotten too high. Moreover, some management companies have grown

Left: Robert M. James, CHA, president of Regal-AIRCOA. Right: Thomas F. Hewitt, president and chief operating officer of The Continental Companies.

in size and power to the point where it makes economic sense for them to own all or part of the properties they manage. As part owners, they can take a share of the hotel's profits in addition to collecting their management fees.

Thomas F. Hewitt, president and chief operating officer of The Continental Companies, says, "I don't think there's a pure management contract that is written in the industry any more, at least not among the major companies. They [management contracts] all involve some degree of ownership, lending, or something that involves risk [for the management company]." Hewitt adds that small management companies don't have the access to capital to work this way, but on the whole, "I genuinely believe a fair formula that recognizes the interests of both the owner and the management company is not only appropriate, but mutually beneficial."[9]

Contract Provisions

The provisions of a management contract are important not only to the owner and the operator, but also to the lenders who finance the project. Lenders—financial institutions and insurance companies—want assurance that both parties have a reasonable opportunity to make a profit. They also want to be sure that differences between the owner and the operator have been resolved in advance; otherwise, the viability of the project may be jeopardized.

Contract provisions detail the exact terms that the parties have agreed upon. Although the fundamental provisions of all management contracts are similar to those identified by Eyster, there are significant differences from contract to contract. These differences include the amounts invested by the owner and the operator; the nature and amount of control exercised by each party; and fee structures, including the incentive arrangement.

In the following sections, we discuss some of the major terms and provisions often addressed in hotel management contracts.[10]

Operating Term. This provision defines the length of the initial term of the contract and its renewal options. The operator usually prefers a long initial period, while the owner usually prefers a shorter one. Eyster explains that while a long-term contract offers stability for both parties, it is a disadvantage to the owner if the owner wants to remove the operator before the contract comes up for renewal. Operators generally favor long-term contracts because such contracts give them more time to recover a return on their investment. The lenders' concern is that the term of the contract and the term of the loan coincide, making it probable that the hotel will be run by only one operator throughout the loan's payback period. Such a stable situation makes it more likely that there will be an uninterrupted flow of revenues and profits to cover debt payments.

The length of the contract is often a serious negotiating point. Although the industry standard was once 20 years, it now varies from as little as 1 year to as much as 30 years. Chain operators demand longer contracts because it takes them at least eight to ten years to recoup their start-up costs and produce a reasonable profit. Eyster's research shows that the median contract term for a chain operator with some equity in the hotel it is managing is still 20 years. However, for independent operators who do not have established brand names, the median contract length is only 8 years, even when they have invested some of their own funds.

Fee Structure. The fee structure—the fees the owner must pay to the operator for managing the property—makes up one of the most important contract provisions because it affects both the owner's and operator's profits. The fee structure is negotiable, and will vary from contract to contract depending on the bargaining power of the parties. Eyster categorizes the payments owners make to operators into three areas.

Technical assistance fees. Technical assistance fees cover the time and expertise of the operator as a consultant in the design of the facilities. Architectural and interior design are the services most commonly rendered, although equipment selection and help with security concerns such as lighting and locking systems are often involved as well.

Pre-opening management fees. Pre-opening management fees are similar to technical assistance fees in that they cover work done by the operator before the hotel opens. Pre-opening management activities include planning, staffing, training, marketing, budgeting, and other activities that the operator needs to perform before the property is ready to receive guests. These activities are very important—especially for hotel owners with no previous experience—since they may well influence the hotel's long-term success.

Post-opening management fees. Also known as simply "management fees," post-opening management fees are the fees paid to the operator for managing the property. In the case of a chain operator such as Hilton or Westin, the fee also covers the use of the established brand name. As has been noted, an independent management company does not bring a recognizable name to the negotiating table. If the owner wants a franchised name like Hampton Inn or Embassy Suite, or wants the property to be part of a referral reservation system like that of Best Western, he or she must deal directly with the franchisor or reservation system. That cost is distinct and separate from the management fee. This is the main justification for a chain operator's higher management fee—a chain operator gives the owner's hotel an already established name.

Today's post-opening management fees are almost always based on some kind of formula. Eyster says the formula is usually structured in one of the following ways:

- A basic fee only

- A basic fee plus an incentive

- A basic fee or an incentive fee, whichever is greater

- An incentive fee only[11]

The important thing in determining an equitable management fee is to relate the fee to the services received and to define the level of profit upon which the incentive fee is based.

The basic fee plus an incentive formula is the most commonly used. The amount of the basic fee ranges from 3% to 5% of gross revenues for chain management companies, 2½% to 4½% for independent companies. Although exact contract details are proprietary information, James and Hewitt indicate that for their companies, which are independent operators, incentive fees range from 2% to 5% of income before fixed charges. Hewitt says, "We look for a profit based on a percentage of gross revenues, or income, or cash flow. It's very dependent on the property, the revenue mix the property has, the project's financing, and so forth. There are different provisions in each contract, but we try to include all of these considerations in most contracts."[12]

In some cases where an operator has taken over a property that is failing or in bankruptcy, the operator, who is expected to turn the operation around, may also ask for an ownership interest. Hewitt notes that "these situations are becoming more common because of [financial] problems in the industry."[13]

Reporting Requirements. This provision defines the types of reports and the frequency with which they are to be provided by the operator to the owner. These reports include budgets, financial statements, variance reports between budget and actual performance, market plans, audited statements, and in some cases weekly and daily activity reports.

Approvals. Since the management contract is an agreement between owner and operator, decisions relative to the hotel's development or operation generally require input from both parties or at least an approval from one party of the other's decision. The agreement should define in what areas approvals are necessary. It is very common for a contract to call for the owner's approval of the general manager. In many cases owners are concerned about restaurant concepts and marketing and pricing strategies as well.

Some owners want to be much more involved than others. According to Hewitt, "In the '70s and '80s a management company presented a marketing program and then told the owner, 'We'll see you next year.'" He says things are dramatically different today. "We insist when we write a contract that the owners should have a degree of participation, sometimes weekly, maybe quarterly. Our regional and divisional people communicate with owners on a regular basis. The day-to-day decisions are of course left to management."[14] James says that there should be no surprises. "Owners should be kept informed about what the operator is doing. Those that are successful, communicate," he points out.[15]

Even when communication between the owner and the operator is good, there might be times when they do not agree, so the contract should contain provisions for settling disputes. According to Eyster, a number of management contracts contain arbitration provisions, specifying that the arbitration come from a hotel accounting or consulting firm or from the American Arbitration Association.[16]

Termination. There are three provisions in all management contracts that allow either party to terminate the management agreement:

1. Non-performance of a contract provision by the other party

2. One of the parties filing for bankruptcy

3. One of the parties causing licenses to be suspended or revoked[17]

Some contracts include other reasons for termination. These relate to the damage or loss of the property, or the sale of the property. Sometimes there is a "termination without cause" provision. This is likely to appear in contracts between operators and owners-in-foreclosure. Owners-in-foreclosure are often lenders who have taken over a property from the developer, usually due to bankruptcy, and require the freedom to dispose of the facility as soon as they can. If a contract is terminated without cause, the owner must pay a penalty fee to the operator to compensate for the loss of profits anticipated by the operator.

Operator Investment. Operators or management companies are in the business of managing, not investing. On the other hand, owners prefer a good-faith investment on the part of the operator. Today, more operators are investing in the properties they manage, usually in the form of loans or equity. When an operator loans money to an owner, the management contract specifies the amount; how the loan will be used (working capital, inventories, furniture, fixtures, and equipment); the term of the loan; and the interest rate. When the investment is an equity contribution, it may be in the form of cash, free technical services, waived pre-opening management fees, or even conversion of incentive fees.[18]

Operating Expenses. In addition to the normal costs of operating a hotel, an operator will incur expenses in its home office or on the premises of the property itself. Expenses such as centralized reservation systems, bulk purchasing, national advertising campaigns, and computer and accounting services are typical of the costs that an operator charges to the hotel's owner. The operator should clearly state the operating expenses it will pass on to the owner—this helps avoid challenges by the owner later on.

Employees. The hotel employees can be on the owner's payroll or the operator's payroll. Usually they are on the owner's payroll unless the owner is an insurance company or a government agency. In the United States, the law prohibits insurance companies and real estate investment trusts from operating hotels or any other properties; a government might be required to use civil service employees under some circumstances, which could prove difficult for the operator. Usually, even if employees are paid by the owner, the hotel's general manager is employed and paid by the operator. The general manager's salary is then charged back to the owner.

Although the employees may be on the owner's payroll, the operator is solely responsible for managing and administering the employees, including hiring, training, supervising, and—if necessary—firing them. It is usually clearly understood that under no circumstances may the owner interfere with the day-to-day operation of the hotel by issuing instructions to the staff. There have been several instances in the industry where owners have tried to do this and have caused severe disruptions in operations.

Other Provisions. Other major provisions of most management contracts include those that:

- Restrict the operator from competing in the same market area by operating another property within the area

- Specify the methods of transferring ownership or management interests to others by either party through a sale or a lease

- Stipulate exclusive rights to work with each other on future hotels

- Define the rights of each party in case the property is damaged or condemned

- Provide indemnification for the adverse performance of the other party

- Lay out a plan for a cash reserve for the replacement of furniture, fixtures, and equipment

Advantages and Disadvantages

Management contracts have advantages and disadvantages for each of the parties involved.

One of the primary disadvantages for owners is that while a management contract relieves them of day-to-day operating responsibilities, they still have to carry all or most of the financial burden. Although in recent years operators have increasingly provided loans and equity investments, owners are still primarily responsible for funding their properties. They must make up for losses or insufficient revenues to cover operating costs. In addition, management fees reduce owner profits.

Owners do, however, benefit from management contracts. The primary advantage is that they buy the services of an established hotel operator with a proven track record and a good reputation. Although a management fee must be paid, the potential for profit is increased by this arrangement.

An experienced operator can offer marketing expertise and systems of cost control that would otherwise not be available to the owner.

At first it may appear that operators have few serious disadvantages in a management contract arrangement. One of the greatest advantages from an operator's point of view is that it can control a large number of properties with a relatively limited investment. The operator's financial risk is much lower than the owner's.

Nevertheless, there are disadvantages to a management contract for operators as well. An operator's reputation is on the line every day at every hotel it manages. The operator must look to the owner for funding when there is a shortfall in revenues. If the owner refuses to supply it, or doesn't have it, the resulting sub-standard services and facilities will reflect on the operator. In addition, today the operator's real opportunity for profit lies in the incentive fee. An operator dealing with a difficult or poorly financed owner will probably never realize the anticipated profits.

A further disadvantage is that, unless the operator has provided equity, the owner may make decisions regarding the property's development or sale without the operator's input. The owner can also dismiss the operator or not renew the contract at the end of its term, possibly damaging the operator's reputation and taking away its opportunity to realize profits from the work it has done. A hotel is rarely an overnight success; it usually takes many years to plan, construct, and realize an operating profit, and only those who are in it for the long haul are likely to reap the rewards.

Chapter Summary

Hotels are a special kind of real estate. They are small, self-sufficient communities, and they need people with hotel expertise to operate them. In the last half of the twentieth century, inexperienced hotel owners such as investors and real estate developers began to acquire hotel properties. These owners realized that the best way to gain hotel management expertise was to bring in experienced hotel operators by (1) leasing the hotel to them, or (2) signing a management contract with them that allowed them to run the hotel. With the first leasing agreements, the operator paid rent for the building but kept whatever profits were made. With the first management contracts, operators did not pay rent and did not keep all of the hotel's profits—they received a basic fee to cover their overhead costs plus a share of the profits or an incentive fee.

A management contract is a written agreement between an owner of a hotel or motor inn and a hotel management company (operator) in which the owner employs the operator as an agent to assume full responsibility for managing the property. The operator can be a hotel chain with an established brand name or an independent management company.

Management contracts have three fundamental provisions: (1) the operator has the sole and exclusive right to manage the property without ownership interference; (2) the owner pays all operating and financing expenses and assumes ownership risks; and (3) the operator is indemnified from its actions except for gross negligence or fraud.

Management contracts are still evolving, for several reasons. Most new hotel owners are only interested in short-term involvement. Hotel development has slowed because the tax structure and business climate have changed and environmental concerns have become more important. In addition, owners are no longer willing to take all of the financial risks by themselves; operators are now sharing these risks.

The most important provisions in a management contract are those dealing with the operating term, the fee structure, reporting requirements, approvals, termination of the contract, operator investment, operating expenses, and employees.

From an owner's point of view, the advantage of hiring a management company is that it relieves him or her of the burden of running the hotel and provides experienced management personnel and operating systems. The disadvantages are that (1) the owner is still responsible for paying the bills even though the management company operates the hotel, and (2) management fees reduce the owner's profits.

Hotel management companies benefit from management contracts because the companies can grow without putting up large amounts of capital, keeping their financial risk low. However, difficult or under-financed owners can damage an operator's reputation and deprive it of profits it has earned. The owner can also dismiss the operator who built the business, even if the hotel is showing a profit.

Endnotes

1. *Hotel and Motel Management,* June 11, 1990, p. 43.

2. Robert M. James, personal interview, August 8, 1990.

3. James J. Eyster, *The Negotiation and Administration of Hotel and Restaurant Management Contracts,* 3d rev. ed. (Ithaca, N.Y.: School of Hotel Administration, Cornell University, 1988), p. 1.

4. Eyster, p. 1.

5. Eyster, p. 4.

6. Eyster, p. 6.

7. James interview.

8. James J. Eyster, "Sharing Risks and Decision Making: Recent Trends in the Negotiation of Management Contracts," *Cornell Quarterly,* May 1988, p. 43.

9. Thomas F. Hewitt, personal interview, May 26, 1990.

10. These provisions and some of the comments about them are adapted from Stephen Rushmore, "Make Sure Management Contracts Contain These Terms," *Lodging/Hospitality,* April 1988. The authors also wish to acknowledge their debt to Professor James J. Eyster. Many of the observations and comments relating to these provisions are based on Eyster's *The Negotiation and Administration of Hotel and Restaurant Management Contracts,* 3d rev. ed. (Ithaca, N.Y.: School of Hotel Administration, Cornell University, 1988).

11. Eyster, p. 48.

12. Hewitt interview.

13. Hewitt interview.

14. Hewitt interview.

15. James interview.

16. Eyster, *Negotiation and Administration,* p. 77.

17. Eyster, *Negotiation and Administration.*

18. Eyster, *Negotiation and Administration,* p. 43.

Key Terms

approval provisions
incentive fee
management contract
operating term
operator investment

post-opening management fees
pre-opening management fees
reporting requirements
technical assistance fees
termination provisions

Discussion Questions

1. How can a hotel owner who is not a hotelier ensure that the property is managed effectively?

2. What is an incentive fee?

3. What three provisions are common to almost every management contract?

4. What are the differences between a lease and a management contract?

5. What are some of the industry-wide changes responsible for the evolution of management contracts?

6. In negotiating a management contract, which party prefers a long-term contract and which party prefers a short-term contract? Why?

7. What are four types of fees owners pay to operators?

8. What are four formulas for calculating the post-opening management fee(s)?

9. What do the "approvals," "termination," and "employees" provisions of a management contract cover?

10. What are the advantages and disadvantages of management contracts, from both the owner's and operator's points of view?

Part IV

Business Ethics and
Future Trends

Chapter Outline

14 Ethics in Hospitality Management

In this chapter we define and discuss ethics in the hospitality industry. The chapter distinguishes ethics from social responsibility, and explores how values are arrived at. Concepts such as whether it is ever right to lie are examined. Ethical issues in hospitality such as discrimination, AIDS, advertising claims, and truth-in-menu laws are discussed. Finally, an ethical litmus test is offered.

What Is Ethics?

There is a children's story about a group of blind men from "Indostan" who by touching an elephant attempt to describe to each other what it is like. The first man, falling against the elephant's side, says the elephant is like a wall. The second, feeling the elephant's tusk, tells the others that the elephant is like a spear. The third, with the animal's trunk in hand, says the elephant is like a rope. The fourth is certain an elephant is like a tree, having touched a leg, while the fifth blind man feels the elephant's ear and concludes elephants are like fans. The sixth, seizing its tail, pronounces that an elephant is like a snake:

> So these men of Indostan
> Disputed loud and long
> Each in his own opinion
> Exceedingly stiff and strong;
> Though each was partly in the right
> And all were in the wrong![1]

Trying to describe ethics is similar to the blind men describing the elephant. Depending on how we approach the question and our own system of values, we can come up with very different answers.

Ethics is a set of moral principles and values that we use to answer questions of right and wrong. Ethics can also be defined as the study of the general nature of morals and of the specific moral choices to be made by the individual in his or her relationship with others. We like this definition because it focuses on moral choices and relationships with others.

There is evidence that many people have forgotten the true meaning of ethics. Today we tend to think of ethics in pragmatic terms—our choices are based on what seems reasonable or logical to us according to our own personal value system. This is called "ethical relativism" because it casts ethics in the role of being relative to what the situation is or how we feel about it. In truth, ethics is something different. The very concept of ethics suggests that there is a real distinction between good and bad, right and wrong, and that it is our obligation to do our best to distinguish between these and then always try to do what is right. Although we all have different personal values and morals, we should recognize that there are some universal principles that virtually all religions, cultures, and societies agree upon. These principles form the basis of ethical behavior. The foundation of all of these principles is the belief that other people's rights are as important as our own and that it is our duty not to harm others if we can avoid it. In fact, it is our duty to help them whenever possible. This idea is at the heart of the value system of most societies, tribes, and organizations. Without it, it would not be possible to live and work together.

Social Responsibility and Business Ethics

It is important to distinguish between social responsibility and business ethics. The concept of social responsibility suggests that "at any one time in any society there is a set of generally accepted relationships, obligations, and duties between the major institutions and the people. Philosophers and political theorists have called this set of common understandings 'the social contract.'"[2] This contract differs among societies and may change over time. For example, today we expect that businesses will take care (1) not to pollute the air we breathe or the water we drink, (2) not to damage the ozone layer, (3) to offer fair wages and employee benefits, (4) to provide a satisfactory product or service at a reasonable price, and (5) to in some way participate in making the community in which they operate a better place. These are not ethical considerations—they are part of a "deal" that says that we as consumers expect companies to act in this manner because they are a part of the society we all share (see Exhibit 14.1).

Many companies recognize this and have stated publicly their belief that it is good business to be a good citizen. They support local arts, build parks, raise funds for charities, and try to put back some of their profits into the community that has made their success possible. Domino's Pizza has formed SCORE, its Strategic Committee on Respecting the Environment. A joint committee of company officials and franchisees, SCORE oversees an environmentally responsible agenda that includes recycling, supplying non-toxic cleaning agents to franchise units, and forming a non-profit wildlife habitat.[3]

Ethical behavior is a whole different matter. During the savings and loan scandals that erupted in the United States in 1990, it was revealed that many savings and loan organizations that lavishly contributed funds to United Way and other charities, sponsored symphony and ballet performances, and generally acted in a socially responsible manner were at the same time stealing millions of dollars from depositors. These companies were trying to create an image of being socially responsible, but were entirely lacking in ethics because, while they were contributing to society with one hand, they were stealing with the other.

Exhibit 14.1   Social Responsibility and McDonald's

McDonald's uses booklets, posters, and other public relations materials to inform its customers of the many ways in which it tries to be socially responsible. Courtesy of McDonald's Corporation, Oak Brook, Illinois.

How We Arrive at Our Values

Author Hunter Lewis says that there are six ways in which we arrive at our values—our personal beliefs about what is "good" and "just." These beliefs are arrived at in the same way as all of our other beliefs. The six kinds of moral reasoning are:

1. *Authority.* Beliefs can be derived from an authority. Here we take someone else's word, such as that of the Bible or the church.

2. *Deductive logic.* Deductive logic is another basis for our beliefs. Here is a simple example of deductive logic: If all chocolate is fattening, and if this is chocolate, then this must be fattening.

3. *Sense experience.* Often beliefs are arrived at through sense experience. In these cases we gain direct knowledge through our five senses. We decide that something is true because we heard it; can see it with our own eyes; or can touch it, taste it, or smell it.

4. *Emotion.* Emotion can dictate our beliefs. We may "feel" that something is true. Sometimes our emotions concerning others color our ideas about them. For example, if we love someone we tend to idealize him or her. Criminals might have parents who say, "He's a good boy" or "She's such a good girl."

5. *Intuition.* Intuition is another way knowledge is arrived at. Here we use our unconscious or intuitive mind to process information and discover the solution to a problem. Sometimes we refer to our intuition as our "gut feeling."

6. *Science.* Science is the basis of some beliefs. When we use the scientific method we use our senses to collect facts, our intuition to develop a hypothesis, our logic to experiment, and our sense experience again to complete the test. Physicians use this process to arrive at their beliefs about the causes of disease and what cures to prescribe.[4]

Although we may use all six techniques of moral reasoning at one time or another, Lewis believes that each of us has a dominant or primary technique. To discover your dominant technique, Lewis suggests you ask yourself who you would confide in if you had a serious personal issue on your mind and wanted advice.

If your answer is a priest, a minister, a rabbi, or another religious leader, your primary mode may be to use authority as the basis for your beliefs. If you would ask a professor of philosophy to help you, you would be looking for someone who could think through your problem in a highly structured or logical way. If your confidant were a professor of history and literature who is also a good friend, you might be relying on his or her own personal sense experience plus the experience of Western culture as contained in its history and literature. Suppose you turn to a family member or very close friend. Here your dominant reasoning style could be characterized as emotional. Clearly you are looking for empathy from a member of your peer group. Some people would seek an answer from a Buddhist or guru of immense calm and unspoken wisdom. They would be hoping to use meditation and other tools to unlock their powers of intuition. If you don't recognize yourself in any of these groups, perhaps you would consult a psychiatrist who could offer an appraisal based on social science methods and principles.[5]

The point is that we are all likely to have a different set of values or ethics depending on which moral reasoning technique is our dominant one. To some of us, some actions are wrong because the Bible or the Torah or the Koran says so. To others, only those actions that our friends and family might condemn if they knew about them would be wrong. Many believe that anything goes "so long as it isn't against the law" or even "so long as you don't get caught." Nearly everyone agrees that it is a good idea to tell the truth, and that stealing from others is wrong.

Is Business Like Poker?
There is a school of thought that recognizes that honesty is the best policy and it is never right to lie or steal, but holds that the rules of business are different and that behavior that is unacceptable elsewhere is legitimate in the business world.

In 1968, business writer Alfred Carr attracted a good deal of attention by comparing business to a poker game:

> No one expects poker to be played on the ethical principles preached in churches. In poker it is right and proper to bluff a friend out of the rewards of being dealt a good hand. Poker's own brand of ethics is different from the ethical ideals of civilized human relationships. The game calls for distrust of the other fellow. It ignores the claim of friendship. Cunning, deception and concealment of one's strength and intentions, not kindness and open-heartedness, are vital in poker. No one thinks any worse of poker on that account. And no one should think any the worse of the game of business because its standards of right and wrong differ from the prevailing traditions of morality in our society.[6]

While this argument may seem to make sense at first glance, Robert Solomon and Kristine Hanson—authors of *It's Good Business,* a book about business ethics—point out that it shows a misunderstanding of both poker and business:

> Bluffing isn't lying, which is as forbidden in playing poker as it is in business. Most business is conducted in conversation where truth and mutual trust are essential. . . . A poker game involves only its players; business is essential to the well-being of the entire society. The rules of poker protect the game and its players; the rules of business protect everyone else too. Carr's suggestion ignores that core of ethics that does not vary from community to community— which we call 'morality.' Morality consists of those basic rules which are not merely a matter of a single game or practice, but provide the preconditions of every game, every practice. Carr may be trivially correct when he says the rules of poker are different from the rules of other games and practices, but he is quite wrong when he suggests that this constitutes a divergence from morality.[7]

In other words, Solomon and Hanson point out that the goals of business are to promote a good life for every individual and wealth for the nation as a whole. The goal of poker is to redistribute the wealth among a small group of players. Because the goals are different, and because much more is at stake, the rules of poker and business should and must be different as well.

Is Honesty Always the Best Policy?
According to some moral philosophers, honesty is the only acceptable policy. They argue that all lying, whether "little white lies" or vicious falsehoods, injures both the liar and the person lied to and may indeed injure society as well. When someone lies to Congress about the extent of the United States' military involvement in an area, or the cost of a weapon or social welfare program, the result is that our elected officials do not have the information they need to protect our interests, which is what we have elected them to do. The principle involved here is described by Sissela Bok— author of *Lying: Moral Choice in Public and Private Life*—who writes, "All our

choices depend on our estimates of what is the case; these estimates must in turn often rely on information from others. Lies distort this information and therefore our situation as we perceive it, as well as our choices."[8]

When we lie to others, Bok argues, we take away their right to make their own choices and instead manipulate them by giving them false information on which to base their decisions. In a real sense we are taking away their freedom. Unless we have a very strong reason for doing so, lies cannot and should not be tolerated.

Liars like to believe that their reasons for lying are sound. Most liars do not believe anyone ought to lie to them, but justify their own behavior on the grounds that they are protecting someone else's feelings or confidences, or that their lie is necessary to protect their business or their employees. But according to Bok, when we lie for any reason we run risks that we may be found out and our credibility will be damaged. Even worse, very few lies are solitary ones. The first lie "must be thatched with another or it will rain through."[9] Eventually

> psychological barriers wear down; lies seem more necessary, less reprehensible; the ability to make moral distinctions can coarsen; the liar's perception of his chances of being caught may warp. . . . For all these reasons, I believe that we must at the very least accept as an initial premise Aristotle's view that lying is "mean and culpable" and that truthful statements are preferable to lies in the absence of special considerations. . . . Only where a lie is a last resort can one even begin to consider whether or not it is morally justified.[10]

Solomon and Hanson take a slightly more liberal view of lying. "Lying may always be wrong, but some lies are more wrong than others."[11] While they too believe that it is never right to lie, they suggest that sometimes it may be prudent or preferable to telling the truth. A sales representative, for instance, might understandably sound more enthusiastic about a product than he or she really is, and most people understand that salespeople present the favorable side of a product or service, not all sides. On the whole, however, they take the position that in business as in personal life, "telling a lie always requires extra thought and some very good reasons to show that this cardinal violation of the truth should be tolerated.[12]

Each person must decide for themselves what such a good reason would be. Clearly, if a robber walks into your business and asks for all your money and you say all you have is in the cash register, when in fact there is a considerable amount stored in the back room, this is a matter of self-preservation and one can justify lying. What about telling an employee who you are letting go that you haven't got enough work, when in fact your real reason is that the person is incompetent? In this case it might be easier to lie, but one can argue that such a lie is easily seen through and it might be kinder in the long run to be honest with the employee so that he or she can look for more suitable work. Each case needs to be looked at individually, with our bias always on the side of telling the truth.

The Search for a Common Moral Ground

Despite the fact that everyone may use a different set of values to determine what is ethical, many philosophers and educators who have spent their lives thinking about ethics have concluded that there are some universal moral imperatives or obligations that form the basis of civilized behavior and are necessary for any society to function. Michael Josephson is an attorney and founder of the Joseph and Edna Josephson Institute for the Advancement of Ethics, a non-profit institute that has been at the forefront of defining ethical behavior for businesses. In an interview with Bill Moyers on the Public Broadcasting System (PBS), Josephson said:

> History, theology, philosophy will show that every enlightened civilization has had a sense of right and wrong and a need to try to distinguish them. Now we may disagree over time as to what is right and what is wrong—but there has never been a disagreement in any philosophy about the importance of knowing the difference. The things that are right are the things that help people and society. They are things like compassion, honesty, fairness, accountability. They are absolute universal ethical values.[13]

Josephson points out that the Golden Rule, which says "Do unto others as you would have them do unto you," occurred in Greek culture and in Chinese culture thousands of years before Christ articulated his version.[14]

Josephson believes that most people have a built-in sense of what is right and wrong. The proof, he says, is that we feel guilt and shame when we do the wrong thing. Despite that knowledge, we often ignore our ideals about what constitutes proper behavior for a number of reasons. We have become a rights-oriented society. Sometimes we feel we have a right to certain things, but we have forgotten that with those rights come certain responsibilities. Too often, says Josephson, we measure our lives by what we get, what we acquire, and who we know. "It's the need to win, to be clever, and to be successful in other people's eyes that sometimes causes people to sacrifice the fundamental ideals," he says.

Sometimes businesspeople feel that the only way to be competitive and win is to be completely selfish—put their own interests above those of everyone else. Josephson tells the story of a lawyer who goes on a camping trip with a friend. They both have their backpacks on their backs, and suddenly they see a cougar about 20 yards away. The lawyer takes off his backpack, and the friend says, "What are you going to do?" The lawyer says, "I'm going to run for it." The friend says, "But you can't outrun a cougar." And the lawyer says, "I don't have to outrun the cougar. I just have to outrun you."[15]

Some justify the philosophy of putting our own interests ahead of everyone else's by saying that life is like having your hand in a bucket of water—when you remove it, the water settles down within moments and no one knew you ever lived. Therefore you should try to get everything you can for yourself because it will make no difference to anyone else in the long run. There is another way of looking at the world and your place in it that holds that you can make a permanent and positive impact on society by doing what you can to make differences in the lives of the people who you come in contact with. You can bring some of them happiness and joy, and help alleviate the pain and suffering of others.

Sometimes people argue that when you are dealing with unethical people, you have to be unethical too or you will be stepped on. Josephson says, "There is usually a choice of ethical and unethical behaviors. We tell people, unless you have three alternatives to every major problem, you haven't thought hard enough. As soon as you have three, you can find one of them that's ethical."[16]

In the long run it is the philosophy of helping people rather than taking advantage of them or using them for our own benefit that most of us come to believe in, but the sad thing is that for many of us this occurs late in life, when we have learned that accomplishing a particular task or career goal did not bring us all the satisfaction we had hoped for. "We know that nobody on a deathbed says, 'I wish I had spent more time at the office.' People's values begin to change when they reflect upon how futile most of the flurry of activity was. And the fact is that a good conscience is the best pillow. Living a good life is the most important thing for us."[17]

Deontology versus Utilitarianism. Donald Robin, professor of marketing at Mississippi State, and Eric Reidenbach, Director of the Bureau of Business Research at the University of Southern Mississippi, point out that there are two major traditions that dominate current thinking in moral philosophy. These are called deontology and utilitarianism.[18]

Deontology holds that there are basic or universal ideals that should direct our thinking. It is based on the beliefs of Immanuel Kant, an eighteenth-century German philosopher. Kant believed that the human mind could not possibly comprehend or arrive at the truth about God or the universe through pure logic or thought. He said that the only judgments we were capable of making were those based on evidence that we could see or prove the existence of. Kant believed in the existence of God, but in effect said we have to take this on faith since we can't prove it by pure logic. Once one admits there is a God, then it is possible to make logical and reasonable assumptions about what is expected of us and how we are required to act. In short, there is a scientifically-arrived-at ideal that is necessary for humans to adhere to and for which adequate evidence exists, once one admits there is a God. Deontology proposes that ethical behavior is simply a matter of doing God's will. Since most of us believe that God is good, then goodwill or loving other human beings as God loves us is the universal principle on which all moral behavior must be based.

Along with the concept of goodwill goes a concept of duty to keep one's promises, which is known as Kant's categorical imperative—an absolute and universally binding moral law. Kant believed in always telling the truth because if we cannot believe what others tell us, then agreements and even conversations between people are not possible. Would you loan money to anyone if you knew that he or she had no intention of repaying it, even though he or she promised to? Deontology, in effect, says that the only way to measure whether an action is ethical is to ask whether we would be willing to live in a world where *everyone* routinely did the same thing. If our actions would be acceptable to us as a universal law, then they are correct and ethical.

Conversely, utilitarianism does not seek universal principles that can be applied to all situations, but instead says that ethical behavior consists of the greatest good for the greatest number. One determines this by "performing a social cost/benefit analysis and acting on it."[19] Robin and Reidenbach show that this philosophy is grounded in the ideas of Adam Smith, who said that "capitalistic systems, by providing the greatest material good for the greatest number, are considered ethical from a perspective of economic philosophy."[20] They point out, however, that there are some major criticisms of utilitarianism that need to be considered. One is that an action might do a small amount of good for a large number of people while at the same time severely injuring a small group. Is it always ethical to replace a small office or apartment building in a suburban neighborhood with a large high-rise? Such a building might benefit the occupants, but be a disaster for the neighborhood by bringing in large amounts of unwanted traffic and accompanying noise and pollution. Moreover, utilitarianism suggests that each action should be judged on its own merits. When we do this there is a lack of consistency which opens the door to generalizations and excuses. One cannot say that anything is either moral or immoral, ethical or unethical, if "it all depends." For example, can an accountant embezzling company funds be excused because he or she believes the company is "ripping people off, so why shouldn't I?" Generally we reject that kind of rationalization because it is entirely subjective.

Ethical Relativism. Ethical relativists suggest that there are no universal ethical principles at all; each issue must be considered in its situational or cultural context. For example, it might be unethical to bribe a government official in the United States to obtain a building permit or zoning variance, but quite acceptable in some other countries where bribes are a routine part of doing business. (Students should note that while one can debate whether bribing government officials is ethical or not, it is most definitely against U.S. law for any American corporation or citizen to do so.) This kind of reasoning is also known as situational ethics. It is a convenient ethical code for those who are not sure what their ethical values are or how they are arrived at, but, like utilitarianism, it provides little guidance for those who believe in a clear and consistent code of ethics.

Ethical Issues in Hospitality

Each day hospitality managers are faced with a variety of business decisions with ethical overtones. Too often, in making these decisions ethical considerations are ignored.

Here are a few examples of decisions that a hotel general manager or someone in a similar position at a club or restaurant might make in the ordinary course of business:

New Menu
You have just approved a new menu that retains many of your favorite high-calorie, high-cholesterol, high-sodium foods. There are no nutritious alternatives on the menu. You reason that hotel guests liked what was on the old menu and they will keep coming back as in the past.

Bumped Reservation
You have just been approached by an influential guest regarding a birthday party he would like to hold at the hotel two months from now. Unfortunately, the hotel's meeting room was booked for that date just yesterday. The guest asks you to bump the person who

reserved the room. He suggests you tell that person the sales manager made a mistake in booking the room when it had previously been reserved. You agree to do so.

Cashier's Integrity

You decide to test a cashier's integrity. The cashier has been with the club ten years and has a flawless record. You slip a $50 bill in the register receipts. At the end of the day, the cashier shows a $5 overage. Upon questioning, the cashier admits to pocketing the $45 difference.

Free Wine

You recently purchased 20 cases of wine for the hotel from a new beverage supplier. Without your advance knowledge, the supplier delivers one free case of wine to your residence. You decide to keep the free case for your personal use, since it did not influence the purchase of the 20 cases for the hotel.[21]

In a *Lodging* magazine poll, 400 lodging managers were asked if they agreed with the ethics of the manager's decision in each of these hypothetical scenarios. The results of that poll are shown in Exhibit 14.2.

The "new menu" scenario considers how much responsibility each of us must take for the welfare of others. We may not consider ourselves our brother's keeper, but it can be argued that as hospitality professionals it is our duty to include low-calorie, nutritious meals on the menu and encourage their purchase.

We were told by one knowledgeable hotelier that meeting room reservations get "bumped" all the time. That may be so, but if we are going to respect the rights of others, the fair thing is to allow the person who made the reservation first to keep it. Moreover, it is wrong to lie and say the other reservation was made earlier when it was not. On the other hand, if we are ethical relativists we might argue that if we do not go along with this influential guest we may lose a substantial amount of business, which could mean laying off employees and other consequences that may hurt others.

The case of the cashier's integrity also bears on the rights of others. Is it fair to put a loyal employee to a test of this nature without warning him or her in advance, especially when there is no evidence that anything is wrong? Would we like to be treated this way?

The free wine scenario poses the question of what constitutes honesty. The wine may have been delivered after the hotel's wine was ordered, but it still represents an unauthorized payment to the manager for "services rendered." The manager could return the free case and ask the supplier to give the hotel an appropriate discount on its wine purchases if he or she wants to show appreciation. Or the manager might give the extra case of wine to the hotel so that the hotel could profit from its sale. One test of whether it is ethical to keep this wine for personal use would be for the manager to ask how it would feel if other managers at the hotel found out about it.

Linda K. Enghagen, an attorney and member of the faculty at the University of Massachusetts, surveyed 113 four-year colleges and universities on ethical issues in hospitality and tourism. While a total of 35 different issues were raised, the ten that received the most mentions were:

Exhibit 14.2 Ethics Poll of Lodging Managers

The New Menu, Bumped Reservation, Cashier's Integrity, and Free Wine scenarios are four scenarios lodging managers were asked to respond to by *Lodging*. When rating the manager's decision in each of the scenarios, the polled managers were asked whether they (a) strongly agreed, (b) moderately agreed, (c) were unsure, (d) moderately disagreed, or (e) strongly disagreed. Here are the results.

New Menu

(a) Strongly agree   6.1%
(b) Moderately agree   15.5%
(c) Unsure   8.9%
(d) Moderately disagree   24.9%
(e) Strongly disagree   44.6%

Comment: The responses suggest a fairly high level of health consciousness among hotel managers.

Bumped Reservation

(a) Strongly agree   1.3%
(b) Moderately agree   5.1%
(c) Unsure   4.6%
(d) Moderately disagree   13.7%
(e) Strongly disagree   75.3%

Comment: Clearly, managers believe that guest favoritism leads to guest dissatisfaction.

Cashier's Integrity

(a) Strongly agree   36.5%
(b) Moderately agree   25.6%
(c) Unsure   9.4%
(d) Moderately disagree   11.7%
(e) Strongly disagree   16.8%

Comment: A minority of managers evidently believed that the test put too much pressure on the employee; however, 62.1% agreed with the manager's test.

Free Wine

(a) Strongly agree   7.4%
(b) Moderately agree   16.5%
(c) Unsure   10.6%
(d) Moderately disagree   17.5%
(e) Strongly disagree   48.0%

Comment: 65.5% of respondents apparently felt that acceptance of the wine could influence future beverage purchases by the hotel.

Source: Adapted from Ray Schmidgall, "Hotel Scruples," *Lodging*, January 1991, pp. 38–40.

- Managing an ethical environment
- Relations with customers and employees
- Honesty
- Employee privacy rights
- Alcohol/drug testing
- Environmental issues
- Relations with foreign governments
- Codes of ethics and self-governance
- Employee abuse of alcohol/drugs
- Conflicts of interest[22]

These issues reflect the academic perspective. Industry leaders have cited many other ethical problems that concern them. These include:

- Sanitation
- Travel agent commissions

- Overbooking

- AIDS

- Employment discrimination by age, sex, or race

- Kickbacks

- Concealing income from the Internal Revenue Service

- Yield management

- Advertising claims

- Raiding of competition's staff

- Truth-in-menu laws

- Meeting the needs of disabled customers and employees

- Adequate safety and security measures

Let's take a closer look at some of these industry issues.

Discrimination

Even though it is unlawful, and a company may have policies forbidding it, discrimination of one sort or another can still occur simply because some managers may have value systems that lead them to discriminate in certain instances, perhaps unconsciously.

Indeed, discrimination may be one of the most common violations of ethics found in the hospitality industry. Because there are so many subtle forms of discrimination—based on age, race, religion, gender, sexual preference, nationality, or physical attributes—discrimination is often difficult to recognize, and in many cases it is neither malicious nor intentional. That does not excuse it, however, and managers must know where they are likely to find it and how to eliminate it.

Almost all discrimination involves fear of one sort or another. We live in uncertain times in which huge political and social upheavals have taken place. These changes are bound to make us uneasy. Many of us are afraid of losing our jobs. Others are afraid of losing power or prestige, or simply not "belonging" anymore. One way these fears manifest themselves is through discrimination. Discrimination allows us to express those fears and rationalize them by giving them faces and names. Unfortunately, many opportunists have made a career out of exploiting our concerns and thus have muddied the waters even more. Their ideas fuel our fears and these fears sometimes express themselves in the workplace.

One of the most serious and blatant forms of discrimination still practiced in many parts of the world is racial. Many societies now recognize that affirmative action may need to be taken to restore to minority groups the freedom and opportunities that have been denied them in the past. The hospitality industry faces the same challenges as the rest of society. With the number of new jobs available every year, there is ample opportunity to give everyone a chance at a better job—no matter what their color—if they want and deserve it.

Discrimination also occurs in policies sometimes found in clubs and hotels that try to restrict the use of their facilities by certain racial and ethnic groups. Hotels have been known to discourage group business from certain groups of people because "our regular guests might feel uncomfortable." While some managers may think in these terms when making a business decision, ethical managers must ask if they can in good conscience be a party to a policy that clearly conflicts with ethical standards.

Sex discrimination is another problem that needs to be addressed. For years, most male chefs believed that women had no place in professional kitchens, and even today that belief is widely held. Sometimes this is based on fallacies such as "it's a man's world" or "those large pots are too heavy for a woman to lift." But discrimination is not confined to the kitchen. Female hotel general managers are still relatively scarce when one considers that more than 50% of most hotels' employees are women. There are also questions of salaries and promotions. Male managers often assume that, since a married woman has a husband to help support her, she is in less need of a raise. Sometimes a female manager is not offered a promotion that involves a transfer to another city because it is wrongly assumed that her husband's job dictates where the family will live. Women have been denied sales positions because it was felt that men were better suited for traveling and going out drinking with clients. In other words, a female manager is just not "one of the boys." Discrimination on this basis is clearly unethical, as well as being unlawful in the United States.

Sexual Harassment

Another ethical problem that needs to be addressed in the workplace is sexual harassment. Men as well as women can be victims of sexual harassment by superiors of the opposite sex. Sexual harassment by employers includes asking their employees for dates, making sexual jokes or comments, touching employees inappropriately, or suggesting that sex will result in a promotion. The pressure to not complain when one's job and economic well-being are on the line is sometimes overwhelming. Companies cannot and should not allow anyone to believe for a moment that such behavior will go unnoticed or will be excused.

AIDS in the Workplace

AIDS is a good example of how prejudice and hysteria have affected some managers' ability to make fair and impartial decisions. There is no doubt that the fear of contracting AIDS is a prevalent one. As of July 1990 the U.S. Public Health Service reported 143,286 AIDS cases, and it is estimated that somewhere between 390,000 and 480,000 Americans will be counted as new AIDS cases by 1993.[23] But by now most of us are aware that AIDS is not contracted easily, that there are many reasonable precautions that can be taken to protect ourselves, and that the epidemic is for the most part limited to certain high-risk groups.

A major issue for hospitality managers has been the subject of testing employees for AIDS. Some people believe that carriers ought to be identified so that they can be informed and prevented from spreading the disease. But as columnist William Schneider points out, "What about their right not to be forced to learn whether they are under a probable sentence of death?"[24] There are other rights involved as well. Should employees who have tested positive for the HIV virus, but have not yet come down with AIDS (and may never come down with it), be promoted? One could argue that they should not be because they may not be able to stay in their new position long enough to benefit the employer, but this is the worst kind of discrimination. No one knows how long a person in this situation will remain healthy, and to deny him or her a well-deserved promotion seems unfair by any standard. The issue is most often not one of promotion but simply of keeping one's job. It is illegal in the United States to discriminate against AIDS-infected workers, since (1) they are considered to be "handicapped," and (2) their condition cannot be transmitted via food or casual contact, according to the latest scientific studies. Nevertheless, many hotel and restaurant operators have no written or expressed policy on the subject. A few operators are quite explicit about their attitudes. Fuddruckers, a hamburger chain based in Wakefield, Massachusetts, clearly states that "the company's policy is not to discriminate in any way against someone infected with AIDS, and if asked, to provide a list of AIDS-related social services."[25]

Advertising Claims

The purpose of advertising is to sell products and services. Most people understand this and therefore are skeptical about advertising claims. They are used to puffery and know that some restaurants that claim to serve "gourmet" meals may offer quite ordinary fare, and that resorts that offer "a luxury vacation" may in reality offer a mediocre one. Most people rely on recommendations from friends, relatives, and travel agents when making dining or travel plans, and take the claims made in brochures and advertising with a grain of salt.

There is a difference between puffery and outright deception. Resorts that advertise that they are "on the beach" should be on the beach and not across the street from it. Some resorts advertise that they offer golf, but neglect to mention that the course they use is 20 miles away and starting times are difficult to come by. If a rate is advertised, it should be one that is readily available.

Unlike a television set, which can be returned if it is not satisfactory, a vacation is not returnable and could represent an investment in time and money that cannot be replaced. Hoteliers have a moral duty to disclose all of the relevant details of their properties so that consumers can make a fair judgment as to whether their expectations are going to be met.

Truth-in-Menu Laws

Many states have enacted truth-in-menu laws, and in some cases fines can be as high as $500 for misrepresenting an item on the menu. But beyond legal obligations, there is a moral one to present what is being sold fairly and honestly. People have a right to know what they are eating, as well as to have enough information to make a fair evaluation about whether they are getting their money's worth. If a menu offers a 12-ounce sirloin steak, it ought to be 12 ounces every time it is served. Honest restaurateurs are proud of the fact that their gulf shrimp really comes from the Gulf of Mexico and their prime beef really is prime and not a lower grade. These may seem like minor points to some, but consumers have indicated that they are important.

Must There Be a Code of Ethics?

Hospitality businesses that do not already have a code of ethics should develop one to live by and to make decisions with. Without such a code, how can a manager know what the company considers ethical or unethical? If every manager makes decisions based on his or her own code of ethics, then a corporation may have no ethics at all, or a lot of different ethical codes, depending on who is calling the shots. Like other management issues, a company's ethics need to reflect the company's mission and must be communicated to those who are responsible for carrying it out. Hospitality is a "people business"; ethics deals with our relationships with other people. For this reason a code of ethics is almost mandatory to achieve a unified direction and a satisfactory level of control over the conduct of business.

There is ample evidence to suggest that without a code of ethics some managers will make unethical decisions. According to a survey done by *Personnel Journal* magazine, middle managers—especially those 40 to 45 years old—are the most likely executives to do something unethical.[26] Some of these managers have a desire to "make it before it's too late" and thus strive to advance by shortcuts. In addition, they may have developed the attitude that "the company owes me" and therefore may be prone to making special purchasing deals involving personal benefits or cheating on expense accounts.[27]

One business that has a very strict and explicit code of ethics is the Sheraton Corporation, a division of ITT. Sheraton's managers are expected to strictly comply with all the business ethics policies of both ITT and Sheraton. The policies are quite lengthy and include the following:

Conflicts of Interest
ITT employees are to exercise sound judgment guided by the highest ethical standards of honesty and integrity in all matters affecting ITT. No employee may abuse a corporate position for personal advantage or promote any actions contrary to ITT's stated ethical standards. . . .
Employees and their immediate families shall not accept any gifts of cash or items of more than token value from third parties in connection with ITT business. All employees shall report immediately to their supervisors any offer or gift of more than token value.

Quality
ITT's success as a corporation in fulfilling its obligation to shareholders is ultimately measured in terms of customer satisfaction. It is ITT policy to provide products and services that satisfy needs and expectations of our customers; conform to appropriate specifications and contractual agreements, including reliability requirements; are safe for intended use and foreseeable misuse; and meet all applicable statutory requirements of local, regional, and national agencies.[28]

Stephen S. J. Hall, a quality assurance consultant and the founder of the International Institute for Quality and Ethics in Service and Tourism (IIQEST), has proposed the ethics code for hotels shown in Exhibit 14.3.

Some Ethical Litmus Tests

Even with laws and company policies and rules, ethical behavior is an intensely personal matter that every manager and employee must wrestle with. There are no easy guidelines that apply equally well in all circumstances. Ethical philosophers often talk about the moral duty of taking into account the interests of all stakeholders in arriving at a decision. A stakeholder is anyone who has a stake in the outcome of a given decision. These could be your employees or your boss, the owners of the company you work for, the families of your employees, or the community in which the business

Exhibit 14.3 Sample Ethics Code for Hotels

1. We acknowledge ethics and morality as inseparable elements of doing business, and will test every decision against the highest standards of honesty, legality, fairness, impunity, and conscience.

2. We will conduct ourselves personally and collectively at all times such as to bring credit to the service and tourism industry at large.

3. We will concentrate our time, energy, and resources on the improvement of our own products and services, and will not denigrate our competition in the pursuit of our own success.

4. We will treat all guests equally regardless of race, religion, nationality, creed, or sex.

5. We will deliver all standards of service and product with total consistency to every guest.

6. We will provide a totally safe and sanitary environment at all times for every guest and employee.

7. We will strive constantly, in words, actions, and deeds, to develop and maintain the highest level of trust and understanding among guests, clients, employees, employers, and the public at large.

8. We will provide every employee at every level all of the knowledge, training, equipment, and motivation required to perform his or her own tasks according to our published standards.

9. We will guarantee that every employee at every level will have the same opportunity to perform and advance, and will be evaluated against the same standard as all employees engaged in similar tasks.

10. We will actively and consciously work to protect and preserve our natural environment and natural resources in all that we do.

11. We will seek a fair and honest profit, no more, no less.

Source: IIQEST Ltd., Twenty Country Way, Scituate, Massachusetts 02044.

operates. Sometimes managers or employees who are forced to implement unethical policies become whistleblowers and let other stakeholders know what is happening rather than be a silent part of an unethical action or plan.

Blanchard and Peale, in their book *The Power of Ethical Management*, have three simple questions that they believe managers ought to ask themselves when making a decision:

1. *Is it legal?* Will I be violating either civil law or company policy?

2. *Is it balanced?* Is it fair to all concerned in the short term as well as the long term? Does it promote win-win relationships?

3. *How will it make me feel about myself?* Will it make me proud? Would I feel good if my decision were published in the newspaper? Would I feel good if my family knew about it?[29]

Chapter Summary

Ethics is a set of moral principles and values that we use to answer questions of right and wrong. It focuses on moral choices and relationships with others. Although we all have different personal values and morals, there are some universal principles which virtually all religions, cultures, and societies agree upon. The basis of all of these principles is that other people's rights are as important as our own, and that it is our duty not to do anything to harm others.

Social responsibility is not the same as ethics, although the concepts are related. Companies have an unwritten social contract with society covering their rights and obligations. Ethics consists of "doing the right thing" in areas that may be entirely unrelated to that social contract, such as dealing with employees and customers.

There are six ways in which we arrive at our values about what is "good" and "just": authority, deductive logic, sense experience, emotion, intuition, and science. One of these ways is usually dominant within an individual and tends to influence the way he or she arrives at personal values. Although everyone is likely to have different values, on the whole most agree that it is a good idea to tell the truth whenever possible, and that stealing from others is wrong.

While some have argued that business is like poker and thus principles of ethical behavior do not apply in business, a careful examination shows that because businesses have different goals and there is much more at stake, the rules of business and poker must and should be different.

Honesty is always the best policy. When we lie we manipulate other people and impair their ability to make choices based on true information. You should think very carefully before telling a lie, and have some very good reasons for violating this cardinal rule of ethics.

The most basic ethical rule is the Golden Rule: Do unto others as you would have them do unto you.

There are two major traditions that dominate current thinking in moral philosophy. These are deontology and utilitarianism. Deontology holds that there are basic or universal ideals that should direct our thinking. These include keeping one's promises (Kant's categorical imperative) and always telling the truth. Utilitarianism says there are no basic or universal ideals; ethical behavior consists of doing the greatest good for the greatest number. This philosophy is based on the ideas behind capitalism.

Many people who cannot choose between these two traditions prefer ethical relativism, also known as situational ethics. However, by definition situational ethics are ambiguous and thus cannot be incorporated into any management system.

Hospitality managers are faced with a variety of ethical decisions daily. One of the most serious of these is discrimination, not only in hiring and promotion, but in treatment of guests. Discrimination can be based on race, ethnicity, gender, or other characteristics. AIDS is another problem that forces managers to make ethical decisions in regard to such things as testing and promotion policies. Advertising claims should not misrepresent the truth or create unrealistic expectations. Menus should honestly describe what is being sold.

Companies should adapt an ethical code such as the one suggested by IIQEST. A fair litmus test of an ethical decision is: (1) Is it legal? (2) Is it balanced? and (3) How will it make me feel about myself?

Endnotes

1. John Godfrey Saxe, *The Blind Men and the Elephant* (New York, N.Y.: McGraw-Hill, 1963).

2. George A. Steiner, "Social Policies for Business," *California Management Review*, Winter 1972, pp. 17–24, cited by Donald P. Robin and Eric Reidenbach in "Social Responsibility, Ethics, and Marketing Strategy: Closing the Gap Between Concept and Application," *Journal of Marketing*, January 1987, p. 45.

3. "The Green Revolution," *Restaurant Hospitality*, September 1990, p. 30.

4. Adapted from Hunter Lewis, *A Question of Values* (New York: Harper & Row, 1990), pp. 10–11.

5. Lewis, pp. 16–17.

6. Alfred Carr, "Is Business Bluffing Ethical?" *Harvard Business Review*, January/February 1968, cited by Robert C. Solomon and Kristine R. Hanson in *It's Good Business* (New York: Atheneum, 1985), p. 91.

7. Solomon and Hanson, pp. 90–93.

8. Sissela Bok, *Lying: Moral Choice in Public and Private Life* (New York: Random House, 1979), p. 20.

9. Bok, p. 26.

10. Bok, pp. 26–27, 32–33.

11. Solomon and Hanson, pp. 93–94.

12. Solomon and Hanson, p. 96.

13. Bill Moyers, "Ethical Dilemmas," *New Age Journal*, July/August 1989, p. 45.

14. Moyers, p. 45. The phrase Josephson is referring to appears in the New Testament: "Therefore all things whatsoever ye would that men should do to you, do even so to them: for this is the law and the prophets." Matthew 5:12.

15. Moyers, p. 97.

16. Moyers, p. 97.

17. Moyers, p. 97.

18. Donald P. Robin and Eric Reidenbach, "Social Responsibility, Ethics, and Marketing Strategy: Closing the Gap Between Concept and Application," *Journal of Marketing*, January 1987, p. 46.

19. Robin and Reidenbach, p. 46.

20. Robin and Reidenbach, p. 47.

21. Adapted from Ray Schmidgall, "Hotel Scruples," *Lodging*, January 1991, pp. 38–40.

22. Linda K. Enghagen, "Ethics in Hospitality/Tourism Education: A Survey," supplied by author. Professor Enghagen—who teaches a course in hospitality ethics at the University of Massachusetts at Amherst in the Department of Hotel, Restaurant, and Travel Administration—was most helpful in the formulation of some of the ideas presented here.

23. "Policies for AIDS-Infected Workers," *Restaurant Hospitality*, September 1990, p. 46.

24. William Schneider, "Homosexuals: Is AIDS Changing Attitudes?" *Public Opinion*, July/August 1987, p. 59.

25. "Policies for AIDS-Infected Workers," p. 48.

26. Study by *Personnel Journal*, November 1987, cited in "Survey: Middle Managers Most Likely to Be Unethical," *Marketing News*, November 6, 1987, p. 6.

27. "Survey: Middle Managers Most Likely to Be Unethical," p. 6.

28. Reproduced with permission of the ITT Sheraton Corporation.

29. K. Blanchard and N. V. Peale, *The Power of Ethical Management* (New York: Morrow, 1988), p. 27.

Key Terms

categorical imperative
deontology
ethical relativism
ethics
stakeholder
utilitarianism

Discussion Questions

1. What is ethics?

2. What is the difference between social responsibility and business ethics?

3. What are the six techniques of moral reasoning?

4. Is business like poker?

5. Is honesty always the best policy?

6. What is the difference between deontology and utilitarianism?

7. What is ethical relativism or situational ethics?

8. What are some typical ethical dilemmas that come up for hospitality managers?

9. Why should businesses have a code of ethics?

10. What three questions should managers ask themselves to test whether they are making an ethical decision?

Chapter Outline

15 The Industry's Future

This chapter addresses the economic, social, and technological trends that will have an impact on the hospitality industry in the twenty-first century. We will examine the globalization of trade and discuss the European Economic Community. We will also discuss the changing composition of the labor force and the consumer base, and the hospitality industry's responses. The chapter concludes with a section on technology in hotels and restaurants.

Changing Times

Only one thing is certain about the future: change is inevitable. Since the beginning of time the world has been on an evolutionary path. But at no time has the phenomenon of change been as dramatic as in the twentieth century—more specifically, the period following World War II. The pace of change from 1945 to 1991 has been unprecedented—and there are no signs it will slow down as we move into the twenty-first century.

More than any other factor, technology is responsible for transforming the way we live. What drove much of the world from an agrarian to an industrial society and, beginning in the 1950s, into an information society was technological advancement.

Technology has provided us with the means to travel faster, produce more food with fewer farmers, manufacture goods more efficiently, and communicate with one another almost instantaneously. Fax machines, teleconferencing, voice messages, portable telephones, and computer linkage enable us to exchange information almost as fast as thoughts are conceived. Satellites and fiber-optic telephone cables across the Atlantic and Pacific Oceans link North America, Europe, and the Far East, carrying voice and electronic communications faster and clearer than previously possible. Even more significantly, these new information-transfer technologies can carry a much greater volume of calls. "We are moving toward the capability to communicate anything to anyone, anywhere by any form—voice, data, text or image—at the speed of light," write futurists John Naisbitt and Patricia Aburdene, authors of *Megatrends 2000.*[1]

The world's population is changing. There are more of us than ever before and the population continues to grow. In 1980 there were approximately 4.5 billion people on the planet. By 1990 the figure had

"*Philippe, dice the potatoes.*"

Drawing by Ed Fisher; ©1988, The New Yorker Magazine, Inc.

grown to approximately 5.3 billion. In the year 2000 we can expect a world population of around 6.1 billion.[2]

Characteristics of the world's population are also changing. In the next decade there will be more affluent people than ever before, but also more people below the poverty line; it is the middle class that is losing ground. In the United States, for example, the number of households with incomes of $50,000 or more per year doubled between 1970 and 1988, while at the same time households with incomes of less than $15,000 increased. In all U.S. population groups there will be a larger percentage of older people; because of the low U.S. birth rate, the number of young people will diminish.

Significant political changes have occurred in the international arena in recent years. The early 1990s saw Soviet President Mikhail Gorbachev hasten the process (which began in 1988) of moving his country from a controlled economy to a free-market economy. *Perestroika* was the term used to describe that economic restructuring. At the same time, *glasnost* (openness) allowed Russians and citizens in Eastern Europe to criticize the old ways. Poland, Hungary, and Romania were allowed self-determination. They began to change from a socialist system to a market economy. With the reunification of East and West Germany in 1990, all of Eastern Europe started a slow but steady transformation towards a more open and traveler-friendly society.

In the Far East, Hong Kong, one of the great financial centers of the world, will lose its status as a British Crown Colony and become part of the People's Republic of China in 1997. While no one knows for certain what will happen, it is expected that little change will occur since Hong Kong represents a major source of foreign capital for China and will serve it well as a "window to the West."

The balance of economic power between nations has changed as well. Wealth has been shifting. The United States, once the world's dominant economic force, now shares that position with Japan and Germany. To compete with the economic superpowers, other countries are considering dramatic changes that may lead to a single global economy.

The Global Economy

The globalization of the world's economy is moving closer to fruition as the twentieth century comes to an end. Trade barriers between countries are being dissolved at a rapid rate. In 1988, Australia and New Zealand's free trade agreement effectively abolished all trade restrictions between the two nations. That same year a free trade agreement was signed between the United States and Canada that dropped all tariff and trade barriers. In late 1990 the United States began negotiating with Mexico to forge a similar agreement. If successfully concluded, the alliance of Canada, the United States, and Mexico would establish North America as a free trade zone of enormous power, producing $6 trillion in goods and services a year.

December 1992 holds the spotlight among the world's industrial nations. That is the month when the European Economic Community (EEC) is scheduled to become a reality, and trade barriers between the 12 member countries will collapse.[3] What will emerge is a Europe that will allow the free movement of money, goods, services, and people. The scale of this still stuns economists and historians: "By means of a mere 300 directives, 12 independent and richly diverse nations with a 1,500 year history of conflict and tension will come together as a united economic power."[4] Naisbitt and Aburdene compare the EEC to the United States, but without the political attachment of the states, the common language, or the common currency. Nevertheless, people and goods will move as easily between England and Germany, France and Ireland, or any other combination of the 12 member nations as they can between any of the 50 American states. When the EEC is created, the world's economic superpowers will be the United States, Japan, and Europe.

There are, of course, numerous obstacles to European unity, many of which are covered in the directives that are still being negotiated. Tariffs—the costs added to goods that cross national borders—are thorny issues. They must either be standardized or be eliminated. The value-added tax (VAT)—the cost added to an item before it is purchased by a consumer (somewhat similar to the sales tax in the United States)—must be standardized. While tariffs and VATs are being negotiated, there remains the goal of a common European currency, which is a much harder issue to resolve and undoubtedly will not come into being for quite a while.

If the lack of a common currency will slow down complete integration, one thing that is bound to speed it up is the "Chunnel." In 1993 the Channel Tunnel between England and France will carry its first passengers underneath the English Channel in what is expected to be part of a high-speed European rail network. The tunnel will allow passengers to travel between London and Paris in half the time it takes today, and open up new auto and freight routes between the United Kingdom and the other EEC members.

How will the creation of the European Economic Community affect tourism? Thus far, the EEC commission has dealt with only a few areas that affect tourism. For example, they have "eliminated police and tax checks at the borders of member states, increased duty-free allowances, adopted a European passport and simplified currency restrictions for travelers in most states."[5] Although the EEC negotiators have established a Directorate General for Tourism and Commerce, it is not adequately funded or staffed.

While the EEC is limited at the moment to its original 12 members, many observers believe that it is just a matter of time before the Eastern Bloc nations, which are progressing toward more democratic societies and market economies, will wish to join and move their countries closer to the West in terms of trade and travel.

The economic implications of the new global trade regions are still not clear. There is some concern that free trade agreements within these regions will become new alliances for setting up trade barriers around the regions instead of expanding trade internationally. While there is no indication yet that protectionism will occur, many companies—including hospitality companies—are establishing a presence in each of the emerging trade regions. According to Bernard Wysocki, Jr., of the *Wall Street Journal*, "U.S. companies are intensifying their efforts in Europe and Asia. European companies are pushing hard into the U.S. and Asia. And Japanese companies, once focused heavily on exports to the U.S., are buying and building aggressively almost everywhere."[6]

Globalization and Hospitality

Operating in the global arena is not new for the travel and hospitality industries. Since the advent of mass trans-Atlantic travel—first by ocean liner, then by aircraft—tourism businesses such as airlines, hotels, and restaurants have dealt with international markets. In the United States, Pan American World Airlines and TWA were pioneers in international travel. Inter-Continental Hotels (IHC) and Hilton International Hotels (HIH) were the first major global hotel companies to bring the modern twentieth-century hotel with its efficient operating standards to many parts of the world. In many cases, the airline routes forged by Pan American and TWA and the presence of an IHC or HIH hotel at the destination were catalysts for economic development and tourism in the destination areas. For example, Puerto Rico enjoyed an increase in tourism and business activity after Hilton built the Caribe Hilton there in the mid-1950s.

Since those pioneering days of the mid-twentieth century, the world of travel and hospitality has evolved into a multinational market where Chinese travelers can fly from New York to London on Air India and stay at a hotel owned by a Canadian company. The globalization of the hospitality industry is already an accomplished fact. There are Pizza Hut restaurants in Beijing and Moscow, McDonald's franchises in Tokyo and Paris. There are Hyatts, Sheratons, and Marriotts throughout the world. Inter-Continental hotels are found in 47 countries, including Gabon, Kenya, Korea, Sri Lanka, and the United Arab Emirates.

The top 50 airlines operating internationally are owned by corporations or governments from 29 different countries.[7] A number of those airlines have multinational ownership. For example, the American-based carrier Northwest Airlines is partially owned by KLM Royal Dutch Airlines.

The hospitality industry has long been global. The Sheraton hotel on the left is in Paris; the one above is in Waikiki. Photos courtesy of ITT Sheraton Corporation, Boston, Massachusetts.

Swissair, Delta, and Singapore Airlines have all bought interests in each other. Scandinavian Airlines Systems (SAS) now owns a piece of Continental Airlines. An extreme example of how far this globalization of the airline business has gone was reported by the *New York Times*: "British Airways, an airline renowned for service, and Aeroflot, a carrier known for lack of it, said yesterday that they were discussing the creation of an international airline. The carrier to be called Air Russia would be organized by the privately owned British airline in cooperation with the Soviet monopoly carrier."[8] Other mergers and affiliations will be forged as deregulation of the EEC member airlines is accomplished and the airlines of other countries compete for the growing international markets. It is anticipated that all major U.S. carriers will seek to expand services to Europe and Asia in the coming years as those markets develop.

Travel agencies are an important link in moving travelers around the globe. It is estimated that by the year 2000 there will be 50,000 travel agencies in the United States alone, booking over $130 billion a year in total sales—$15 billion (or more) of that in hotel room nights.[9] One can only imagine how big the travel agency industry will be worldwide. In preparing for the global surge in travel, some agencies are merging and becoming multinational. The U.S. firm Carlson Travel Group purchased controlling interest in one of Britain's largest agencies, A. T. Mays, and Britain's venerable Thomas Cook organization merged with Crimson/Heritage Travel, headquartered in Boston.

As airlines and travel agencies become more globally oriented, so do attractions, resorts, restaurants, and hotel chains. The Walt Disney Company's first international project, a "Magic Kingdom" in Tokyo, is a great success. A second Disney international amusement park, Euro Disney, is scheduled to open in May 1992 just outside of Paris.

Hotel companies based in England, India, Switzerland, Germany, Hong Kong, and Japan own (and in some cases, operate) hotels in the United States. U.S. companies such as Hyatt and Marriott continue to expand globally. As mentioned in Chapter 2, Bass PLC, a British company, became the world's largest hotel company when it acquired Holiday Inn. In 1990 The Continental Companies (TCC), a U.S. hotel management company based in Miami, Florida, joined with Tobishima Corporation of Japan to develop seven golf resorts in France, Germany, and Italy. The resorts will be operated by the Grand Bay Management Company—a joint venture between TCC and Tobishima—and the golf courses will be operated by Luxembourg-based International Golf Associates, which is in part owned by Amer Group Ltd. of Finland.

Grand Metropolitan, a British company, sold Inter-Continental Hotels (having purchased it from the founder of the hotel chain, Pan American Airlines) to the Saison Group of Japan to raise the capital to purchase Pillsbury, the parent company of Burger King. The Japanese food service company Kyotaru purchased controlling interest in Restaurant Associates (RA). RA operates 120 restaurants on the East and West Coasts of the United States through six divisions. One of their most popular and well-known restaurants is Mamma Leone's in New York City.

These multinational companies have been labeled "consortia," described as "parent companies without national loyalty that own and co-ordinate business assets in multiple countries."[10] As a result, in order to compete in the marketplace of the future, hospitality companies must not only own properties worldwide but think on a global scale. Companies must learn how to function in foreign countries in such vital areas as finance, labor, and marketing. Even the political and social climate must be understood. For example, the aggressive U.S. marketing method does not work in Japan, where a more patient and subtle approach is needed to develop customer appreciation over a period of time.

Hospitality Careers. What are the implications of globalization for those of you who have or want to have a managerial career in the hospitality industry? For some, it may mean working at a U.S.-owned property in a foreign country. For others, it may mean working for a foreign-owned hotel, restaurant, or other hospitality business in the United States, which means the owners and many if not all of the company officers will have a different nationality and culture than you and most of the other staff. Foreign ownership may have little effect on day-to-day operations, since the purpose of the investment in most cases is to establish an economic base and global link in another international market. However, you must be sensitive to the owners' social and cultural differences, including the corporate culture of their company. And if you wish to progress to the highest corporate levels you will almost certainly need to master the language and etiquette of the home office.

Understanding the cultural and social differences of other nations is most critical in serving guests. A case in point is the way money is handled. With a few exceptions, American hotels have lagged behind European and Asian hotels in their ability to deal with the currency exchange needs of

Exhibit 15.1 America's Aging Population

	1960	1970	1980	1990	2000	Percentage Change 1960–2000
Under 5	20,341	17,166	16,458	18,408	16,898	–17%
5–17	44,184	52,596	47,237	45,630	48,815	+10
18–34	39,047	50,034	67,976	70,065	62,380	+60
35–54	44,799	46,466	48,622	63,384	81,134	+81
55–74	26,678	31,175	37,415	39,737	42,401	+59
75 +	5,622	7,614	10,051	13,187	16,639	+196
Total	180,671	205,051	227,759	250,411	268,267	+48
Note: Figures in thousands.						

Source: *Future Scope*, p. 29.

visitors from abroad. If the U.S. hospitality industry is to share in the growing international travel which will arise from increased globalization of business and pleasure travel, currency exchange must be made convenient for travelers.

But settling currency issues is only the beginning. The social customs and tastes of foreign guests must be understood. Some U.S. hoteliers have already reacted to the special needs of their international guests. The La Quinta Golf and Tennis Resort in La Quinta, California, in recognition of its increasing number of Japanese guests, has added to its room service menu a traditional Japanese breakfast of grilled salmon, miso soup, rice, a Japanese omelette, pickled vegetables, and fresh fruit. A growing number of hotels and resorts accustomed to dealing with international guests have recruited multilingual staffs. Others will need to follow that example.

The Baby Boomers

As we approach the year 2000, changing demographics and lifestyles will require hospitality enterprises to adapt to the needs and desires of the new traveling public or face going out of business. For American and foreign-owned companies operating in the United States, special attention will have to be paid to the baby-boom generation.

As mentioned in earlier chapters, the major demographic phenomenon in America is the aging of the population (see Exhibit 15.1)—a trend also occurring in Europe. By 2000, the median age in the United States will be 36.3 years. Up until World War II, the median age was in the 20s. However, between 1946 and 1964 seventy-six million babies were born—the "baby boom."

The baby-boom generation gave us the flower children and hippies of the 1960s, when politics, fashion, values, and attitudes were influenced by that large and vocal population segment. The 1960s and 1970s also saw tremendous fast-food restaurant growth. This new generation felt it was entitled to everything it could get after the deprivation their parents had felt as a result of the war, and, echoing their sentiments, McDonald's told them "you deserve a break today," while Burger King promised to sell them hamburgers prepared "your way."

In large part because of the baby boomers, the U.S. birthrate began declining in the 1970s and has continued to decline. One of the things the new generation did not want was the responsibilities of marriage and children. The number of unmarried-couple households increased by 117% in the 1970s and another 63% between 1980 and 1988, when the total reached 2.6 million households.[11] Those couples that did marry did so later in life and they postponed having children, if they had them at all. The average American family today has 3.17 members, the fewest in history.

By 2000 the baby boomers will be between 35 and 54 years old and will represent 66% of the total population. These middle-agers should be well established in careers and in their peak earning years. By 2012 the baby boomers will start retiring from work. But unlike many of their parents, they will not pull up a rocking chair or move into a nursing home. This generation has learned how to keep physically fit and eat more nutritious foods. Fewer of them smoke or consume alcoholic beverages. Moreover, there have been huge strides in medicine. We have much more success treating many formerly fatal diseases, and new types of genetic therapy promise to cure or at least alleviate other chronic diseases and illnesses. The bottom line is that the baby boomers will stay healthier and live longer.

How will the baby boom generation affect the hospitality industry in the near future? Two of the most affected areas will be labor, and products and services.

Labor Implications

Because many baby boomers chose to have few or no children, there are fewer young workers available to take their place as they move through their careers and retire. Therefore, hospitality businesses must start earlier and work harder to attract their share of the dwindling number of young people. One answer is to support high school programs that introduce students to the hospitality industry. Graduates of these programs can enter the industry directly or go on to college for additional schooling. In the future, local chapters of hotel and restaurant associations will be forced to take a more active role in their community schools.

Competition among hospitality businesses for young entry-level workers may cause wage inflation, which could translate into higher prices for rooms, food, and services. One alternative will be to look at other population groups for employees.

Senior citizens represent a growing potential labor market. Already, companies feeling the effects of having fewer young workers in the labor pool have turned to older persons, offering them an opportunity for a new career. As mentioned in Chapter 9, McDonald's with its "McMasters" program offers special job training for senior citizens that prepares them for jobs ranging from line servers and cooks to management positions. Days Inn has successfully recruited retirees to answer telephones and take reservations. In many cases, seniors have retired from careers outside the hospitality industry. Therefore, in the near future hospitality businesses will have to develop training programs (if they haven't already) to meet the special needs of seniors.

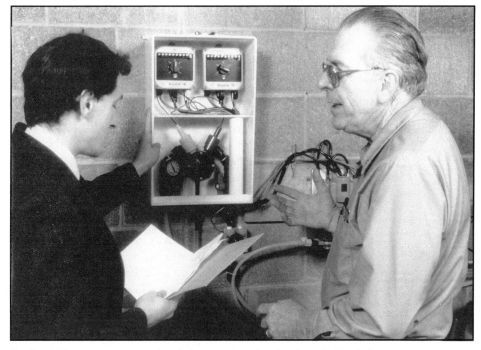

Senior citizens are a growing labor market for the hospitality industry.

Single parents and working mothers are another source of new work-ers. In the past two decades the divorce rate has doubled in the United States, and demographers now estimate that about half of all marriages from the early 1970s will end in divorce.[12] Today most mothers with chil-dren under 18 work either to supplement their husbands' incomes or pro-vide the sole support for their family. These mothers will need training and either flexible schedules to accommodate their parenting obligations or child care at the workplace.

Another source of new employees will be immigrants. For most of U.S. history, immigrants typically came from Europe. America was built by waves of British and Spanish colonists, followed by Irish, Italian, German, Scandinavian, and Russian immigrants. In recent years, as a result of po-litical and economic disasters in the Far East, Mexico, Central and South America, and the Caribbean, these regions have provided the major sources of immigrants. From 1981 to 1985, 800,000 immigrants entered the United States from Hispanic countries south of the border (not including Puerto Ricans, who are U.S. citizens).[13] Although still a small segment of the population, the number of Asian immigrants is growing at the fastest percentage rate of all immigrant groups, and their numbers will double by the year 2010.[14] Most of this group comes from the Philippines and settles in California. Asian-Americans typically are more highly educated than other immigrants. Not only do more of them arrive with college de-grees, but more attend college in the United States than immigrants from other parts of the world.

Most immigrants are eager to take entry-level jobs, not only for the pay but to acquire new work skills. Immigrants are not likely to under-stand how to perform their jobs in their new careers so, again, training will take on a much more important role in the future. Of course, many immigrants will not only require job training but training in English as a second language.

Product and Service Implications

The lifestyle developed by the baby boomers bodes well for the hospitality industry. As we have pointed out, they were the major influence in the spectacular growth in restaurant dining in the 1970s and 1980s. Free-standing restaurant sales went from $22 billion in 1970 to an estimated $150 billion in 1990.[15] Baby boomers are used to eating out frequently. While they are expected to continue to patronize restaurants, whether they will remain loyal to fast food remains to be seen. To hang on to the baby boomers, fast-food operators have conducted extensive marketing research to identify the concerns of the older baby boomers. Menus have been expanded. Salads and chicken sandwiches have been added. Saturated fats are being replaced by healthier oils for cooking potatoes and other deep-fried products. McDonald's is even testing a brand new kind of franchise—a modern version of an old-fashioned diner that serves entrées like meat loaf and mashed potatoes.

"*If there are sixteen moons, it must be Jupiter.*"

Drawing by Ed Fisher; ©1988, The New Yorker Magazine, Inc.

Baby boomers and their families will continue to be important for the restaurant industry. However, they will require convenience and moderate prices. Restaurants should be concerned about the growing number of store-front establishments in strip malls and other locations that prepare entire dinners for take home, as well as the expanding market in prepared foods—including the frozen dinners sold in supermarkets. As mentioned in earlier chapters, some cafeteria chains have created take-out menus and have started home delivery services. Since the growing number of working families have a growing number of dining alternatives, it is estimated that "by 2000, the most important appliance in putting dinners on the table will not be the kitchen range or the food processor but the telephone and the car."[16]

With baby boomers growing older and their parents in many cases taking early retirements, there is a growing market for travel packages and hotels targeting older guests. Although the over 50 group controls much of the nation's discretionary income, they are sensitive to price and value. While the senior citizens of 2000 will be used to more activity than their parents or grandparents, they will be concerned about health and exercise and will probably drink fewer alcoholic beverages. They will want more meaningful recreational programs at resorts. The Mohawk Mountain House, the venerable resort in New Paltz, New York, now offers packages that include the study of languages and other self-improvement activities. A travel company in Chevy Chase, Maryland, has packaged safaris to Kenya and barge trips through Holland (among other trips) for grandparents and their grandchildren.

As the average hotel guest gets older, managers must adjust to meet the needs of these guests. Senior citizens look for good lighting in rooms and public areas; signs with large print; highly visible hazard-warning signs on stairs, glass doors, and other places that pose potential hazards; wide aisles; security; and a controlled level of noise.

The growth of the elderly population has presented opportunities for hotel companies to enter yet another market niche—continuing-care retirement communities, which we described in Chapter 3. Marriott and Hyatt are already committed to a substantial number of these facilities, and other hotel chains and independent hotels are expected to follow.

Hospitality Technology

As the hospitality industry moves into the twenty-first century, technology is being utilized to make hospitality businesses more efficient, to improve guest service, and to provide the technically adept traveler an office on the road.

In *Megatrends*, John Naisbitt coined the phrase "high tech/high touch" to describe the balance required between the adoption of technological advances and the "spiritual demands of our human nature."[17] Nowhere is that balance more important than in the hospitality industry. Initially, the hotel industry applied technology in areas that guests could not see, such as the accounting, reservations, sales, and purchasing offices. Eventually technology came to the front of the house and computers were placed at the front desk to handle guest check-in and check-out. Guest demands for better hotel security led to electronic and mechanical card/key systems

Drawing by Ed Fisher; ©1988, The New Yorker Magazine, Inc.

tailored for each guest in each room. As guests became more accustomed to hotel technology, more innovations were introduced. Computer-controlled wake-up calls and voice messages are becoming commonplace. In some hotels a guest can order room service, check messages, review hotel charges, and check out by using a guestroom keyboard or even touching the screen of the television set in his or her room.

As mentioned in Chapter 6, restaurants have introduced hand-held server terminals with a transmitter so that a server can send an order electronically from the guests' table to the bar or any number of stations in the kitchen. Fast-food restaurants are introducing similar technology in the form of terminals for customers to use in making selections at counters or drive-through windows. Technology was originally viewed as a means to control if not reduce labor and other operating costs. That role has been expanded to include improving both the speed and convenience of guest service.

How much technology are customers willing to accept? In a poll of business travelers conducted by the *Wall Street Journal* for Red Lion Hotels and Inns, respondents suggested that they would welcome technology that made business travel easier. They would like computerized airline ticket dispensers and a convenient way to make airline reservations at hotels. They wanted baggage automatically delivered to the hotel from their plane and taken back to their plane upon check-out. They wanted their preferences for type of room noted in the reservation and acted upon. They wanted voice mail. They wanted guestroom televisions to provide information about airlines, monitor fire and other safety systems, and tell them who is knocking on the guestroom door. In other words, these business travelers were ready for an integrated technological system of vast capabilities.

However, not all guests are embracing new technology to that extent, and some properties are meeting their needs. At hotels in the upscale Four Seasons chain, guests never see computers—even at the front desk—because management feels they detract from their hotels' personalized and luxurious service. Some advanced technology is used, but it is well-hidden and only used by the staff.

In future years we can expect to see hospitality businesses tighten their embrace of technology in a number of areas:

- *Property Management Systems (PMS).* There will be more integration of front and back office systems, especially reservations, front desk, housekeeping, and accounting systems. Motel 6 and Thriftlodge are testing a computerized drive-through night check-in system that operates somewhat like a bank automatic teller.

- *Marketing.* Technology will provide easier access to market segmentation analysis and become an important factor in adopting yield management systems, which help to maximize revenue.

- *Call Accounting Systems.* Call accounting systems will be more widely used. They make it possible for hotels to accurately track and compute the charges for telephone calls made by guests and hotel staff. This technology continues to provide the means to make the telephone department a profit center for some hotels.

- *Safety Systems.* Technology has provided monitoring systems that can notify hotel guests and staff of the location of hazards such as fires. As older properties are refurbished and upgraded, these systems will be added.

- *Energy Management Systems.* Energy management systems will become more sophisticated and gain wider use as energy costs continue to increase.

- *Key Systems.* Electronic guestroom card/key systems will become more prevalent because they provide greater security than a conventional lock-and-key system.

- *Smart Cards.* Major airlines and banks have begun testing a system that will allow travelers to purchase airline tickets directly from the banks' ATM machines using existing credit cards or new "smart cards." Smart cards are credit-card-like devices that promise to make travelers' lives easier. They may even be used to make hotel reservations in the near future. With smart cards, travelers will be able to enter their personal code into a hotel's computer, make guestroom reservations, note the type of room they prefer, and input their expected time of arrival. The system will verify their credit line and automatically register them. When they arrive at their hotel, travelers can go directly to their guestroom and use the smart card as a key. Insertion of the card in the door lock will notify the front desk of their arrival.

Chapter Summary

Since the beginning of time the world has been on an evolutionary path. More than any other factor, technology has been responsible for transforming the way we live. Technology has provided us with the means to travel faster, to produce more food with fewer farmers, to manufacture goods more efficiently, and to communicate with one another almost instantaneously.

People are redefining and changing the way they live and think about themselves. The new society of the next decade will contain more affluent people then ever before, but also more people below the poverty line.

The balance of economic power between nations has changed and will continue to change. The most dramatic change in the near future is the coming together in December 1992 of 12 European countries into a unified market: the European Economic Community. However, the economic union of the United States, Canada, and Mexico is also a distinct possibility. Countries in eastern Europe are trying to establish market economies, and in 1997 Hong Kong will be united with the People's Republic of China.

Since the advent of mass trans-Atlantic travel, first by ocean liner then by aircraft, tourism businesses such as airlines, hotels, and restaurants have dealt with international markets. Pan American, TWA, Hilton, and Inter-Continental are examples of airlines and hotels that have been globally oriented since their inception. Travel agencies too are merging and buying interests into their counterparts overseas.

U.S. hotel chains such as Hyatt and Marriott and fast-food companies such as McDonald's and Pizza Hut continue to expand globally. Many companies are adapting a strategy of building a presence in all of the world's trade regions.

What are the implications of globalization for those interested in a managerial career in hospitality? Some managers may work at a U.S. property located in a foreign country. Others may work for a foreign-owned hospitality business in the United States. In either case, hospitality managers must sensitize themselves to the different social and cultural values of hotel guests and staff from other countries. Moreover, to serve guests from many nations it will be necessary for managers to more aggressively address issues such as foreign currency exchange and food preferences when designing guest services.

The major demographic phenomenon in America is the aging of the population. Between 1946 and 1964 seventy-six million babies were born—the "baby boom." Now that generation is growing old and hospitality businesses must adjust. Labor, and products and services are the two industry areas that the baby boomers will affect the most.

Because most baby boomers chose to have few or no children, there are fewer young workers to take their place as they move through their careers and retire. Therefore, hospitality businesses must work harder to attract their share of the dwindling number of young people. They can do this by supporting high school programs that introduce students to the industry and taking a more active role in community schools.

The industry is also exploring alternatives to young workers. Senior citizens represent a growing potential labor market. Seniors will need training, and may hospitality companies such as McDonald's have already developed special training programs for them. Single parents, working mothers, and immigrants are other sources of new workers. All of these groups will need training and perhaps special programs such as day care or flexible shifts.

The industry will have to adjust products and services to the needs of the aging baby boomers. Fast-food companies are using healthier cooking methods and including more nutritious items on their menus. Many small food businesses are springing up to sell take-out food to busy two-income families. Restaurants are responding by creating their own take-out menus and in some cases providing home delivery services.

Resorts are establishing special programs for those baby boomers who want to improve themselves physically or intellectually. Hotel managers are adjusting to meet the needs of older guests by providing good lighting in rooms and public areas, signs with large print, highly visible hazard-warning signs in appropriate places, wide aisles, security, and quiet. There is a growing market for travel packages created especially for retirees.

Initially, technology in the hospitality industry was applied in areas that guests could not see. Later it was added to the front of the house and it will continue to grow in the following areas: property management systems, marketing, telephone call accounting, safety, energy management, card/key systems, and smart cards.

Endnotes

1. John Naisbitt and Patricia Aburdene, *Megatrends 2000* (New York: Morrow, 1990), p. 23.

2. *1990 World Almanac* (New York: Pharos Books, 1990), p. 773.

3. The countries that will initially join the European Economic Community are the United Kingdom, the Republic of Ireland, France, Portugal, Spain, Denmark, Germany, Italy, Netherlands, Greece, Belgium, and Luxembourg.

4. Michael Silva and Bertil Sjogren, *Europe 1992 and the New World Power Game* (New York: Wiley, 1990), p. 15.

5. Peter Akerhielm, Chekitan S. Dev, and Malcolm Noden, "Europe 1992: Neglecting the Tourism Opportunity," *The Cornell Hotel and Restaurant Administration Quarterly*, May 1990, p. 104.

6. Bernard Wysocki, Jr., "Going Global in the New World," *Wall Street Journal*, September 21, 1990, p. R-3.

7. William Woods, "Taking Off Overseas," *Fortune*, September 24, 1990, p. 52.

8. "British Air Plan with Aeroflot," *New York Times*, October 13, 1990, p. 17.

9. Melinda Bush, "The 1990's Will Be the Age of Information for Hotels and Travel Agents," *The Cornell Hotel and Restaurant Administration Quarterly*, May 1990, p. 1.

10. Silva and Sjogren, p. 56.

11. Joe Cappo, *Future Scope* (New York: Longman Financial Services Publishing, 1990), p. 60.

12. Cappo, p. 100.

13. Cappo, p. 44.

14. Cappo, p. 46.

15. Cappo, p. 66.

16. Cappo, p. 67.

17. John Naisbitt, *Megatrends* (New York: Warner Books, 1982), pp. 40–41.

Key Terms

baby boomers
consortia
European Economic Community (EEC)
globalization
smart cards

Discussion Questions

1. What recent changes discussed in the chapter have occurred on the world scene in technology, politics, and economics?

2. What new trade regions are being set up around the globe?

3. Is globalization new to the hospitality industry?

4. What are some examples of international hospitality and travel companies?

5. What implications does globalization have for hospitality managers?

6. What is the major demographic phenomenon in America?

7. What effect have the baby boomers had on the labor supply for the hospitality industry? How is the industry responding?

8. What effect have the baby boomers had on hospitality products and services?

9. How have hotels and restaurants used technology to date?

10. What are some likely technological trends for hospitality businesses in the near future?

Appendix
Hospitality Associations and Periodicals

The following is a list of some of the associations and periodicals that may be of interest to hospitality students, managers, and employees. Phone numbers are not included because they change somewhat frequently.

ASSOCIATIONS

American Bed and Breakfast Association (ABBA)*
16 Village Green, Suite 203
Crofton, MD 21114

American Franchise Association (AFA)
2730 Wilshire Blvd., Suite 400
Santa Monica, CA 90403

American Hotel & Motel Association (AH&MA)
1201 New York Ave., N.W., Suite 600
Washington, DC 20005

American School Food Service Association
(ASFSA)
1600 Duke St., 7th Floor
Alexandria, VA 22314

American Society for Hospital Food Service
Administrators (ASHFSA)
c/o American Hospital Association
840 N. Lake Shore Drive
Chicago, IL 60611

American Society of Bakery Engineers (ASBE)
Two N. Riverside Plaza, Rm. 1733
Chicago, IL 60606

American Society of Heating, Refrigerating and
Air-Conditioning Engineers (ASHRAE)
1791 Tullie Circle, N.E.
Atlanta, GA 30329

American Society of Sanitary Engineering (ASSE)
P.O. Box 40362
Bay Village, OH 44140

American Society of Travel Agents (ASTA)
1101 King St.
Alexandria, VA 22314

American Travel Inns (ATI)
640 W. North Temple
Salt Lake City, Utah 84116

Association of Corporate Travel Executives (ACTE)
P.O. Box 5394
Parsippany, NJ 07054

Association of Group Travel Executives (AGTE)
c/o Arnold H. Light
A. H. Light Co., Inc.
424 Madison Ave., Suite 705
New York, NY 10017

Association of Retail Travel Agents (ARTA)
1745 Jefferson Davis Hwy., Suite 300
Arlington, VA 22202

Bed and Breakfast League/Sweet Dreams and
Toast (BBL)
P.O. Box 9490
Washington, DC 20016

Center for Hospitality Research and Service
(CHRS)
c/o Department of Hotel, Restaurant and
Institutional Management
Virginia Polytechnic Institution and State
University
Blacksburg, VA 24061

Chinese American Restaurant Association (CARA)
173 Canal St.
New York, NY 10013

Cruise Lines International Association (CLIA)
500 Fifth Ave., Suite 1407
New York, NY 10110

Council on Hotel, Restaurant, and Institutional
Education (CHRIE)
1200 17th St., N.W.
Washington, DC 20036

---

*All association names and addresses have been quoted from Deborah M. Burek, ed., *Encyclopedia of Associations*, 25th ed. (Detroit, Mich.: Gale Research Company, 1991). This encyclopedia is updated each year.

Food Industries Suppliers Association (FISA)
P.O. Box 2084
Fairfield Glade, TN 38555

Food Processing Machinery and Supplies
Association (FPM&SA)
200 Daingerfield Road
Alexandria, VA 22314

Foodservice and Lodging Institute (FLI)
1919 Pennsylvania Ave., N.W.
Washington, DC 20006

Franchise Consultants International Association
(FCIA)
5147 S. Angela Road
Memphis, TN 38117

Hospitality Lodging and Travel Research
Foundation (HLTRF)
c/o Raymond C. Ellis, Jr.
American Hotel & Motel Association
1201 New York Ave., N.W.
Washington, DC 20005

Hotel-Motel Greeters International (HMGI)
P.O. Box 20017
El Cajon, CA 92021

Hotel Sales and Marketing Association (HSMAI)
1300 L St., N.W., Suite 800
Washington, DC 20005

International Association of Holiday Inns (IAHI)
3796 Lamar Ave.
Memphis, TN 38195

International Association of Hospitality
Accountants (IAHA)
Box 27649
Austin, TX 78755

International Caterers Association (ICA)
220 S. State St., Suite 1416
Chicago, IL 60604

International Franchise Association (IFA)
1350 New York Ave., N.W., Suite 900
Washington, DC 20005

International Society of Hotel Association
Executives (ISHAE)
P.O. Box 1529
Tallahassee, FL 32302

Mexican Food and Beverage Board (MFBB)
314 E. 41st St.
New York, NY 10017

Mobile Industrial Caterers' Association (MICA)
7300 Artesia Blvd.
Buena Park, CA 90621

National Association of Black Hospitality
Professionals (NABHP)
P.O. Box 5443
Plainfield, NJ 07060

National Association of Catering Executives
(NACE)
5757 W. Century Blvd., #512
Los Angeles, CA 90045

National Association of Concessionaires (NAC)
35 E. Wacker Dr., Suite 1545
Chicago, IL 60601

National Association of Institutional Linen
Management (NAILM)
2130 Lexington Rd., Suite H
Richmond, KY 40475

National Association of Pizza Operators (NAPO)
P.O. Box 114
Santa Claus, IN 47579

National Association of Restaurant Managers
(NARM)
5322 N. 78th Way
Scottsdale, AZ 85253

National Bed-and-Breakfast Association (NB&BA)
P.O. Box 332
Norwalk, CT 06852

National Black McDonald's Operators Association
(NBMOA)
5434 King Ave., No. 3
Pennsauken, NJ 08110

National Food Service Association (NFSA)
P.O. Box 1932
Columbus, OH 43216

National Restaurant Association (NRA)
1200 17th St., N.W.
Washington, DC 20036

National Soft Serve and Fast Food Association
(NSSFFA)
516 S. Front St.
Chesaning, MI 48616

Preferred Hotels Association (PHA)
1901 S. Meyers Rd., Suite 220
Oakbrook Terrace, IL 60181

Roundtable for Women
Food-Beverage-Hospitality (RWFBH)
145 W. First St., Suite A
Tustin, CA 92680

Shakey's Franchised Dealers Association (SFDA)
5820 Wilshire Blvd., #500
Los Angeles, CA 90036

Small Luxury Hotels Association (SLHA)
c/o Jayne Levant
337 S. Robertson Blvd., Suite 202
Beverly Hills, CA 90211

Society for Cuisine in America (SCA)
304 W. Liberty St., Suite 301
Louisville, KY 40202

Society for Food Service Management (SFM)
304 W. Liberty St., Suite 301
Louisville, KY 40202

Society for the Advancement of Food Service
Research (SAFSR)
304 W. Liberty St., Suite 301
Louisville, KY 40202

Tourist House Association of America (THAA)
R.D. 2, Box 355A
Greentown, PA 18426

Travel and Tourism Research Association (TTRA)
P.O. Box 58066
Salt Lake City, UT 84158

Travel Industry Association of America (TIA)
Two Lafayette Center
1133 21st St., N.W.
Washington, DC 20036

U.S. Travel Data Center
Two Lafayette Center
1133 21st St., N.W.
Washington, DC 20036

Washington Ethical Society (WES)
7750 16th St., N.W.
Washington, DC 20012

PERIODICALS

Airline/Ship Catering & Onboard Service
P.O. Box 188
Hialeh, FL 33011

Annals of Tourism Research
Pergamon Press (Journals)
Maxwell House, Fairview Park
Elmsford, NY 10523

Business Travel News
600 Community Drive
Manhasset, NY 11030

Casino World
P.O. Box 2003
Madison Square Station
New York, NY 10159

Club Management
Club Managers Association of America
Commerce Publishing Company
408 Olive Street
St. Louis, MO 63102

Contemporary Hospitality Management
MCB University Press Limited
62 Toller Lane
Bradford BD8 9BY
England

Convention World
63 Great Rd.
Maynard, MA 01754

Cook's Magazine
2710 North Avenue
Bridgeport, CT 06604

Cooking for Profit
P.O. Box 267
Fond du Lac, WI 54935

Cornell Quarterly
327 Statler Hall
Cornell University
Ithaca, NY 14853

FIU Hospitality Review
Florida International University
Tamiami Trail
Miami, FL 33199

Food Executive Newsletter
3017 W. Charleston Blvd., Suite 50
Las Vegas, NV 89102

Food Management
Edgell Communications, Inc.
1 East First Street
Duluth, MN 55802

Food Management Magazine
Edgell Communications, Inc.
270 Madison Avenue
New York, NY 10016

Foodservice and Hospitality
980 Yonge St., Suite 400
Toronto
Ontario, Canada

Food Service News
8 Highland Avenue
Randolph, MA 02368

Foodservice News
2233 N. Hamline Avenue, Suite 615
Roseville, MN 55113

Gaming and Wagering Business
254 West 31st St.
New York, NY 10001

Hospitality Education and Research Journal
Council on Hotel, Restaurant and Institutional
Education
311 First Street NW
Washington, DC 20001

Hospitality Educator
CHRIE
311 First Street NW
Washington, DC 20001

Hospitality Law
Magna Publications
2718 Dryden Drive
Madison, WI 53704

Hotel & Motel Management
P.O. Box 6195
Duluth, MN 55806

Hotel and Resort Industry
488 Madison Avenue
New York, NY 10022

Hotel & Travel Index
500 Plaza Drive
Secaucus, NJ 07096

Hotelier
Kostuch Publications
980 Yonge St., Suite 400
Toronto
Ontario, Canada

Hotels
P.O. Box 173305
Denver, CO 80217

Innkeeping World
P.O. Box 84108
Seattle, WA 98124

International Journal of Hospitality Management
Pergamon Press (Journals)
Maxwell House, Fairview Park
Elmsford, NY 10523

Journal of Travel Research
College of Business and Administration
University of Colorado
Campus Box 420
Boulder, CO 80309

Lé Chef Magazine
252, Route 171
St. Ettienne DeLauzon
Quebec, Canada

Lodging Hospitality
Penton Publishing
P.O. Box 95759
Cleveland, OH 44101

Lodging Magazine
American Hotel & Motel Association
1201 New York Avenue, NW
Washington, DC 20005

Lodging Outlook
Smith Travel Research
P.O. Box 1529
Hendersonville, TN 37077

Meeting News
P.O. Box 8391
Boulder, CO 80329

Military Clubs and Hospitality
825 Old Country Road
Westbury, NY 11590

Military Clubs and Recreation
1438 Duke Street
Alexandria, VA 22314

Military Market
Circulation Department
6883 Commercial Drive
Springfield, VA 22159

Nation's Restaurant News
Lebhar-Friedman
305 Madison Ave., Suite 535
New York, NY 10165

Resort Condominiums International
P.O. Box 80229
Indianapolis, IN 46280

Resort Management
Western Specialty Publications, Inc.
2431 Morena Blvd.
San Diego, CA 92110

Restaurant Business
Circulation Department
633 Third Avenue
New York, NY 10017

Restaurant Hospitality
Penton Publishing
P.O. Box 95759
Cleveland, OH 44101

Restaurant Management
One East First Street
Duluth, MN 55802

Restaurant Personnel Management
Lebhar-Friedman, Inc.
425 Park Avenue
New York, NY 10022

Restaurants & Institutions
Cahner's Publishing Company
270 St. Paul Street
Denver, CO 80206

Restaurants USA
National Restaurant Association
1200 Seventeenth Street, NW
Washington, DC 20036

Sales & Marketing Management
P.O. Box 1025
Southeastern, PA 19398

School Food Service Journal
5600 S. Quebec St., Suite 300-B
Englewood, CO 80111

Successful Hotel Marketer
111 E. Wacker Dr., 17th Floor
One Illinois Center
Chicago, IL 60601

Successful Meetings
633 3rd Avenue
New York, NY 10017

Teleprofessional
209 West 5th Street
Waterloo, IA 50701

Tour and Travel News
600 Community Drive
Manhasset, NY 11030

Travel Agent Magazine
825 7th Avenue, 3rd Floor
New York, NY 10019

Travel Digest
1654 S.W. 28 Avenue
Ft. Lauderdale, FL 33312

Travel Trade
6 East 46th St.
New York, NY 10017

Travelage
888 7th Avenue, 29th Floor
New York, NY 10106

Glossary

A

ACCOUNTING DIVISION

Responsible for keeping track of the many business transactions that occur in a hotel and managing the hotel's finances.

ADDED-VALUE

What advertising adds to the value and reputation of the product, service, or company advertised.

ADVERTISING

Planned communication activity in which messages in mass media are used to persuade audiences to adopt goods, services, or ideas.

AIRLINE-RELATED GUESTS

Airplane crew members and passengers who need emergency accommodations.

AIRPORT HOTELS

Hotels built near airports. These hotels are full-service and are more likely than other hotels to have in-room movies, computerized property management systems, and call accounting systems.

ALL-SUITE HOTELS

Hotels that feature rooms larger than typical hotel rooms, with a living space separate from the bedroom. They can also have kitchenettes.

AMBIENCE

The decor, lighting, furnishings, and other factors that create a feeling about or an identity for an establishment.

APPROVAL PROVISIONS

The provisions of a management contract specifying which operator decisions require management approval. The mechanism for settling owner/operator disputes is sometimes included in these provisions.

AREAS OF DOMINANT INFLUENCE (ADI)

A term used in the television industry to describe areas covered by the signals of major television stations as measured by Arbitron, a national TV rating service.

ASSESSMENT

A one-time or periodic charge imposed on private club members to cover operational shortfalls or raise capital for improvements to the club.

B

BABY BOOMERS

Those individuals born during the "baby boom" after World War II. Between 1946 and 1964 seventy-six million babies were born, a generation that by its sheer numbers affected many demographic and social changes in the United States.

BACK OF THE HOUSE

The areas of a hotel or restaurant in which personnel have little or no direct guest contact, such as kitchen areas and the accounting department.

BALANCE SHEET

A financial statement that provides information on the financial position of a business by showing its assets, liabilities, and equity on a given date.

BARNARD, CHESTER I.

One of the founders of the behavioral school of management.

BAR PAR

The amount of each type of beverage established for behind-the-bar storage, based on expected consumption.

BEHAVIORAL MANAGEMENT SCHOOL

Management theorists who sought to develop better ways to motivate workers than the rules, systems, and wages proposed by the classical management theorists.

BLIND RECEIVING

A receiving system in which the supplier gives the receiving clerk a list of items being delivered, but not the quantities or weights, thereby forcing the clerk to count or weigh the incoming products and record the results. These results are later compared with the supplier's invoice received by the accounting office.

BODY COPY

The main text of an ad.

BUSINESS-FORMAT FRANCHISE

An ongoing business relationship between a franchisor and a franchisee in which the franchisor sells its products, services, trademark, and business concept to the franchisee in return for royalties and other franchise fees.

C

CAFETERIA

A food service operation in which guests pass through serving lines and help themselves to food items or receive food items from service staff.

CARD KEYS

Plastic cards, resembling credit cards, used in place of metal guestroom keys. Card keys require electronic locks.

CAREER PATH

A series of positions an individual may take on the way to his or her ultimate career goal. Some companies lay out sample career paths for their employees.

CASINO HOTELS

Hotels that feature legalized gambling, with the hotel operation subordinate to the gambling operation.

CATEGORICAL IMPERATIVE

One must keep one's promises.

CATERING

Part of the food and beverage division of a hotel. Responsible for arranging and planning food and beverage functions for (1) conventions and smaller hotel groups, and (2) local banquets booked by the sales department.

CATERING MANAGER

Promotes and sells a hotel's banquet facilities and uses his or her expertise to plan, organize, and perform hotel banquets.

CENTER CITY HOTELS

Full-service hotels located in downtown areas.

CHEF DU PARTIE

The chef in charge of a particular food production area in the kitchen.

CHEF DU RANG

In French service, the employee responsible for taking orders, serving drinks, preparing food at the table, and collecting sales income. If there is no sommelier or wine steward, he or she may serve wine.

CHIEF ENGINEER

Responsible for a hotel's physical operation and maintenance.

CLASSICAL MANAGEMENT SCHOOL

A school of management thought in which workers are seen as rational people interested primarily in making money. This management approach addresses an employee's economic and physical needs, but not his or her social needs or need for job satisfaction.

CLOSING DATE

The day when all copy and other ad components must be delivered to the media if the ad is to appear on its scheduled date.

CLUB MANAGER

The hired professional responsible for guiding all of the elements of a private club's operation.

CLUTTER

The proliferation of commercials in media. Clutter reduces the impact of any single ad.

COGENERATION SYSTEM

A generator to which heat recovery equipment has been added to increase the efficiency of the system.

COMMERCIAL AGENCY

A travel agency that specializes in commercial business and usually has little or no walk-in clientele.

COMMIS DU RANG

In French service, the employee who assists the *chef du rang*. He or she may take food orders to the kitchen, pick up the food when it is ready, and take it to the cart at tableside for further preparation. A *commis du rang* may also deliver drink orders and serve food to guests.

COMMISSIONS

Retailers located off the hotel site (such as gift shops, car rental agencies, and photographers) that pay a commission to the hotel based on a percentage of their gross sales to guests.

COMPETITIVE PRICING

Basing prices on what competitors charge.

CONCESSIONS

Facilities that might well be operated by the hotel directly, such as a beauty salon or fitness club, but are turned over to independent operators who are responsible for the concession's equipment, personnel, and marketing. The hotel may receive a flat fee, a minimum fee plus a percentage of the gross receipts over a specific amount, or a percentage of total gross sales.

CONDOMINIUM HOTELS

Hotels in which an investor takes title to a specific hotel room, which remains in the pool to be rented to transient guests. The investor expects to receive a gain from the increase in value of the hotel over time, as well as receive ongoing income from the rental of his or her room.

CONFERENCE CENTERS

Specialized hotels, usually accessible to major market areas but in less busy locations, that almost exclusively book conferences, executive meetings, and training seminars.

CONSORTIA

Parent companies without national loyalty that own and coordinate business assets in many countries.

CONSTRUCTION LOAN

A short-term loan to be used while the hotel is being built, with repayment to be made in three years or less.

CONSUMER-BASED PRICING

Pricing based on what consumers are willing to pay.

CONTINGENCY THEORY

According to this theory, every management situation is different and every manager is different. Therefore, there are few universal management principles.

CONTINUING-CARE RETIREMENT COMMUNITIES (CCRCs)

Living facilities for retired individuals. Some are like residential hotels, except that they offer special safety features, structured group activities, meals that conform to special dietary needs, and readily available medical care.

CONTRIBUTION MARGIN

A food or beverage item's selling price minus the cost of the ingredients that went into preparing the item.

CONTROLLER

Manages the accounting department and all of its functions, including management of credit, payroll, guest accounts, and cashiering activities.

CONVENTION AND ASSOCIATION GROUP

A group of businesspeople attending a convention or association meeting. The number of people attending can run well into the thousands.

CORPORATE GROUPS

Groups of people traveling for business purposes, usually to attend small conferences or meetings.

CORPORATE—INDIVIDUALS

Individuals traveling for business purposes.

COST CENTERS

Divisions or departments within a hotel that do not directly generate income. They provide support for the revenue centers. Also known as support centers.

COST PER THOUSAND (CPM)

The cost to reach 1,000 people one time. CPM is a measure of audience used to price advertising space.

COST-PLUS PRICING

Determining a price by taking the total cost of providing a product or service and adding to it (1) a percentage to cover overhead or fixed expenses, and (2) a predetermined gross profit margin.

COUNTRY CLUB

A private recreational and social facility for individuals and families who live in the surrounding area.

CRUISE-ONLY AGENCY

A travel agency that only sells cruises.

CRUISE SHIPS

Passenger ships designed for vacationers. Today's cruise ships feature lots of activities and entertainment and can be thought of as floating resort hotels.

CULTURAL MOTIVATORS

Travel motivators based on the desire to know about the culture of other areas.

"CUME"

A marketing term used as a verb to express the accumulation of an audience. It is the number of unduplicated people or households that is achieved by an ad or advertising schedule over a period of time.

CYCLE MENU

A menu that changes every day for a certain number of days, then repeats the cycle. A few cycle menus change regularly but without any set pattern.

D

DEONTOLOGY

A system of ethics that assumes God exists and holds that there are basic or universal ideals.

DIRECT PURCHASE

Food sent directly from the receiving area to the kitchen or dining room rather than to a storage area.

DIRECT-RESPONSE AGENCY

A travel agency that markets its products exclusively through the mail, usually to senior citizens.

DOGS

Unpopular menu items with a low contribution margin.

E

ECONOMY/LIMITED SERVICE HOTELS

Hotels that offer few amenities or services and charge 20% to 50% below mid-market rates for their rooms.

ELASTICITY OF DEMAND

A measure of customer responsiveness to changes in price.

ENGINEERING DIVISION

Responsible for taking care of the hotel's physical plant and controlling energy costs.

EQUITY CLUB

A non-profit private club whose members buy shares in the club and invest any revenues left over after expenses have been paid into improving the club's facilities and services.

ESCOFFIER, GEORGES AUGUSTE

Chef Georges Auguste Escoffier (1847–1935) is considered the father of twentieth-century cookery. His two main contributions were (1) the simplification of classical cuisine and the classical menu, and (2) the reorganization of the kitchen.

ETHICAL RELATIVISM

Making ethical choices based on what seems reasonable or logical according to one's own value system.

ETHICS

(1) A set of moral principles and values that we use to answer questions of right and wrong; (2) the study of the general nature of morals and of the specific moral choices to be made by individuals in their relationships with others.

ETHNIC RESTAURANT

A restaurant featuring a particular cuisine such as Chinese, Mexican, or Italian.

EUROPEAN ECONOMIC COMMUNITY (EEC)

Twelve European nations that in 1992 will form a trade community in which money, goods, services, and people will be able to move freely across the national borders of the member countries.

F

FAMILIARIZATION (FAM) TOUR

A free or reduced-rate travel program designed by hotel personnel to acquaint travel agents and others with the hotel and stimulate sales.

FAYOL, HENRI

One of the first to define the duties and functions of managers. Much general management theory is based on his 14 principles of management.

FEASIBILITY STUDY

A study commissioned by developers and prepared by consultants that seeks to determine the potential success of a proposed hotel on a proposed site.

FINANCIAL CONTROLS

Financial statements, operating ratios, and other financial statistics that managers can use to keep track of operations and make sure financial goals are being attained.

FIRST-IN, FIRST-OUT (FIFO)

An inventory system for rotating and issuing stored food that requires items that have been in storage the longest to be used first.

FIXED MENU

A menu with a set list of items that is used for several months or longer before it is changed. Also known as a static menu.

FOOD AND BEVERAGE DIVISION

Responsible for preparing and serving food and beverages within a hotel. Also includes catering and room service.

FOOD AND BEVERAGE MANAGER

Directs the production and service of food and beverages.

FOOD COST

The cost of food used in the production of a menu item.

FOOD COST PERCENTAGE

A ratio comparing the cost of food sold to food sales, which is calculated by dividing the cost of food sold during a given period by food sales during the same period.

THE FOUR Ps

The four basic marketing responsibilities: product, place, price, and promotion.

FRANCHISE

Refers to (1) the authorization given by one company to another to sell its unique products and services; or (2) the name of the business format or product that is being franchised.

FRANCHISEE

The individual or company granted a franchise.

FRANCHISOR

The franchise company that owns the trademark, products, and/or business format that is being franchised.

FRONT OFFICE

A hotel's command post for processing reservations, registering guests, settling guest accounts, and checking guests in and out.

FRONT OF THE HOUSE

The areas of a hotel or restaurant in which employees have extensive guest contact, such as the front desk (in hotels) and the dining room(s).

FULL-MENU RESTAURANT

A restaurant that (1) has more than a dozen or so main-course items on the menu, and (2) cooks to order.

FULL-SERVICE AGENCY

A travel agency that handles all types of travel for consumers.

FULL SERVICE/LUXURY HOTELS

Hotels with high room rates that feature exceptional service and amenities.

FULL-TIME-EQUIVALENT (FTE) EMPLOYEE

A measure used for statistical purposes in which two or more part-time employees whose hours add up to 40 hours a week (the number of hours one full-time employee would work) equal one full-time-equivalent (FTE) employee. For example, four part-time employees who each work ten hours a week would for statistical purposes be recorded as one FTE employee.

G

GANTT, HENRY

Devised a control system for production scheduling so that management could forecast how much work should be expected from employees. His Gantt chart is still used today.

GENERAL MANAGER

The chief operating officer of a hotel.

GILBRETH, FRANK

An efficiency expert who studied worker productivity and created ways to improve it.

GILBRETH, LILLIAN

A management theorist who studied worker fatigue and advocated reforms such as standard work days, lunch periods, and regular breaks for all employees.

GLOBALIZATION

Refers to the international consolidation of big businesses as well as the growing trend for countries to allow the free transfer of goods and services across national borders.

GOLF COMMITTEE

A private country club committee composed of club members who establish golf course policy, review golf course budgets and operations, and oversee the care of the golf course(s).

GOVERNMENT AND MILITARY TRAVELERS

Travelers in government or the military who typically are reimbursed for hotel and other travel expenses on a fixed per diem allowance—that is, they receive a certain amount of money to pay for their hotel room no matter what the rate is.

GREAT-EXPECTATIONS SYNDROME

The greater travel expectations of the new, more educated and well-traveled American tourist.

GROUP AND INCENTIVE AGENCY

A travel agency that specializes in creating customized travel programs for groups and corporations.

GUEST MIX

The variety or mixture of guests that stay at a hotel or patronize a restaurant.

H

HARRIED TRAVELERS

New parents and working couples stretched for time. Harried travelers are more likely to make last-minute travel plans and take mini-vacations.

HAWTHORNE EFFECT

The link between supervision, morale, and productivity.

HAWTHORNE STUDIES

Studies of workers conducted by the Western Electric Company involving Harvard Business School professor George Elton Mayo. The studies were originally designed to assess the affects of lighting conditions on worker productivity, but subsequently were broadened to include other working conditions such as rest periods and type of supervision.

HEADLINE

The most prominent part of a print advertisement in which a promise or benefit is often expressed. Used to get attention.

HENDERSON, ERNEST

A Boston investor who founded the Sheraton hotel chain.

HIGHWAY HOTELS

Hotels built next to highways. These hotels typically feature large property signs, an entrance where travelers can leave their cars while they check in, and a swimming pool. Parking space is plentiful and the atmosphere is informal.

HILTON, CONRAD

A hotel-chain pioneer.

HOSPITALITY

The cordial and generous reception of guests. Derived from the Latin term *hospes*, "a guest."

HOSPITALITY INDUSTRY

Lodging and food service businesses that provide short-term or transitional lodging and/or food.

HOSPITIA

Early Roman inns that had rooms and sometimes food for travelers.

HOTEL CHAIN

A group of affiliated hotels.

HOUSE COMMITTEE

A private club committee made up of members whose job it is to monitor the maintenance and operation of the clubhouse and its services.

HOUSEKEEPING

A department of the rooms division, responsible for cleaning the hotel's guestrooms and public areas.

HUMAN RESOURCES DIVISION

Responsible for recruiting, orienting, training, evaluating, motivating, rewarding, disciplining, developing, promoting, and communicating with hotel employees.

HUMAN RESOURCES MANAGER

In charge of employee relations within an organization.

I

INCENTIVE FEE

That portion of the management fee (paid by hotel owners to hotel management companies) that is based on a percentage of income before fixed charges (also known as gross operating profit), or on a percentage of cash flow after debt service.

INDEPENDENT HOTEL

A hotel that is not connected with any hotel company and is owned by an individual or a group of investors.

INITIATION FEE

A typically non-refundable charge that new members must pay to join a private club.

IN-PLANT AGENCY

A branch office of a travel agency typically located in the offices of large corporations.

INTERPERSONAL MOTIVATORS

Travel motivators that include a desire to meet new people, visit friends or relatives, escape from routine or from family and neighbors, and make new friends.

J

JOB BREAKDOWN

The specific, step-by-step procedures for accomplishing each task of a particular job.

JOB DESCRIPTION

A recruiting and training tool that outlines for a particular job (1) the title that goes with the job, (2) the person to whom the employee reports, (3) the work to be performed (in general terms), and (4) the education or skills the employee must possess.

JOB LIST

A list of the tasks that must be performed by the individual holding a particular job.

JOB RESTRUCTURING

A method of increasing productivity by changing the nature of a task or the way it is done.

JOHNSON, HOWARD

A restaurant-chain pioneer and one of the first franchisors. The food, building, decor, and seating arrangements of his Howard Johnson's restaurants were all standardized.

K–L

KROC, RAY

Founder of McDonald's. The success of McDonald's is due in large part to Kroc's emphasis on quality, service, cleanliness, and value.

LEISURE TRAVELERS

Travelers—often entire families—that typically spend only one night at a hotel unless it is a hotel at their destination.

LIMITED-MENU RESTAURANT

A restaurant with a small selection of food and limited services. Limited-menu restaurants emphasize speed of preparation and delivery, making convenience one of the main reasons for their appeal.

LOGOTYPE (LOGO)

A unique trademark, name, symbol, signature, or device used to identify a company or other organization.

LONG-TERM STAY/RELOCATION GUESTS

Individuals or families relocating to an area who require short-term lodging until permanent housing can be found.

LOSS LEADERS

Items sold at or below cost in order to attract customers to a business.

LUXURY RESTAURANT

A restaurant that features fine dining; an exciting menu (not necessarily French or haute cuisine, however); and employs well-trained, creative chefs and skilled food servers. Luxury restaurants are generally small and independently operated, with more employees per guest than other types of restaurants.

M

McGREGOR, DOUGLAS

A management theorist who created Theory X and Theory Y to represent traditional and more progressive management assumptions about employees.

MANAGEMENT COMPANY

A company that manages hotels for owners, typically for a combination of fees plus a share of revenues. A management company may or may not have any of its own funds invested in a hotel it manages.

MANAGEMENT CONTRACT

A written agreement between an owner and an operator of a hotel or motor inn by which the owner employs the operator as an agent (employee) to assume full responsibility for operating and managing the property.

MANAGEMENT TRAINING PROGRAMS

Education programs developed by large hospitality organizations to provide further training to their manager trainees. The best management training programs teach general management skills as well as technical skills.

MARKETING

The effort to determine and meet the needs and wants of present and potential customers. Marketing includes sales and a great deal more.

MARKETING DIVISION

Responsible for (1) identifying prospective guests for the hotel, (2) conforming the products and services of the hotel as much as possible to meet the needs of those prospects, and (3) persuading prospects to become guests.

MARKETING MANAGER

Develops and implements a marketing plan and budget.

MARKETING MIX

The mixture of marketing activities a business engages in.

MASLOW, ABRAHAM

Created the theory that there is a priority to the needs people have, and that we satisfy our most basic physiological needs first before attending to a sequence of higher-level needs.

MAYO, GEORGE ELTON

A Harvard Business School professor involved in studies on employee behavior at the Western Electric Company's plant in Hawthorne, Illinois.

MEGA RESTAURANT

A large restaurant, usually characterized by elaborate or unusual decor, that enjoys a high level of patronage.

MEMBERSHIP DUES

The cost to a private club member for the exclusivity provided by the club's limited membership. Membership dues subsidize all of the club's operating costs and fixed charges.

MENU ENGINEERING

A method of menu analysis and food pricing that considers both the profitability and popularity of menu items.

MILITARY CLUB

A club for officers or non-commissioned officers operated by the armed services.

MOMENTS OF TRUTH

Instances when important personal contact is made between customers or guests and employees.

MULTIPLIER EFFECT

The hidden or indirect benefits of a travel and tourism business to a community, measured by adding up all the expenditures of travelers in the community and then multiplying that figure by a factor (known as the multiplier) to arrive at the amount of income that stays in the community and is generated by these expenditures.

N–O

NIGHT AUDIT

An accounting task usually performed between 11 p.m. and 6 a.m. A night audit verifies that guest charges have been accurately posted to each guest's account and that the income is properly credited to the division or department that earned it.

ONE-STOP PURCHASING

A convenience offered to food service operations by food distributors that have broadened and expanded their product lines so that a purchaser can buy everything from produce to kitchen equipment from one supplier, rather than going to separate ones.

OPERATING TERM

The provision of a management contract that defines the length of the initial contract and its renewal options.

OPERATOR INVESTMENT

The provision of a management contract outlining the details of the operator's investment in the property.

OWEN, ROBERT

A Scottish cotton mill manager who thought that a manager's job was one of instituting reform. Owen was one of the first management theorists.

P

PERFORMANCE REVIEW

A meeting between a manager and one of his or her employees to (1) let the employee know how well he or she has learned to meet company standards, and (2) let managers know how well they are doing in hiring and training employees. Typically held every three, six, or twelve months, depending on the employee's performance and experience.

PERPETUAL INVENTORY SYSTEM

A system for tracking inventory by keeping a running balance of inventory quantities—that is, recording all additions to and subtractions from stock.

PETERS, THOMAS H.

Along with Robert A. Waterman, Jr., was the first management theorist to emphasize the primary importance of the customer in determining how a company should be managed.

PHYSICAL MOTIVATORS

Travel motivators that lead people to reduce tension through physical activities. People with physical motivations seek out physical rest, sports participation, beach recreation, and other active and healthy activities while on vacation.

PLOWHORSES

Popular menu items with a low contribution margin.

POINT-OF-SALE (POS) SYSTEM

A network of electronic cash registers and precheck terminals capable of capturing data at point-of-sale (POS) locations.

POSITIONING

A marketing term used to describe how consumers perceive the products and services offered by a particular advertiser in relation to similar products and services offered by competitors. Positioning strategies attempt to establish in the minds of consumers a particular image of an advertiser's products and services.

POST-OPENING MANAGEMENT FEES

Fees paid by an owner to a management company for managing the property. In the case of a chain management company, the fees also cover the use of the established brand name.

PRE-OPENING MANAGEMENT FEES

Fees paid by an owner to a management company for work done by the company before the opening of the hotel, including planning, staffing, training, marketing, budgeting, and other activities that the management company must perform before the property is ready to receive guests.

PRICE AND SIGHTS GROUP

The group of travelers that are interested in doing the most things for the least amount of money while on vacation.

PRIME COSTS

The cost of food sold plus payroll cost (including employee benefits). These are a restaurant's largest costs.

PRIVATE CLUB

A gathering place for members only.

PRODUCTIVITY STANDARD

A measurement that tells managers how long it should take an employee to complete a task using the best methods management has devised, and how many tasks an employee can perform in a given time period. This measurement differs according to the task the employee is performing.

PRODUCT OR TRADE-NAME FRANCHISE

A supplier-dealer arrangement whereby the dealer (franchisee) sells a product line provided by the supplier (franchisor) and to some degree takes on the identity of the supplier.

PROFESSIONAL CLUB

A private dining or social club for people in the same profession.

PROMOTION

All the ways a business persuades people to buy its products and services.

PROPERTY MANAGEMENT SYSTEM (PMS)

A computerized system that helps managers and other personnel carry out a number of front-of-the-house and back-of-the-house functions. A PMS can support a variety of applications software that helps managers in their data-gathering and reporting responsibilities.

PROPRIETARY CLUB

A for-profit private club owned by a company that sells memberships in the club.

PSYCHOGRAPHIC RESEARCH

Research that attempts to classify people's behavior in terms of their lifestyles and values.

PUBLICITY

The editorial mention in the media of an organization's people, products, or services.

PUBLIC RELATIONS (PR)

A systematic effort by a business to communicate favorable information about itself to various internal and external publics in order to create a positive impression.

PURCHASE ORDER

An order for food or other supplies prepared by an operation's purchasing staff and submitted to suppliers.

PURCHASE SPECIFICATIONS

A detailed description for ordering purposes of the quality, size, weight, and other characteristics desired for a particular item.

PURCHASING DEPARTMENT

Responsible for buying, receiving, storing, and issuing all the products used in a hotel.

PUZZLES

Unpopular menu items with a high contribution margin.

Q–R

QUALITY CONTROLS

Standards of operation, quality assurance programs, and other controls that seek to establish and maintain products and services at quality levels established by management.

QUALITY GROUP

The group of travelers for whom the quality of their vacation is of paramount importance. They want and are willing to pay for first-class accommodations and service.

QUANTITATIVE MANAGEMENT SCHOOL

A school of management that tries to integrate the management theories of the classical and behavioral management schools. The two main theories of the quantitative school are the systems theory and the contingency theory.

REFERRAL SYSTEMS

Independent properties or small chains that do not share common operating systems, decor, purchasing systems, etc., but are linked together (1) by a common reservation system, and (2) by a common marketing strategy. The reservation system and marketing campaigns are funded by the hotels in the system.

REGIONAL GET-AWAY GUESTS

Guests who check into a hotel close to home in order to enjoy a weekend away from children and other responsibilities.

RENTALS

Enterprises such as offices or stores that pay rent to a hotel.

REPORTING REQUIREMENTS

The provision of a management contract that stipulates the types of reports the management company must give to the owner and how often they must be submitted.

REQUISITION

A written order used by employees identifying the type, amount, and value of items needed from storage.

RESERVATIONS OFFICE

A department within a hotel's rooms division staffed by skilled telemarketing personnel who take reservations over the phone, answer questions about facilities, quote prices and available dates, and sell to callers who are shopping around.

RESIDENT MANAGER

In charge of the rooms division in a mid-size to large hotel. Sometimes resident managers are also in charge of security.

RESORT HOTELS

Hotels, usually located in desirable vacation spots, that offer fine dining, exceptional service, and many amenities.

RETURN ON INVESTMENT (ROI)

The profits earned by the investors in a business, or, more generally, the gain associated with an investment of capital.

REVENUE CENTERS

Divisions or departments within a hotel that directly generate income through the sale of products or services to guests.

ROGERS, ISAIAH

Designer of the Tremont House in Boston (opened in 1829), which is considered the first modern hotel in America. Rogers went on to design many other hotels and become one of the most influential hotel architects of the nineteenth century.

ROOMS DIVISION

The largest, and usually most profitable, division in a hotel. It typically consists of four departments: front office, reservations, housekeeping, and uniformed service.

ROOM SERVICE

The department within a food and beverage division that is responsible for delivering food or beverages to guests in their guestrooms. May also be responsible for preparing the food and beverages.

RUN-OF-PAPER (ROP)

The basis on which most newspaper advertising space is sold, in which the newspaper staff picks the ad's position.

S

SAINT JULIAN THE HOSPITALLER

The patron saint of innkeepers, travelers, and boatmen.

SAINT NOTBURGA

The patron saint of food servers.

SALES

Activities for getting rid of what you have.

SALES MANAGER

Conducts sales programs and makes sales calls on prospects for group and individual business. Reports to the marketing manager.

SALES PROMOTION

Sales tools and techniques such as contests, extra commissions, familiarization tours, and loyalty marketing programs that are designed to generate an immediate response.

SATELLITE TICKET PRINTER

A travel agency's ticket printer located in a client's office.

SCALAR CHAIN

The chain of authority in a business that extends unbroken from the ultimate authority to the lowest employee ranks. One of Fayol's 14 management principles.

SECURITY DIVISION

Responsible for the protection of (1) guests and their property, (2) employees and their property, and (3) the hotel itself.

SIGNATURE

The name of the advertiser as it appears at the bottom of a print ad.

SMART CARDS

A credit-card-like device that can be read by a computer, enabling its user to (1) buy an airline ticket, and/or (2) make a hotel reservation, check into the guestroom, pay the bill, and perform other functions.

SPECIALTY MENU

A menu that differs from the typical breakfast, lunch, or dinner menu. Specialty menus are usually designed for holidays and other special events or for specific guest groups. Examples include children's, beverage, dessert, and banquet menus.

STAKEHOLDER

Anyone who has a stake in the outcome of a given decision.

STANDARD INDUSTRIAL CLASSIFICATION CODE

The basis of government classification of all businesses in the United States, based on U.S. census reports.

STANDARD RECIPE

A formula for producing a food or beverage item specifying ingredients, the required quantity of each ingredient, preparation procedures, portion size and portioning equipment, garnish, and any other information necessary to prepare the item.

STARS

Popular menu items with high contribution margins.

STATEMENT OF INCOME

A financial statement of the results of operations that presents the sales, expenses, and net income of a business for a stated period of time.

STATLER, ELLSWORTH

A hotel-chain pioneer who opened the first Statler hotel in Buffalo, New York, in 1908, and soon thereafter built others in Cleveland, Detroit, St. Louis, and Boston. Statler's genius was his ability to increase service and simplify operations on a chain-wide basis.

STATUS AND PRESTIGE MOTIVATORS

Travel motivators that concern ego and personal development needs. People with these motivators take trips related to business, conventions, study, and the pursuit of education or hobbies.

STRATEGIC TRAVELERS

Travelers who look for the best value, not the lowest price. Strategic travelers are information-oriented consumers.

SUBURBAN HOTELS

Hotels somewhat smaller than downtown hotels (typically 250 to 500 rooms), usually part of a chain, with restaurants, bars, and other amenities found at downtown hotels.

SUN AND SURF GROUP

The group of travelers that seek a vacation spot where there is good weather, guaranteed sunshine, and a beautiful beach.

SYSTEMS MANAGER

Manages a hotel's computerized management information systems. May write simple computer programs and instruction manuals for employees.

SYSTEMS THEORY

Proposes that a company is a system of many interrelated parts, which in turn is part of a larger external environment (system). Therefore, managers cannot act independently; what they can accomplish depends on factors inside and outside the company.

T

TACTICS

Specific plans created to carry out objectives. Also called action plans.

TAKE-OUT

(1) The permanent financing secured for a new hotel; (2) food prepared by a food service business for consumption off-site.

TAYLOR, FREDRICK W.

An American industrial engineer who revolutionized the manufacturing process by coming up with scientific principles of management.

TECHNICAL ASSISTANCE FEES

Fees paid by an owner to a management company covering the time and expertise of the company as a consultant in the design and plan of the facilities.

TELEPHONE DEPARTMENT

Responsible for providing telephone and other services (such as wake-up calls) to hotel guests.

TERMINATION PROVISIONS

The provisions of a management contract stating the circumstances under which a party may terminate the contract.

THEME RESTAURANT

A restaurant distinguished by its combination of decor, atmosphere, and menu.

THEORY X

A traditional set of assumptions some managers make about human nature that governs their management style. According to Theory X, the average employee (1) dislikes work and must be directed and threatened with punishment in order to put forth adequate effort, and (2) avoids responsibility and values security above anything else.

THEORY Y

A set of assumptions some managers make about human nature that governs their management style. According to Theory Y, (1) the average employee does not inherently dislike work, (2) external control is not necessary if employees are committed to the organization's objectives, and (3) commitment to objectives is achieved by associating rewards to the attainment of those objectives.

THEORY Z

Author William Ouchi's term for the Japanese management style, which is characterized by employing people for a lifetime, promoting managers slowly, and making decisions on a collective or consensus basis.

THREE POSITION PLAN OF PROMOTION

A plan developed by Frank and Lillian Gilbreth in which workers not only perform their jobs, but also (1) learn the next higher job, and (2) train a worker below them to take over their present job when they are promoted.

TIME-SHARE CONDOMINIUMS

Condominiums in which an owner can purchase a portion of time at the condominium—typically one month or one week—for one-twelfth or one-fiftieth of the condominiums's price, and share the condominium with other owners. Owners have the right to stay at the condominium during their assigned time during the year or trade their time slot with another owner.

TOURIST COURTS

The forerunners of motels, built along highways in the 1920s and 1930s. Tourist courts were usually a simple row of small cabins that often had no private baths.

TOUR OPERATOR

A business that puts together travel tours and sells them directly to individuals or through travel agencies.

TRADE-OFF SYNDROME

The tendency to postpone vacations in order to purchase some other product or service. Even with the increase in two-earner families, many Americans are finding that they can't have it all.

TRAVEL AND TOURISM INDUSTRY

A collection of organizations and establishments that derive all or a significant portion of their income from providing goods and services to travelers.

TRAVEL CLUB

A travel agency that charges an annual fee to its members and in return offers packaged vacations to members at reduced prices.

TREMONT HOUSE

A 170-room Boston hotel that opened in 1829. It was the first hotel to have bellpersons, front desk agents, locks on guestroom doors, and free soap for guests. It is considered the first modern American hotel.

TURNOVER

The number of workers hired within a period by a work unit to replace those leaving or dismissed; also, the ratio of this number to the average number in the work unit.

U–V

UNIFORMED SERVICE

A hotel department within the rooms division that deals with guests' luggage and transportation and provides concierge services. Also referred to as the guest service department.

UNIFORM FRANCHISE OFFER CIRCULAR (UFOC)

A prospectus that outlines certain vital aspects of a franchisor and the franchise agreement, which by law must be given to a potential franchisee before the franchisee signs the franchise agreement.

UNIVERSITY CLUB

A private club for university graduates.

UTILITARIANISM

A system of ethics based on the greatest good for the greatest number.

VISITORS' FEES

Charges to non-members of a private club who are guests of members and use rooms, buy food or beverages, or use recreational facilities.

W–Y

WATERMAN, JR., ROBERT A.

Along with Thomas H. Peters, was the first management theorist to emphasize the primary importance of the customer in determining how a company should be managed.

WILSON, KEMMONS

Founder of the Holiday Inn hotel chain. He was also among the first to offer standardized roadside restaurants.

WORK-SAMPLING TESTS

Tests that require prospective employees to perform a "sample" of the kind of work they will be doing if hired. Using video simulations and other techniques, candidates respond to test situations as they would if they were actually on the job.

YACHT CLUB

A private club located near a large body of water, whose main purpose is to provide facilities such as marinas to boat owners.

YIELD MANAGEMENT

A hotel pricing system adapted from the airlines that uses a hotel's computer reservation system to track advance bookings and then lower or raise prices accordingly—on a day-to-day basis—to yield the maximum average daily rate.

Index

M

Macaulay, James F., 272
McClean, Bill, 268
McDonald, Maurice, 349
McDonald, Richard, 349
McDonald's
  advertising and, 312
  decor, 169–179
  employee titles and, 269
  employee training and, 265
  founding of, 31
  franchise construction and, 353
  franchise standards and, 358
  globalization and, 412
  goodwill, 360
  growth, 363
  intangibility and, 36
  job programs, 260
  leasing programs, 47
  manager salaries, 47
  marketing and, 145, 236, 283
  new product development and, 145–146
  number of units of, 145, 347
  public relations and, 334–336
  recruiting employees and, 257–258
  secrets of success, 158
  service standards, 237
  student food service and, 153
  training and, 354
  unit openings of, 355
  unit sales of, 47
McGrath, Michael R., 239
McGregor, Douglas, 228–229, 234
McIntosh, Robert, 15
McMasters Job Program, 260, 416
McRecycle USA, 336
Magazines, 325–327
Mailing lists, 331, 333
Management
  behavioral school of, 225–229
  by objectives (MBO), 234
  classical school of, 224–225
  companies, 85, 371–383 (Exhibit 13.1)
  contracts, 373, 375–383
  14 principles of, 225, 226 (Exhibit 8.2)
  manufacturing vs. service, 232–236
  quantitative school of, 229–230
  roles, 239–240 (Exhibit 8.3)
  scientific, 224
Management information systems (MIS), 230
Management by Menu, 182
Management theories, 223–231
  contingency, 230
  customers first, 231
  systems, 230
  X, 229
  Y, 229
  Z, 230–231
Management theorists
  Barnard, Chester I., 225
  Fayol, Henri, 225
  Gantt, Henry, 224
  Gilbreth, Frank, 224
  Gilbreth, Lillian, 224
  Maslow, Abraham, 228
  Mayo, George Elton, 225–228
  McGregor, Douglas, 228–229

Owen, Robert, 223
  Taylor, Fredrick W., 224, 231
Management training programs, 50–51, 139
Managers
  applicant evaluation and, 262–263
  applicant interviewing and, 261–262
  developing people and, 222–223
  employee evaluation and, 272–273
  employee hiring and, 263
  employee motivation and, 268–272
  employee references and, 263
  employee training and, 264–268 (Exhibits 9.7–9.8)
  job applications and, 261
  jobs of, 219–223 (Exhibit 8.1)
  measuring performance and, 222
  motivating and communicating and, 222
  organizing and, 220–222
  recruitment of, 259–260
  screening interview and, 261–262
  setting objectives and, 220
  vs. supervisors, 220
Managing by walking around (MBWA)
Managing in the Service Economy, 233
Mankarios, Astef, 149
Mansion on Turtle Creek, 149
Margittai, Tom, 156
Market segmentation, 71, 73–74, 236–237, 315–317
Marketing and sales division, 287
Marketing and sales manager, 44
Marketing
  concept, 277–283
  controls, 286
  division, 119–121 (Exhibit 4.7)
  loyalty programs, 339
  objectives, 285–286
  plan, 283–286
  strategies, 286
  vs. selling, 277–278
Marketplace analysis, 283–284
Marriott, 11, 42, 71, 73, 78, 84, 151, 152, 156
  advertising and, 318
  career paths and, 258
  Guest Satisfaction Index (GSI), 222
  job programs, 260
  management training programs, 51
  service standards and, 238
  travel agencies and, 302
Marriott, J. W. "Bill," Jr., 222, 223, 271
Marriott, J. Willard, 223
Martinez, Frank, 203
Marx, Groucho, 197
Maslow, Abraham, 228
Mayo, George Elton, 225–228
Meal plans, 111
Mega restaurants, 143
Megatrends 2000, 409
Megatrends, 419
Mellman, Richard, 140
Membership dues, 209
Mentor role, 240
Menu
  categories, 174–175 (Exhibit 6.4)
  design, 175–176
  dogs, 181
  doorknob, 113–114
  items, 159, 160 (Exhibit 5.6)
  planning, 180–181

plowhorses, 181
preferences, 172–174 (Exhibit 6.3)
prices, 176–177
puzzles, 181
rules for creating a, 170–172
stars, 181
Mid-price/extended stay hotels, 73
Middle Ages, 4, 26, 348
Military clubs, 204
Military food service, 155
The Millions, 5
Mississippi Management, 222
Mizner, Addison, 170
The Mobley, 29
Modified American Plan, 111
Molloy, John T., 292
Moments of truth, 236
MONITOR, 18–19
Monitor role, 240
Moore, Robert Lowell, 29
Moral reasoning, 391–393
Morrison's Custom Management, 148
Motel 6, 72
Motels, 68, 72, 338
Moyers, Bill, 395
Multinational companies, 412–414
Multiplier effect, 9
Mystery shoppers, 133–134, 338

N

Naisbitt, John, 409, 411, 419
National School Lunch Program, 49
Networking, 260
New restaurants, 155–163 (Exhibit 5.5)
Newspapers, 321, 322–325
Nielson, 162–163
Nutrition, 172

O

Ocean liners, 5
Ogilvy, David, 319, 320–321, 330
Oldag, Karl, 153
Olds, R. E., 7
One Hudson Cafe, 169
Ongoing franchise fees, 360
Operating standards, 131
Operating term, 379
Operator investment, 381
Organization charts, 101 (Exhibit 4.1), 102–103 (Exhibit 4.2), 104 (Exhibit 4.3), 107 (Exhibit 4.4), 112 (Exhibit 4.6), 121 (Exhibit 4.7), 125 (Exhibit 4.10), 206 (Exhibits 7.1–7.2)
Organizing, 220–222
Ouchi, William, 230–231
Overhead expenses, 128
Overseas travel, 10, 11 (Exhibit 1.3)
Owen, Robert, 223
Owentsia Country Club, 204
Owners-in-foreclosure, 381
Oxford Dictionary of Saints, 25

452 *Index*

P

Package tours, 303
Pan American Airlines, 8
Parsons, W. Craig, 67
Patti, Charles H., 312
Payroll control, 238–239
Peale, 404
People skills, 40, 222
Pepsico, 347
Perestroika, 410
Performance reviews, 272–273
Perishability, 37
Permanent financing (take-out), 93
Perpetual inventory system, 191
Personal selling, 282, 286–297
    vs. advertising, 309
Personality types, 288–291 (Exhibit 10.1)
Peters, Thomas H., 231, 233, 239, 269, 270
Peterson, Herb, 358
Piccadilly, 148
Pilgrimages, 4
Pizza Hut, 146–147, 151, 238, 412
Place, 279–280
Pleasure travelers, 16, 17 (Exhibit 1.5)
Plowhorses, 181
Point-of-sale (POS) systems, 180–181, 186–187
Poker vs. business, 393
Polling, 179
Polo, Marco, 4
Poloroid, 339
Population shift, 249
Positioning, 314–315
Post-opening management fees, 379
The Power of Ethical Management, 404
Pre-opening management fees, 379
Press tours, 337–338
Price, 280–282
Price and sights group, 18
Price segmentation, 73–74
Pricing
    menu items, 176–177
    strategies, 235
Prime costs, 180 (Exhibit 6.6)
Print advertising, 318–319, 320, 322–327, 331–333
Prison food service, 155
Private clubs, 197–212
Private employment agencies, 259
PRIZM, 163
Producer role, 240
Producing, food, 185
Product, 278–279
Product or trade name franchise, 346
Product or trade name franchising, 348–349
Product segmentation, 11–12, 40
Product-driven pricing, 280
Productivity standards, 254–257 (Exhibit 9.5)
Professional clubs, 199–200
Promotion, 282–283
Property management systems (PMS), 103, 124, 230, 421
Proprietary clubs, 205, 206 (Exhibit 7.2)
Prospecting, 294–295
Psychographic research, 18
Public relations, 282, 333–336 (Exhibit 11.3)

Publicans, 347–348
Publicity, 336–338 (Exhibit 11.4)
    vs. advertising, 336
Purchase specification, 182 (Exhibit 6.8), 183
Purchasing
    department, 114
    food, 181–183
Puzzles, 181

Q

Qualifying, 294–295
Quality
    assurance, 131–132
    control, 37, 129–134
    group, 18
    objectives, 285–286
    standards, 131
Quality International, 353, 356
Queen Elizabeth II, 82
Queen Mary, 5, 6, 170
Quinn, Robert E., 239

R

Radice, Judi, 176
Radio, 321 (Exhibit 11.2), 328–330
Railroads, 28
Ramada, 335
Receiving, 183–184
    clerks, 183–184
Reciprocal agreements, 205
Regal-AIRCOA, 373, 374 (Exhibit 13.1)
Regional getaway guests, 77
Reidenbach, Eric, 396
Renaissance, 5
Rentals, 118
Repetitiveness, 37
Reservations department, 106
Residence Inn, 40, 73, 76, 78, 315
Resident manager, 44
Resort hotels, 5, 40–41, 63–68 (Exhibits 3.1–3.3), 315
Resort Report, 271
Restaurant
    atmosphere, 142–143, 169–170
    balance sheet, 178
    career options, 44–47
    chains, 46, 145, 146 (Exhibit 5.2)
    feasibility study, 162–163
    guest expenditures, 34
    guests, 167–168, 172–174 (Exhibit 6.3)
    menu, 170–172
    organization, 167–191
    site selection, 160–163
    statement of income, 178–179 (Exhibit 6.5)
Restaurants
    concept of, 159–160
    cost of, 157–158 (Exhibit 5.5)
    cruise lines and, 149
    ethnic, 143
    failure of, 157
    family, 45–46

financial controls and, 177–179 (Exhibit 6.5)
food costs and, 180–189 (Exhibit 6.7)
full-menu, 141–143, 144–145 (Exhibit 5.1)
independent, 156
limited-menu, 46–47, 143, 145–147
lodging operations and, 148–149
luxury, 45, 141, 176
mega, 143
operational controls and, 179–180
theme, 143
24-hour, 145
Return on investment (ROI), 93, 312
Revenue centers, 100–119
    concessions, rentals, and commissions, 116, 118
    fitness and recreation facilities, 118–119
    food and beverage division, 109–116 (Exhibits 4.5–4.6)
    rooms division, 100–109 (Exhibit 4.3)
    telephone department, 116
    vs. cost centers, 100
Ries, Al, 314
Robin, Donald, 396
Rogers, Isaiah, 27
Romans, 3, 4, 26, 63, 197, 347
Room
    attendants, 107, 108
    inspectors, 107
    service, 113–114
Rooms division, 100–109 (Exhibit 4.3)
Rosen, Harold, 358
Royal Castle, 168
Royce, Sir Henry, 7
Run-of-paper (ROP), 323

S

Saint Julian the Hospitaller, 25
Saint Notburga, 25
Sales
    call, 294–297
    department, 120
    preparation, 295–296
    presentation, 296
    promotion, 282, 338–339
    strategies, 291
Salespeople
    asking for the sale and, 297
    follow-up and, 297
    overcoming objections and, 296–297
    qualities of, 288, 291–294
    super, 288
Sambo's, 168
Satisfaction Guaranteed Eateries, Inc., 220
Scharfe, Walter P., 142
Schneider, William, 401
Scientific management, 224, 231
Screening interview, 261–262
Security
    division, 126–127
    officers, 127
Segmentation
    guest, 333
    market, 71, 315–317
    price, 73–74
    product, 11–12, 40

The Educational Institute Board of Trustees

The Educational Institute of the American Hotel & Motel Association is fortunate to have both industry and academic leaders, as well as allied members, on its Board of Trustees. Individually and collectively, the following persons play leading roles in supporting the Institute and determining the direction of its programs.

Howard P. "Bud" James, CHA
Chairman of the Board
Chairman
Global Hospitality Corporation
San Diego, California

William N. Hulett, CHA
Vice Chairman - Industry
President
Stouffer Hotels & Resorts
Cleveland, Ohio

Anthony G. Marshall, CHA
Vice Chairman - Academia
Dean, School of Hospitality
    Management
Florida International University
Miami, Florida

Jack J. Vaughn, CHA
Treasurer
President
Opryland Lodging Group
Nashville, Tennessee

Philip Pistilli, CHA
Secretary
Chairman
Raphael Hotel Group
Kansas City, Missouri

E. Ray Swan
President & CEO
Educational Institute of AH&MA
East Lansing, Michigan

George R. Conrade, CHA
Assistant Treasurer
Executive Vice President
Educational Institute of AH&MA
East Lansing, Michigan

David J. Christianson, Ph.D.
Dean, William F. Harrah
    College of Hotel Administration
University of Nevada, Las Vegas
Las Vegas, Nevada

Ronald F. Cichy, Ph.D., CHA
Director
School of Hotel, Restaurant and
 Institutional Management
Michigan State University
East Lansing, Michigan

Robert C. Hazard, Jr., CHA
Chairman & CEO
Choice Hotels International, Inc.
Silver Spring, Maryland

Douglass C. Cogswell, CHA
General Manager
The Westin Resort
Vail, Colorado

Arnold J. Hewes
Executive Vice President
Minnesota Hotel & Lodging
 Association
St. Paul, Minnesota

Caroline A. Cooper, CHA
Department Chair
Hospitality/Tourism
Johnson & Wales University
Providence, Rhode Island

Richard M. Kelleher
President
Guest Quarters Suite Hotels
Boston, Massachusetts

Edouard P.O. Dandrieux, CHA
Director & Founder
H.I.M., Hotel Institute Montreux
Montreux, Switzerland

Donald J. Landry, CHA
President
Manor Care Hotel Division
Silver Spring, Maryland

Ronald A. Evans, CHA
President & CEO
Best Western International, Inc.
Phoenix, Arizona

Bryan D. Langton, C.B.E.
Chairman
Holiday Inn Worldwide
Atlanta, Georgia

Lawrence B. Magnan, CHA
Chief Operating Officer
Spa Suites Corporation
Mercer Island, Washington

M.O. "Bus" Ryan, CHA
Senior Vice President
Marriott Hotels-Resorts-Suites
Atlanta, Georgia

Jerry R. Manion, CHA
Executive Vice President - Operations
Motel 6
Dallas, Texas

William J. Sheehan
President & CEO
Omni Hotels
Hampton, New Hampshire

Joseph A. McInerney, CHA
President & CEO
Travelodge International
El Cajon, California

Thomas W. Staed, CHA
President
Oceans Eleven Resorts, Inc.
Daytona Beach Shores, Florida

John A. Norlander, CHA
President
Radisson Hotels Corporation
Minneapolis, Minnesota

William R. Tiefel
President
Marriott Hotels & Resorts
Washington, D.C.

Michael B. Peceri, CHA
Chairman of the Board
Marquis Hotels & Resorts
Fort Meyers, Florida

The Educational Institute Fellows

Respected experts dedicated to the advancement of hospitality education

Michael J. Beckley, CHA
President
Commonwealth
 Hospitality,Ltd.
Toronto, Ontario
Canada

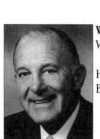
William H. Edwards, CHA
Vice Chairman and
 Director Emeritus
Hilton Hotels Corporation
Beverly Hills, California

John L. Sharpe, CHA
Executive Vice President
Four Seasons
 Hotels & Resorts
Toronto, Ontario
Canada

Stephen W. Brener, CHA
President
Stephen W. Brener
 Associates, Inc.
New York, New York

Creighton Holden, CHA
President, Hotels Division
Encore Marketing
 International
Columbia, South Carolina

Larry K. Walker, CHA
President
Cypress Hotel Management
 Company
Orlando, Florida

Melinda Bush, CHA
Executive Vice President,
 Publisher
Hotel & Travel Index
Reed Travel Group
Secaucus, New Jersey

Allen J. Ostroff
Senior Vice President
The Prudential Property
 Company
Newark, New Jersey

Paul E. Wise, CHA
Director
Hotel, Restaurant &
 Institutional Management
University of Delaware
Newark, Delaware

Robert S. DeMone, CHA
President, Chairman & CEO
Canadian Pacific Hotels
 & Resorts
Toronto, Ontario
Canada

Harold J. Serpe, CHA
President
Midway Hospitality
 Corporation
Brookfield, Wisconsin